Individuals, Families, and Communities in Europe, 1200–1800

The Urban Foundations of Western Society

In this new interpretation of European family and society, Katherine A. Lynch examines the family at the center of the life of "civil society." Using a variety of evidence from European towns and cities, she explores how women and men created voluntary associations outside the family – communities, broadly defined – to complement or even substitute for solidarities based on kinship. She shows how demographic, economic, religious, and political features of European urban society encouraged the need for collective organizations for mutual protection, and how men and women acted to fulfill this need. She also suggests the central place that family issues played in the creation of larger communities, from the "confessional" communities of the Reformation to the national "imagined" community of the French Revolution. Based on a wide range of research, this is an ambitious integration of the history of the family into the history of public life.

KATHERINE A. LYNCH is Professor of History at Carnegie Mellon University, Pennsylvania. Her previous publications include *Family, Class, and Ideology in Early Industrial France: Social Policy and the Working-Class Family, 1825–1848* (1988) and (with J. Dennis Willigan) *Sources and Methods of Historical Demography* (1982) as well as articles in the fields of family history and historical demography.

Cambridge Studies in Population, Economy and Society in Past Time 37

Series Editors

Richard Smith
Cambridge Group for the History of Population and Social Structure
Jan de Vries
University of California at Berkeley
Paul Johnson
London School of Economics and Political Science
Keith Wrightson
Yale University

Recent work in social, economic and demographic history has revealed much that was previously obscure about societal stability and change in the past. It has also suggested that crossing the conventional boundaries between these branches of history can be very rewarding.

This series exemplifies the value of interdisciplinary work of this kind, and includes books on topics such as family, kinship and neighbourhood; welfare provision and social control; work and leisure; migration; urban growth; and legal structures and procedures, as well as more familiar matters. It demonstrates that, for example, anthropology and economics have become as close intellectual neighbours to history as have political philosophy or biography.

For a full list of titles in the series, please see end of book.

Individuals, Families, and Communities in Europe, 1200–1800

The Urban Foundations of Western Society

Katherine A. Lynch

Carnegie Mellon University

CAMBRIDGE
UNIVERSITY PRESS

PUBLISHED BY THE PRESS SYNDICATE OF THE UNIVERSITY OF CAMBRIDGE
The Pitt Building, Trumpington Street, Cambridge CB2 1RP, United Kingdom

CAMBRIDGE UNIVERSITY PRESS
The Edinburgh Building, Cambridge, CB2 2RU, UK
40 West 20th Street, New York, NY 10011–4211, USA
477 Williamstown Road, Port Melbourne, VIC 3207, Australia
Ruiz de Alarcón 13, 28014 Madrid, Spain
Dock House, The Waterfront, Cape Town 8001, South Africa

http://www.cambridge.org

First published 2003

Printed in the United Kingdom at the University Press, Cambridge

Typeface Times 10/12 pt.   *System* LATEX 2$_\varepsilon$ [TB]

A catalogue record for this book is available from the British Library

ISBN 0 521 64235 3 hardback
ISBN 0 521 64541 7 paperback

For my mother, Gladys Berlin Lynch, and to the memory
of my father, Donald Charles Lynch

Epigraph

"What, else, I ask you, is a city than a great monastery?"
Erasmus, quoted in Lee Palmer Wandel,
Always among Us (Cambridge, 1990), 14

"How beautiful a day when the king announces his wish to command a free people and create one vast lodge out of his superb empire in which all *good* Frenchmen will truly be brothers."
Speech before the Masonic Lodge,
"The Perfect Union," Rennes,
France, 23 July 1789, quoted in Marcel David,
*Fraternité et Révolution française,
1789–1799* (Paris, 1987), 88

Contents

Illustrations

Maps

Tables

x

Preface and acknowledgments

This study represents the convergence of research interests I have pursued since graduate school in the fields of family history and historical demography. It was during research for my doctoral dissertation on nineteenth-century France that I first came across the Société de Saint Vincent de Paul, a voluntary association of young men in France who assisted the poor in their homes. From that research, I learned that this charitable association had roots in the seventeenth-century Catholic Reformation, and was intrigued that men of the nineteenth century were attempting to reinvent a kind of organization that had thrived centuries previously. Although I pursued other research, my interest in precedents for the nineteenth-century organizations I had studied remained.

My work in historical demography also prepared me to write the present book, not through any special quantitative focus that this study has, but rather through the habits of thinking that the study of demographic questions often imparts. In particular, my work in this field has taught me that demographic regimes usually change only very slowly. The study of historical demography thus led me almost inexorably to think in terms of the "*longue durée*," and to believe that studying continuities in human societies is just as interesting as studying changes.

A summer grant from the National Endowment for the Humanities permitted me to work on the French Revolution portion of the present work. During research on the family during the Revolution I encountered striking similarities between problems of working-class family poverty during the Old Regime and those I had studied for nineteenth-century France. Additional reading on the comparative history of poor relief in the European past finally convinced me to change what I had originally intended to be a monograph on the family during the French Revolution into a comparative, interpretive work about European family and society over the long term.

I was also encouraged to write this book by Peter Laslett's enthusiasm for a paper I gave at a conference on the "History of the Family" organized by Rod Phillips at Carleton University in Spring 1992. Since that time, I have had the pleasure of presenting my work in a number of forums in the United States and abroad including: the "State and Society" Group of the Pittsburgh Center for

Social History, Brock University, the Economic History Workshop at Indiana University, the International Institute for Social History (IISG), the University of Nijmegen, the Economic History Seminar at the University of Munich, and the Amsterdam School for Social Science Research. A month spent at the Ecole des Hautes Etudes en Sciences Sociales allowed me to present my work in seminars there and at the University of Paris – IV (Sorbonne). For invitations to present my ideas in these stimulating venues, I thank Stephan Curtis, John Sainsbury, Elyce Rotella, George Alter, Lex Heerma van Voss, Paul Klep, John Komlos, Jan Breman, Jean-Pierre Bardet, and Patrice Bourdelais.

I also had the opportunity to discuss my work in the context of two conferences on "Social Control in Early Modern Europe," held at the Villa Vigoni and in Amsterdam, sponsored by the Volkswagen Foundation. I thank Pieter Spierenburg for including me in this interesting forum, and for welcoming me for a semester as an invited researcher at the N.W. Posthumus Institute, which allowed me time to write. During my semester in Amsterdam, the International Institute for Social History provided an office away from home and a congenial setting for writing. My thanks go to its executive director, Lex Heerma van Voss and staff for their cordial reception.

Special thanks go to the staff at Hunt Library, Carnegie Mellon University who contributed their skills to helping me with this project, including Sue Collins, Geri Kruglak, and the staff at the Inter-Library Loan department. Mary Catharine Johnsen and Mo Dawley helped early on in my search for illustrations. I also thank Elaine Engst, Director, and the staff of the Division of Rare and Manuscript Collections, Carl A. Kroch Library, Cornell University, who expedited my requests for illustrations. Gil Shapiro helped with the interpretation of findings from his and John Markoff's study of the French *cahiers de doléances*. I wish to acknowledge the University of Chicago and Barbara B. Diefendorf for permission to reproduce an extract from Barbara B. Diefendorf, "Give us Back our Children: Patriarchal Authority and Parental Consent to Religious Vocations in Early Counter-Reformation France," *Journal of Modern History* 68 (June 1996): 265–6.

Other debts are longer term. Over the years, my life and work as a family historian and historical demographer have been enriched by the friendship and collegiality of Jean-Pierre Bardet, Anders Brandström, Lars-Göran Tedebrand, Patrice Bourdelais, Jean-Noël Biraben, and Jacques Dupâquier.

For research assistance at various stages of this project, I thank Steve Beaudoin, Sabine Marx, and most notably Darrell Meadows. His contributions went well beyond those of research assistance to include excellent advice, both scholarly and editorial, for improving the manuscript. For their help in reading and commenting upon parts or all of earlier versions of this book, I thank Tom Adams, Mary Lindemann, Hal Parker, Nicholas Terpstra, Richard M. Smith, Leslie Moch, Joel Harrington, Phil Gavitt, Carter Lindberg, John Gillis, and

Daniel Scott Smith. The book has been much improved by their thoughtful suggestions, most of which I have tried to incorporate. The responsibility for remaining errors is my own.

The members of my own family – Cynthia, Joel, Rob, Toby, and Sarah – have been a source of joy and support to me during the years I have spent working on this study. I dedicate this book to my mother, and to the memory of my father, for providing examples of how to live out obligations to both family and community.

Introduction

This study investigates European family and social life by examining families and their members against a background of other kinds of relationships and institutions that have long typified western Europe. It explores families as groups of individuals related by marriage, blood, or adoption. It considers groups of people who lived together in households, and moves beyond the household to study extended kinship bonds as well.

The book also puts family relations into larger perspective by viewing them as only one of multiple foundations of solidarity in western society. I am interested in how individuals and families used other associations and institutions – communities, broadly defined – to complement or even fulfill some of the fundamental missions that families have historically provided, such as a place to live, assistance in times of need, and a sense of identity.

I suggest that there has been a deep and enduring tendency among Europeans, especially urbanites, to form communities that often used the terminology of fictive or invented kinship to express moral solidarity. Examples of these relationships range from godparenthood to bonds of "brotherhood" and "sisterhood" among members of monastic communities, invented kinship ties created in religious confraternities of laymen and women, or ties of "brotherhood" that bound together civic communities.

The kinds of communities that men and women created varied across time, space, and social group. Confraternities, which were associations of laymen and women designed for purposes of religious association, mutual assistance, charitable outreach, or burial, depending upon time and place, are a good example. For poorer inhabitants of towns and cities – often lone individuals – these communities could serve as substitutes for family bonds that were weak or nonexistent. Husbands and wives of the middling ranks of urban society frequently joined confraternities together, treating them as extensions of their conjugal bonds. Certain urban patricians, on the other hand, often used social networks that their confraternities provided as a welcome refuge from lives dominated by dense kinship ties.

Whether studying the families and larger social lives of the poor or wealthy, this book tries to show how family forms and organizational or "community" forms developed together as interdependent parts of the same society. One of the book's goals is therefore to expose the symbiotic relationship between western household and family forms on the one hand, and the diverse sorts of communities that supported them and made them possible. I think of the interdependent development of family and community relationships as structural in the sense that Fernand Braudel defined it:

> By *structure*, observers of social questions mean an organization, a coherent and fairly fixed series of relationships between realities and social masses. For us historians, a structure is of course a construct, an architecture, but over and above that it is a reality which time uses and abuses over long periods. Some structures, because of their long life, become stable elements for an infinite number of generations: they get in the way of history, hinder its flow, and in hindering it shape it. Others wear themselves out more quickly. But all of them provide both support and hindrance. As hindrances they stand as limits . . . beyond which man and his experiences cannot go. Just think of the difficulties of breaking out of certain geographical frameworks, certain biological realities, certain limits of productivity, even particular spiritual constraints: mental frameworks too can form prisons of the *longue durée*.[1]

The persistent structural features of European family life's links to larger patterns of community building seem to have appeared most clearly in urban settings, for several reasons. First of all, some of the community forms I am studying seem to have required populations to be of a certain size and diversity before they could develop. Second, it may well be that what economists call the "demand" for various sorts of communities – particularly those designed for mutual assistance – was stronger in towns and large cities because of the demographic conditions prevailing there. As I discuss in Chapter 1, higher rates of mortality, and the greater presence of migrants in urban areas often reduced the size of households and weakened bonds of family and kinship, making extrafamilial networks of solidarity more vital to individual survival. However, I also believe that we may simply be more aware of the urban versions of these organizations and other forms of associations in urban settings because they were more likely to become formalized there, producing records and accounts that permit historians to study them.

Some kinds of voluntary communities could be found in rural areas, where the vast majority of the population lived, and were imported into the city by streams of migrants. Evidence suggests, however, that extrafamilial forms of solidarity were more often nurtured in the city and then exported to the surrounding countryside, brought there both by return migrants, or, in the case of some Christian organizations, by clergy eager to build community ties that extended beyond those of blood and descent.

---

[1] Fernand Braudel, "History and the Social Sciences: The Longue Durée," in *On History*, trans. Sarah Matthews (Chicago, 1980), 31.

Temporal and spatial limits

My study draws on evidence for western Europe from the Middle Ages to the end of the eighteenth century. Such an ambitious task requires justification in an age of the specialized monograph. As copious references attest, this study would have been impossible without the specialized research of scholars in family history, urban history, demographic history, gender history, the history of charity and poor relief, and religious history. The availability of excellent recent studies of societies whose fundamental features I am trying to lay bare has inspired me to try to integrate these findings into an interpretation that makes sense of evidence from these different fields.

Why the choice of time period, and why extend the study back to the Middle Ages? The answer is quite simple. It seems to me that the factors that have combined to create western patterns of family and community structures were already beginning to animate and shape European culture and society in the thirteenth century. Although this book does not seek the exact origins of these patterned relationships, it does try to see some of them in their infancy. However, I try to avoid the criticism that Marc Bloch leveled against historians obsessed with the origins of things. He wrote: "To bring the seed to light is not the same thing as to show the causes for its germination."[2] This study is more interested, therefore, in the processes of germination and flowering of key relationships between family forms and community building than in uncovering the exact origins of such relationships.

I draw most of my evidence from the history of France, England, Germany, Italy, the Low Countries, and Spain. I focus on these parts of western Europe, and have largely excluded eastern Europe, because of my greater familiarity with these areas; the greater impact of urbanization in this part of Europe; and a sense that certain key demographic and political factors were configured rather differently in eastern and western Europe.

But why focus on continuities in family history instead of concentrating on changes, given most historians' belief that what we need to explain are transformations in families' affective relations, gender relations, and the demographic, economic, and political systems of western Europe that have shaped them? The simplest answer is that evidence of important continuities is there in the historical record, but with few exceptions such as studies of continuities in the basic demography underlying European family life, or

---

[2] On the overemphasis on "origins," see Marc Bloch's "A Contribution towards a Comparative History of European Societies," in C. Lane and Jelle C. Riemersma, eds., *Enterprise and Secular Change* (Homewood, IL, 1953), 504–5, and Marc Bloch, *The Historian's Craft*, trans. Peter Putnam (New York, 1971), 29–35 on the "Idol of Origins."

the size and structure of domestic groups, historians have explored them less fully than changes.[3]

This relative lack of attention to historical continuities over what *Annales*-school historians call the *longue durée* results mainly from historians' practice of specializing in the study of narrowly defined times and places. Although specialization at its best leads to mastery of particular times and places, it sometimes leaves the community of scholars relatively unfamiliar with the wide range of evidence and case studies needed to become more aware of continuities or recurring patterns in the past. Furthermore, historians seem to prefer observing and studying change rather than continuities, which sometimes drives us to devote more attention to what appear to be novelties in the historical record than to what is familiar. Finally, the very deeply rooted sense of linear time that pervades the consciousness of western historians makes stories of progressive change more compatible with our fundamental worldview.[4] Change, we often think, calls for explanation, while continuity is just "there." While fully acknowledging the impact of such critical changes in European family and social life as secularization, the growth of what Lawrence Stone called "affective individualism," or, later, the Industrial Revolution of the eighteenth and nineteenth centuries, I argue that the social history of the family in the West has also been marked by important elements of continuity that remain to this day.[5]

Weberian perspectives

The concepts of western culture or western society have so many historical and ideological associations that it is wise to specify what I mean by them beyond the simple temporal and spatial limits of the study indicated above. The work of Max Weber, who believed that there was something distinctive about European society, has shaped my view of some of the key structural continuities of European history. I am particularly interested in his discussions of urban life, his musings about the relative weakness of lineages or clans in Europe, and his belief in the importance of Christianity in shaping the society as a whole.

Weber's analysis of these topics appeared in his well-known *Economy and Society*.[6] Here, he laid out the argument that occidental cities differed from

---

[3] For continuities in the history of the domestic group, see Peter Laslett, "Introduction: The History of the Family," and "Mean Household Size in England since the Sixteenth Century," in Laslett and Richard Wall, eds., *Household and Family in Past Time* (Cambridge, 1972), 49, 139, 142, 156–8; Linda A. Pollock, *Forgotten Children: Parent–Child Relations from 1500 to 1900* (Cambridge, 1983), 33–67, 262–71.

[4] On the appeal of models of linear time, see Joyce Appleby, Lynn Hunt, and Margaret Jacob, *Telling the Truth about History* (New York, 1994), 55–64.

[5] Lawrence Stone, *The Family, Sex and Marriage in England, 1500–1800* (New York, 1977), 221–69.

[6] Max Weber, *Economy and Society: An Outline of Interpretive Sociology*, ed. Guenther Roth and Claus Wittich, 2 vols. (Berkeley, 1978).

those in Asia by the development of several key features, which included a notion of "community," a high level of "autocephaly," and specific forms of law and economic policy.[7] Although Weber realized that Asian urbanites often banded together and challenged officials of their central governments, he argued that they had developed no *de jure* right to do so. Higher political powers, he believed, were never forced to recognize the legitimacy of the kinds of community interests for which urban dwellers in many parts of medieval Europe struggled.[8]

Weber distinguished between cities of northern and southern Europe, distinctions that will also emerge occasionally in this study. He noted, for example, that the "occidental" type of city as he defined it was most developed north of the Alps, and argued that southern European cities were somehow transitional between Asiatic and North European forms. This stemmed, he believed, mainly from the continuing presence in southern European cities of a nobility of rural origins and mentality whose values differed from those of thoroughly urbanized patriciates found in northern Europe. Despite such differences between cities in north and south, however, Weber's main distinction lay between Western cities on the one hand and Asian ones on the other. His view of the importance of this broader distinction also informed his discussion of the relative strength of clan, kin, and caste groups in Asia and Europe.[9]

Weber characterized the history of lineage and clan relations in the West by hypothesizing their progressive weakening. He argued that several factors distinguished Europe from Asia in this regard. Important among them were migration, the feudal system, and the development of state organizations, which combined to demystify and weaken kin groups in Europe as early as the Middle Ages.[10]

He believed that the power of kindreds also declined under the impact of Christianity, whose adherents' notions of community challenged claims of solidarity based solely on biological descent.[11] Weber seemed to imply that Christianity's emphasis on extra-kin solidarity would have been inadequate by itself to shatter strong clan structures, but that these structures were already weakened when Christian ideology and institutions dealt their own blows. Whether Christian models of community by conversion appealed to individuals who were part of societies already characterized by loosely bound kin networks,

---

[7] *Ibid.*, vol. II, 1212–20. Citations refer to the Roth and Wittich edition. I prefer to translate *Gemeinde* as "community," as in Max Weber, *The City*, trans. and ed. Don Martindale and Gertrud Neuwirth (Glencoe, IL, 1958).

[8] Weber, *Economy*, 1228–30.   [9] *Ibid.*, 1236–8.   [10] *Ibid.*, 1244.

[11] *Ibid.*, 1244; Alan Macfarlane, *The Origins of English Individualism: The Family, Property, and Social Transition* (New York and Cambridge, 1978), 45–50. On the demystification of biological descent in Christianity, see Michael Mitterauer, "Christianity and Endogamy," *Continuity and Change* 6, 3 (1991): 314, 325, and Michael Sheehan, "The European Family and Canon Law," *Continuity and Change* 6, 3 (1991): 356.

or whether the Christianization of Europe further weakened such networks, is impossible to demonstrate. Probably, it was a bit of both.

Weber thus portrayed a society whose kin groups and clans gradually encountered a belief system and a church organization whose principles provided a potential challenge to models of solidarity based on ties of blood and descent. Importantly, Weber believed that this pattern marked the experience of Europe's upper as well as lower classes. He argued that neither the nobility nor the lower classes of western society displayed the high levels of patrilineal solidarity and ancestor worship found in many other civilizations. Weber observed that medieval nobilities ascribed increasing importance to patrilineal descent and hereditary claims to titles during their rise to power, but rejected the idea that their obsession with these ties compared in intensity to practices of ancestor worship found elsewhere in the world.[12]

Weber also emphasized how the fundamental relationship between free men in many parts of western Europe of the Middle Ages – that of lord and vassal – was based not on ties of blood, but rather on a public, contractual relationship sworn between two unrelated individuals face-to-face. It was a form of invented solidarity between men that joined those who did not share membership in the same clan or descent group.[13] Thus, in his view, the evolution of a form of urban political community, a demystified kinship system, and the presence of other forms of solidarity such as contractual relationships between unrelated free men, constituted several of western society's distinctive features.

The problem of "essentialism"

In recent years, no scholar has done more than Jack Goody to challenge Weber and those who would use Weber's work to understand family and kinship within a comparative framework. In *The Oriental, the Ancient and the Primitive*, Goody sought to document the many similarities between the development of family groups in East and West, focusing on ways that Eurasians living in socially stratified societies passed property on to their children, dwelt in conjugal families, and granted women surprisingly liberal rights to property. He believes that it is best to see Eurasia as one region when it comes to understanding how families and lineages functioned across time, how they transmitted property through generations, and how they organized family and gender relations.

---

[12] On the nobility's growing sense of lineal solidarity in eleventh-century Europe, see Georges Duby, *La Société aux XIe et XIIe siècles dans la région mâconnaise* (Paris, 1953), 215–27.
[13] On the kinship model informing the symbolism of rituals of lordship and vassalage, see Marc Bloch, *Feudal Society*, trans. L. A. Manyon (Chicago, 1961), vol. I, 137–42; Jacques Le Goff, "The Symbolic Ritual of Vassalage," in *Time, Work and Culture in the Middle Ages*, trans. Arthur Goldhammer (Chicago, 1980), 260–1.

Interestingly, in this work, Goody drew his European examples exclusively from Mediterranean Europe, allowing it, or more precisely, the eastern Mediterranean, to "stand" for Europe. The absence of northern Europe from this magisterial comparative study surely did not result from the author's lack of familiarity with northern Europe, since his earlier writings, including *The Development of the Family and Marriage in Europe*, drew important contrasts between southern and northern Europe, emphasizing resemblances among societies within the Mediterranean basin.[14] Perhaps Goody believes that similarities between Europe and Asia are most obvious in the Mediterranean area. In this respect, he would concur with many, including Weber himself, who identified what he saw as Europe's peculiarities most of all with its northern areas.

Despite Goody's desire to diminish what I believe are radical differences between the family histories of Europe and Asia, he has ironically done more than any other scholar to reemphasize the institution that was most responsible for shaping the peculiar way that Europe's families – and especially its urban families – evolved over time. It was Goody who, in *The Development of the Family and Marriage in Europe*, reminded historians of the Church's central role in shaping family life in Europe north and south. Here, Goody demonstrated the impact of the Church on patterns of property holding and devolution, noting its success in convincing lay property owners to will to it the wealth that in most other societies would have passed to kin or spouses. The Church thereby distorted normal (in world cultural terms) patterns of property devolution and ensured its own enrichment. Over the centuries, the accumulation of property helped the Church become ever more powerful in imposing many features of its worldview on European culture and society.[15]

My study bears the stamp of this important theme of Goody's, though my own treatment of the Church's impacts emphasizes its success in providing the laity with both a worldview promoting extrafamilial forms of association and practical models for their construction. Moreover, while this study is informed by certain Weberian views, and is focused on the West, I have tried to heed Goody's admonition to avoid the "essentialism" that he deplores in the work of those who are convinced of some of the West's peculiarities. Goody recommends that instead of simply positing the West's essential "uniqueness,"[16] social scientists need to work empirically to identify a carefully delimited number of factors or "variables" that, when taken together, shaped western family and society in peculiar ways.[17]

[14] Jack Goody, *The Development of the Family and Marriage in Europe* (Cambridge, 1983).
[15] *Ibid.*, 91–133.
[16] Jack Goody, *The Oriental, the Ancient and the Primitive: Systems of Marriage and the Family in the Pre-Industrial Societies of Eurasia* (Cambridge and New York, 1990), xix, 1, 357, 465, 483–5.
[17] Jack Goody, "Comparing Family Systems in Europe and Asia: Are there Different Sets of Rules?" *Population and Development Review* 22, 1 (March, 1996): 9, 13.

In search of a western family form

The writing of the family history of Europe for the last thirty years has been built in large part upon the monographic study of particular times and places. The field has also benefited, however, from investigations that tried to generalize from results of case studies to find broader patterns or models. The most celebrated and widely studied of these models appears in John Hajnal's work, which used a variety of genealogies and census records to formulate a model of marriage that he called the "European Marriage Pattern." This pattern, which Hajnal and others believe emerged in the sixteenth century, had two main characteristics: a relatively high age at first marriage for women (over 23–24) and men (26 and over), and a relatively high proportion (10–15 percent) of "permanently celibate" people – that is, people who never married.[18]

A second major effort to build a model of western family history came from research identified with the Cambridge Group for the History of Population and Social Structure. Members of this group focused largely upon family relations as they could be observed from listings of households. In a series of publications, they and other historians of the family and household in many parts of the world determined that for most of the documentable past, households in western Europe had been nuclear in form. Stem family households, those in which one heir usually remained in the household throughout his life, existed in some areas. The most statistically representative household form in western Europe, however, was one that was nuclear in structure and likely to contain servants or other employees rather than large numbers of kin.[19] Over the years, additional research on both household and family led the leader of the Cambridge Group, Peter Laslett, to propose a model of the "western family" that included: a nuclear family household, a mother who was relatively old during her child-bearing years, a relatively small age gap between spouses, and the frequent presence in the household of persons who were not members of the immediate family and often not kin at all.[20]

Although Hajnal's work referred to Europe north and south and emphasized east–west differences, his model of "European Marriage" has been found to be predominant mainly in the north. This fact led quite logically to more intensive

---

[18] John Hajnal, "European Marriage Patterns in Perspective," in D. V. Glass and D. E. C. Eversley, eds., *Population in History: Essays in Historical Demography* (Chicago, 1965), 101–43, and Hajnal, "Two Kinds of Preindustrial Household Formation System," *Population and Development Review* 8, 3 (1982): 449–94.

[19] For an aggressive rejection of the idea of the ubiquity of nuclear families in western Europe, see Pierre Goubert, "Family and Province: A Contribution to the Knowledge of Family Structures in Early Modern France," *Journal of Family History* 2, 3 (1977): 179–95.

[20] Peter Laslett, "Characteristics of the Western Family Considered over Time," in Laslett, *Family Life and Illicit Love in Earlier Generations: Essays in Historical Sociology* (Cambridge and New York, 1977), 13–14.

efforts to find and elaborate a model of marriage and household formation that corresponded to southern or Mediterranean Europe. Research to date has failed to find such a model, however. Rather, it seems that southern Europe has been characterized by a variety of household formation systems in different subregions.[21] The family formation system that seems to have predominated in parts of southern Spain and southern Italy partially resembled that in northern Europe. Like young people in northwestern Europe, newly married couples in southern Italy and southern Spain tended to set up new households rather than live with parents after marriage. However, women there tended to marry at significantly younger ages than women in the north, resulting in couples where the age difference between wives and husbands was usually greater than in northern Europe.

Households in other areas of southern Europe seem to have differed from northern Europe even more profoundly. Parts of central Italy, northern Spain, and some mountainous areas of southern France were home to more complex households, including stem family households.[22] In this system, adult brothers and sisters of the heir usually had the right to co-reside with him, but were required to remain celibate if they did. In "joint" families typical of certain landowning groups in central and northern Italy, brothers brought their spouses and reared their children together in the same large households. Research on household formation systems in southern Europe has thus revealed that important elements of Laslett's "western family" or Hajnal's "European Marriage Pattern" did exist in many areas of southern Europe, but that there was more apparent regional variation than in the north. Features such as wider disparities between husbands' and wives' ages, and generally lower proportions of women who remain unmarried seem to be quite general, however.

Historians and anthropologists have also looked beyond systems of household formation to uncover the presence of different models of family relations. Of particular interest are relations between individuals and their kin who did not live in the same household. Inspired by the work of Max Weber as well as empirical studies of kin relations, some observers have proposed that kin networks in northern Europe were generally loosely knit. This view emerged

[21] David I. Kertzer and Caroline Brettell, "Advances in Italian and Iberian Family History," *Journal of Family History* 12, 1–3 (1987): 87–120; Francesco Benigno, "The Southern Italian Family in the Early Modern Period: A Discussion of Co-residential Patterns," *Continuity and Change* 4, 1 (1989): 165–94; Rosella Rettaroli, "Age at Marriage in Nineteenth-Century Italy," *Journal of Family History* 15, 4 (1990): 409–25; Pier Paolo Viazzo and Dionigi Albera, "The Peasant Family in Northern Italy, 1750–1930: A Reassessment," *Journal of Family History* 15, 4 (1990): 461–82.
[22] David Kertzer, *Family Life in Central Italy, 1880–1910: Sharecropping, Wage Labor, and Coresidence* (New Brunswick, NJ, 1984), 188–94. On variations in marriage systems in Spain and Portugal, see Robert Rowland, "Sistemas matrimoniales en la Península Ibérica (siglos XVI–XIX). Una perspectiva regional," in Vicente Pérez Moreda and David-Sven Reher, eds., *Demografía histórica en España* (Madrid, 1988), 72–137.

most strongly in discussions of English social history in the work of Alan Macfarlane, who argued that from late medieval times onward, English life and law were distinguished by the primacy of the individual over the family grouping, and by the absence of the sort of "familism" found among peasantries of the European continent.[23] Market forces, Macfarlane believed, regulated the ownership and transfer of land between individuals in England, whereas differing systems of law and "family strategies" that subordinated individuals to their families or kinship groups predominated elsewhere. His study of the life of one seventeenth-century English clergyman, Ralph Josselin, vividly showed how very little contact or apparent sense of identity Josselin shared with his extended kin.[24]

Research on a later period of English history suggested a model of kin relations in which people who did have sustained interactions with their kin frequently displayed an "instrumental" attitude. In his study of urban working-class households in nineteenth-century industrial Lancashire, Michael Anderson developed a "rational actor" model of kin behavior. He argued that the sorts of services that extended kin provided for one another depended on calculations of individual interests, which could result in the refusal as well as the proffering of assistance in "critical life situations," including the death of key wage earners, their unemployment, or the need for lodgings in the case of migrants who came to the city.[25] Members of the families that Anderson studied valued kin solidarity, and believed in a certain level of obligation to fairly close relatives whenever possible. Beyond these obligations to immediate family, however, assisting other relatives where obligations were not so clear meant a certain amount of negotiation. Anderson's findings about the ways individuals tried to balance their own needs or those of their conjugal family with those of extended kin illustrated nicely Hans Medick and David Sabean's model of kinship solidarity that had room for both "interest and emotion."[26] Moreover, as Peter Laslett suggested, the likelihood of giving or receiving help in money, services, or housing to or from one's kin depended on many factors having nothing to do with the desire to help. To be able to provide assistance, kin had to be alive, in physical proximity, and of an age and financial status to offer it.[27]

---

[23] Macfarlane, *The Origins*, 51, 81, 83, 94.

[24] Alan Macfarlane, *The Family Life of Ralph Josselin: An Essay in Historical Anthropology* (New York and Cambridge, 1970), 126–43.

[25] Michael Anderson, *Family Structure in Nineteenth-Century Lancashire* (Cambridge, 1971), 136–61.

[26] Hans Medick and David Warren Sabean, "Interest and Emotion in Family and Kinship Studies: A Critique of Social History and Anthropology," in Medick and Sabean, eds., *Interest and Emotion: Essays on the Study of Family and Kinship* (Cambridge, 1984), 9–23.

[27] Peter Laslett, "Family, Kinship, and Collectivity as Systems of Support in Pre-Industrial Europe: A Consideration of the 'Nuclear-Hardship' Hypothesis," *Continuity and Change* 3, 2 (1988): 157.

Laslett based his belief in the looseness of extended kin relations in England on the widespread practice of "life cycle" servanthood. In England, as in many other parts of northern Europe, young women and men of the English lower and middling classes often left their households of origin as teenagers to work for pay in households of employers who were generally not their kin. The experience of employment at young ages outside their families of birth weakened ties with parents and other kin. The ideal of neolocal residence, whereby young married people founded a new independent household, also contributed, he believed, to loosening individuals' relations with their kin.[28] However, other historians and historical anthropologists have come forward with evidence to dispute this finding. Their studies of wills, diaries, and letters suggest the existence of important face-to-face relationships and a formal recognition of kin relations in testaments and legacies.[29]

It is difficult to disentangle these conflicting interpretations. First, it can be hazardous to generalize from sources such as letters to assess the strength of extended kin relations in the past. Historians can never be sure whether these sources were representative of the population as a whole. On the other hand, measuring the strength of extended kinship ties solely from the evidence of written documents fails to capture the quotidian provision of services or the small amounts of property that changed hands within kin networks without leaving traces in letters or formal legal documents.

Moreover, research has cast some doubt on the dichotomy that Macfarlane drew between England and the Continent on the issue of "familism" there. A recent intensive study of one west-European peasant community where nearly all social relations involved interactions with kin, portrays a world that contained a great deal of individual negotiation and intra-kin strife.[30] Clearly, societies where extended kin relations were densest were not necessarily the same as places where individuals could count on the support of their kin. Indeed, Michel Verdon has recently suggested that relations among extended family members are likely to be most cordial in societies where households are small and nuclear in form and kin interactions loosest.[31] He believes that, as a rule, societies where kinship ties are weaker have more family harmony. In contrast, where strong, formalized kinship ties exist across household boundaries, conflict among extended kin is more likely to erupt.

Despite work suggesting that English and continental kin systems were not dichotomous, the belief that there have been broad and enduring regional variations in the strength of family and kinship ties continues to mark the scholarship.

---

[28] Laslett, "Characteristics," in *Family Life*, 12–49.

[29] David Cressy, "Kinship and Kin Interaction in Early Modern England," *Past and Present*, no. 113 (November, 1986): 38–69; Stone, *The Family, Sex, and Marriage*, ch. 4.

[30] David Warren Sabean, *Property, Production, and Family in Neckarhausen, 1700–1870* (New York and Cambridge, 1990), 420–1.

[31] Michel Verdon, *Rethinking Households: An Atomistic Perspective on European Living Arrangements* (London and New York, 1998), 134–5.

In a recent, wide-ranging essay, David Reher argues for the enduring importance of "weak" family systems in the north and "strong" family systems in the south, differences that still leave traces in opinions that the elderly give to pollsters about their residential preferences. In the south, the majority of the elderly favors co-residence with their children, while the elderly in most of northern Europe do not. Interestingly, however, Reher shows that these responses and other evidence of "strong" family ties in southern Europe do not correspond to subregional differences in family formation systems in southern Europe referred to above. Evidence of the ideal of strong family ties is as obvious in areas of southern Europe where nuclear families have long predominated as those where stem families are found.[32] To account for this, Reher appeals to the importance of cultural mores to explain the "path-dependency" that seems to distinguish northern from southern Europe in these matters.[33] For Reher, the "realities" of northern and southern Europe differed sufficiently over a long enough period to yield significantly different sorts of ties among extended kin that have survived into the twenty-first century.

Here, Pierre Bourdieu's distinction between "official" and "practical" kin seems quite useful.[34] Official kin are those whom one can call upon and who will agree to appear on narrowly defined ritual sorts of occasions: in the European setting, such events as baptisms or legal proceedings where property rights or the guardianship of children were being discussed. Practical kin, on the other hand, are those whom we can call upon for assistance in daily life, kin to whom one is bound rather tightly and with whom one maintains an ongoing face-to-face relationship. Although official kin bonds can certainly be useful, practical kin are even more so. It is the strength of practical kin bonds that Reher is describing in distinguishing between north and south.

As Reher acknowledges, the strength of practical kin bonds has important consequences for social policy, both past and present. In societies where individuals enjoy secure relationships with members of their own households and extended kin, these practical bonds will help to shield them in the sort of "critical life situations" that Michael Anderson studied. Conversely, where bonds of practical kinship are weak, individuals and their households will be more vulnerable. Indeed, they may need to look outside their networks of kin to find practical assistance.

Households, extended kin relations, and the "collectivity"

Peter Laslett formalized this sort of argument in his work on what he termed the "nuclear-hardship hypothesis." He suggested that the nature of a society's

[32] David Sven Reher, "Family Ties in Western Europe: Persistent Contrasts," *Population and Development Review* 24, 2 (June, 1998): 209–11.
[33] *Ibid.*, 221.
[34] Pierre Bourdieu, *Outline of a Theory of Practice*, trans. Richard Nice (Cambridge, 1977), 32–8.

household organization strongly shapes patterns of dependency of household members upon assistance from others during times of need. He argued that, especially in societies in which nuclear households were the norm, people depended upon kin outside the household as well as larger "collectivities" such as the parish, confraternal organizations, or other charitable and poor relief institutions for material assistance. The practice of neolocality, which prescribed that newly married young people set up their own households, also contributed to making nuclear households more vulnerable. He wrote: "the more widespread the nuclear family, and the more strictly neolocal rules are applied, the more important collective institutions will be for the security of the individual." In fact, "[t]he collectivity provided just those forms of assistance which might be supposed to belong to the responsibilities of family and kin." "The family and the collectivity complement each other."[35]

According to Laslett, households formed at the time of marriage and then consisting ordinarily of parents and children or even one generation were, *ceteris paribus*, more vulnerable than complex or extended households to Anderson's "critical life situations." Individuals living in smaller households were less able to spread the risks associated with life's critical situations than those who lived in large, complex households. Thus, "[t]he collectivity was normally the only agency other than the immediate family . . . which stood in an insurance relationship to the individual."[36]

Laslett's hypothesis seems to illuminate very well the interdependencies of family and community in areas where nuclear households predominated, principally northern Europe. But what relevance does his hypothesis have for societies with larger, more complex household structures, such as parts of northern Spain, central Italy, or entire social groups such as urban patricians? Were large stem or extended families in these societies or among these social groups able to care for their members without recourse to community or collective institutions?[37]

As this study will try to show, the evidence is not so clear. Organizations and institutions that cared for the poor in urban Europe included regions where some people lived in large, complex households. One of the reasons that Laslett was so sanguine about the ability of complex family systems to care for their members was his failure to differentiate among the fates of people of different genders, ages, or statuses. The need for assistance beyond household or family boundaries could differ widely between males and females, married and widowed, heirs and nonheirs. Thus, we will not be surprised to find that in some areas such as central Italy where family bonds were strong and complex households widespread, there were still many collective institutions for the care

---

[35] Laslett, "Family, Kinship," *Continuity and Change*, 156, 166.   [36] *Ibid.*, 166.

[37] For a discussion of Laslett's hypothesis for an understanding of poor relief in southern Europe, see Pier Paolo Viazzo, "Family Structures and the Early Phase in the Individual Life Cycle: A Southern European Perspective," in John Henderson and Richard Wall, eds., *Poor Women and Children in the European Past* (London and New York, 1994), 31–50.

of particular categories of individuals (young, elderly, females) or entire house-holds whose extended kin were unable or unwilling to do so. In towns and cities of both southern and northern Europe, then, a variety of "collective" or community organizations evolved to provide assistance beyond boundaries of household or extended kinship.[38]

Studying communities

The best known, if rarely read, model of how the lives of individuals, families, and communities were intertwined in the past remains Ferdinand Tönnies' classic *Community and Society*, mainly because of the distinction he drew between preindustrial life based in a tightly knit community (Gemeinschaft) and modern life lived in a loosely knit society (Gesellschaft).[39] Although Tönnies believed that "the town" could constitute a type of "community," he focused nearly exclusively on rural life, portraying preindustrial urban areas as little more than overgrown villages bearing scant resemblance to modern cities.[40]

Beyond its failure to consider seriously the importance of preindustrial towns and cities in shaping Europeans' ideas about and experience of community life, Tönnies' work presents major methodological difficulties. Particularly trouble-some is Tönnies' essentialist notion of community, which suggests that indi-viduals in communities were somehow "organically" bound to one another. In Tönnies' portrait, preindustrial communities appear as closed geographical en-tities with collective minds of their own and nearly complete internal harmony. While evocative to some, this model of community is useless for historians, since it is not clear what organic unity would look like in the historical record. Many historians, including myself, frequently accept the convenient fiction of "collective actors" such as families or communities, when members seem to be acting out of shared goals at particular times. We use these terms when we are unable to document the views of all individuals who compose those groups. This is a far cry, however, from the notion of individuals organically joined to one another within families or villages. Tönnies' model is simply too ahistorical and his concept of organic unity impossible to match with evidence from his-torical sources. Thus, it seems necessary to find other approaches to the study of the "phenomenon of community."[41]

Here, I believe that seeing communities as networks of individuals will help. It is true that historians lack access to the living informants whose testimonies

[38] Ronald Lesthaeghe, "On the Social Control of Human Reproduction," *Population and Devel-opment Review* 6, 4 (1980): 531.
[39] Ferdinand Tönnies, *Community and Society (Gemeinschaft und Gesellschaft)*, trans. and ed. Charles P. Loomis (New Brunswick, NJ and Oxford, 1988 [1957]).
[40] *Ibid.*, 62.
[41] Craig Calhoun, "History, Anthropology and the Study of Communities: Some Problems in Macfarlane's Proposal," *Social History* 3, 3 (1978): 370.

allow sociologists to reconstruct and measure people's networks of association. Nonetheless, seeing communities as networks of people helps to accomplish several things.[42] It frees us from Tönnies' overly mystical and largely unusable model. It expresses the idea that communities are, at their foundation, composed of conscious individuals. The notion of community as a network of relationships also has the advantage of accommodating flux and change as community members come and go. Finally, it suggests that communities are not just "there," but are the product of conscious efforts to invent and maintain them.[43]

For most of this book, I consider communities that were composed of individuals who actually knew and interacted with one another. But as the study proceeds, I focus on communities of increasing size and scope, culminating in my discussion, in Chapter 5, of a nation in the making. Thus, not all communities of interest to me were necessarily small or intimate, though most examples I discuss are smaller than entire countries. As I have already suggested, large, citywide confraternities in Italy appealed to many upper-class men of the fifteenth and sixteenth centuries precisely because they were neither small nor parochial, and because they facilitated wide, financially and politically useful networks of association. These latter kinds of association, based on what Mark Granovetter famously called "weak ties," were attractive for reasons that he adduced in his research on late twentieth-century society. He showed that networks of association in the city do not have to be small and intensive to be useful.[44] Friends of friends or "mere" acquaintances can be extremely valuable to those facing perennial challenges of urban life – looking for work or business connections, seeking out lodgings and material assistance to tide one over, or simply looking for a friend or a mate.

My interest in how civic communities were constructed also requires going beyond the small, face-to-face group. Once urban settlements had grown beyond a population of several thousand – perhaps the outward limit of true "face-to-face" communities – the civic community began to take on some of the qualities of an "imagined community" that Benedict Anderson has so memorably associated with the creation of the modern nation-state.[45] From the late eleventh century onwards, efforts to establish privileges of self-government often led to

---

[42] For an example of formal network analysis with historical data, see John F. Padgett and Christopher K. Ansell, "Robust Action and the Rise of the Medici, 1400–1434," *American Journal of Sociology* 98, 6 (1993): 1259–1319.

[43] Otto Gerhard Oexle, "Les Groupes sociaux du Moyen Age et les débuts de la sociologie contemporaine," *Annales, ESC* 47, 3 (1992): 761.

[44] Mark S. Granovetter, "The Strength of Weak Ties," *American Journal of Sociology* 78, 6 (1973): 1360–80; Mark Granovetter, "The Strength of Weak Ties: A Network Theory Revisited," in Peter V. Marsden and Nan Lin, eds., *Social Structure and Network Analysis* (Beverly Hills, 1982), 105–30.

[45] Benedict Anderson, *Imagined Communities: Reflections on the Origin and Spread of Nationalism*, rev. edn. (London and New York, 1991).

an increasingly self-conscious and formal articulation of urban communities as "moral persons," in which citizens had a vital interest. Urban rituals confirmed such facts. The swearing of oaths of allegiance to the civic community demonstrated ritually the voluntary nature and the strength of solidarity among members. Such ceremonies made it clear to new arrivals fortunate enough to earn the status of citizen that becoming a member of the civic community bore strong resemblances to joining an association. As one observer noted: "Like the medieval guilds, the cities and towns were based on a covenant, a solemn collective oath (or series of oaths) to a publicly expressed charter. This was not so much a social contract as a 'kind of sacrament; it both symbolized and effectuated the formation of the community and the establishment of the community's law.' "[46] Various forms of cultural expression reflected this aspiration for unity of heart and purpose. Portraits of cities and the writing of town histories both conveyed a sense of solidarity and collective identity that urban communities were supposed to embody, despite or perhaps because of the many threats of disunity among their constituent parts (see Plate 1).[47]

Considering these elements of conflict exposes another important feature of community building – that of discerning their boundaries or understanding exclusion as well as inclusion. Although this study devotes very little attention to religious minorities or the completely destitute who were largely excluded from most of the kinds of community life discussed, it does pay attention to certain elements of this problem. We will see, for example, how civic communities used their powers of regulation to banish or expel those (the poor, the religiously deviant, political enemies) who did not have sufficient wealth or demonstrate behaviors needed to belong. My discussion of women's work patterns in the city also demonstrates the close relationship between the construction of civic communities, the power of men's work communities, and the exclusion of women workers from higher-status work positions. Discussions of the religious and civic views that divided cities during the Protestant Reformation, and tensions created by attempts to construct a poor relief system in revolutionary France show vividly that building communities often entailed coercion or violence.

The coercive elements often associated with the process of community building were not limited to the oppression of subordinate or marginal groups, however. I am also interested in the fact that forging urban civic and religious

---

[46] Harold J. Berman, cited in Carter Lindberg, *Beyond Charity: Reformation Initiatives for the Poor* (Minneapolis, 1993), 53. On the sacral character of late-medieval government in the German imperial cities, see Bernd Moeller, *Imperial Cities and the Reformation*, ed. and trans. Erik Midelfort and Mark U. Edwards Jr. (Philadelphia, 1972), 44–9.

[47] See, for example, Richard C. Trexler, *Public Life in Renaissance Florence* (Ithaca, NY, 1980), xxi–xxvi, 240–70, especially his description of the functions of the feast of St. John in expressing the unity of citizens and the glory of the commune.

Plate 1 View of Nuremberg, from Petrus Bertius, *Commentariorum rerum Germanicarum* (Amsterdam, 1616).

communities often entailed pressure on the wealthy. Forcing wealthy patrician families to give up their right to settle disputes with outsiders with armed violence, or strongly encouraging (for all practical purposes forcing) those with financial resources to share some of their money with the poor, were important goals for those determined to forge community bonds. The willingness of the relatively powerful to submit to such constraints and to assist others was often grudging, especially when they were asked to extend it to those they did not consider to be full community members.

Here, I suggest that the main question is not whether such people submitted cheerfully or entirely voluntarily to demands that leaders sometimes placed on them, but whether they submitted at all. For, as Abram de Swaan has suggested in his work on charitable and social welfare systems in the West, many programs for the relief of the poor, however repressive and inadequate in the eyes of modern observers, served to create a "collective good" for their societies as a whole.[48] Religious or civic programs to feed, house, make work, or assist the

---

[48] See Abram de Swaan, *In Care of the State: Health Care, Education and Welfare in Europe and the USA in the Modern Era* (New York, 1988), 22–3.

poor in their own homes accomplished more than simply stifling social rebellion and regulating labor markets.

Many of these programs, especially ones that assisted those of the community who were considered to number among the "respectable poor" by virtue of their birth, long-term residence, or family connections in the city, conferred important entitlements to assistance. Evidence suggests that the "respectable poor" took these entitlements very seriously, and often used them creatively as one of a bundle of resources that they tried to cobble together in order to get by. Indeed, even those "dishonorable poor" who were excluded from entitlements to assistance based on urban citizenship or residency learned to use various assistance programs of the urban community for their own good. The level and security of entitlements for the poor in different urban areas, the strength of individuals' and families' claims to membership in networks of community, and their ability to use poor relief institutions could spell the difference between life and death.

Individuals and families in civil society

As these reflections on the importance of community suggest, this study rejects the idea that the family is a topic whose development should be considered as a topic in the history of "private life."[49] It argues instead for integrating family history more fully into the history of the public world. Employing the concept of "civil society" is an excellent way to effect this reorientation. The concept of civil society as formalized in western political theory has a history dating back to the seventeenth century. For John Locke, civil society was synonymous with political society, being distinct from the "state of nature."[50] Writers of the Scottish Enlightenment such as Adam Smith emphasized the natural sociability of human beings in civil society and how face-to-face relations both rested upon and reinforced bonds between individuals.[51]

On the Continent, however, observers often conceived of relations among individuals in civil society as providing the foundations of social life in a sphere that was both actually and conceptually separable from the state.[52] Well-known observers such as Rousseau, Hegel, and Marx expressed a negative view of it, seeing civil society mainly as the seat of tensions among particularistic interests that included loyalties to family and self-interest in the pursuit of financial gain.

---

[49] Philippe Ariès and Georges Duby, eds., *The History of Private Life*, 5 vols. (Cambridge, MA, 1987–1992); Katherine A. Lynch, "The Family and the History of Public Life," *Journal of Interdisciplinary History* 24, 4 (1994): 665–84.

[50] Krishan Kumar, "Civil Society: An Inquiry into the Usefulness of an Historical Term," *British Journal of Sociology* 44, 3 (1993): 376.

[51] Adam B. Seligman, *The Idea of Civil Society* (New York, 1992), 33.

[52] Kumar, "Civil Society," 390.

For Rousseau and Hegel, social life in civil society remained ethically inferior to life in the state.[53] They sought a universalistic sort of community in a state composed of citizens: one based on Reason or the "general will," which they believed was capable of transcending purely individualistic interests. This view emerged concretely during the republican phase of the French Revolution when, under the inspiration of their spiritual father Rousseau, Jacobin leaders sought to suppress the kind of "factionalism" that they believed stemmed from lingering "private" loyalties of individuals to family, friends, associations or social class. For them, solidarities of civil society were antithetical to the interests of the revolutionary Jacobin state. In their view, newly constructed solidarities of citizenship were the only legitimate ties that should bind men and women together in a new national community.[54]

My use of the term "civil society" incorporates both positive and negative features that have marked its history as a reality and a concept. I see civil society as a public sphere where individuals forged communities, and where competition, rivalry, and patterns of social inequality also developed. I use the term to refer to a sphere of public life lying outside the narrow confines of household or family, but that is distinguishable from formal political life. Seeing the life of families against the background of civil society captures individuals in their neighborhoods, at the marketplace and workplace, in their religious practices, and in voluntary associations.

The value of this approach is several-fold. First, it allows me to trace the larger social significance of family ties beyond the domestic sphere. It is also critical for understanding the position of women in European towns and cities. Largely excluded from the formal political sphere of public life, women nevertheless carried out important public functions: working inside the home contributing to the production of goods for sale; working outside the home as earners of wages or sellers of goods; participating in associational life. All of these activities allowed many women in towns and cities to create a relatively high level of autonomy for themselves compared to women in many other societies.

Such an assertion in no way minimizes restrictions that women encountered, which I discuss in a number of places in this study. Rather, it confirms key findings of cross-cultural inquiries that have identified women's access to some sort of public life, and the permeability of boundaries between domestic and public life, as an important determinant of women's social standing. In her well-known

---

[53] On Hegel's view of civil society, see Zdravko Planinc, "Family and Civil Society in Hegel's *Philosophy of Right*," *History of Political Thought* 12, 2 (Summer, 1991): 311–12 and Kumar, "Civil Society," 378–9.

[54] On the relationship between Rousseau and the Jacobin state, see Charles Taylor, "Modes of Civil Society," *Public Culture* 3, 1 (Fall, 1990): 116; and Michael Walzer, "Citizenship," in Terrence Ball, James Farr, and Russell L. Hanson, eds., *Political Innovation and Conceptual Change* (Cambridge and New York, 1989), 212.

introduction to *Woman, Culture, and Society*, for example, Michelle Rosaldo identified women's ability to cross the boundaries between domestic and public life as one of the most important determinants of women's status. She wrote:

[W]omen's status will be lowest in those societies where there is a firm differentiation between domestic and public spheres of activity and where women are isolated from one another and placed under a single man's authority, in the home. Their position is raised when they can challenge those claims to authority, either by taking on men's roles or by establishing social ties, by creating a sense of rank, order, and value in a world in which women prevail. One possibility for women, then, is to enter the men's world or to create a public world of their own. But perhaps the most egalitarian societies are those in which public and domestic spheres are only weakly differentiated, where neither sex claims much authority and the focus of social life itself is in the home.[55]

My belief that women's family roles provided them with inspiration and models for their more public relations in civil society leads me to differ somewhat with other observers of women's associational life. For example, where Linda Nicholson sees women's participation in charitable or voluntary associations as activities that were entirely consistent with the increasing "privatization" of women's lives in the nineteenth century, I argue that for centuries, these kinds of activities enabled women to combine with one another, and to develop what I think of as a kind of "shadow citizenship" within civil society, if not the formal state.[56] These kinds of experiences are no substitute for actual political entitlements, but I suggest that they deserve more attention for their importance in helping individuals forge enduring bonds of community and identity beyond domestic life. Only by limiting one's notion of public life to formal political participation can one conclude that most women in western society have ever been literally consigned to a separate, or "private" sphere of the family. Requirements of families as they developed in the West, indeed the growth of a sphere of civil society itself, depended upon women and men's presence as individuals in the public world.

But it was not just material factors, such as urban economies' dependency on women's paid labor, that led to the emergence of a sphere of public life where women and men forged community ties. Religious ideals and popular religious traditions also militated against women's relegation to a separate private sphere. Formative ideas and practices of western Christianity also figured importantly in the development of the strange notion that the individual was "an autonomous

---

[55] Michelle Z. Rosaldo, "Women, Culture and Society: A Theoretical Overview," in Rosaldo, Louise Lamphere, and Joan Bamberger, *Woman, Culture, and Society* (Stanford, 1974), 36; and Peggy Reeves Sanday, *Female Power and Male Dominance: On the Origins of Sexual Inequality* (Cambridge and New York, 1981), 113–14.

[56] Linda Nicholson, *Gender and History: The Limits of Social Theory in the Age of the Family* (New York, 1986), 3.

entity secure in his or her individuality beyond communal ties and referents."[57] Despite the strongly misogynist content of much Christian patristic writings, medieval and early modern church practices nonetheless demonstrated a conviction of at least the spiritual individuality of both men and women. Although the *concept* of civil society emerged in its thoroughly secularized form only in the seventeenth and eighteenth centuries, its moral and intellectual foundations, such as the idea of the autonomous individual, had deep historical roots. Although liberal theories of the individual citizen as the seat of political entitlement privileged males and excluded females, the idea of the autonomous individual originated long before natural rights theory.[58]

This study suggests that boundaries between domestic sphere and public life became quite permeable not only because of the participation of family members in the public life of civil society, but also through the purposeful intervention of a variety of agents and ideas into family relations. Neighbors and extended kin intervened to assist families' physical survival; clergy, city fathers, or even voluntary associations of which people were members, could act to shore up their morals, or punish various family members for violations of formal laws and informal norms.

The long-standing openness of European families to intervention by a variety of outside forces made it nearly inevitable that those who envisioned building new sorts of communities were ineluctably drawn to consider exactly how the family would fit into that new community, since ways that family members are bound to one another affects the kind of bonds one can build beyond those of kinship itself. Chapters of western history as diverse as the Protestant and Catholic Reformations and the French Revolution, to be considered here, were marked by highly charged ideological and practical efforts to build communities while defining how the bonds of family and wider community should figure in the lives of those who would be members.

The book is organized as follows. Chapter 1, "Fundamental Features of European Urban Settings," lays out the principal demographic and economic factors that characterized those settings in which family and community forms developed. It studies the importance of migration and high mortality in shaping the urban demographic system. It argues that a distinctive and enduring feature of European urban economies was their dependency upon the paid work of women. The chapter then turns to a discussion of major household and family forms typical of urban Europe. Although I argue for the dominance of relatively small nuclear households in the city, I also consider a competing kind of "patrician" household and family form among urban elites and trace patterns of neighborhood life that corresponded to both of these family forms.

---

[57] Seligman, *The Idea*, 66.
[58] On the Christian foundations of natural rights theory, see Elaine Pagels, *Adam, Eve, and the Serpent* (New York, 1988), xx, 81.

Chapter 2, "Church, Family, and Bonds of Spiritual Kinship," investigates fundamental religious values and forms of organizational life in medieval and early modern Europe. It focuses on the experience of laymen and -women in voluntary communities that were themselves often modeled on the family, and the Church's effort to elevate bonds of spiritual kinship to a status nearly equal, or sometimes even superior to that binding "natural" families. It examines in detail two movements that exemplified how urban dwellers used clerical models to build networks of community to help them face practical problems of urban life. My discussion of a movement of urban women called "beguines," and of the participation of men and women in confraternities, suggests how these associations complemented and sometimes even substituted for ties of blood.[59]

Chapter 3, "Charity, Poor Relief, and the Family in Religious and Civic Communities," examines what I see as some of the fundamental and continuous features of poor relief in western Europe from the Middle Ages through the Protestant Reformation. It begins with a discussion of the idea of charity, and focuses on the critical role that poor relief – especially relief to the domiciled or "respectable" poor – played in the construction of communities both civic and confessional from the Middle Ages to the Protestant Reformation of the sixteenth century. It examines the long-standing participation of secular authorities and ordinary laypeople in poor relief in Europe's towns and cities, and the general collaboration between civic and religious authorities in these matters. The discussion of the Reformation, particularly in areas affected by Reformed Protestantism, provides the opportunity to investigate some of the tensions that could arise between those seeking to maintain bonds of civic community and those committed to the construction of newer kinds of "confessional" communities.

Chapter 4, "Individuals, Families, and Communities in Urban Europe of the Protestant and Catholic Reformations" is set against the background of civic authorities' growing concerns about urban social order. It discusses working women's declining fortunes in urban labor markets and the rising association of women's roles with domestic life, while pointing out the renewed appeal of "maternalist" efforts within both Protestant and Catholic cities. It describes the growing intervention of confessional and civic authorities in the domestic lives of urban residents in the interests of building community. Finally, it suggests that the growth of new confessions involved a heightening of tensions among individual desires and identity, family loyalty, and community membership.

Chapter 5, "Constructing an 'Imagined Community': Poor Relief and the Family during the French Revolution" extends the terms of my study of family

---

[59] Beguines were laywomen who took temporary religious vows, often lived in communities together, and frequently worked in the textile industries. They are discussed in detail in Chapter 2.

and community in the city to an understanding of the French Revolution of 1789–94. While some observers quite rightly identify the family-based national poor relief system developed by French revolutionaries as the ancestor of the modern European welfare state, I show how revolutionaries used an older, urban, civic model of home assistance to the poor to build a new community at the level of the nation itself. As in the past, revolutionaries used the provision of assistance to the "deserving poor" to help build bonds of solidarity among individual citizens and between citizens and the nation itself.

This study makes no claims to providing an exhaustive account of community building in European society or to the history of the family's importance to that process. There are important chronological gaps in the analysis, which focuses on episodes and not on linear developments over time. However, I hope to show that the examples and larger episodes of community building analyzed here reflected recurring patterns that have been fundamental in shaping European society's particular characteristics.

1   Fundamental features of European urban settings

This chapter introduces the main features of the urban settings in which fundamental individual, family, and community relationships originated and experienced their "germination." After defining town and city, it discusses long-standing features of an urban demographic system, including migration and mortality, marriage systems, and sex ratios. It suggests that the structural features of cities' demographic regimes helped to reduce the size of households and kinship groups of the common people, making many individuals and families in the city socially and financially vulnerable in "critical life situations."

The economic system of urban places, particularly the availability of paid work for women, was inextricably tied to these patterns of urban demography, since women as well as men migrated from countryside to city to find work. The discussion of women's work identifies broad continuities and also explores variations over space and time. Variations in women's standing in urban labor markets was strongly affected by the ability of organized groups of male workers and civic governments to control access to skilled work. Women's access to relatively high-paid work may well have shaped patterns of marriage as well.

The majority of town and city dwellers lived in households with few other people, constituting what I term a "plebeian" model of household and family that was nuclear in form. However, many towns in northern and southern Europe also contained patrician families which, though they were a minority, provided another model of family life and solidarity, one that was stronger and larger. Despite these families' ideals of strength and solidarity, keeping large, extended family households together was not an easy task. The demographic, social, and even political pressures of life in late medieval and early modern cities sometimes conspired to disrupt urban patriarchs' best-laid strategies to build and maintain their family bonds.

Defining town and city

Historians of urban life have come to a fairly high level of agreement about basic demographic features that have helped distinguish European towns and cities from rural areas. Following from the work of Max Weber, historians have generally emphasized towns' economic functions, the division of labor within them, and the size, density, and relative heterogeneity of their populations when compared with rural areas.

This study uses a demographic definition of urban places, choosing a threshold population of 2,000 inhabitants to distinguish the smallest towns from rural areas. Similarly, it distinguishes town from city mainly on the basis of population size. It uses the term "town" to refer to settlements of at least 2,000 persons and "city" to refer to places with approximately 10,000 or more inhabitants. In economic terms, town connotes a kind of place that most likely served local market functions, while cities provided these services in a wider, perhaps even international network.[1] Such a distinction between town and city is most appropriate for the medieval period, when only about 21 percent of the total urban population in northern Europe lived in places with populations of 10,000 or more inhabitants.[2] By the sixteenth and seventeenth centuries, however, places with populations as large as 20,000 could feel like mere towns in the sense of their regional economic functions and outlook. Mack Walker's study of "home towns" in early modern Germany best illustrates the point. He identified home towns not only by their population size of fewer than 15,000 inhabitants, but also by the political organization, social outlook, and economic function that distinguished them from true cities of the period. Home towns of the early modern era were less likely than cities to contain entrenched patriciates; they had a higher proportion of inhabitants who were citizens; and generally exercised more control over the comings and goings of people across their borders.[3]

The main hazard of considering places with a population of 2,000 as urban is that it may lead to an overestimation of Europe's level of urbanization, particularly in the earliest periods covered by this study, when the smallest towns figure so importantly in the calculations. A threshold this low risks including places that were essentially large agglomerated villages, especially the "agro-cities" of the Iberian and Italian peninsulas, whose populations contained large numbers of people working in agriculture.[4] The two major studies which provide estimates of levels of urbanization in Europe over time agree, however, that the main barrier to including the smallest towns (population 1,000–2,000) in calculations of European urbanization is not that these places lacked urban

---

[1] Edward Whiting Fox made this distinction in a slightly different way, referring to the "trade" functions of towns and the "commerce" functions of cities. See *History in Geographic Perspective: The Other France* (New York, 1971), 34; Paul M. Hohenberg and Lynn Hollen Lees, *The Making of Urban Europe, 1000–1950* (Cambridge, MA, 1985), 4–5, 47–73.

[2] This figure is calculated from data in Hohenberg and Lees, *The Making*, table 2.1, 53.

[3] Walker notes that by 1800 one-quarter of the German population, including German-speaking parts of Austria, lived in 4,000 such towns, while 7 percent lived in thirty-six "cities." See Mack Walker, *German Home Towns: Community, State, and General Estate, 1648–1871* (Ithaca, NY, 1971), 32.

[4] Jan de Vries, *European Urbanization, 1500–1800* (Cambridge, MA, 1984), 54.

characteristics, but that the sources to study the size and composition of their populations are faulty or lacking.[5]

Research on settlements that had even fewer than 2,000 people suggests that some of these places possessed characteristics of towns. In his study of England on the eve of the plague epidemics of the fourteenth century, for example, Rodney Hilton detailed the extensive division of labor that existed in places whose populations numbered even fewer than 1,000. Beyond a wide range of food service workers such as bakers, brewers, and fishmongers who lived in the town of Halesowen, a market town of England's West Midlands, there was a lively and diverse production and trade in woolens, leather, flax and linen, metal and wood. Halesowen also contained large numbers of that cast of characters who would figure prominently in the urban setting for centuries to come – servants, "disreputable elements," migrants attempting to settle in the town (illegally in the eyes of seigneurial authorities), and respectable burghers, many of whom were themselves migrants.[6] The choice of a 2,000-person threshold of an agglomerated population as an urban baseline, particularly before the nineteenth century, therefore seems reasonable. It also has the advantage of corresponding with definitions used in later official statistics.[7]

Choosing the correct threshold for considering places as urban is not purely a statistical task, however. It has important consequences for the interpretation of Europe's urban past.[8] The lower the population size threshold chosen for identifying places as urban, the more continuous the history of European urban life appears to be (see Table 1.1).

From approximately 1300 to 1800, the proportion of the European population dwelling in places with 2,000 or more inhabitants increased only modestly, from approximately 14 to 17.5 percent of the total. Taking the figure of 5,000 as the cutoff point for defining a "town" yields a similar portrait of stability in levels of urbanization over time. The two available estimates for the proportion of the European population dwelling in towns and cities with populations over 5,000

---

[5] See Paul Bairoch, Jean Batou, and Pierre Chèvre, *La Population des villes européennes: banque de données et analyse sommaire des résultats, 800–1850* (Geneva, 1988), 300 for a defense of their use of the threshold of 2,000 souls for defining a town. De Vries' decision to focus on cities of at least 10,000 was also based on source problems. See *Urbanization*, 21–2. For a discussion of typologies and thresholds of city types, see Roger Mols, *Introduction à la démographie des villes d'Europe du XIVe au XVIIIe siècle* (Louvain, 1954–56), vol. II, 39–40.

[6] R. H. Hilton, "Small Town Society in England before the Black Death," *Past and Present*, no. 105 (November, 1984): 53–78; R. H. Hilton, "Medieval Market Towns and Simple Commodity Production," *Past and Present*, no. 109 (November, 1985): 3–4. David Herlihy and Christiane Klapisch-Zuber explored the urban status and functions of Tuscan communities with populations as small as 800: see *Tuscans and their Families: A Study of the Florentine Catasto of 1427* (New Haven, CT, 1985), 53–4.

[7] Philip Benedict, "Was the Eighteenth Century an Era of Urbanization in France?" *Journal of Interdisciplinary History* 21, 2 (Autumn, 1990): 183–4.

[8] For a critical evaluation of de Vries' and Bairoch *et al.*'s methods see Benedict, "Eighteenth Century," 183.

Table 1.1. *Size and relative weight of the urban population, Europe 1300–1800*

Year	1300	1400	1500	1600	1700	1800
Population living in towns of 2,000 and above (in millions)	[10.6][a]	[10.3]	11.4	15.4	16.9	26.6
Percent of total population living in category	[14.0]	[18.4]	15.1	17.1	16.7	17.5
Population living in towns of 5,000 and above (in millions)	7.8	7.6	8.4	11.6	13.2	20.9
Percent of total population living in category (est. 1)[b]	10.3	13.6	11.2	12.9	12.9	13.8
Percent of total population living in category (est. 2)[c]	—	—	9.6	10.8	11.9	13.0
Percent of total population living in towns of 10,000 and above[d]	—	—	5.6	7.6	9.2	10.0
Percent of population living in towns of 40,000 and above[e]	—	—	1.9	3.5	5.2	5.6

Notes:
[a] Bairoch *et al.* note that figures in brackets have "a higher . . . margin of error than other figures for the same period."
[b] Bairoch *et al.*, table B2, 254.
[c] De Vries, table 4.14, 76.
[d] De Vries, table 3.7, 39.
[e] De Vries, table 4.14, 76.

Sources: Paul Bairoch, Jean Batou, and Pierre Chèvre, *La Population des villes européennes: banque de données et analyse sommaire des résultats, 800–1850* (Geneva, 1988), table B2, 254; Jan de Vries, *European Urbanization, 1500–1800* (Cambridge, MA, 1984), table 4.14, 76.

Table 1.2. *Percent of population living in cities of 10,000 inhabitants and above, Europe 1500–1800, by region*

Year	1500	1600	1700	1800
Central[a]	3.7	5.0	7.1	7.1
Eastern[b]	1.1	1.4	2.6	4.2
Mediterranean[c]	9.5	13.7	11.7	12.9
North and West[d]	6.6	8.2	13.1	14.9

Notes:
[a] Germany, France, Switzerland.
[b] Austria-Bohemia, Poland.
[c] Italy, Spain, Portugal.
[d] Scandinavia, England and Wales, Scotland, Ireland, Netherlands, Belgium.
Source: Jan de Vries, *European Urbanization, 1500–1800* (Cambridge, MA, 1984), table 3.7, 39.

differ somewhat in their figures for 1500 (11.2 versus 9.6 percent urban), but converge at a figure of approximately 13–14 percent by the year 1800.

In contrast, defining levels of urbanization by focusing on cities of 10,000 or larger sharpens the impression of discontinuity. By this measurement, the urban population of Europe nearly doubled as a proportion of the total population between 1500 and 1800, from 5.6 to 10 percent. A sense of discontinuity also emerges in figures for cities of 10,000 or more inhabitants broken down by broad subregions, with the possible exception of the Mediterranean area, which has had a longer history of large agglomerations (see Tables 1.2 and 1.3).[9] Considering places with populations as low as 2,000 or even 1,000 as truly urban and including them in this study therefore emphasizes continuities.

Continuity does not mean stasis, however. Nor were patterns of growth linear, despite what figures in Tables 1.1 and 1.2 suggest. Although useful for tracking the "big picture" of urban history, calculating aggregate levels of urbanization by comparing population figures at 100-year intervals can be quite misleading. With the possible exception of England, western Europe's history of urbanization was quite cyclical at least up to the late eighteenth or nineteenth century.[10] What was most constant was a system of alternating phases of expansion and decline that affected the proportions of Europe's population who resided in towns and cities.[11] Periods of greatest increase in these proportions occurred

[9] On spatial variations in levels and patterns of urbanization, see Bairoch *et al.*, *La Population*, 253.
[10] De Vries, *Urbanization*, 38–40, notes that any idea of a gradual urbanization of Europe is a statistical artifact. See also Jan de Vries, "Problems in the Measurement, Description, and Analysis of Historic Urbanization," in Ad van der Woude, Akira Hayami, and de Vries, eds., *Urbanization in History: A Process of Dynamic Interactions* (Oxford, 1990), 44–8.
[11] See Hohenberg and Lees' suggestive model of alternating phases of economic expansion in rural and urban sectors, in *The Making*, 113–20.

Table 1.3. *Percent of the population living in (a) towns of 5,000 and above and (b) cities of 10,000 and above, 1300–1850, by country or region*

	1300	1400	1500	1600	1700	1800	1850
Belgium							
(a)	22.4	39.0	28.0	29.3	30.6	21.7	
(b)			21.1	18.8	23.9	18.9	20.5
England and Wales							
(b)			3.1	5.8	13.3	20.3	40.8
France							
(a)	8.0	10.8	8.8	10.8	12.3	12.9	
(b)			4.2	5.9	9.2	8.8	14.5
Germany							
(a)	7.9	11.1	8.2	8.5	7.7	9.4	
(b)			3.2	4.1	4.8	5.5	10.8
Ireland							
(b)			0.0	0.0	3.4	7.0	10.2
Italy							
(a)	20.8	24.1	22.1	22.6	22.6	21.9	
(b)			12.4	15.1	13.2	14.6	20.3
Netherlands							
(a)	13.8	21.7	29.5	34.7	38.9	34.1	
(b)			15.8	24.3	33.6	28.8	29.5
Portugal							
(a)	8.0	14.4	15.0	16.7	18.5	15.2	
(b)			3.0	14.1	11.5	8.7	13.2
Scandinavia							
(a)	0.8	1.7	2.2	3.8	4.8	6.2	
(b)			0.9	1.4	4.0	4.6	5.8
Scotland							
(b)			1.6	3.0	5.3	17.3	32.0
Spain							
(a)	21.5	26.3	18.4	21.3	20.3	19.5	
(b)			6.1	11.4	9.0	11.1	17.3
Switzerland							
(a)	2.7	8.3	6.8	5.5	5.9	6.9	
(b)			1.5	2.5	3.3	3.7	7.7
United Kingdom							
(a)	4.4	5.7	4.6	7.9	11.8	20.8	

Sources: Bairoch, Batou, and Chèvre, *La Population des villes européennes*, table B5, 259; De Vries, *European Urbanization*, tables 3.7, 39; 3.8, 45–8. Figures for Italy computed from tables 3.2, 30; and 3.6, 36–7.

from the eleventh through the thirteenth centuries, during the sixteenth century, and most explosively during the nineteenth century.[12]

Cross-sectional measures of the proportion of the urban population at any point in time also underestimate the number of people in the population who had had some experience, however temporary, with urban life and mores. Efforts to calculate net rates of migration between rural areas and towns, useful for estimating the relative demographic size of urban and rural sectors of the economy, are no exception. Using a method pioneered by Tony Wrigley, Jan de Vries attempted to estimate what proportion of rurally born Europeans could have been predicted to migrate to a town or city based on certain assumptions about fertility and mortality rates in urban and rural sectors, and the relative sizes of those sectors. For the period 1500–1800, de Vries' calculations showed a net permanent migration to urban areas of less than 10 percent of the rurally born who survived to twenty years of age, with estimates for northern Europe below those for Mediterranean Europe, except for the period 1600–1650.[13] The problem with such estimates, as de Vries shows, is that they are designed to assess only net permanent migration to towns and cities and do not count the number of actual incidents of in- and out-migration, nor the importance of temporary migration from countryside to town and city.[14]

Interestingly, according to one estimate, the proportion of people dwelling in places that can reliably be thought of as towns was often not far below the maximum number that could be accommodated in them given the capacity of agricultural and transportation systems to produce and supply food. One set of calculations for Europe as a whole (minus Russia) estimated that the proportion of the population that *could* have lived in towns was approximately 15 percent for towns of 5,000 or more and 20 percent in towns of 2,000 or more for areas not dependent upon agricultural imports from abroad and not practicing any agricultural employment themselves.[15]

Beyond a relative stability in the proportions of Europeans living in towns of 2,000 or more and the system of cyclical urban development that sustained them, lies a third continuous element in the history of European urban life – the persistence of the actual towns and cities in which urban life took place over the long term. As Jan de Vries observed: "The high middle ages endowed most of

---

[12] *Ibid.*, 7–9.   [13] De Vries, *Urbanization*, 200–9, tables 10.2, 10.3.

[14] *Ibid.*, 202–6. On the extraordinarily high number of individual moves underlying net levels of migration, see Ingrid Eriksson and John Rogers, "Mobility in an Agrarian Community: Practical and Methodological Considerations," in Kurt Ågren, David Gaunt, Ingrid Eriksson, John Rogers, Anders Norberg and Sune Åkerman, eds., *Aristocrats, Farmers, Proletarians: Essays in Swedish Demographic History* (Stockholm, 1973), 60–87.

[15] Bairoch *et al.*, *La Population*, 257.

Map 1 European towns and cities

Europe with a stock of urban settlements and market towns that was little altered
until the rise of the factory system."[16] Although urban populations experienced
very high rates of turnover, the set of places in which this turnover occurred
remained quite stable until the nineteenth century, enhancing the growth of
forms of urban sociability and outlook that themselves endured over time.

Links between countryside and city

Many observers have seen something distinctive about life in urban areas. However, they have not always agreed on what accounted for it. In the introduction
to a well-known collection of essays in urban history, Philip Abrams warned
about the dangers of searching for a conceptual model of "the town" or "the
city." He believed that such a search risked reifying the concept, leading to

[16] De Vries, *Urbanization*, 69.

a view of the town as an autonomous reality removed from the rural world that surrounded it. Instead, he suggested that scholars approach urban areas "as fields of action integral to some larger world...within which the interactions and contradictions of that larger world are displayed with special clarity."[17]

One way of gaining better insight into these interactions is to pay special attention to the movements of people between countryside and city, which increased and declined along with oscillations in the economy or changes in social conditions. Philip Benedict's observations about the sixteenth-century town could just as well be applied to those of earlier times. He noted: the sixteenth-century town was an "accordion, expanding when harvest failures or warfare led inhabitants from the surrounding countryside to seek refuge or charity behind city walls, shrinking when plagues sent the rich fleeing to the safety of their country estates or prolonged economic difficulties provoked the emigration of skilled artisans."[18] The in- and out-migration of people between countryside and city helped to integrate rural and urban areas and to intermix rural and urban habits and beliefs. In-migrants helped build and replenish urban working- and upper-class populations and kept urban economies functioning. Indeed, their presence in European towns and cities as servants, unskilled workers, business people, government officials, and clergy was part of what lent towns and cities their distinctiveness.

Towns and cities were not unique in being sites of migration. Nor did their attraction as poles of migration for those looking for work distinguish them entirely from rural areas of western Europe. However, the numbers and proportions of migrants in urban populations generally outweighed those in most rural areas. It was therefore a difference of scale and often permanency of settlement. Migrants may have been most obvious in the vast seaports or "network" cities of the late medieval and early modern world, which attracted newcomers from far-reaching areas of the globe. However, even the most provincial towns required migrants to fulfill their labor needs. This fact of migration's impact on European society has not always appeared with sufficient emphasis, however.

For example, most of the best social-historical inquiries into the *ancien régime démographique* inadvertently obscured the importance of migration by organizing themselves around the study of rural places rather than rurally born

[17] Philip Abrams, "Introduction," in Abrams and E. A. Wrigley, eds., *Towns in Societies: Essays in Economic History and Historical Sociology* (New York and Cambridge, 1978), 3. He also criticizes Weber, among others, for his emphasis on the formal properties of towns and cities (28).

[18] Philip Benedict, "French Cities from the Sixteenth Century to the Revolution: An Overview," in Benedict, ed., *Cities and Social Change in Early Modern France* (London and Boston, 1989), 13.

people.[19] Because of the data requirements of family reconstitution studies, which needed to follow married couples through time to understand their reproductive behavior, many studies excluded migrants from analysis, focusing instead on men and women who remained in their villages of origin for their whole married lives. Studies of the preindustrial rural world that focus exclusively on those who lived out their lives in their places of birth, however, leave out of consideration migrants whose departure, whether temporary or permanent, often helped perpetuate family and inheritance systems in their rural places of birth. Only a few family reconstitution studies of the urban world gave migration in and out of towns and cities the attention that it deserves.[20]

Migration to search for work has been a key part of western European demographic and family systems since the beginning of the end of serfdom in the eleventh and twelfth centuries.[21] In one of its best-known and most long-standing forms, farm servants, particularly in northern Europe, circulated within rather small, well-defined geographical areas seeking yearly contracts for work. Although the author of the best study of this kind of population movement characterized it as "mobility" rather than "migration" because of its circumscribed areal extent and short-term nature, it is clear that this mobility captured some of the essential features of the migration experience. Its goal was paid work. It was not random in nature, but was usually based on information about job availability.[22]

Short-distance migration was not the only type of movement involving agricultural laborers, however. Annual long-distance migrations of groups of harvest workers such as those between the German province of Westphalia and

---

[19] Katherine A. Lynch, "The European Marriage Pattern in the Cities: Variations on a Theme by Hajnal," *Journal of Family History* 16, 1 (1991): 79–96; Leslie Page Moch, *Moving Europeans: Migration in Western Europe since 1650* (Bloomington, 1992), 22–36 for discussions of the problems of leaving migrants out of village studies and of underestimating the importance of migration in early modern and modern Europe.

[20] They include: Alfred Perrenoud, *La Population de Genève du seizième au début du dix-neuvième siècle: étude démographique* (Geneva, 1979) and Jean-Pierre Bardet, *Rouen aux XVIIe et XVIIIe siècles: les mutations d'un espace social* (Paris, 1983), vol. I, 210–17. Steve Hochstadt notes that migration did not even figure as a part of Michael Flinn's well-known work on the European Demographic System: see Hochstadt, "Migration in Preindustrial Germany," *Central European History* 16, 3 (1983): 196.

[21] Jean Lestocquoy noted that it took ten years for freed serfs to earn citizenship in medieval Florence. See: *Aux origines de la bourgeoisie: Les Villes de Flandre et d'Italie sous le gouvernement des patriciens (XIe–XVe siècles* (Paris, 1952), 47. Richard M. Smith, however, notes that even serfdom did not inhibit migration for marriage, at least in England. See: "Some Reflections on the Evidence for the Origins of the 'European Marriage Pattern' in England," in Chris Harrison in association with Michael Anderson *et al.*, eds., *The Sociology of the Family: New Directions for Britain* (Keele, 1979), 97.

[22] A. S. Kussmaul estimated that farm servants who were hired on an annual basis in eighteenth and early-nineteenth-century England migrated approximately 5–15 kms at a time between successive employers. See "The Ambiguous Mobility of Farm Servants," *Economic History Review* 34, 2 (1981): 228, tables 4–5.

Dutch province of Holland complemented the more widespread practices of short-distance migration.[23] Migration for work did not require that one be born near a town or city, but only that one have the information, the motive, and means to travel to where one's labor might be needed.[24]

Systems of migration linking rural and urban regions even grew up in areas where they might be least expected, in parts of Europe that at first view seem to have been most removed from contact with urban influences. Despite the lack of urban development, mountainous regions were often part of migration systems linking them to the larger urban world. One study of the western Alpine region in the early modern period, for example, showed the importance of long-distance seasonal migration involving men who trekked from mountain villages to work as plasterers and masons in towns and cities below. In what has been termed the "Alpine paradox," villages' altitude and distance from urban destinations were good predictors neither of the direction and numerical importance of migrants, nor of which mountain settlements were most linked to urban labor markets. Although men living in villages at medium altitudes migrated for short-term work as harvest laborers in adjacent villages, men from the most physically "remote" villages, those at 1200–1600 meters, were more apt to migrate in to work in towns and cities.[25]

Certain of these mountainous regions were known for the presence of "stem" families, those in which one child was designated heir and made responsible for the care of aged parents for as long as they survived. Heirs were also responsible for the ancestral "house" and for supporting their unmarried siblings who co-resided there. In his depictions of this "stem family" type, nineteenth-century conservative commentator Frédéric Le Play portrayed them as a powerful source of stability in a changing world, one far removed from the disintegrative forces that weakened urban nuclear families.[26]

However, more finely meshed analysis has revealed the critical importance of urban migration to the success of these rural families and lineages. Indeed, those families that were best able to survive across generations and whose members

---

[23] Moch, *Moving Europeans*, 40–3.

[24] These are some of the characteristics distinguishing migration from vagrancy, though vagrancy was sometimes the result of failed efforts at migration. See A. L. Beier, *Masterless Men: The Vagrancy Problem in England 1560–1640* (London, 1985), 29.

[25] Pier Paolo Viazzo, *Upland Communities: Environment, Population and Social Structure in the Alps since the Sixteenth Century* (New York and Cambridge, 1989), 142.

[26] On stem families, see Antoinette Fauve-Chamoux, "Les Structures familiales au royaume des familles-souches: Esparros," *Annales, ESC* 39, 3 (May–June, 1984): 513–28; and Fauve-Chamoux and Emiko Ochiai, eds., *House and the Stem Family in EurAsian Perspective*. Proceedings of the C18 Session, Twelfth International Economic History Congress (Kyoto, 1998). On Le Play, see Peter Laslett, "Introduction: The History of the Family," in Laslett and Richard Wall, eds., *Household and Family in Past Time* (Cambridge, 1972), 16–23; and Louis Assier-Andrieu, "Le Play et la famille-souche des Pyrénées: politique, juridisme et science sociale," *Annales, ESC* 39, 3 (May–June, 1984): 495–512.

were most successful in amassing property were often the ones most apt to involve selective out-migration. In what some observers have seen as families' migration "strategies," certain members of each generation migrated out of their families and villages of birth – often for years at a time – and returned with financial resources that could be used to bolster their own and their relatives' chances of survival.

This was illustrated in Emmanuel Le Roy Ladurie's study of one fourteenth-century village in southern France. Here, the out-migration of nonheirs served first to relieve their households of the burden of supporting them. Ideally, after an absence working for wages either in the immediate region or across the Pyrenees in Spain, adult migrants returned home with cash earned elsewhere, or sometimes settled permanently in their destination. Similarly, in her study of the Pyrenees region, Anne Zink showed that in some areas where stem families predominated, the majority of younger children chose to work either temporarily or permanently outside the familial home. They preferred this even though they could have counted on a more secure material life by residing in the family home and accepting permanent celibacy and dependency on the heir.[27]

During periods of harsh weather or in cases of severe imbalances between households' number of mouths to feed and their labor requirements, individual out-migration could sometimes turn rapidly into the sort of vagrancy or "subsistence" migration that was driven mainly by poor conditions at home. Yet poor mountainous areas of Europe also spawned important networks of organized kinds of migration even more elaborate than the seasonal migration of gangs of male workers.[28] By the eighteenth century, for example, family networks originating in one village in the mountainous province of the French Dauphiné became deeply involved in both the itinerant and more settled urban aspects of book selling, the success of such a business being based on the dispersal of individual family members over a wide territory.[29]

Shifting the focus of analysis from the study of places to the study of people over time and space broadens our understanding of migration's effects on rural and urban society. Stem families or other complex family forms associated with parts of Europe far removed from towns or cities, and that can appear so autarkic, were often deeply linked to urban economies through the movement of their members.

---

[27] Emmanuel Le Roy Ladurie, *Montaillou: village occitan de 1294 à 1324* (Paris, 1975), 108–98; Anne Zink, *L'Héritier de la maison: géographie coutumière du sud-ouest de la France sous l'Ancien Régime* (Paris, 1993), 167–75.

[28] D. J. Siddle, "Migration as a Strategy of Accumulation: Social and Economic Change in Eighteenth-Century Savoy," *Economic History Review* 50, 1 (1997): 17, usefully distinguishes between "crisis" and "organized" migration.

[29] Laurence Fontaine, "Droit et stratégies: la reproduction des systèmes familiaux dans le Haut-Dauphiné (XVIIe–XVIIIe siècles)," *Annales, ESC* 47, 6 (November–December, 1992): 1259–77.

Apprentices constituted one of the most recognizable migrant groups. Although large numbers of urban fathers and mothers passed on their occupations to their children, apprenticeships also attracted young people from outside towns and cities from rural and small-town populations. In fourteenth- and fifteenth-century Toulouse, for example, notarial apprenticeship contracts reveal that over half of all apprentices and young male servants who came into the city for a two- or three-year training period came from outside the town and its immediate suburbs. By later standards, many of them were very young, from 8 to 12 years old, and came to the city from other towns and small hamlets, oftentimes with the help of relatives residing in Toulouse.[30]

The size of urban places seems to have affected the extensiveness of the distances from which migrants came. While towns usually attracted most migrants from their immediate hinterlands, larger cities' fields of attraction were correspondingly greater. Among a sample of apprentices who migrated into sixteenth-century London, for example, fully two-thirds had come at least eighty miles, and one-half from homes at least ninety miles away from the capital.[31] Some seasonal migrants also walked long distances. Wealthier migrants, who were more likely to circulate among different cities, used more expensive modes of transport to move among places located hundreds of miles apart.

Although families of urban elites frequently based their claims to political hegemony in urban society on their families' long-term residence in cities they governed, many of these groups consisted of families only a generation or two removed from an ancestor who had been admitted to citizenship or to political office. In a study of the southern French town of Aix-en-Provence based on a sample of men who practiced law or held public office in the years 1400–1535, only about one-third of their families had resided in the town for three generations or more, though only 16 percent of actual office holders were themselves migrants. However, fully 75 percent of such in-migrants had wives who had been born in the town.[32]

Sixteenth-century citizenship records of London show that of 1,055 newly sworn citizens whose birthplace could be determined, five-sixths had migrated to the capital.[33] Estimates of the proportion of migrants among those who earned full citizenship status in early modern German towns ranged from a low of 15 to 20 percent for the Swabian town of Nördlingen (population about 10,000

---

[30] Philippe Wolff, *Commerces et marchands de Toulouse (vers 1350–vers 1450)* (Paris, 1954), 78–81.
[31] Steve Lee Rappaport, *Worlds within Worlds: Structures of Life in Sixteenth-Century London* (New York and Cambridge, 1989), 80. The author notes that the majority were coming from a "rural-and semirural-to-urban" situation (81). His sample of apprentices traveled an average of 115 miles to London in the early 1550s (77).
[32] Lucie Larochelle, "L'Intégration des étrangers au sein de l'oligarchie d'Aix-en-Provence (1400–1535)," in *Les Sociétés urbaines en France méridionale et en péninsule ibérique au Moyen Age* (Paris, 1991), 340.
[33] Rappaport, *Worlds*, 77. The sample is from 1551–3.

in 1579) to about 50 percent for a sample of citizenship lists (*Bürgerbücher*) for twenty-four medieval and early modern German towns and cities.[34] Estimates of *annual* rates of migration for a sample of German cities and towns range from 3 to 8 percent, with little apparent variation by period or town size.[35] The same study showed that the proportion of German workers who did not desire or could not afford full citizenship rights was even higher, totaling nearly five-sixths of the working-class populations in these areas.[36]

Figures for a later period are even higher. For example, dispensary and hospital records for seventeenth- and eighteenth-century London or Bordeaux, which overrepresent the most impoverished portions of the population, show that nearly 75 percent of those treated had migrated in from outside.[37] Thus, although migrants usually constituted an especially large proportion of the urban working classes, no social group in town or city was without important numbers of newcomers.

Migration levels would probably have been even higher than they were had town and city officials allowed them to be, since many urban governments did not eagerly welcome all newcomers at all times. Local legislation, as in the case of many early modern German towns, regional statutes regulating the numbers and qualities of migrants admitted to Italian towns, and national laws, such as England's Tudor Poor Laws, enabled authorities to expel migrants for reasons ranging from poverty or immoral conduct to officials' fear of unemployment and disorder.[38] Workers in western Europe were freer to circulate through the countryside than servile rural labor forces of eastern Europe. However, their movements into towns and cities sometimes occurred despite repressive laws of settlement that officials could bring out and dust off when economic crises or fear of urban rebellion made it seem wise to expel the poor or the troublemakers from city premises. Governments in large cities were probably less able, willing, or eager to effect this sort of police control over their borders.

[34] Christopher R. Friedrichs, "Immigration and Urban Society: Seventeenth-Century Nördlingen," in Etienne François, ed., *Immigration et société urbaine en Europe occidentale, XVIe–XXe siècle* (Paris, 1985), 69–71, and *Urban Society in an Age of War: Nördlingen, 1580–1720* (Princeton, 1979), 38; Hochstadt, "Migration," 199.

[35] Hochstadt, "Migration," 209. [36] *Ibid.*, 199–203.

[37] John Landers, *Death and the Metropolis: Studies in the Demographic History of London, 1670–1830* (New York and Cambridge, 1993), 47–8; Colin Jones and Michael Sonenscher, "The Social Functions of the Hospital in Eighteenth-Century France: The Case of the Hôtel-Dieu of Nîmes," *French Historical Studies* 13, 2 (Fall, 1983): 181–2; Jean-Pierre Poussou, *Bordeaux et le sud-ouest au XVIIIe siècle: croissance économique et attraction urbaine* (Paris, 1983), 50–1, notes the various problems involved in inferring migrant status from deaths in urban hospitals.

[38] E. Fasano-Guarini, "Politique et population dans l'histoire des villes italiennes aux XVIe et XVIIe siècles," *Annales de démographie historique* (1982): 77–90; on England, Philip Styles, "The Evolution of the Law of Settlement," in *Studies in Seventeenth–Century West Midlands History* (Kineton, 1978), 175–204.

The migration of women to work in towns and cities, coupled with higher rates of mortality for men, created an urban setting where females generally outnumbered men, according to fragmentary evidence on the ratio of males to females generally available only since the sixteenth century (see Table 1.4). There were, of course, some exceptions, generally in southern Europe in cities with high numbers of male clergy, such as Rome. Port towns and those where soldiers were garrisoned also represented exceptions to this "rule."[39] Whether this characteristic of towns and cities existed as early as the medieval period is impossible to say. Given the long-standing participation of women in urban labor markets and the higher mortality of men in urban as well as rural places in the European past, it seems very likely.[40]

Urban mortality

Once arrived in an urban environment, men and women new to the city encountered a mortality regime that was generally more unfavorable to survival than that of rural areas. High rates of urban mortality stemmed from the deleterious effects of population density, including poor sanitation, and the agglomeration of people in sufficient numbers to support a disease regime of endemic infection. Medieval towns were often more densely inhabited than some modern cities. A study of medieval Winchester, an English town of 7,000–8,000 in 1400, showed 29 persons per acre within the town's walls, and up to 81 in the town's center.[41]

High rates of mortality were linked to migration to towns and cities in several ways.[42] First, high mortality in the towns and cities itself stimulated in-migration from the countryside. In the most orthodox statement of what has been termed

---

[39] Eugenio Sonnino, "Between the Home and the Hospice: The Plight and Fate of Girl Orphans in Seventeenth- and Eighteenth-Century Rome," in John Henderson and Richard Wall, eds., *Poor Women and Children in the European Past* (London and New York, 1994), 96; Antoinette Fauve-Chamoux, "Le Surplus urbain des femmes en France préindustrielle et le rôle de la domesticité," *Population* 53, 1–2 (1998): 359–78 and the numerous references therein.

[40] On migrant women in the medieval city and their precarious financial position, see Sharon Farmer, *Surviving Poverty in Medieval Paris: Gender, Ideology, and the Daily Lives of the Poor* (Ithaca, NY and London, 2002), 20–5, 136–64.

[41] Christopher Dyer, *Standards of Living in the Later Middle Ages: Social Change in England, c. 1200–1520* (New York and Cambridge, 1989), 189. The author notes that this density figure for medieval Winchester, "exceeds the densities in modern British cities." Additional figures on the densities of urban populations before 1500 show totals ranging from a low of 38 for Danzig in 1380 to a high of 176 for Lübeck with the median around 100. See Mols, *Introduction*, vol. III, table 1, 189–96, and vol. II, 92–3.

[42] On the interaction of mortality and migration in the demographic histories of western Europe and the United States, see Katherine A. Lynch, "Geographical Mobility and Urban Life: Comparative Perspectives on American and European Demographic Trends in the Past," in A. Bideau, A. Perrenoud, K. A. Lynch, and G. Brunet, eds., *Les Systèmes démographiques du passé* (Lyon, 1996), 203–23.

Table 1.4. *Sex ratios (males/females) for selected European cities*

City/Town	16th Century			17th Century			18th Century		
	Year	Total Pop.	Adult Pop.	Year	Total Pop.	Adult Pop.	Year	Total Pop.	Adult Pop.
Amsterdam									
(Christians)							1795	0.806	0.725
(Jews)							1795	0.901	0.833
Bern							1764	0.714	0.641
Bologna	1581	0.962		1600	0.935		1708	0.909	
				1645	0.909				
Bruges							1784	0.847	0.758
Florence	1551	0.826		1622	0.820		1710	0.781	
	1562	0.806		1631	0.840		1738	0.901	
				1632	0.826	0.787	1766	0.909	
				1642	0.870	0.746	1794	0.926	
				1661	0.855	0.787			
Lille				1677	0.935	0.746			
				1686	0.917	0.794			
Louvain	1597		0.714	1631		0.794	1784	0.926	0.909
Marseille							1765	0.971	0.952
Naples							1765	1.031	
							1780	0.980	
							1796	0.990	

City	Year	Index	Index	Year	Index	Index	Year	Index
Rome	1592	1.724		1602	1.515		1702	1.389
				1627	1.667		1727	1.282
				1652	1.449		1752	1.266
				1677	1.449		1777	1.235
Venice	1563	1.075	1.020	1606	0.971	0.870	1766	0.980
	1581	1.064	0.962	1642		0.862	1771	1.087
	1586	1.042	0.943	1655	0.901	0.787	1790	0.962
	1593	1.149	0.980					
Verona				1616	0.909		1716	0.943
							1770	0.917
							1790	0.935
Ypres				1689	0.833	0.758		
Zurich				1637	0.813	0.735		
				1671	0.741	0.833		

Source: Roger Mols, *Introduction à la démographie historique des villes d'Europe du XIVe au XVIIIe siècle*. 3 vols. (Louvain, 1955), II:183–93.

the "urban graveyard" or the "urban deficit" effect, chronically high "normal" rates of infant and child mortality and the more lethal intensity of epidemic and endemic diseases striking adults in European towns and cities, combined to create environments where fresh recruits were usually in high demand. Evidence of population extinction and high population turnover is available from some medieval sources. For example, Plague epidemics in Albi in the fourteenth century were responsible for eliminating nine-tenths of family names there. In Chalon-sur-Saône, approximately three-quarters of household heads in 1381 bore names that had not been present in the town twenty years earlier. Studies of medieval tax records yield the same impression, showing that a 50 percent turnover in family names within ten years was not unusual.[43]

The urban graveyard hypothesis has met with some criticism, however. In a well-known but still unresolved debate, Allan Sharlin challenged the hypothesis, arguing that migration was more cause than remedy of high urban mortality. In his view, migrants, many of whom remained in the towns only temporarily, helped to cause towns' and cities' inability to sustain themselves demographically because so many remained unmarried during their time in the city. They thereby contributed many deaths but few births to the cities' demographic ledgers. Other scholars have rejected Sharlin's own logic, however. In addition to evidence of inter-marriage between migrants, they also show that even the native inhabitants of many towns, whom Sharlin identified as the source of urban populations' ability to replace themselves, were unable to maintain their own numbers in large part because of high mortality rates.[44] Although towns could experience natural increase in their populations over a number of years, high mortality seems to have been a hallmark of Europe's urban demographic regime until well into the eighteenth century, especially in the larger cities.[45] Although there were certainly "good years" when urban economies were flourishing and mortality was on the decline, it was not until this period that

[43] Jacques Rossiaud, "Crises et consolidations, 1330–1530," in Georges Duby, ed., *Histoire de la France urbaine*, vol. II, *La Ville médiévale: des Carolingiens à la Renaissance*, ed. André Chédeville, Jacques Le Goff, and Jacques Rossiaud (Paris, 1980), 474–5.

[44] The most dramatic statement of the "urban graveyard" hypothesis is Mols, *Introduction*, vol. II, 333–4. For the more recent debate, see Allan Sharlin, "Natural Decrease in Early Modern Cities: A Reconsideration," *Past and Present*, no. 79 (1978): 126–38; and Sharlin, "Debate: Natural Decrease in Early Modern Cities," *Past and Present*, no. 92 (1981): 169–80; Alfred Perrenoud, "Croissance ou déclin? Les Mécanismes du non-renouvellement des populations urbaines," *Histoire, économie et société* 4, 4 (1982): 581–601; A. M. van der Woude, "Population Developments in the Northern Netherlands (1500–1800) and the Validity of the 'Urban Graveyard' Effect," *Annales de démographie historique* (1982): 55–75.

[45] The best recent statement of the "urban graveyard model" with application to English data is found in Chris Galley, "A Model of Early Modern Demography," *Economic History Review* 48, 3 (1995): 448–69. For an interesting simulation of the differential effects of a constant "normal" infant mortality rate versus episodic mortality crises in a metropolitan environment, see Roger Finlay, *Population and Metropolis: The Demography of London, 1580–1650* (New York and Cambridge, 1981), 111–13.

the majority of European towns and cities would have been able to maintain their populations without high net migration from outside their borders.

Good estimates of age-specific mortality rates are unusual before the later medieval period for Italy or the early modern period for northern Europe. While London's mortality averaged about 35 per 1,000 in the sixteenth and seventeenth centuries, this rate could rise by a factor of 4–7 times during recurrent epidemics of Plague that visited the city.[46] During this period, London's and Geneva's overall mortality rates represented a life expectancy at birth of 18–36 years, varying by social background. Under such a regime, normal infant mortality rates ranged above 250 or even 350 per thousand, with much lower rates for children of 1–14 years of age. This combination of rates meant, however, that fewer than 50 percent of children survived to marriageable age.[47]

Catastrophic epidemic diseases such as the bubonic plague became increasingly identified with cities by the early modern period. And although the impact of epidemics was temporarily devastating both to individual lives and urban demographic and economic systems, rapid recovery of town and city population sizes was the rule because of the immediate increase in migration that would occur after epidemics had ended. More important over the longer term was the toll taken on urban populations by the year-in year-out effect of high "normal" mortality, particularly of the very young.[48]

There was another important link between mortality and migration. Migrants, especially young adult migrants to larger cities, appear to have experienced higher rates of mortality than urban-born adults because they bore less immunity to infectious diseases. In his work on London, John Landers used William McNeill's model of a "metropolitan epidemiological regime" to distinguish an urban mortality regime. This model:

predicts that, relative to more thinly settled regions, mortality in such populations is likely to be high – especially in childhood – due to the maintenance of endemic foci of infection, which will also reduce the level of short-run instability displayed by mortality levels. Such high mortality may lead to natural decrease among the population and thus to a dependence on immigration if numbers are to be maintained, but the immigrants themselves are likely to lack immunological defenses against many "metropolitan" infections and suffer substantially higher mortality than their "native" peers.[49]

---

[46] Herlihy and Klapisch-Zuber, *Tuscans*, 270, note Florence's (population about 40,000 in the early fifteenth century) minimum mortality rate at the same level, showing that a "major epidemic" of Plague, such as that of 1400, increased the number of deaths by a factor of 10, and less severe epidemics by a "factor of 4 or 5."

[47] Finlay, *Population*, 107–8, 138.

[48] Alfred Perrenoud, "The Attenuation of Mortality Crises and the Decline of Mortality," in Roger Schofield, David Reher, and Alain Bideau, eds., *The Decline of Mortality in Europe* (Oxford, 1991), 18–37.

[49] Landers, *Death*, 125; William H. McNeill, "Migration Patterns and Infection in Traditional Societies," in N. F. Stanley and R. A. Joske, eds., *Changing Disease Patterns and Human Behaviour* (New York and London, 1980), 27–36.

Research on other towns and cities of late medieval and early modern Europe suggests that during epidemics of the Plague, mortality among the young rose most sharply, while adults who survived exposure to the disease thereby acquired some immunity.[50] Exposure to and survival of the Plague in infancy or childhood would thus have conferred some advantage on the urban-born.

Not enough is yet known about urban mortality rates to estimate how populous towns and cities had to be for the "urban penalty" or "high potential mortality model" to occur, since the base size of agglomerated populations, the density of settlement, and the nature of the diseases to which inhabitants were exposed all helped maintain this kind of regime. Common sense suggests a gradient in which increasing size and population density would raise the likelihood of creating conditions in which severe infectious disease would become endemic. However, historical research on cholera, a modern source of high urban mortality, found that a town or city's vulnerability to that nineteenth-century urban killer was shaped as much by its being part of a larger system of migration as by its population size or density.[51] If this finding can be extended to earlier periods and other infectious diseases, it suggests that rural areas and small towns most closely linked to larger ones by chains of migration were also the most vulnerable to the kinds of high, crisis mortality typical of urban areas.

Patterns of celibacy and marriage

As already noted, Sharlin's focus on the "urban deficit" debate brought special attention to the fact that early modern towns and cities often harbored large populations of unmarried people, many of them migrant men and women of the lower classes. Moreover, the presence of relatively high proportions of permanently single people in European populations was one of the principal characteristics of Hajnal's model of the "European Marriage Pattern."[52] While it is clear that many of the single migrants in their twenties who dwelt in European towns and cities would, if they gained the financial resources, eventually marry, towns and cities probably represented an exaggerated form of this key part of Hajnal's pattern for much of their history, especially in northern Europe.

One of the questions is whether the "European Marriage Pattern," including relatively high ages at marriage for both men and women, existed anywhere

---

[50] Herlihy and Klapisch-Zuber, *Tuscans*, 273–4.

[51] Patrice Bourdelais, "Choléra des villes et choléra des champs: faits et représentations," in Michel Pouvain, René Leboutte, Henriette Damas, and Eric Vilguin, eds., *Historiens et populations: Liber amicorum Etienne Hélin* (Louvain-la-Neuve, 1991), 225.

[52] John Hajnal, "European Marriage Patterns in Perspective," in D. V. Glass and D. E. C. Eversley, eds., *Population in History: Essays in Historical Demography* (Chicago, 1965), 101–43, and Hajnal, "Two Kinds of Preindustrial Household Formation System," *Population and Development Review* 8, 3 (1982): 449–94; Lynch, "The European Marriage Pattern," *Journal of Family History*, 79–96.

in Europe before the sixteenth century. Some medieval data for rural England suggest the early emergence of the European Marriage Pattern there.[53] Other sources on urban England, however, imply that women of higher social standing married earlier than models of the European Marriage Pattern predict. For example, women of the London merchant class in the fifteenth century married in their late teens, while men were more likely to be in their mid-twenties.[54] These results may not be generalizable, however, since women of the upper-middle and upper classes of European society historically married at younger ages than poorer women. Nor is it clear whether medieval women in general married earlier than women of the early modern period, when evidence of the European Marriage Pattern is more abundant.

French data suggest that in medieval towns and cities, women generally married around age 20 while men were closer to age 30.[55] Late medieval evidence for central Italy shows that city girls there generally married before age 20, and usually to men who were at least six and more likely ten years older than they. Men's marriage ages, on the other hand, seem to have varied directly with the size of the settlement where they lived. Grooms marrying in the Tuscan capital, for example, had an average age of 34 while the figure for the surrounding rural area was 23.[56]

Several circumstances combined to yield this medieval urban variant of the European Marriage Pattern in which men's but not women's ages at marriage were quite high. Contrasting the economic functions of family in rural and urban Tuscany of the late medieval period, David Herlihy and Christiane Klapisch-Zuber noted that while in the countryside male peasants needed a wife and children to run a farm and to achieve some measure of economic independence, this was not the case for working-class men in the city.[57]

Moreover, evidence from late-medieval Tuscany seems to suggest that women's marriage ages, in particular, moved inversely with mortality conditions. The higher the mortality, the lower the marriage ages. As Plague-related mortality declined from the late fourteenth into the fifteenth century, young women's average ages at first marriage in the cities of Florence and Prato, for example, increased from 16 or 17 to 20 or 21. As conditions of life improved,

---

[53] Richard M. Smith, "Some Reflections," 89–103.

[54] Sylvia Thrupp, *The Merchant Class of Medieval London, 1300–1500* (Chicago, 1948), 192, 196; Vivien Brodsky Elliott, "Single Women in the London Marriage Market: Age, Status and Mobility, 1598–1619," in R. B. Outhwaite, ed., *Marriage and Society: Studies in the Social History of Marriage* (New York, 1981), 86. By the late sixteenth and early seventeenth century, Elliott shows, a sample of London wives from the middling ranks of the population had an average age at marriage of 20.5 for the London-born and 24.2 for migrant women.

[55] Rossiaud, "Crises et consolidations," in Duby, ed., *Histoire de la France urbaine*, vol. II, 484–5; David Herlihy, *Medieval Households* (Cambridge, MA, 1985), 103–11.

[56] Herlihy and Klapisch-Zuber, *Tuscans*, 202–11.   [57] *Ibid.*, 221.

the proportion of persons never marrying also rose.[58] Moreover, during periods of higher mortality, the Florentine situation also differed from the other predictions of the European Marriage Pattern in the low proportion of women who never married. In the early fifteenth century, when the city was still greatly affected by intermittent outbreaks of the Plague, permanently single adult women constituted less than 2 percent of the population.[59] By the sixteenth century, however, 11 to 13 percent of Florence's female population was permanently celibate as a result of their entry into religious orders.[60]

Although the European Marriage Pattern in its most orthodox form does not seem to have emerged before the early modern period in most of Europe, data from medieval cities suggest that, even at this early date, marriage ages of men, or women, or both were responsive to economic and/or mortality conditions. Furthermore, organizations affecting men and their work careers had begun to exert upward pressure on men's ages at marriage in some areas. In addition to young tradesmen and merchants having to accumulate sufficient property to marry within their social milieu, guild members were under pressure to remain unmarried until training was completed and their transition to master status confirmed.[61] These systems placed constraints not only on men's but also on women's likelihood of marrying, and the ages at which they married.

Women's labor and urban marriage markets

Broad continuities seem to characterize the work that most women did to earn income in European towns and cities.[62] From the medieval period until the eighteenth century, urban women were present in large numbers in a range of commodity manufacturing based on the production of linen, wool, silk, and, by the eighteenth century, cotton thread and cloth, and in lace-, glove-, and dressmaking. Especially in towns of northern Europe, domestic service employed a large number of single young women who generally worked in this capacity for only part of their lives. Women worked in the sale of food and its distribution both within official city markets and by hawking their wares independently. Women in the food trades often got into trouble with larger, more

---

[58] *Ibid.*, *Tuscans*, 86–7. Elliott, "Single Women," in Outhwaite, ed., *Marriage and Society*, 98, hypothesizes the same relationship between high mortality and relatively low marriage ages in early modern London.

[59] Herlihy and Klapisch-Zuber, *Tuscans*, 216.

[60] Richard Trexler, "Le Célibat à la fin du Moyen Age: les religieuses de Florence," *Annales, ESC* 27, 6 (1972): 1348.

[61] Lynch, "The European Marriage Pattern," *Journal of Family History*, 79–96.

[62] On continuity and cyclicality in women's history, see Judith M. Bennett, "'History that Stands Still': Women's Work in the European Past," *Feminist Studies* 14, 2 (Summer, 1988): 269–83; and Amanda Vickery, "Golden Age to Separate Spheres? A Review of the Categories and Chronology of English Women's History," *The Historical Journal* 36, 2 (1993): 383–414.

established male provisioners because of their involvement in "huckstering," which involved selling small quantities of food in the streets and alleyways or even door-to-door, thus violating the terms of many tightly controlled urban food markets.[63] In the larger towns and cities and those with large numbers of unmarried clerics and students, prostitution was an everpresent occupation that included both professionals and other women who used it as an occasional or part-time activity to make ends meet when wages proved inadequate. Women involved in the most capital-intensive sorts of industries were generally married women who worked alongside their husbands in family-based workshops, especially if their husbands held positions as masters in urban guilds.

There seems to have been a widespread belief among the working-class and middling ranks of European society that women's presence in the urban workforce was a normal feature of life. Women's money-earning activities were necessary for large numbers of those living on their own as well as for the majority of married women whose husbands' wages were inadequate to support wife and children through the entire life of the family. This was true even though wage-earning women generally could earn only about one-third to one-half of what men earned on a daily basis at roughly comparable levels of skill.

Although wives and daughters of bourgeois and patrician families had little or no experience of wage work or production for the market, they were a small minority and quite unrepresentative of urban women as a whole. Their absence from an urban labor market did not mean, however, that they spent their days in idleness. The larger residences and numbers of persons and servants living in households of upper-class urban dwellers meant more demands on the time and energies of married women of this milieu.

Like the work of many men in towns and cities, women's work often took place within some sort of domestic or familial setting, though not necessarily their own homes. The portrait of the married woman working alongside her husband, often accompanied in the same shop by several apprentices and journeymen, was accurate for households headed by married men who were skilled workers and owners of capital. In households such as these, the wife's labor input proved critical to the family's survival. Evidence for the importance of the wife's labor in a small shop was expressed in the permission given to one fifteenth-century founder in the city of York, who was allowed by his guild to have two apprentices serve him since he had no wife.[64]

---

[63] For examples of the minutiae of regulations on the sale of food and drink in early modern German towns, see Merry E. Wiesner, *Working Women in Renaissance Germany* (New Brunswick, NJ, 1986), 113, 116–47.

[64] P. J. P. Goldberg, *Women, Work, and Life Cycle in a Medieval Economy: Women in York and Yorkshire c.1300–1520* (Oxford, 1992), 128.

However, married women who were gainfully employed did not always work alongside their husbands but oftentimes in completely unrelated fields. This was especially the case for those numerous working-class couples in which the man worked outside his own home earning wages elsewhere.[65] Court records from seventeenth- and eighteenth-century London show that many married women there labored quite on their own account, occupying a specific age-related niche in the urban labor market. Younger single women dominated the field of domestic service; married women were concentrated in the needle trades; and older women, including many widows, worked as washerwomen, nurses, and street vendors.[66] Furthermore, when questioned, many of these women made it quite clear that they depended upon their ability to earn wages. A sample of female court deponents here showed fully 72 percent either wholly or partially dependent upon income they themselves earned, with percentages "wholly dependent" reaching 78 percent for spinsters, 33 percent for married women, and 73 percent for widows.[67]

Changes in women's occupational distributions over the life course also existed for towns in southern Europe. In fourteenth-century Montpellier, for example, single women who had migrated in from the surrounding countryside worked as apprentice bakers, textile finishers, spinners of gold thread, and basket weavers. As was true of women in many towns in both north and south, women here were excluded from the more highly paid and skilled occupations that recruited male apprentices such as moneychangers, apothecaries, merchants, or drapers. On the other hand, married women and especially widows did appear in contracts involving business partnerships and foreign trade, thus showing their familiarity with credit instruments and other practices of the international business world.[68]

Regional variations

Although labor force participation for women was a familiar part of European urban life, conditions in north and south may have been somewhat different. Recent work has dispelled an older notion that southern European women were unlikely to participate in wage labor markets. Yet a lingering sense still remains that a combination of economic and cultural features of Mediterranean

---

[65] Charles Phythian-Adams, *Desolation of a City: Coventry and the Urban Crisis of the Late Middle Ages* (New York and Cambridge, 2002 [1979]), 88.

[66] Peter Earle, "The Female Labour Market in London in the late Seventeenth and Early Eighteenth Centuries, *Economic History Review* 42, 3 (1989): 343.

[67] *Ibid.*, 337. An additional 6, 27, and 12 percent of spinsters, married women, and widows were "partially maintained by employment."

[68] Kathryn L. Reyerson, "Women in Business in Medieval Montpellier," in Barbara A. Hanawalt, ed., *Women and Work in Preindustrial Europe* (Bloomington, IN, 1986), 120, 122, 137.

Europe made women's urban labor force participation there lower than was characteristic of women in the north.

Beginning with one of the most important female workforces – domestic servants – several studies of southern Europe show interesting contrasts with the north. In the fourteenth and fifteenth centuries, approximately one-quarter to one-third of Florentine households employed domestic servants, with the norm being one or two per household. Female house slaves constituted about 10 percent of this labor force and formed its lowest echelon. These women, whose numbers dwindled in the course of the fifteenth and sixteenth centuries, sometimes played the role of domestic concubine to their patrician employer or his son.[69]

The workforce of female domestic servants in Renaissance Tuscany looked quite different from that in cities of the north in other ways as well. The city's domestic servants included women born in both city and countryside, in contrast with urban household servants in northern towns, who generally came from rural areas. Farther north, urban-born women or longer-term in-migrants usually rejected domestic service as an occupation, especially when they could earn better wages in crafts production or market activities that also allowed them more physical autonomy.

In Florence, moreover, household service sometimes involved a kind of employer–servant relationship not found in northern towns. At the end of the fifteenth century, adolescents or even very young girls aged 8 to 10 were sometimes sent by their own families to serve in the homes of Florentine employers for five to ten years, culminating in the employer paying the girl a small dowry at the time she completed the contract and entered marriage. This kind of contract seems rarely to have reached its completion, however. Most of these girls left their original employers' houses before marriage, even though that meant departing with only their clothes or a small prorated payment decided on by the employer alone. Over time, Florence's female domestic service labor force came to include more married and widowed women living with their own families, again in distinction to trends in northern European cities, where female domestic servants nearly always lived in their employer's home as an unmarried person.[70]

As in Renaissance Florence, Rome's youngest female servants entered the homes of their employers less as wage employees and more as dependents who

[69] On slaves working as house servants, see Jacques Heers, *Esclaves et domestiques au Moyen-Age dans le monde méditerranéen* (Paris, 1981), 144–63, 193–221; and Philip Gavitt, "'Perche non avea chi la ghovernasse': Cultural Values, Family Resources and Abandonment in the Florence of Lorenzo de' Medici, 1467–85," in Henderson and Wall, eds., *Poor Women and Children*, 65–93.

[70] Christiane Klapisch-Zuber, "Women Servants in Florence during the Fourteenth and Fifteenth Centuries," in Hanawalt, ed., *Women and Work*, 60–3, 68.

required the employer's moral guardianship. Like their Tuscan counterparts, these youngest teenage servants often received only food, lodging, and clothing for their work and tended to marry young and within an urban milieu of domestic service. The domestic labor force of Rome did not consist solely of these sorts of dependents, however, but was diversified by age as well as gender, at least up until the eighteenth and nineteenth centuries. A second group of Rome's female domestics more closely resembled those of northern towns in that they migrated to the city on their own. This second group also married later than the first, thereby experiencing the kind of temporary "life cycle" service characteristic of northern Europe. Female domestics in Rome who were willing to accept prolonged or even permanent celibacy changed employers often, building a wide personal network of urban acquaintances. Those who did marry often contracted marriages with older widowed artisans. Those who remained permanently celibate could, like their unmarried male counterparts, become members of a relatively highly paid "elite" within the domestic service labor market.[71] The labor force of domestic servants in southern European towns and cities seems to have included more males than in the north, especially in cities such as Rome which, because of the importance of the Church, had long had an unusually high sex ratio.

Evidence from southern Italy suggests how a combination of household formation and cultural practices shaped the labor market for domestic servants in this region. Like urban households in towns of northern Europe, households in both rural and urban southern Italy were largely nuclear in form. As in northern Europe, young married couples here generally set up their own households at the time of marriage, thus conforming to the practice of "neolocality." However, age at marriage for women was quite low compared to northern Europe, around 20 years in the seventeenth century, rising to the early twenties by the mid-eighteenth century. Moreover, in contrast to both rural and urban practices in northern Europe, southern Italy had almost no tradition of young people going out to work as wage laborers in the homes of others.

Southern Italian mores viewed domestic service outside one's household with suspicion, especially when it involved unmarried girls. As Giovanna Da Molin observed: "In southern society, to go into service was considered to be humiliating and a disgrace; in some cases it was almost better to starve. To leave one's own home to work as a servant in another home was considered to be

---

[71] Angiolina Arru, "Serviteurs et servantes à Rome: différences de 'genre', Life Cycle et pouvoirs (1650–1860), in Erik Aerts, Paul M. M. Klep, Jürgen Kocka and Marinia Thorborg, eds., *Women in the Labour Force: Comparative Studies on Labour Market and Organization of Work since the 18th Century* (Leuven, 1990), 109–21. Judith C. Brown estimates that as early as the sixteenth century, two-thirds of Florentine domestic servants were females. See: "A Woman's Place was in the Home: Women's Work in Renaissance Tuscany," in Margaret W. Ferguson, Maureen Quilligan, and Nancy J. Vickers, eds., *Rewriting the Renaissance: The Discourses of Sexual Difference in Early Modern Europe* (Chicago, 1986), 211.

absolutely unforgivable."[72] Particularly for unmarried young women, going into service violated deeply held notions regarding the preservation of a woman's sexual honor and the honor of her family.

Thus, it was not surprising that few households in the small towns and cities of southern Italy had resident female servants. Only households of male clerics, of the wealthy aristocratic elite, and the small number of professionals of the peninsula's southern towns and cities regularly employed co-resident servants. In this region, domestic service was less a temporary phase of one's life course and more a profession for a lifetime, as was the case among a portion of Florence's domestic servants.

Comparative studies of women in northern and southern European cities suggest that regional differences in women's control of property varied positively with their participation in wage labor. They suggest that single, and perhaps also married, women enjoyed greater legal and physical autonomy in towns and cities of northern Europe than in the south. Indeed, the capacity of women to act relatively independently in financial terms seems to have varied less by period than by region because of systems of inheritance, property transmission, and laws governing women's pursuit of commercial activities. Unmarried women in cities and towns of northern Europe were more likely to dispose of property through wills than those in the south, a fact stemming in large part from different inheritance customs. In many areas of Mediterranean Europe governed by Roman law, women reached adulthood and received property in the form of dowries at the time of their marriage or, for certain upper-class women, at the time they entered religious orders. In contrast, women in many areas of northern Europe inherited property from their parents no matter what their marital status.

A comparison of Genoa with the city of Douai in the thirteenth and fourteenth centuries illustrates this contrast. Genoa's patrilineal system of inheritance conferred property on daughters in the form of dowries. Although husbands had the right of administration over dowries, with any luck women would have an intact dowry to help support them during their widowhood. They also had the authority to dispose of this property in their wills. Under this system, however, sons or other patrilineal male kin inherited the bulk of the property. In contrast, under Douai's customary law system, daughters generally received no dowries, but enjoyed more equal treatment with brothers in inheriting from their parents.[73] The greater importance of the spousal versus the lineal relationship in Douai was evidenced in the fact that wives and their husbands served as each other's heirs. Moreover, husbands in Douai named their wives as executors of their wills more often than did men in Genoa.

---

[72] Giovanna Da Molin, "Family Forms and Domestic Service in Southern Italy from the Seventeenth to the Nineteenth Centuries," *Journal of Family History* 15, 4 (1990): 521.

[73] Ellen E. Kittell, "Testaments of Two Cities: A Comparative Analysis of the Wills of Genoa and Douai," *European Review of History* 5, 1 (1998): 70.

Plate 2 *Market Life in Cologne*, Abraham Aubry, "Marketleben . . . *c.* 1655."

These differences in the two cities' inheritance and will-making systems were entirely consistent with the more active role that unmarried women played in Douai's economy. In Douai, a higher proportion of unmarried women made wills because they had more property to dispose of. Single women's participation in the labor market is also suggested by the fact that women will-makers in Douai sometimes identified themselves by their occupational affiliations, such as "maker and seller of oil" or "measurer of wheat for the market," whereas Genoese wills identified women almost always solely in relation to a named father, husband, or son.[74] Evidence from wills in early modern England also suggests that parents there had a rather flexible notion of adulthood for their daughters. Many wills provided that daughters could inherit parental property at a certain age rather than at the time of their marriage, illustrating the fact that parents considered the possibility that their daughter might remain single. In any case, she did not have to be married to achieve adulthood.[75]

Married women throughout Europe commonly engaged in commercial activities in food markets or the sale of clothing, and not necessarily with their husbands (see Plate 2). And though married women in legal principle were not

[74] *Ibid.*, 65.
[75] Christine Peters, "Single Women in Early Modern England: Attitudes and Expectations," *Continuity and Change* 12, 3 (1997): 334–5.

autonomous individuals, special laws allowing them to adopt *"feme sole"* status facilitated their engagement in commerce on their own by allowing them to incur debts for which their husbands could not be held liable. To acquire the status of *feme sole*, women had sometimes to declare it to civic authorities before they could carry on a business of their own. In other instances, requirements were not so formal, with public reputation as an independent dealer or peddler sufficient to designate women as such. The existence of this status is known in great part by records of commercial disputes in courts of late medieval and early modern Europe. Those involving married women often resulted when angry creditors attempted to collect debts from husbands, who attempted to escape responsibility for their wives' debts based on their claims to *feme sole* status.[76]

While unmarried women in northern European towns were more likely to engage in paid labor outside their homes and control property than those in southern European towns, it is not clear that these differences were quite as marked for married women or for widows in the two regions, though evidence of the entitlements of *feme sole* arrangements seems more abundant in cities of the north.

Variations in women's paid work over time

The discussion so far has suggested that while the kinds of work that urban women performed showed great continuity over time, some regional variations stemming from differences in family formation rules and cultural patterns distinguished north from south.[77] But what about variations over time? Although evidence on temporal variations in the levels or nature of women's paid work in European towns and cities is difficult to interpret, one thing seems clear. The history is neither linear nor progressive in any simple way. As Michael Roberts noted in his study of women's work in England in the sixteenth century: to study the interrelationship between work and gender in the urban past "is inevitably to be forced away from a linear, progressive reading of urban history, towards its cyclical rhythms and impermeable structural features."[78] In the study of women's work, continuity has been the rule. However, notable variations may have occurred in the proportions of women working for payment, and in the occupational distribution and consequent economic position of working-class

---

[76] Maryanne Kowaleski and Judith M. Bennett, "Crafts, Gilds, and Women in the Middle Ages: Fifty Years after Marian K. Dale," in Judith M. Bennett *et al.*, eds., *Sisters and Workers in the Middle Ages* (Chicago, 1989), 161; Wiesner, *Working Women*, 25–30.

[77] Kittell, "Testaments," 47.

[78] Michael Roberts, "Women and Work in Sixteenth-Century English Towns," in Penelope J. Corfield and Derek Keene, eds., *Work in Towns, 850–1850* (London and New York, 1990), 95–6, who argues that the late sixteenth century witnessed a "crisis of gender." Mary Elizabeth Perry sees "heightened anxiety about order and gender in Seville in the sixteenth and seventeenth centuries." See *Gender and Disorder in Early Modern Seville* (Princeton, 1990), 6.

and middle-class women relative to men. Some evidence suggests that these variations have been cyclical in nature, corresponding to turns in business cycles and the ability of work communities of men to claim a dominant position or even a monopoly of skilled positions in certain industries.

In a study of York in the fifteenth century, Jeremy Goldberg used the results of his local study to suggest a pattern of alternating periods in European women's relative standing in wage-labor markets. York had the economy of a typical district market center containing little manufacturing but a great deal of occupational diversity.[79] Some division of labor by gender had always existed. Few women worked as bakers or butchers, or participated in trades requiring a high level of capital investment, which was usually outside the reach of single women. Women worked on their own as bread sellers and "hucksters." Those who engaged in brewing were usually wives working with their husbands or widows of "more substantial" artisans and traders. Women spinners figured among the poorest workers, while women weavers who worked alongside their husbands were better off.[80]

Nonetheless, despite longer-term structures that divided labor by gender, women's relative standing in the labor force varied over time in three rather distinct phases. In the first phase of Goldberg's model, whose midpoint fell around the year 1379, broad demographic decline following recurring plague epidemics and a consequent shortage of male labor expanded the range of occupations available to women. In the second phase, from 1420–50, York's working women began to fill positions formerly held only by men. The third phase, involving economic decline and a reversal of women's gains, followed these years, however. After the middle of the fifteenth century, women workers were gradually driven out of better jobs under pressure from men who were organized into formal work communities. Guild restrictions on women's work enabled men to exclude women from the lucrative wool labor market, for example.[81]

Goldberg hypothesized that different phases of his model produced different effects on the urban marriage market, though this hypothesis must remain largely speculative. In the first and second phases, he argued, unmarried women earning relatively good wages doing semiskilled or skilled work were more likely to remain single or to postpone marriage or remarriage. Conversely, in the third phase, when men's access to better wages was rising relatively, women, losing power in the labor market, may have married earlier and at higher rates.[82]

---

[79] Goldberg, *Women*, 24. The city fathers of early modern Seville exercised similar sorts of restrictions on female "hucksters" there. See Perry, *Gender*, 18–19.
[80] Goldberg, *Women*, 113, 117.   [81] *Ibid.*, 336–7.
[82] *Ibid.*, 337–8. Pamela Sharpe ascribes rising proportions of unmarried women in the town of Colyton, Devon, in the seventeenth century to the presence of work for women in lacemaking as well as a low sex ratio encouraged, by this same factor, through female in-migration. See

Goldberg's model has incurred criticism for its slim empirical foundations and its lack of fit with conditions in other contemporary cities in England or on the Continent. The phases of variation in York's labor market did not occur during the same years as trends elsewhere in Europe, for example in Florence. Nor does its portrait of fourteenth- and fifteenth-century trends accurately describe the economic history of either northern or southern Europe as a whole.[83] Furthermore, it is important to remember that women continued to participate in wage labor after they married, though not necessarily in the same sort of work nor with the same level of commitment, especially after giving birth to children.[84]

However, the lack of temporal fit of Goldberg's phases with the history of Florence and Tuscany or with other regions seems less important than the value of his broader suggestion of cyclical variations in the relative fortunes of women and men in urban labor markets and their effects on levels and ages at marriage. Goldberg's association of relatively good financial opportunities for women and their postponement of marriage also deserves a closer look.[85]

Examining the possible functioning of such a phased model in diverse places and times requires towns and cities with well-developed markets for women's labor, since it focuses as much on the relative as the absolute well-being of men and women. This makes the model perhaps more appropriate for understanding trends in northern Europe. Indeed, parts of Mediterranean Europe where even many women of the lower classes did not engage in paid labor before marriage may have experienced a *permanent* version of "phase three" of this model. Indeed, a lack of labor force opportunities outside the home for many single women in Mediterranean Europe may have encouraged their patterns of marrying at ages younger than those of northern European urban women.[86]

When women's wage-earning opportunities declined relative to those of men, a number of things could have happened. Women may have been more willing

---

"Literally Spinsters: A New Interpretation of Local Economy and Demography in Colyton in the Seventeenth and Eighteenth Centuries," *Economic History Review* 44, 1 (1991): 51–5.

[83] For critiques of Goldberg's model, see Samuel Kline Cohn, "Women and Work in Renaissance Italy," in Judith C. Brown and Robert C. Davis, eds., *Gender and Society in Renaissance Italy* (London, 1998), 107–26; Maryanne Kowaleski, "The History of Urban Families in Medieval England," *Journal of Medieval History* 14, 1 (1988): 58.

[84] Mark Bailey, "Demographic Decline in Late Medieval England: Some Thoughts on Recent Research," *Economic History Review* 49, 1 (1996): 1–19.

[85] Richard M. Smith, "Marriage in Late Medieval Europe," in P. J. P. Goldberg, ed., *Woman is a Worthy Wight: Women in English Society c. 1200–1500* (Wolfeboro Falls, NH, 1992), 44. Smith focuses on the importance of different levels of employment of women as servants in northern and southern Europe.

[86] For a discussion of women's labor market participation in cross-national perspective, see Jack A. Goldstone, "Gender, Work, and Culture: Why the Industrial Revolution Came Early to England but Late to China," *Sociological Perspectives* 39, 1 (1996): 1–22; David S. Landes, *The Wealth and Poverty of Nations: Why Some Nations Are so Rich and Some so Poor* (New York, 1998), 56, 412–13.

to marry in the city to the extent that likely male partners were themselves enjoying better financial prospects. Women who had migrated to the town might decide to migrate back to their place of origin to try their chances in the labor or marriage market there. Evidence suggests that women who stayed in the city and remained actively engaged in paid work during relative or absolute declines in the availability of higher-paid work might have to shift to lower-paid occupations such as casual street sellers, domestic servants, or prostitution, and to work even harder to survive in an "economy of expedients," as Olwen Hufton so aptly termed it.[87] The availability of work for women and the relative status of women in urban labor markets may therefore have played an important role in shaping practices related to ages at marriage and the proportion of women who remained single.

The capacity of male workers to organize themselves into their own work communities supported by urban civic governments also proved to be critical in shaping urban labor and marriage markets. As early as the thirteenth century, formally organized groups of male workers were attempting to oppose the wage-earning activities of beguines in the textile trades of such Rhineland towns and cities as Töss, Unterlinden, and Colmar. Italian houses of Poor Clares, nuns associated with the Franciscan order, who devoted part of their energies to work in industrial pursuits, also aroused the anger of male guild members. They argued on behalf of themselves and their families that the work of communities of nuns represented unfair competition. This antipathy grew particularly acute in the fourteenth century during the economic depression following the Black Death.[88]

City councils, for their part, sometimes expressed a sense of concern about men, and especially married men with dependents, when they were perceived to be losing the competition with women for scarce work in times of economic downturn. In tight labor markets, certain urban dwellers had greater entitlements than others to what work there was. City authorities of fifteenth-century Bristol, for example, decried the influx of wives and daughters of weavers into the craft of broadloom weaving there, lamenting that some of the men who fought in the King's service risked being put out of work.[89]

Workingmen's guilds proved especially able to exclude women workers from various occupations when their access to political power was on the rise, and they were able to bring pressure on city governments that oversaw and regulated the power of local corporations. As Martha Howell noted in her comparative

[87] Olwen Hufton, "Women and the Family Economy in Eighteenth-Century France," *French Historical Studies* 9, 1 (1975), 19–21.
[88] Jo Ann Kay McNamara, *Sisters in Arms: Catholic Nuns through Two Millennia* (Cambridge, MA, 1996), 282–3; also Wiesner, *Working Women*, 191–2.
[89] Heather Swanson, "The Illusion of Economic Structure: Craft Guilds in Late Medieval English Towns," *Past and Present*, no. 121 (November, 1988): 45.

study of access to work and requirements for citizenship in various northern European towns and cities, there was a close relationship among: guild membership and citizen status; the power of guilds to exclude women from selected occupations; and women's exclusion from eligibility for citizen status. Towns or cities that had once had relatively open admissions to citizenship rights for both men and women began to guard their citizenship entitlements more tightly, reserving them exclusively for men who were members of gender-segregated guilds. Thus, at the same time as guilds won the right to help control the conferral of citizenship rights, they gradually excluded women from their ranks. Conversely, women were more likely to participate in guild membership in cities where guild membership conferred no such citizenship rights.

The tightening of restrictions on women's entry into work reserved for guild workers or to citizenship itself occurred in fourteenth-century Frankfurt am Main. Here, workingmen's guilds sought and gained seats for their representatives on the city council while enhancing "fraternal" ideals of urban citizenship. The guilds' espousal of ideals of civic "brotherhood" created an equality among citizens that was more symbolic than real. However, one of the consequences of their effort to build an urban political community on ties forged in the world of work was the gradual exclusion of women workers from guild-dominated industries as well as from the path leading to urban citizenship. Whereas "citizens" had once stood politically as representatives of their households or families in the civic community, an emerging "fraternal" model implied a network of individual male citizens who represented only themselves.[90]

The working lives of women, their ages at marriage, and their probabilities of marrying were all interrelated. Demographic facts of life, especially high mortality, may have been more important in determining women's relatively low ages at marriage in southern Europe. However, single women's lack of access to wage labor outside their homes in many areas of southern Europe probably affected this pattern as well. In the north, where single women participated more actively in wage-labor markets, their relative status in those markets was strongly shaped not only by cyclical oscillations in the urban economy, but by the desire of male workers and civic governments to ensure their access to work as a key component of "fraternal" communities in the making.

High levels of migration and mortality proved vital to shaping the environment of medieval and early modern towns and cities. The structural integration of women into the wage-labor force was also fundamental, though levels of

---

[90] Martha C. Howell, "Citizenship and Gender: Women's Political Status in Northern Medieval Cities," in Mary Erler and Maryanne Kowaleski, eds., *Women and Power in the Middle Ages* (Athens, GA, 1988), 48–51.

employment varied by region. Families in towns and cities were shaped by political forces as well, whether in the form of urban policy that regulated in migration, citizenship entitlements, or access to work, especially during periods when civic governments were seeking to establish their authority.

Household size and composition

Histories of the urban family and household over the *longue durée* suggest that they were generally quite small. Evidence from tax records, wills, urban surveys, and partial censuses leads to the conclusion that, from the Middle Ages on, most urban households included relatively few people overall and only small numbers of children. The most complete survey of late-medieval findings indicates the following figures for the average number of persons per household: for fifteenth-century Reims (population 12,000–15,000), 3.6 and 3.8 for different parishes; for Ypres (population 10,000) in the early fifteenth century: 3.2, 3.4, and 3.6; for Zurich (population 5,000) in 1467: 2.5; for Basel (population 10,000) in 1446 and 1452: 3.3 and 3.6 respectively; for Carpentras (population 3,000) in 1473: 5.1; for Prato (population 15,000) in 1298–1305: 4.1 and for the same city in 1372, after its population had shrunk dramatically: 3.5 and in 1427: 3.7. The vast majority of households in late medieval cities included fewer than four persons.[91]

Evidence from late medieval Tuscany suggests that urban households there were smaller than rural ones in the same region. In the towns and cities, household size averaged fewer than four persons, and nearly five in the countryside. While the vast majority of households in the area were nuclear in structure, rural households were more likely to contain three generations and to include relatives.[92]

However, towns and cities in southern Europe also contained larger and more complex households, especially among the wealthy. The average size of households in the city of Florence was raised by the simple fact that most of the wealthiest Tuscan households were located in the towns, and especially in the capital.[93] Calculating the proportion of urban dwellers who lived in households of different sizes rather than the average number of persons per household brings out the importance of these larger groups. For city and countryside combined, persons living in fifteenth-century Tuscan households of six or more persons constituted more than one-half the total. While the mean household size of

---

[91] Rossiaud, "Crises et consolidations," in Duby, ed., *Histoire de la France urbaine*, vol. II, 484.

[92] Herlihy and Klapisch-Zuber, *Tuscans*, tables 10.1, 10.2, 290–8; table 10.5, 308,

[93] *Ibid.*, 283, 295–6, 320. They note, however, that 20 percent of Florentine households in 1427 consisted of solitaries (91).

Carpentras cited above was only 5.1, over 21 percent of its population lived in households containing ten to fifteen people. This latter example of the presence of large, complex households occurred in a time of rapid population growth and an increase in the density of the town's settlement.[94]

High rates of mortality, and in particular, infant and child mortality were among the more important demographic determinants of the small average number of persons found in urban households, and especially the small number of children. They helped to create conditions in which a higher proportion of households were headed by widows or contained only one or two members than was the case in rural areas. Figures calculated from one study of wills in the city of Toulouse in the fourteenth and fifteenth centuries show that in an urban society where will-making was a familiar practice for both women and men, nearly 74 percent of men and 89 percent of the women will-makers in the years 1330–1450 left one or no children. Of men with a living spouse at the time they made their wills, 71 percent left one or no children. The figure was 89 percent for women with a living spouse.[95] Work on other late medieval populations has confirmed these findings. Burgher households in Nuremberg in the mid-fifteenth century counted fewer than two children on average, while the figure was two for one neighborhood in Ypres in the early sixteenth century. The figure was approximately the same for London's merchant class in the same period, even among the wealthiest who had been married at least once and often multiple times. Their historian noted: "at no part of the period [from 1288–1527] did the average number of heirs that a merchant left behind in the direct male line reach two" (see Plate 3).[96]

Although there were variations across time and social class in the percentage of urban households headed by married and unmarried people and in the presence of servants and unrelated persons in medieval and early modern urban households, the picture is generally of a household that was nuclear in structure and contained a small number of children and a small total number of members.[97] This portrait is roughly similar for the majority of urban people in southern Europe, though as shown for late medieval Carpentras, periods of population increase could stimulate the growth of larger and more complex units among the wealthiest inhabitants. The emergence of a rather small, residential

---

[94] Figures are from Rossiaud, "Crises et consolidations," in Duby, ed., *Histoire de la France urbaine*, vol. II, 484, and Herlihy, *Medieval Households*, 143–4. In contrast, Le Roy Ladurie found an increase in complex family types in rural Languedoc during periods of de-population. See *Les Paysans de Languedoc* (Paris, 1966), vol. I, 163–7.

[95] Rossiaud, "Crises et consolidations," in Duby, ed., *Histoire*, vol. II, 484; figures calculated from data in Wolff, *Commerces*, Appendix, 102–12.

[96] Thrupp, *Merchant Class*, 199–200.

[97] Richard Wall, "European Family and Household Systems," in Michel Pouvain, René Leboutte, Henriette Damas, and Eric Vilquin, eds., *Historiens et populations: Liber amicorum Etienne Hélin* (Louvain-la-Neuve, 1991), 617–36.

Plate 3 Burgher Household, *Bürgerstube mit Familie: Der Vater rechnet, der Sohn buchstabiert, Mutter und Tochter spinnen* (Burgher house with family: the father counting, the son reading a book, mother and daughter spinning).

family in the consciousness and in the record-keeping systems of medieval Europe, well documented by David Herlihy and others, seems to have had clear demographic causes as well as cultural roots.[98]

Plebeian and patrician models of family and kinship

Family members living in the same household generally compose the most tightly knit network of relationships of solidarity.[99] Nonetheless, household members' interactions with the larger world of kin, neighbors, and others are also vital to individuals' and households' survival. The most important single determinant of kin solidarity is doubtless sheer physical proximity. For kin members to enjoy strong ties of effective solidarity, they need to be close enough to aid one another. As the discussion of Laslett's "nuclear hardship" hypothesis suggested, when kin are not present as a result of death or migration or are too poor to lend assistance, individuals have to seek other persons with whom to join for purposes of mutual support. One study of late medieval France suggests that thirty kilometers was about the greatest distance a man could be depended upon to come to help avenge crimes committed against a friend or kinsman.[100]

For most people of the lower and middling ranks of society, household and family relations provided a launching ground for a larger world of neighborhood interdependency. Evidence from medieval Genoa shows that lower-class people very often migrated to the city from rural areas on their own in the kind of classic short-distance migration discussed earlier. Migrants to the city from the same villages tended to cluster together in hilltop neighborhoods there, and often preserved close relations with their villages of origin. Men who had migrated to Genoa usually sought wives in their communities of origin or alternatively married women from their villages who had also moved to the city. Children of these twelfth- and thirteenth-century migrants often took up occupations quite different from those of their parents and freely migrated to other neighborhoods of the city. Like the urban households of northern Europe, households of these lower-class migrants were simple nuclear units and their domestic "ideals" deeply conjugal.[101]

The first generations of urban migrants, like those of medieval Genoa, might not necessarily have kin in their neighborhood. Indeed, until a migration system

---

[98] David Herlihy, *Medieval Households*, 56–62; Jacques Le Goff, "L'Apogée de la France urbaine médiévale," in Duby, ed., *Histoire*, vol. II, 360.

[99] Michel Verdon, *Rethinking Households: An Atomistic Perspective on European Living Arrangements* (London and New York, 1998), 34–7.

[100] Claude Gauvard, "Violence citadine et réseaux de solidarité: l'exemple français aux XIVe et XVe siècles," *Annales, ESC* 48, 5 (1993): 1115.

[101] Diane Owen Hughes, "Domestic Ideals and Social Behavior: Evidence from Medieval Genoa," in Charles E. Rosenberg, ed., *The Family in History* (Philadelphia, 1975), 126.

between rural sending areas and specific urban neighborhoods has functioned over generations, many new urbanites might not have any members of their extended kin living in their neighborhoods. With the passage of time and a favorable mortality climate, however, bonds of extended kinship could proliferate in any town or city.

The working classes of medieval Genoa tried quite consciously to use what family they had to build bonds of obligation to help them in their old age. For example, artisans and their wives often had formal contracts drawn up with their sons to support them during retirement. They also signed similar contracts with sons-in-law who co-resided in their household and who agreed to work for and obey their parents-in-law in exchange for receiving their wives' dowries. Given the conjugal ideals of lower-class migrants, however, this kind of household extension was viewed as only temporary.[102]

Neighbors were also vital to urban migrants. At key times of their lives when lower-class urban dwellers needed witnesses to legal procedures, executors for their estates, or legal counsel, they seem to have been quite willing to seek out neighbors, fellow workers, or priests as well as their kinsmen.[103] Evidence from large cities of the seventeenth and eighteenth centuries suggests a similar importance of neighbors and friends in the lives of urban dwellers of the lower or middling ranks. In one area of seventeenth-century London, men chose overseers of their wills or witnesses to legal procedures from among neighbors, or, if the men belonged to one of the City's guild companies, from a fellow member. By this time, London drew on a vast territory for its peopling and had a high degree of population turnover, with only approximately 27 percent of household heads living in the same dwelling after ten years. Persistence within the same district of the capital after ten years was higher, however, reaching between 28 and 49 percent according to the size and social composition of the specific neighborhood.[104]

For lower-class Parisians of the eighteenth century, kinship relations and relations with neighbors seem to have been complementary. Relations with adult siblings were the most important, particularly in working-class neighborhoods that contained large numbers of more geographically stable people, such as the working-class district of the Faubourg St. Antoine in the eastern part of the capital. Here, networks of kin relations were able to develop, often overlapping with those of craft and residence. Where extended kin were

---

[102] *Ibid.*, 128.

[103] *Ibid.*, 125; Diane Owen Hughes, "Kinsmen and Neighbors in Medieval Genoa," in Harry A. Miskimin, David Herlihy, and Abraham L. Udovitch, eds., *The Medieval City* (New Haven, CT, 1977), 104.

[104] Jeremy Boulton, *Neighbourhood and Society: A London Suburb in the Seventeenth Century* (New York and Cambridge, 1987), 210, 217, 235–57.

present, obligations to them were generally held to be stronger than ties between neighbors.[105]

Urban men and women of the popular classes experienced the worlds of kinship and neighborhood rather differently. From their youth, lower-class city women seem to have had more intensive relations with neighbors. This was in large measure due to the fact that girls' and women's lives tended to be more spatially circumscribed than men's, leading them to develop more and tighter connections with people residing in the same area. Girls raised in the city seem to have lived at home longer than their brothers, and their behavior was subject to stricter scrutiny by neighborhood women who constituted the "public opinion" of the area.

Women's more extensive relationships with their neighbors often had important consequences for resolving family conflicts. Lower-class women in eighteenth-century Rouen, for example, depended on neighbor women to intervene in domestic disputes before their lives were endangered. As Roderick Phillips observed:

> Women... had an interest in ensuring that the family remained open to social scrutiny and social control, since on the neighbourhood level this was their guarantee of assistance in times of crisis. Men, on the other hand, might well have preferred that their familial activities be insulated from public observation, so that they could exercise their domestic authority without hindrance.[106]

Women's stronger links with their neighbors also appeared in records of witnesses called upon to testify for parties to domestic disputes. In complaints they filed against abusive husbands, women commonly included signatures of neighbors or local merchants in denunciations of their husbands' violent behavior. In contrast, men filing against their wives' misconduct usually named members of their own kin.[107]

Studies also suggest the greater importance of friends and neighbors than kin in certain vital moments of a family's history. Evidence from French revolutionary courts set up by 1790 legislation to resolve domestic conflicts demonstrated this fact quite well. While the courts had been set up explicitly to involve kinship groups in the resolution of these conflicts, records indicate that husbands and wives tended to use friends and neighbors to serve as witnesses and arbiters.[108] In these instances, it is not clear whether kinship bonds were

---

[105] David Garrioch, *Neighbourhood and Community in Paris, 1740–1790* (New York and Cambridge, 1986), 59–68, 87–95.

[106] Roderick G. Phillips, "Gender Solidarities in Late Eighteenth-Century Urban France: The Example of Rouen," *Histoire Sociale/Social History* 13, 26 (1980): 335.

[107] Arlette Farge and Michel Foucault, *Le Désordre des familles: lettres de cachet des archives de la Bastille au XVIIIe siècle* (Paris, 1982), 35–6.

[108] Roderick G. Phillips, "Tribunaux de famille et assemblées de famille à Rouen sous la Révolution," *Revue historique de droit français et étranger* 58, 1 (1980): 69–79.

simply not very strong, kin members were not living close enough to take part in the deliberations, or there were no kin actually alive. In cases where relatives were involved, they tended to be members of the same generation as the couple involved.

While this "plebeian" model of the household and family characterized the majority of households in urban Europe both north and south over the long term, evidence of a larger, more complex "patrician" model suggests not only a different size and composition of the household or family, but also different relations of the family to kin and the larger neighborhood. This sort of family–kin–neighborhood model is best documented for families and households of urban elites living in the cities of northern and central Italy in the late medieval period. In these families, males who headed household and family networks seem to have pursued multiple goals of building bonds of solidarity among extended kin and neighbors as well. They sought to strengthen their own patrilineal groups while at the same time ensuring that lineage members, wives, and offspring were well integrated into the neighborhood of the city where they were living by cultivating relations of clientage with less powerful neighbors.[109] Indeed, districts of Florence and Genoa in the thirteenth and fourteenth centuries were often dominated architecturally, socially, and demographically by a single lineage, whose house and tower contained extended kin living in separate households that were linked by marriage and clientage to neighbors.[110]

Although these large family enclaves seem to have represented an ideal in the minds of heads of medieval Italian patrician families, this model linking an extended family to a neighborhood dense with clientage relationships proved devilishly difficult to maintain through several generations. What one or two generations of family heads worked laboriously to construct could be swept away by the birth of too few or too many male heirs, mortality crises, conflicts between brothers, armed conflict among factions within the city, or the out-migration of heirs.

Father–son relationships in these joint patriarchal families were often strained as the result of competition for scarce family resources. The family head's strategy for the perpetuation of his lineage and his decisions about when to transfer property to heirs did not necessarily conform to the wishes of adult sons impatient to receive their inheritances and freedom from paternal control. Wealthy patrician fathers had therefore to try to adjust whatever strategies they had for their families to these sorts of realities.

Difficulties of maintaining joint families, and problems of weakened or shrinking lineage groups among blood kin sometimes led to attempts to create

[109] Hughes, "Domestic Ideals," 118, and "Kinsmen," 101.
[110] Richard A. Goldthwaite, "The Florentine Palace as Domestic Architecture," *American Historical Review* 77, 4 (1972): 977–1012.

lineages artificially. From the thirteenth century on, for example, some Genoese patricians tried to construct artificial clans out of fragments of lineage groups on the decline. These *alberghi* joined together people who were, or claimed to be, distant relatives, and who were very often neighbors. The consolidation of such clans often necessitated constructing new family enclaves as both vehicles for and architectural symbols of lineage and neighborhood power.[111]

Patrician plans for integrating members of their kin group solidly into their neighborhoods allowed more variety and flexibility. One practice that some Genoan patricians preferred was to arrange marriages between impoverished members of their own lineages with neighborhood clients, many of whom were of modest financial means. The inherent value of having one's kin in physical proximity was attested to by the importance that patrician family heads attributed to these links with neighbors through strategic marriage bonds.

Various social developments seem to have gradually changed the neighborhood-based strategies of patrician family heads in some places, however. In fifteenth-century Florence, certain upper-class families began to abandon their deep attachment to particular neighborhoods that had been the historic seats of their power. Examining a sample of Florentine marriage records, for example, Samuel Cohn noted declining levels of neighborhood endogamy in that city by the end of the fourteenth century, especially among patricians. At this time, while 44 percent of the city's marriages joined brides and grooms from the same city district, figures were only 6 percent for the city's "ruling class," lower than they had been a century earlier.[112] The Florentine patriciate did not give up its ideal of family rootedness in a specific urban territory altogether, but did apparently seek wider alliances within the city to serve as a source of power within changing political circumstances. Relations of clientage within their home neighborhoods, however, remained important to many patricians.[113]

Elements of this patrician household model also appeared north of the Alps, though there is less evidence that northern European patricians avidly cultivated the same degree of kinship density or neighborhood clientage relations as those of northern Italy. In Ghent, Europe's second largest city for much of the fourteenth century, extended family enclaves existed among some members of the city's ruling elite. Here, as elsewhere, extended kin were often available to step in and help in crises. Nonetheless, despite a certain level of

---

[111] Hughes, "Domestic Ideals," 119, 124, and "Kinsmen," 108–9.

[112] Neighborhood here is defined as the district (*gonfalone*) which comprised approximately two parishes. See Samuel Kline Cohn, *The Laboring Classes in Renaissance Florence* (New York, 1980), 58.

[113] D. V. Kent and F. W. Kent, *Neighbors and Neighborhood in Renaissance Florence: The District of the Red Lion in the Fifteenth Century* (Locust Valley, NY, 1982), 51–3, 117.

solidarity within and across household lines, wealthy parents in Ghent also had to make formal arrangements with adult children or extended kin to ensure that they would be cared for during their old age. They also used their formidable financial resources to pay for services in their old age from hired caregivers.[114]

Glimpses of urban life in the eighteenth century suggest the persisting distinction between the family and neighborhood ties of upper- and lower-class urban dwellers. In parts of Europe where patrician families did not necessarily dominate a neighborhood in the fashion of northern Italian elites, there may have been a tendency for them to withdraw from the life of the neighborhood. This seems to have been the case among families of the Parisian upper classes, who increasingly restricted their social contacts to those with other members of the upper-middle and upper classes or contained their social life within the home.[115]

Relations of solidarity with those living in close proximity were thus key to the survival or comfort of urban Europeans. While heads of urban patrician families in southern Europe in late medieval times sought to ensure the power and authority of their patrilines through a combination of strategies, lower- and middle-class urban dwellers, especially women, seem to have depended more upon neighborhood solidarities for survival in their everyday lives.

From the late medieval period, the sheer availability of kin in close proximity helped to determine levels of kin solidarity within the city. Urban neighborhoods went through successive phases of growth and decline depending upon prevailing patterns of mortality and in-migration, which affected the durability of kin networks. In cases where migration streams between stable sending areas and towns persisted through multiple generations relatively unscathed, relations of neighborhood could begin to overlap those of kinship or birthplace. Times of high mortality or reverse migration would, however, have worked to destabilize these networks, necessitating individuals' greater reliance upon voluntary ties of support and mutual help with neighbors or friends whom they met in the city.

The high mortality regime of Europe's towns and cities doubtless did not distinguish them from urban areas in other societies during the same eras. However, the vital importance of the migration and waged labor of women as well as men, the relatively low sex ratios in most towns and cities, and the importance of economic forces in shaping urban marriage practices, when taken in combination, seem more unusual. Moreover, as the discussion of guilds and civic governments' cooperation with them has suggested, the formation

[114] David Nicholas, *The Domestic Life of a Medieval City: Women, Children, and the Family in Fourteenth-Century Ghent* (Lincoln, NE, 1985), 176–82.
[115] Garrioch, *Neighbourhood*, 206–9.

of communities of men in European towns and cities also affected the urban demographic system through marriage markets.

In the next chapter, discussion focuses on the role the Church played in providing a rationale and organizational models for the community-building activities of laywomen and -men in European towns and cities. In particular, we shall see how useful these models were for individual men and women facing the insecurities that urban life brought with it.

2   Church, family, and bonds of spiritual kinship

The demographic and economic regimes of medieval and early modern cities, characterized by high rates of mortality, large numbers of temporary and permanent migrants, small families, and large numbers of single people, combined to create a high level of demand in these places for bonds of association that could help protect individuals and their households in times of need. However, simply because people need to reach outside their households, or even the extended kin group, to establish networks of assistance does not mean that they will naturally or inevitably create them. People cannot create such organized relationships out of need alone. They require tools and raw materials to construct viable networks of association such as financial resources, values, and even inspiration.

This chapter suggests that the medieval Church was a fruitful source of ideas and organizational models that laymen and laywomen of European cities would use to construct extrafamilial forms of community life. The Church also provided a vision of community that suggested ways that family bonds could be fitted into a wider array of human relationships among believers. Because of both their viability and their moral prestige, the sorts of religiously inspired organizations explored in this chapter furnished men and women with forms of solidarity that proved quite useful for surviving in the city. Joining these organizations allowed lone individuals or their households to address the insecurities that they might well experience in the normal course of life. Urbanites did not simply adopt readymade organizations handed to them by the Church, however. Rather, women and men seized upon some features of religious organizations, adapting them to their own needs as well as they could to forge bonds of community.

After exploring the development of Christian ideas about community, family, and marriage ties, this chapter traces how the Church tried to teach these ideas, and how laypeople in Europe's cities and towns seem to have received or practiced them. It shows how secular clergy used bonds of "invented kinship" to build ties of solidarity among unrelated individuals while using such bonds to establish higher levels of peace and order. Reducing the power of kinship ties to create violence was the goal of urban governments as well as the Church, which worked together using various powers of persuasion and repression to control the violence of kindred groups. Members of the regular clergy who became spiritual advisors to women and men of the upper classes also used their influence to spread the Church's family ideals.

Following this, the discussion considers two important examples of organizations that urban laywomen and -men adapted from clerical models to fulfill their needs for assistance and moral solidarity. An examination of the beguine movement, which involved the establishment of residential communities for single or widowed women and the growth of confraternities in European towns and cities, shows how urban dwellers seized upon these clerical models to invent familylike bonds among themselves for their mutual protection and edification.

The family as community

As Michael Sheehan observed, there was relatively little systematic thinking in Roman Catholic patristic writing about family relations as we think of them. Indeed, when church fathers and canonists discussed "families," they usually had in mind organized communities such as monasteries or the large households of bishops rather than groups of laypeople related by blood or affiliation. Church fathers were deeply concerned with individuals' sexual relations, but not very much with the families and kin groups that originated from them.[1]

Part of the Church's view of the need for strong bonds among unrelated individuals doubtless stemmed from the organization's history in late classical antiquity. During the first several centuries AD, the search for new foundations of community life represented a major task of the early urban churches. As Peter Brown noted, Christian ethics of the second century AD competed with an older, elite model of community by trying to foster bonds of solidarity across social groups. He wrote:

> Outside the household a sense of solidarity with a wider range of fellow city-dwellers . . . developed, in marked contrast to the civic notables, who continued throughout the period to view the world through the narrow slits of their traditional "civic" definition of the urban community. A sense of solidarity was a natural adjunct of a morality of the socially vulnerable.

One consequence of the growth of this new model of solidarity was the Church's success in establishing itself as a force that "intrude[d] between individual, family, and city."[2]

---

[1] Michael Sheehan, "The European Family and Canon Law," *Continuity and Change* 6, 3 (1991): 348–9, 356.

[2] Peter Brown, "Late Antiquity," in Paul Veyne, ed., *The History of Private Life*, vol. I: *From Pagan Rome to Byzantium* (Cambridge, MA, 1987), 261, 282.

When it came to instructing the laity in issues related to their families, church teaching focused intensively upon the family unit founded by marriage, which itself emerged as a sacrament in the twelfth and thirteenth centuries. Against lay ideals of family and kinship that emphasized ties of blood and descent, the Church encouraged a notion of the family as a fundamentally voluntary association that linked together two individuals.[3]

Moreover, church teaching tried to emphasize similarities between bonds that joined members of the family and those that linked individuals together in the larger community outside the family circle. As David Herlihy noted, according to St. Augustine, the boundary between family and community was to be weak and transparent. "There is little sense of polarity, still less of hostility, between the domestic and the public realms. Only the intensity, not the nature of affection, changes as one moves beyond the domestic circle. Neighbors and strangers are not viewed as heartless and menacing, only as persons whom we are justified in loving less."[4] Thus, early medieval church teaching suggested that bonds that held families together should be stronger but not essentially different from those that bound together individual believers in the larger community outside the family.

The Church's models of household and family seem to have grown from several sources: the notion of a "household" that included people who were possibly unrelated, a family based on a sacrament joining two individuals, and a larger ethic that sought to break down barriers between individuals' loyalties to their families and integrate them into a larger community of believers. Parts of this repertoire of ideas and models of family and household doubtless resonated with varying power among different sorts of people and groups. While the sacramentally based small family model associated with it doubtless corresponded to the daily experience of the common people of medieval towns and cities, the larger household model associated with the clerical elite conformed more to the upper-class households from which they were recruited.

Inventing kinship in countryside and city

The Church sought to teach its vision of household, family, and society through efforts to construct a system of spiritual kinship to rival or at least complement ties of blood. Building ties of godparenthood and co-parenthood, based in the sacrament of infant baptism, helped the Church infuse elements of its own vision of the family into the lives of the European laity. For older Frankish rituals of adoption, the Church substituted baptismal sponsorship, which broke

---

[3] David Herlihy, *Medieval Households* (Cambridge, MA, 1985), 11.
[4] David Herlihy, "Family," *American Historical Review* 96, 1 (1991): 9; Georges Duby, "Two Models of Marriage: The Aristocratic and the Ecclesiastical," in *Medieval Marriage: Two Models from Twelfth-Century France*, trans. Elborg Forster (Baltimore and London, 1978), 3–4.

with the past both by complementing blood bonds of kinship with spiritual ones and involving infant girls on the same terms as boys.[5]

The creation of bonds of godparenthood grew from two beliefs and practices of the early medieval Church. The growth of the doctrine of original sin hastened the development of infant baptism, a ritual in which parents often served as sponsors, receiving the child from the baptismal water. A second doctrinal development was the Church's eagerness to distinguish "mere" biological kinship from the spiritual kinship that resulted from an infant's "rebirth" during the baptism ceremony. As a direct result, the Church became increasingly reluctant to allow parents to sponsor their own infants.[6] Rather, by the ninth century, the Church largely excluded biological parents from sponsoring their children at baptism. As a text of the period noted: "A father or mother must not receive their own offspring [from the baptismal water], so that there may be a distinction between spiritual and carnal generation."[7] As it developed in medieval Europe, infant baptism was an occasion requiring parents to choose two or more people with whom the infant and parents would establish formal bonds of friendship designed to last the child's lifetime. The Church's elaboration of the godparent–godchild relationship gradually emphasized pedagogical and spiritual features of the relationship, with the godparent serving as a "good teacher." In the Church's view, the godparent's principal task was to help raise the child in the faith.

Although not as developed as in many parts of Latin America, the co-parenthood relationship among adults in the European past may have been even more important to the laity than the relationship of godparent and godchild, involving as it did ties of love, friendship, and mutual assistance. As Joseph Lynch observed: "even in the sixth and seventh centuries we can see that co-parents addressed one another in a way that leveled social distinctions, protected one another, acceded to one another's requests, and trusted in one another's good will." Bonds of co-parenthood were thought to involve all parties in a relationship of *amor* or love.[8]

In contrast, the Church showed deep ambivalence about any sense of "alliance" that might grow up among co-parents. Clergy were ambivalent about building bonds among unrelated individuals which, while originating from spiritual sources, risked degenerating into selfish, secular-minded alliances if allowed to escape their control.[9] Moreover, clergy were often dismayed at the

---

[5] Joseph H. Lynch, *Godparents and Kinship in Early Medieval Europe* (Princeton, 1986), 179–81.

[6] *Ibid.*, 134.

[7] Cited in *ibid.*, 279. The extensive incest taboos prohibiting marriage relations between individuals linked by spiritual kinship resulted from this same ethic.

[8] *Ibid.*, 201. He notes (177): "In the fratricidal world of the Franks, such 'love' could be very important."

[9] But *ibid.*, 178–9, notes that the Church was very interested in helping build any set of relationships that would mitigate inter-family violence.

disorder that often punctuated banquets celebrating baptism and the establishment of co-parenthood bonds, seeing them as potential threats to their efforts to render these relationships purely spiritual.[10]

The choice of godparents seems to have involved some real reflection on parents' part. In the early medieval period, holy men and members of the secular clergy were popular sponsors.[11] As the practice spread, however, friends, neighbors, and co-workers also took their place as godparents and co-parents. Despite the Church's preferences, parents often chose godparents and co-parents from relatives of the child such as an aunt or uncle. In cases where there was an existing kinship bond, the relationship of godparent and co-parent could make that bond even stronger. Where no actual kinship bond existed, choosing individuals as godparents and co-parents helped to solidify a relationship. From the parental point of view, it made sense to choose individuals who would be able to help support a child in the event of their deaths, a not inconsiderable issue in an age of high mortality.

There was a reverse movement from the other direction, however, in which the wealthy sometimes used the occasion of their child's baptism to choose godparents from among poorer neighbors. The powerful could thereby use the establishment of spiritual ties of kinship to pursue another of the Church's key values – the practice of charity. In Renaissance Florence, for example, wealthy families frequently chose godparents and relations of co-parenthood from among their needy neighbors as a charitable act "for the love of God." In such a relationship, the wealthier parents of the baptized infant extended gifts to the godparents and not the reverse as was usually the case in relations of greater social equality.[12] The material and moral value of this relationship for both the poor and the wealthy was significant.[13] Although it was not clear where charity ended and patronage began, both values pointed in the same direction. Bonds of charity and bonds of patronage extended ties of solidarity beyond the blood kin group. Thus, the laity of Europe doubtless used ties of godparenthood and co-parenthood to forge purely secular-minded relationships for their mutual advantage. Arguably, however, the Church benefited just as much if not more by fostering ties of invented kinship, infusing them with spiritual meaning and ethical significance, and using them creatively to teach important lessons about constructing larger social bonds beyond the blood kindred.[14]

---

[10] On rituals surrounding the celebration of bonds of godparenthood and co-parenthood, see Agnès Fine, *Parrains, marraines: la parenté spirituelle en Europe* (Paris, 1994), ch. 4.

[11] Lynch, *Godparents*, 150.

[12] Louis Haas, "Il Mio Buono Compare: Choosing Godparents and the Uses of Baptismal Kinship in Renaissance Florence," *Journal of Social History* 29, 2 (Winter, 1995): 344.

[13] *Ibid.*, 346.

[14] John Bossy, "Godparenthood: The Fortunes of a Social Institution in Early Modern Christianity," in Kaspar von Greyerz, ed., *Religion and Society in Early Modern Europe, 1500–1800* (London, 1984), 197; Bernhard Jussen, "Le Parrainage à la fin du Moyen Age: savoir public, attentes théologiques et usages sociaux," *Annales, ESC* 47, 2 (1992): 467–502. On the church community as "artificial kin" in the late classical period, see Brown, "Late Antiquity," 282.

Although the laity's daily experience may have taught them that ties of blood were stronger than those of spiritual kinship, spiritual kinship offered its own advantages as a complement, or even sometimes as a substitute for those relations. For one thing, it was voluntary, at least on the part of parents who chose their child's godparents. Individuals had some choice in matters regarding their spiritual kin that they did not have with their blood kin. Second, and very importantly, while godparents and co-parents characteristically bestowed gifts upon one another in the form of services and material aid, their relations avoided one of the main sources of conflict and violence among blood kin. For while godparents and co-parents owed each other mutual assistance, their relationship with a child conferred no rights of inheritance. Neither godchildren nor their parents had legitimate claims upon the property of those who agreed to serve as baptismal sponsors.[15]

Across the centuries, laymen and -women seized upon the possibilities that relations of godparenthood and co-parenthood offered for friendship and mutual assistance, often using their spiritual kin to serve some of the functions that Pierre Bourdieu identified with the bond of "practical" kinship.[16] It was clear, however, that despite the clergy's efforts to teach lessons of spiritual kinship, their task was particularly difficult to accomplish among the upper classes where lineal ties were usually strongest.

Controlling violence

The Church was not the only force trying to control the power of family and lineage ties. Like the Church, urban governments sought to limit both the capacity and legitimacy of lineage groups to mobilize members in the search for justice, seeing them as a force inimical to establishing and maintaining the larger civic unity. In late medieval Hainaut, for example, the governors of Douai imposed the obligation of temporary truces on men from warring families. They also took the stronger step of seeking to establish longer-lasting "peace and reconciliation," that is, "a moral rapprochement between enemies, a complete forgetting of quarrels, and an engagement to take up normal life again with the [larger system] of urban peace."[17] Although all inhabitants of Douai were eligible for inclusion in such truces, only families that were full members of the urban civic community were included in peace arrangements, at least until the middle of the fifteenth century.[18]

Germanic law had recognized a large place for lineage prerogatives in the settlement of interfamily disputes, a place that was maintained in private law. Nonetheless, urban judicial authorities in Flanders, Hainaut, and Brabant had

---

[15] Lynch, *Godparents*, 190–1.   [16] See above, p. 12.
[17] G. Espinas, "Les Guerres familiales dans la commune de Douai aux XIIIe et XIVe siècles: les trèves et les paix," *Nouvelle revue historique de droit français et étranger* (1899): 419.
[18] *Ibid.*, 421.

little tolerance for violations of the peace, and worked increasingly effectively to identify and bring punishment upon offending individuals. For example, penalties for feuding continued to require payments to victims' kin, an adaptation of Germanic laws of *Wergeld*.

In establishing a formal peace between families, the town government of Douai also drew upon the moral authority of the Church, using its intriguing notion of individual rather than family responsibility for crimes. Punishment of the offending individual often consisted of the penalty and penance of pilgrimage away from the town, thus helping to restore the larger civic peace while offering the offender, his kin, and other townsmen an object lesson about individual responsibility for breaches of law and order.[19] Urban governments in twelfth- and thirteenth-century Ypres and Metz made concerted efforts to break down the power of lineage groups in other ways as well, by enacting laws against the wearing of livery and establishing sumptuary laws limiting excessive displays of wealth by powerful clans.

Progress in repressing the armed conflict of kin groups varied by region, and was not a smooth, linear process in many areas. In Florence, the power of consortial or corporate families among the minor feudal nobility, which held their lands undivided, varied inversely with the ability of urban governments to control it. By the late thirteenth century, the powerful Commune government there succeeded in curbing many noble families' disruptiveness. In the fourteenth and fifteenth centuries, however, under conditions of social disruption, consortial family groupings began to reappear.[20] Even during these times of civil dislocation, however, many weary Florentines had little sense of their kindred group as a haven. Giovanni Morelli, a Florentine of the late fourteenth century, warned that even bonds of kinship were liable to weaken and snap when matters of property and self-interest were at stake. For the families of the Florentine lower classes, of course, years of social crisis saw no similar corporate family formations emerging. For their families, periods of war and pestilence merely exposed the fragility of small family formations in weathering social disorders.[21]

The historic power of lineage groups in some towns and cities was symbolized in the visual representations of urban communities. Whereas in most parts of northern Europe by the fourteenth century, portraits of towns generally emphasized unified communities enclosed by walls, representations of towns in

---

[19] *Ibid.*, 420, 441.

[20] David Herlihy, "Family Solidarity in Medieval Italian History," in David Herlihy, Robert S. Lopez, and Vsevolod Slessarev, eds., *Economy, Society and Government in Medieval Italy: Essays in Memory of Robert L. Reynolds* (Kent, OH, 1969), 178–9. This paradoxically made the earlier period appear more "modern" in terms of the power a civic government could marshal against armed lineage groups.

[21] Herlihy, "Family," 13–14.

parts of north-central Italy, Mediterranean France, and Germany illustrated the power of lineage groups through the fortified towers that distinguished patrician families from those of the common people.[22]

The gradual imposition of a more individuated system of punishment demonstrated communal governments' success in delegitimating lineages' rights of vengeance within the urban community and substituting for them the legitimacy of an emerging urban legal code against individual offenders. Ironically, in this way, late medieval urban governments sometimes helped protect extended families by controlling feuds that could destroy them, establishing rules for making and maintaining peace, and isolating and punishing the most reckless of lineages' own members.[23]

Urban governments and church authorities, who were in some instances the same people or members of the same families, shared the goal of taming the power of kin groups to assert themselves. This was a work lasting centuries, entailing both an adaptation of the daily and ritual life of the Church to the facts of blood and kinship ties, and a simultaneous effort to mold the laity's "habits of the heart" in ways more consistent with the visions of solidarity that lay at the heart of both medieval Christianity and civic communities.

Models of extrafamilial community

Households of the high clergy provided one model of a household that was large and included members who were not all members of the same blood family. The lives of the regular clergy – monks and nuns – living in residential communities also demonstrated a practical and influential model of joint living arrangements based on spiritual ties. Rituals marking the entry of men and women into religious orders were designed to demonstrate individuals' forsaking ties of natural kinship for those of a more spiritualized order.[24] As Michael Sheehan noted:

The ritual by which a candidate joined a monastery was clearly intended to impress upon him or her a complete separation from an earlier form of life and entry into a new one...By putting aside secular garb and assuming monastic dress,

---

[22] Jacques Heers, *Le Clan familial au Moyen Age: étude sur les structures politiques et sociaux des milieux urbains* (Paris, 1974), 140, 197.

[23] Espinas, "Les guerres," *Nouvelle renue historique*, 449.

[24] Herlihy, "Family," 8, cites two critical biblical passages. "He that loveth father or mother more than me is not worthy of me, and he that loveth son or daughter more than me is not worthy of me (Matthew 10.37)"; "If any man come to me and hate not his father, and mother, and wife, and children, and brethren, and sisters, yea, and his own life also, he cannot be my disciple (Luke 14.26)." Clarissa Atkinson argues that as Christianity changed from radical sect to established religion, it accommodated itself more fully with patriarchal structures of family life. See: *The Oldest Vocation: Christian Motherhood in the Middle Ages* (Ithaca, NY, 1991), 17–19, 239–42.

the candidate recognized that henceforth all the necessities for the physical support of life would be supplied by the head of the new household that he or she had entered.[25]

Clarissa Atkinson has concurred, observing: "Monks and nuns built new families to replace families left behind. They carried into the cloister images and meaning attached to such designations as 'sister,' 'brother,' 'mother,' and 'father' and returned new definitions and relationships to the wider community."[26]

The reality of the regular clergy's lives was, of course, a bit more complicated than this. In many instances, family and kinship ties persisted behind monastic walls. Families of the upper classes who were the source of Europe's regular clergy often had close, ongoing relationships with local monasteries. Aristocratic nuns frequently had siblings or other relatives living in the same monastic community with them. Nuns in medieval England often tried to create a domestic environment by setting up private rooms for eating and sleeping, or sought to accumulate family property, all of which violated vows of poverty they had taken as well as their acceptance of life in this sort of spiritual community.[27]

In some urban settings, placing more than one daughter in the same convent could offer families a financial advantage. By placing multiple daughters in the same convent, parents could sometimes get a bargain on the amount they were required to furnish for each girl's entry into religious orders. In cities riven by armed conflict among large family groups, however, the Church had cause to regret such policies, which introduced the same factionalism that was dividing the civic community into religious ones. This sort of problem arose dramatically during the siege of Florence in 1517 in the convent of the Murate, which was divided into two camps: those women who supported the Medici and those who

---

[25] Michael Sheehan, "Sexuality, Marriage, Celibacy, and the Family in Central and Northern Italy: Christian Legal and Moral Guides in the Early Middle Ages," in David I. Kertzer and Richard P. Saller, eds., *The Family in Italy: From Antiquity to the Present* (New Haven, CT, 1991), 182.

[26] Atkinson, *Oldest Vocation*, 65–6. In medieval Ireland, monks' spatial removal from their families was more dramatic than for women religious, who generally lived in communities closer to their blood kin, or established small religious communities composed of kin. See Lisa M. Bitel, "Women's Monastic Enclosures in Early Ireland: A Study of Female Spirituality and Male Monastic Mentalities," *Journal of Medieval History* 12, 1 (1986): 19–20.

[27] Eileen Power, *Medieval English Nunneries, c. 1275 to 1535* (New York, 1964), 14–15, 317–31. The author also notes the small size of English monasteries for women, which lent them a more domestic atmosphere. Daniel Bornstein shows that in late-fourteenth-century Venice, patrician parents often placed two daughters in the same convent "so they would not feel totally deprived of family." See "Spiritual Kinship and Domestic Devotions," in Judith C. Brown and Robert C. Davis, eds., *Gender and Society in Renaissance Italy* (London and New York, 1998), 185. Sandra Cavallo, *Charity and Power in Early Modern Italy: Benefactors and Their Motives in Turin, 1541–1789* (New York and Cambridge, 1995), 158–9, discusses the "private" apartments in Turinese convents.

supported their enemies.[28] Conversely, despite the fact that family and lineage relations could penetrate or even permeate monastic settings, there is ample evidence that many individuals who had contact with monastic life, even those who did not take perpetual vows, might experience a transformation of personal identity or a transfer of primary loyalties from their blood kin group to their spiritual one.

The Church's commitment to the superiority of virginity over the married state, and to "families" held together by spiritual and not biological kinship, gradually made a wide impact on the society and culture as a whole given the regular clergy's "near monopoly" on education and their elite status. In the ideology of ninth-century Christian monasticism, for example, "spiritual motherhood... replaced biological motherhood as a woman's most valuable work."[29] By the twelfth century, the Church's commitment to the cult of the Virgin Mary and the Holy Family signaled a greater willingness to adapt itself to the biological and emotional realities of motherhood and to accommodate values of spiritual motherhood to them.[30] Nonetheless, it still held out its greatest praise for saints such as Elizabeth of Hungary who "[by] turning maternal passion outward toward the sick and poor... transformed mother love from a private, somewhat 'selfish' emotion into holy charity" (see Plate 4).[31]

True spiritualized motherhood, as in the example of St. Elizabeth, looked outward towards the larger community and not inward into a domestic sphere governed by "selfish passions." This particular "turn," which prized the development of values of sociability from motherhood, the strongest tie of blood, exemplified the Church's goal of building a community of believers in which bonds of blood kinship would be transformed by being extended beyond family boundaries. The Church's gradual advocacy of efforts to extend the maternal relationship to a wider society arguably represented the earliest appearance in western society of a set of practices now known as "maternalism."[32]

Extending religiously based ideals of family relations to laymen and -women seems to have been particularly important to new preaching orders of mendicant brothers that grew up in the twelfth and thirteenth centuries. The fortunes of the mendicant orders were intimately connected to those of Europe's towns and cities, which experienced rapid growth during this time. As Jacques Le Goff

---

[28] Richard C. Trexler, "Le Célibat à la fin du Moyen Age: les religieuses de Florence," *Annales, ESC* 27, 6 (1972): 1341–2.

[29] Atkinson, *Oldest Vocation*, 65–6.   [30] *Ibid.*, 99, 163.   [31] *Ibid.*, 168.

[32] Maternalism occurs when upper-middle- or upper-class women organize themselves into associations for the improvement of the lives of poor women and children, based on skills associated with women's domestic identities. On the theory and practice of "maternalism" in the late nineteenth and twentieth centuries, see: Seth Koven and Sonya Michel, eds., *Mothers of a New World: Maternalist Politics and the Origins of Welfare States* (New York, 1993); Kathryn Kish Sklar, *Florence Kelley and the Nation's Work: The Rise of Women's Political Culture, 1830–1900* (New Haven, CT, 1995).

Plate 4 *St. Elizabeth Clothes the Poor and Tends the Sick*, 1390s.

and others have noted, these new preaching brotherhoods chose the town over the countryside for several reasons. In the widely cited opinion of Humbert of Romans, the mid-thirteenth-century general of the Dominican Order, friars went to the city because that was where the need for new spiritual leadership was greatest given the growth of towns and cities. Areas most in need of attention were the rapidly growing suburbs of towns where secular clergy were in shortest supply and parish structures weakest.[33] Second, mendicants went to the towns because that was where the sin was. Or perhaps it was just that sin was most noticeable there, given the scale and density of urban populations. Finally, the mendicants' predilection for town living stemmed from their leaders' down-to-earth and telling assessment of the dynamic relationship between city and countryside. Even at this early stage of Europe's first major spurt of urban growth, the same Humbert observed: "the countryside emulates the town, so that if one had to choose between preaching in town or in the country, it would be better to opt for a town on the chance that some part of the message would be diffused into the surrounding rural area."[34]

Members of the Dominican Order seem to have been especially active in seeking out and maintaining pastoral relationships with women of the upper classes, single, married and widowed. Through these relationships, friars and their layfollowers, sometimes known as "third orders" or "tertiaries," succeeded in introducing important elements of church teaching about family relations into the lives of patrician households. In the aftermath of the devastations of Plague mortality, clergy members involved in active pastorates became more concerned to address issues of practical importance to pious members of the laity, demonstrating a new willingness to show how those living in the married state and in a secular household could nonetheless infuse their households with religious values and their families with spiritual meaning. They authored tracts about domestic morality, child rearing, and spiritual observances within the household that spoke to married women, often using the lives of female saints as exemplars. To be sure, such tracts took liberties with the exact facts of female saints' lives, often transforming charismatic, not to say disruptive, female saints into docile exemplars of the kind of female spirituality the Church wished laywomen to emulate.[35]

[33] On the weaknesses of the parish clergy and parish community, see Gabriel Le Bras, "Esquisse d'une histoire des confréries," in *Etudes de sociologie religieuse*, vol. I (Paris, 1955)," 420, and James R. Banker, *Death in the Community: Memorialization and Confraternities in an Italian Commune in the Late Middle Ages* (Athens, GA and London, 1988), 17. On the fragility of parish organization in the towns, John Bossy, *Christianity in the West, 1400–1700* (New York and Oxford, 1985), 71; Jacques Le Goff, "Ordres mendiants et urbanisation dans la France médiévale: l'état de la question," *Annales, ESC* 25, 4 (1970): 924–46.

[34] Lester K. Little, *Religious Poverty and the Profit Economy in Medieval Europe* (Ithaca, NY, 1978), 187.

[35] Anna Benvenuti Papi, "Mendicant Friars and Female Pinzochere in Tuscany: From Social Marginality to Models of Sanctity," in Daniel Bornstein and Roberto Rusconi, eds., *Women and*

The interpenetration of household by church ideals and of monastic communities by family ideals and behaviors was demonstrated vividly in the life of one late-fourteenth-century Venetian patrician woman. Margarita Paruta and her husband had been patrons of the monastery of Corpus Domini, a house of seventy-odd women members committed to ascetic ideals of the observant Dominican Order. When she became a widow, Paruta entered the convent, granting it all of her sizable estate. What was more, her marriage and earlier role as manager of a large household proved to be exactly the kind of apprenticeship needed for the role she would play in the convent. "Accustomed as she was to managing a large patrician household, she fell naturally into the role of vicaress, repairing and improving the buildings and running the convent on behalf of the elderly prioress."[36] The larger "households" of women religious and those of the urban patriciate required some of the same skills from the women who ran both.

Beguines in towns and cities

One of the more interesting and "original" examples of lay efforts to construct artificial families and communities within an urban setting derived at least part of its inspiration from these same mendicant orders. In many towns, women known as *beguines* formed residential communities that provided opportunities to lead a strict devotional life while remaining part of the larger urban community.[37] Originating in northern Europe in the thirteenth century in such towns as Louvain (1205), Anvers and Tournai (1230), Ghent (1234), Cologne (1246), Frankfurt (1242), and Münster (1248), the beguine movement spread throughout towns and cities of western Europe, though it seems to have been most popular in the north. Although the lives of beguines differed in their particulars across the towns and cities of medieval Europe, there were also common features.[38] Whether living on their own, in houses with relatives or friends,

---

Religion in Medieval and Renaissance Italy, trans. Margery J. Schneider (Chicago and London, 1996), 84–103.

[36] Daniel Bornstein, "Spiritual Kinship and Domestic Devotions," in Brown and Davis, eds., *Gender and Society in Renaissance Italy*, 174, 180–2, 184.

[37] There is a single reference to the existence of beguine houses in villages outside Strasbourg in Dayton Phillips, *Beguines in Medieval Strasburg: A Study of the Social Aspects of Beguine Life*, Ph.D. thesis, Stanford University, 1941, 47. Andreas Wilts, *Beginen im Bodenseeraum* (Sigmaringen, 1994), shows that in the Mittelrhein area, beguines existed in cities, towns, and villages, but that historians have tended to emphasize the more homogeneous urban movement (22). In the Bodensee region, during the decline of the beguine movement in the fourteenth and fifteenth centuries, new foundations increased in the countryside (263, 275).

[38] On distinctions between the beguine movement in various parts of Europe, see Otto Nübel, *Mittelalterliche Beginen- und Sozialsiedlungen in den Niederlanden; ein Beitrag zur Vorgeschichte der Fuggerei* (Tübingen, 1970), 116–19, 133–8, 276; and Wilts, *Beginen*, 21, 268–74.

in small, informal communities of several women, or in large *beguinages* of several hundred women or more, beguines observed practices of chastity and rigorous devotional and sacramental life, attending mass and confession frequently and following strict limitations on their social intercourse with family and friends.[39] Beguines wore somber gray or black garb. When living in beguine convents or beguinages, they were prohibited from receiving adult men in their houses and required to limit the number of social occasions which they gave or attended.[40]

Unlike women of regular religious orders who entered the cloister often before puberty and took formal lifelong vows of poverty, chastity, and obedience, beguines were more likely to be adult women who adopted a religiously observant way of life that distinguished them from the world for only as long as they wished to follow it. They took no formal public vows at all. In this sense, beguines did not join a religious order but rather adopted a status or a "way of life."[41]

Beguines were unlike women religious entering a regular convent in another important respect. They retained rights to whatever property they had at the time they entered the community. If they were able to endow a particular house within the beguinage, they could usually transmit rights to dwell in "their" house to female kin or to other women whom they named in their wills who wished to follow rules of the group. Given these differences between beguine houses and convents, beguine houses are better considered as associations of individual pious women than religious communities, strictly speaking.[42]

Although these distinctions between women religious and beguines were real enough, it is important not to dichotomize their lives too greatly. Recent research suggests that communities of late-medieval women trying to lead a religious or penitential life be viewed as lying along a spectrum, particularly when it came

---

[39] Walter Simons, "The Beguine Movement in the Southern Low Countries: A Reassessment," *Bulletin de l'Institut historique belge de Rome* 59 (1989): 67, usefully distinguishes among beguine houses, beguine convents, and "*curtis* beguinages." If located outside a beguinage wall, beguine convents were often under the supervision of a priest, other religious authority, or "secular persons appointed as trustees." Walter Simons' book on the same subject, *Cities of Ladies: Beguine Communities in the Medieval Low Countries, 1200–1565* (Philadelphia, 2001) appeared too recently to be included in the present discussion. Ernest W. McDonnell, in *The Beguines and Beghards in Medieval Culture, with Special Emphasis on the Belgian Scene* (New Brunswick, NJ, 1954), 480, argues that, strictly speaking, German cities had no real beguinages, since the largest groups of beguines in towns and cities there usually numbered no more than 15–20 women "living together."

[40] Klemens Wytsman, *Des Béguinages en Belgique* (Gand, 1862), 22–4.

[41] Phillips, *Beguines*, 8. Unlike most authors, Phillips denies that widows could be considered beguines, since chastity was an important part of the rules that beguines were required to follow. While widows could and did reside in the beguine houses of Strasbourg, they were not considered full members of the community. Nübel, *Mittelalterliche Beginen,* 166, argues that though the minimum age for admission for beguines was 16, this rule was frequently violated.

[42] Phillips, *Beguines*, 166–7, 175–6.

to adopting rules of strict enclosure. Italian evidence, in particular, shows how communities of women tertiaries, often related to the mendicant orders, could successfully use petitions (sometimes to the pope himself), moral suasion, and the power of local secular authorities to resist the imposition of strict cloistering, whether mandated by papal legislation or male religious orders who sought to control them. Like beguines in the north of Europe, women living in religious communities in southern Europe knew that adopting strict enclosure would threaten their very existence, since it would prohibit them from circulating in the streets, seeking work, or begging for alms. Such a rule would also weaken their relationships with family, kin, and friends in the city.[43]

In areas of the southern Low Countries where larger beguine communities, so-called *curtis* beguinages, were especially numerous, these settlements demonstrated visually the liminality of a beguine's status between that of a pious lay woman living on her own and a woman who was a member of a regular community of religious.[44] Beguinages were usually enclosed by walls and a gate that set them off from the larger urban world. However, their internal architectural organization also reflected norms of secular life. Unlike convents of "true" women religious, beguinages did not generally consist of a building in which women shared sleeping and eating quarters, but rather of separate houses occupied by one or two individuals. Although some beguine houses were multistoried, others, especially those typical of smaller communities, usually resembled houses of the poor or the middling orders of the town or city where they were constructed (see Plate 5).

Beguines generally enjoyed a respected status among most members of the urban laity because of their commitment to ideals of poverty and work. They were the main source of labor in hospitals that served the larger beguinages and in other hospitals established by mendicant orders.[45] In addition, beguines' daily lives resembled more those of ordinary respectable single women and widows of the city than those of women religious who led contemplative lives apart from the larger urban world. Beguines, particularly those associated with the Franciscan order, worked in textile industries, engaging in crafts of spinning, weaving, and lacemaking. Additionally, in many towns and cities they taught

---

[43] Katherine Gill, "*Scandala:* Controversies Concerning Clausura and Women's Religious Communities in Late Medieval Italy," in Scott L. Waugh and Peter D. Diehl, eds., *Christendom and its Discontents: Exclusion, Persecution, and Rebellion, 1000–1500* (Cambridge, 1996), 177–203; and Gill, "Open Monasteries for Women in Late Medieval and Early Modern Italy: Two Roman Examples," in Craig A. Monson, ed., *The Crannied Wall: Women, Religion, and the Arts in Early Modern Europe* (Ann Arbor, 1992), 15–47.

[44] Although there were differences between the larger beguine communities of the Low Countries and the smaller, less formal residences in Germany, the nature of the communities seems to have been quite similar. See Brigitte Hotz, *Beginen und willige Arme im spätmittelalterlichen Hildesheim*, Schriftenreihe des Stadtarchivs und der Stadtbibliothek Hildesheim, vol. XVII (Hildesheim, 1988), 19–20, and the literature cited therein.

[45] Wilts, *Beginen*, 35. The author discusses the importance of beguines to urban health care in general (222–39).

Plate 5 *Beginenhof in Brügge* (Beguine House in Bruges).

young children and distributed alms to the local poor.[46] Beguines' proclivity for work earned them the admiration of a number of religious authorities including the bishop of Lincoln, Robert Grosseteste. He was reported to have stated (albeit privately) his preference for the beguines' approach to poverty over that of the Franciscan Brothers, since the beguines "lived by their own efforts and did not burden the world with their demands."[47]

Grosseteste's comments were especially important given the close association between the beguine movement and the urban missions of the mendicant orders. Many beguine houses were located near Dominican, Franciscan or Augustinian convents, which facilitated women's close relations with members of preaching orders whom many chose as their confessors or as executors of their estates.[48] Some beguinages were, in fact, established by Franciscan or Dominican orders. This did not mean that all male mendicants necessarily

---

[46] Beguines' weaving activities fanned the opposition and enmity of male guild members, who succeeded in restricting beguines' work in weaving to its preparatory processes. See H. Nimal, *Les Béguinages* (Nivelles, 1908), 99; Jo Ann Kay McNamara, *Sisters in Arms: Catholic Nuns through Two Millennia* (Cambridge, MA, 1996), 484; Gaston Robert, *Les Béguines de Reims et la maison Ste-Agnès* (Reims, 1923), 20–1.

[47] Cited in R. W. Southern, *Western Society and the Church in the Middle Ages* (London, 1970), 320.

[48] Phillips, *Beguines*, 45.

approved of them, however. In 1274, for example, one Franciscan, Gilbert of Tournai, complained "there are among us women whom we have no idea what to call, ordinary women or nuns, because they live neither in the world nor out of it."[49]

Their ambiguous status at the boundaries of lay and religious life and other features of the movement introduced conflict into the beguines' history. In the thirteenth century, itinerant beguines and beghards – beguines' male counterparts – were identified with heretical movements particularly in Rhineland Germany, earning them the antipathy of many church authorities who made concerted efforts to quash or at least control the movement. While the Church officially condemned the beguines in the early fourteenth century, including a decree of Pope Clement V in 1311, major church legislation was ambiguous.[50] On the one hand, the General Council of Vienne in 1312 decried some beguines' heterodox beliefs and teaching. On the other hand, this decree and later ones left room open for women's efforts to construct semireligious communities as long as they agreed to accept strict supervision by church authorities.[51] One of the several consequences of church legislation that attempted to increase male ecclesiastical control over the beguines was the encouragement it gave to the establishment of larger beguinages.

Beguines' labor also brought them into certain typically urban conflicts with laymen, however. Particularly acrimonious were those that broke out with guild authorities over the right of beguines to work in textile crafts, particularly weaving. Given their vows of poverty, beguines were limited in the wages they were allowed to accept, which brought them into direct competition with male artisans who sought to limit beguines' participation to less well-paid, secondary tasks of textile production. In several documented instances in the fifteenth century, guilds of weavers were able to drive beguines away from work that competed with their own.[52]

Estimates of the number of beguines in medieval Europe are notoriously hard to make. In 1317, the bishop of Strasbourg estimated that there were 200,000 of them in all of Germany. In other local estimates for the early fourteenth century when the movement was at its height in many parts of northern

---

[49] Quoted in Carol Neel, "The Origins of the Beguines," in Judith M. Bennett *et al.*, eds., *Sisters and Workers in the Middle Ages* (Chicago and London, 1989), 242.

[50] Nimal, *Les Béguinages*, 32–3.

[51] Relevant parts of the 1312 decree are reproduced in Southern, *Western Society*, 330. On the secular clergy, see Wytsman, *Des Béguinages*, 20; and Nimal, *Les Béguinages*, 72, on the control of the bishop. Robert, *Les Béguines*, 12, however, says that some beguines chose Franciscans as executors.

[52] On beguines' relations to guilds, see Phillips, *Beguines*, 21, 159; McDonnell, *Beguines and Beghards*, 270–3; Nimal, *Les Béguinages*, 99; and Hotz, *Beginen*, 88–9. Beguines in Reims who cared for the sick were prohibited from receiving any payment. See Robert, *Les Béguines*, 20.

Europe, the English monk Matthew Paris reported their number at 1,000 in the city of Cologne (population approximately 35,000) and 2,000 in Cologne and "neighbouring" cities. In fourteenth-century Strasbourg, there were 30 beguine houses with a total of 300 women.[53] The "Great Beguinage" of Leiden was so called because it consisted of more than forty houses.[54] Evidence from medieval wills suggests that in the thirteenth century, "true" beguinages such as those in Ghent or Brussels were gigantic in relative terms. The estimate of 800–900 beguines living in the St. Elisabeth's community at Ghent may not be an exaggeration.[55] The establishment of these communities never appears to have become completely obligatory, however. Even after the turbulent period of the 1320s, beguines in many areas continued to dwell on their own outside beguine houses, living alone, with parents, with other kin, or with several other beguines.[56]

Knowledge of the social background of medieval beguines is often lacking and evolved differently over time in various regions. Some evidence suggests that, until the early fourteenth century, beguines were generally women from the rural nobility or urban patriciate who patronized and endowed beguine communities handsomely through donations and wills.[57] This may have been the case in areas that lacked regular communities of women religious and for groups of beguines associated with the Dominican order. By the fourteenth and fifteenth centuries, however, many beguine communities grew more socially inclusive.[58] One of their more important functions by this time was to admit and support poorer women through the wealth left by richer members. Indeed, by the early modern period municipal authorities in some German cities viewed local beguine communities as poorhouses for the support of single and widowed women without families to shelter or support them. Families of these same poor women, similarly, viewed them as convenient places for the care of relatives.

---

[53] Southern, *Western Society*, 318–19; Phillips, *Beguines*, 227. For other local data, see Nübel, *Mittelalterliche Beginen- und Sozialsiedlungen*, 30–1, 147–8, 288.
[54] McDonnell, *Beguines and Beghards*, 550.
[55] Simons, "Beguine Movement," *Bulletin de l'Institut historique*, 78–81. Other estimates include 2,000 beguines in the town of Nivelles in the latter thirteenth century, and beguinages including 100 and 84 women in Champfleury and Mons in 1273 and 1365 respectively.
[56] Simons, "Beguine Movement," 84–91, emphasizes that the desire for control over beguines, and not an evolutionary path over time, led to larger beguinage communities in the southern Low Countries. He suggests that various forms co-existed in the same time period, though not necessarily in the same towns and cities.
[57] Steven Ozment, *When Fathers Ruled: Family Life in Reformation Europe* (Cambridge, MA, 1983), 13–14; Wilts, *Beginen*, 35, 270–1.
[58] McDonnell, *Beguines and Beghards*, 88, 478. This was true in the Bodensee area. The persecutions of the early fourteenth century seem to have made life as a beguine less attractive to women of the rural nobility, urban patriciate, and simple bourgeoisie. See Wilts, *Beginen*, 35, 270–1. The opposite trend seems to have been the case in Hildesheim. See Hotz, *Beginen*, 78–84.

These sorts of functions help to explain the ongoing appeal of beguinages as objects of charitable donations into the fifteenth and sixteenth centuries.[59]

Like the history of towns and cities of which they were part, the history of the beguine movement was marred by depredations of war, which devastated numerous establishments, as well as confiscations of their property by lay and church authorities at different points of their existence.[60] Some beguine communities survived into the seventeenth and eighteenth centuries in parts of the Low Countries where the larger, agglomerated communities had been most numerous. Indeed, in certain cases, renewed Catholic piety associated with the Catholic Reformation of the sixteenth and seventeenth centuries gave new vigor to them. But by this latter date beguine communities that had managed to survive had lost the kind of semireligious character that was part of their original appeal and became nearly indistinguishable from cloistered orders of nuns.[61]

While researchers in the early twentieth century were divided over whether the beguine movement should properly be seen as a religious or a social movement, this debate seems to be quite fruitless. The demand for strict religious observances and restrictions on beguines' freedom made it unlikely that religious piety was entirely lacking from women's choice of this way of life. Clearly, however, the beguine movement also had several practical advantages for women living in towns and cities where beguines were concentrated. Coresidence in a community setting provided residential and physical security. As one of its historians observed: "The beguinage was a retreat, especially well adapted to an urban society, where women living in common could pursue chastity without a vow ... and earn a livelihood by suitable work."[62] Recent research suggests that beguines were often rural in-migrants to the city as well as urban-born women.[63] Yet, as already noted, even the larger beguinages preserved important features of secular domestic life including small individuated households and the right to retain one's property.[64] Finally, life as a beguine offered women a certain flexibility, since they could live as a beguine only temporarily if they chose. In important respects, the lives of beguines exemplified features that many women sought from religious communities – an existence that had real continuity with their everyday lives and tasks, and the possibilities of a more flexible sort of affiliation than that desired by many men who joined regular religious orders.[65]

---

[59] Hotz, *Beginen*, 83–4, 89–92.
[60] On seizures of beguine property, see McDonnell, *Beguines and Beghards*, 486.
[61] Wilts, *Beginen*, 262.   [62] McDonnell, *Beguines and Beghards*, 131.
[63] Simons, "Beguine Movement," 73–5 emphasizes the appeal to migrant women of rural origin, but his data are from the sixteenth to the eighteenth centuries.
[64] Wytsman, *Des Béguinages*, 34.
[65] Caroline Walker Bynum, "Women's Stories, Women's Symbols: A Critique of Victor Turner's Theory of Liminality," in Robert L. Moore and Frank E. Reynolds, eds., *Anthropology and the Study of Religion* (Chicago, 1984), 117.

Although the appeal of this form of semireligious life spread throughout the European continent, its impact was greatest in the areas of northern Europe that were most urbanized, where women seeking the kind of semireligious identity and practical solidarity that only a residential sort of community could provide were sufficiently numerous to leave the "imprint" of their organizations upon the larger society.[66]

Networks of lay confraternal life

The impact of church teachings and organizations on the lives of Europe's laity can be seen in the appeal of another even more widespread form of association, also identified with the missions of urban mendicant brothers, though not originating with them.[67] Lay "confraternities" differed from groups of beguines in that they were not residential in character, but were, rather, associations of individuals who banded together to enhance their devotional lives through participation in special religious services, to assist one another in times of need and especially in times of sickness or death, or to carry out larger charitable projects.

This discussion of confraternal life is limited in several ways. It focuses on confraternities composed of members of the laity rather than clergy, on those that were truly voluntary in nature, and mainly on confraternities in towns and cities. Excluded from consideration are confraternities of men who practiced the same craft and whose confraternity represented a simple extension of ties formed in the workplace. Unlike other groups, membership in these craft confraternities seems to have been automatic or compulsory rather than voluntary. The discussion also touches only briefly on the sorts of rural confraternities which seem to have included all of a village's inhabitants in an association designed to honor a local patron saint, for example.[68] The term "confraternities" as used here refers to lay confraternities. In discussing Europe as a whole, "confraternities" refers to all groups. When discussing England alone, however, the more accepted

---

[66] Simons, "Beguine Movement," *Bulletin de l'Institut historique*, 77. See also Wilts, *Beginen*, 272, on the unusually intensive relationships between town and country in the Bodensee, which helped spread urban developments of different kinds to rural areas.

[67] Jacques Le Goff, "Ordres mendiants," *Annales, ESC*, 927–9. On the relationship between the mendicant orders and the confraternal movement, see also Nicholas Terpstra, *Lay Confraternities and Civic Religion in Renaissance Bologna* (Cambridge, 1995), 39; and Maureen Flynn, *Sacred Charity: Confraternities and Social Welfare in Spain, 1400–1700* (Basingstoke, 1989), 15. Lay confraternal life in Normandy was not stimulated by mendicant orders, but rather by diocesan authorities, older monastic orders, and the construction of private chapels by rich families. See Catherine Vincent, *Des Charités bien ordonnées: les confréries normandes de la fin du XIIIe siècle au début du XVIe siècle* (Paris, 1988), 94–6, 105, 170.

[68] Maurice Agulhon, *La Sociabilité méridionale: confréries et associations dans la vie collective en Provence orientale à la fin du 18e siècle* (Aix-en-Provence, 1966), 173, makes this remark concerning confraternities of different crafts groups.

term "fraternity" is used instead, since there the term "confraternities" generally refers to associations of clergy.[69]

European confraternities have been traced to origins in pre-Christian
Germanic drinking and feasting societies of the early medieval period. First used
by the clergy to bolster solidarity among themselves, their extension to members of the laity enabled the Church to use them in the battle against medieval
heresies, particularly Catharism, in the thirteenth and fourteenth centuries.[70]
Yet their appeal also lay in the increasing sense of control that lay members had
over the organizations, despite their religious origins and the active participation
of members of the clergy as chaplains or full members in some groups.

From the late Middle Ages onward, lay confraternities spread throughout
many parts of rural Europe as well as to towns and cities. Like other forms of
community life devoted to building networks of association, it is difficult to determine whether they spread from countryside to town or town to countryside.[71]
Whatever the exact path of diffusion, confraternities flourished in the towns
and cities as a result of demographic and financial circumstances, the appeal
of clerical models of association, and the need of individuals and families
of different social groups for the sorts of solidarity that confraternities could
provide.

Medieval confraternities appear to have developed along several different
lines.[72] Some focused on regular devotions within a confraternal church or
chapel, and appear to have built upon networks of association based in neighborhood or parish. Another sort of devotional confraternity that emerged especially in southern European cities in the fourteenth and fifteenth century was
penitential confraternities. Members of these groups sought to imitate the piety
of the mendicant orders by participating in rituals of self-flagellation and other
demonstrations of self-mortification, oftentimes in public ceremonies as well
as private. Other confraternities, to be considered more fully in Chapter 3, were

---

[69] Caroline M. Barron, "The Parish Fraternities of Medieval London," in Barron and Christopher
Harper-Bill, eds., *The Church in Pre-Reformation Society: Essays in Honour of F.R.H. Du
Boulay* (Suffolk, 1985), 17–18. While "fraternity" was used to refer to parish-level, grassroots
associations of the laity, "confraternities" involved relations between members of the laity with
religious houses of which they were *confratres*. See also Ludwig Remling, *Bruderschaften
in Franken: Kirchen- und sozialgeschichtliche Untersuchungen zum spätmittelalterlichen und
frühneuzeitlichen Bruderschaftswesen* (Würzburg, 1986), 12–16.

[70] On the formation of confraternities by the lower clergy who were concerned about their own
isolation, see Remling, *Bruderschaften*, 87–111. On the Church's use of confraternities to fight
heresy, see Le Bras, "Esquisse," *Etudes de sociologie religieuse*, 452.

[71] One recent student of French confraternal life argues that "the diffusion [of confraternities] in
the countryside may be taken as the sign of a reproduction of urban behavior by rural people."
See Catherine Vincent, *Les Confréries médiévales dans le royaume de France, XIIIe–XVe siècle*
(Paris, 1994), 44.

[72] Several studies lay out the general types of late-medieval confraternities. For Italy, see John
Henderson, *Piety and Charity in Late Medieval Florence* (Oxford, 1994), 35–7; Terpstra, *Lay
Confraternities*, 33–50; for Germany, Remling, *Bruderschaften*, 16–35.

more outward-looking, specializing in pious works outside the limits of their membership.[73]

Village confraternities and the impact of urbanization

Rural confraternities seem to have been rather loosely knit and inclusive sorts of organizations. Indeed, it is not clear that they should be considered organizations in the strict sense of the word since, beginning in the late medieval period, rural confraternities generally included the whole population of a village. In the diocese of Geneva, for example, a majority of rural dwellers belonged to these "community-confraternities" which have been found in villages as small as ten to thirty households.[74] Here, membership was socially heterogeneous with the local *seigneur* often playing the role of main benefactor. The principal activity of many rural confraternities was to sponsor a banquet on Pentecost or the feast day of the village's patron saint. Banqueting was an important ritual activity of these and nearly all confraternities, raising as it did members' consciousness of ties that bound them together.[75] Moreover, banquets often provided occasions for distributing food and alms to the poor.

Rural confraternities sometimes received legacies that helped pay for donors' continuing membership after death by allowing them to benefit from masses and prayers said on their behalf by the living. Bequests to village confraternities included land, mills, money, and leases of property as well as funds to support annual banquets.[76] In many areas, including Savoy, Dauphiné, the Suisse Romande, the western Alps and Rhône valley, the Auvergne and the Centre, community-confraternities are estimated to have existed in at least half of all rural communes, though this is probably an underestimate, since village groups created very few records. The rural parish fraternities of medieval England resembled their continental counterparts by their inclusiveness, organizing meals on patron saints' feast days, supplying candles for worship services, providing charitable gifts and funeral costs for members who needed them, and in many instances distributing alms for the poor.[77] Although rural confraternities were familiar in many parts of late medieval and early modern Europe, conditions of urban life made them multiply and flourish.

---

[73] On the outward-looking features of late-medieval confraternities, see Banker, *Death*, 5–8.

[74] Louis Binz, "Les Confréries dans le diocèse de Genève à la fin du Moyen Age," in *Le Mouvement confraternel au Moyen Age: France, Italie, Suisse* (Geneva, 1987), 236. Confraternities in rural Italy also seem to have been nearly all-inclusive. See, in the same volume, Charles M. de la Roncière, "Les Confréries à Florence et dans son contado," 302.

[75] Pierre Duparc, "Confréries du Saint-Esprit et communautées d'habitants au Moyen-Age," *Revue historique du droit français et étranger* 36 (1958): 353. The author observes that such confraternities were less frequent in towns and cities.

[76] *Ibid.*, 357.

[77] Barbara Hanawalt, "Keepers of the Lights: Late Medieval English Parish Gilds," *Journal of Medieval and Renaissance Studies* 14, 1 (1984): 35–6.

An apparently structural relationship between urbanization and the elaboration of confraternal life has been well demonstrated in studies of parts of southern France, where a consistent, positive relationship between the level of urbanization and the strength of penitential confraternities is quite evident. Lower Provence in the seventeenth and eighteenth centuries had a particularly high density of these groups, with fully 60 to 70 percent of all communes in the region containing at least one.[78]

The proliferation of penitential confraternities in parts of Provence suggests the presence of some important general relationships between settlements' population sizes and the presence of confraternities. The development of confraternal life in Provence was linked in part to a pattern of urban development there. Provence had a large number of "urbanized villages," part of a larger settlement pattern in which the distinction between town and countryside was less profound than in many other parts of Europe.[79] Provence's urbanized villages generally contained populations of 500 to 800 inhabitants, which would disqualify them from consideration even as towns under the definition used in this study. Not only were these "villages" smaller than towns as I have defined them, their populations also included large numbers of people engaged in agriculture. Nonetheless, villages where penitential confraternities were most abundant fulfilled many local economic and administrative functions associated with urban places. Still, size considerations did play a part. Where populations in these sorts of urbanized villages fell below 500 inhabitants, confraternities seem to have been rare.[80] Habits of confraternal life and the relationship between size of settlements and the presence of confraternities persisted over the centuries in this region. As late as the eighteenth century, 70 percent of villages in Provence with more than 850 inhabitants contained confraternities, while in western Provence, where this hybrid urban form was most developed, the figure was 90 percent.[81]

A similar link between urbanization and the development of confraternities existed in partially urbanized rural areas of central Italy. Here, as in Provence, confraternities flourished in the smaller towns in the dependencies of larger cities, especially those small burgs where artisans and merchants were most numerous. These rurally based confraternities often spilled over parish boundaries, and attracted members from nearly all classes of society.[82] Moreover,

---

[78] The percentage fell, however, as one moved into the less urbanized provinces of Dauphiné and Languedoc. See Marie-Hélène Froeschlé-Chopard, "Pénitents et sociétés populaires du sud-ouest," *Annales historiques de la Révolution française*, no. 267 (January–March 1987): 120.

[79] Agulhon, *La Sociabilité*, 404.   [80] *Ibid.*, 153–4, 506, 537.

[81] Michel Vovelle, *De la cave au grenier: un itinéraire en Provence au XVIIIe siècle. De l'histoire sociale à l'histoire des mentalités* (Québec, 1980), 274, 280.

[82] De la Roncière, "Les Confréries à Florence," *Le Mouvement confraternel*, 299–300. See also Ronald F. E. Weissman, *Ritual Brotherhood in Renaissance Florence* (New York, 1982), 7, on

rural dwellers in these areas sometimes belonged to urban confraternities, though in most instances urban associations seem to have reserved their leadership positions for town dwellers.[83] Thus, evidence from southern Europe where penitential confraternities were most popular suggests that they were likely to appear in rural areas that displayed some "urban" characteristics such as an agglomerated population nearing 1,000, a set of urban functions such as the presence of markets, and a developed division of labor.

Patterns of urban confraternal life

The religious sociologist Gabriel Le Bras, one of the fathers of confraternal studies, believed that between the thirteenth and fifteenth centuries most Christians were members of a confraternity.[84] This may have resulted from what one historian has identified as a main feature of medieval devotional life – the need to express individual piety within the context of a community.[85]

Studies of individual towns and cities furnish a wide array of data on the number of confraternities and the members they attracted. The town of Zamora, in Léon-Castille, for example, saw its first confraternity in 1230. By 1400, there were 10, and by the second half of the sixteenth century, when the town's population was approximately 8,600, there were 150 confraternities, most of them numbering 20 or 30 individuals.[86] Elsewhere in Spain, confraternities grew most rapidly in the fifteenth century in territories won back from the Muslims.[87] In the small Tuscan town of San Sepolcro in the mid-thirteenth century, confraternity membership totaled about 1,200 in a population of fewer than 5,000. At that time, approximately one-third of the town's households were represented by a male confraternity member.[88] The Norman city of Rouen had confraternities in 88 percent of its parishes in the fifteenth century.[89] In medium-sized towns

---

the relationship between confraternal life and the urbanized countryside of Tuscany. Remling, *Bruderschaften*, 91, notes the presence of clerical confraternities in "larger rural market places with small-town character" in Franconia.

[83] Banker, *Death*, 8, 54–6.

[84] Le Bras, "Esquisse," *Etudes de sociologie religieuse*, 433–4.

[85] Caroline Bynum, "Did the Twelfth Century Discover the Individual?" in Bynum, *Jesus as Mother: Studies in the Spirituality of the High Middle Ages* (Berkeley, 1982), 88, 104–5.

[86] Flynn, *Sacred Charity*, 15.   [87] Vincent, *Les Confréries médiévales*, 43.

[88] Banker, *Death*, 59, 64. Flynn, *Sacred Charity*, 16–17, supplies data mainly for the sixteenth century, when Valladolid (population 30,000) boasted "at least 100 confraternities," and Toledo (population 60,000), 143. In the province of Cuenca, there was one confraternity for every 48 households, and one for every 100 households in New Castile. There were 75 confraternities in Florence (population 59,000), 68 in Lyon (population 45,000–65,000), 67 in Lübeck (population 25,000 in 1400), and 99 for Hamburg (population 16,000–18,000) on the eve of the Reformation.

[89] Vincent, *Des Charités*, 58–9. She notes that only 13 percent of other deaneries in the diocese had approved confraternities. This finding may stem, however, from the inequality in the record-keeping between rural and urban parishes, with the rural parishes producing and preserving fewer documents.

of the fourteenth and fifteenth centuries, the number of confraternities usually ranged from thirty to forty.[90] In fifteenth- and sixteenth-century Bologna, 10 to 20 percent of the adult population belonged to a confraternity, though membership varied by gender and social class, with wealthier men being most likely to join multiple groups.[91] In late sixteenth-century Geneva there were sixty confraternities in a city of 10,000–12,000.[92]

London's parish confraternities were especially numerous in the extramural parishes and are estimated to have included approximately 10 percent of the parishioners there. Membership in a confraternity in these larger parishes may well have provided laymen and -women with a smaller, more intimate devotional group experience than the parish experience could provide.[93] Indeed, by their size and mixed-gender composition, parish- or neighborhood-based confraternities of northern Europe seem to have represented, perhaps even consciously, the kind of community networks associated with early urban Christian groups.[94]

Membership in these sorts of parish- or even neighborhood-based confraternities mainly required evidence of good character and the desire to live in harmony with other members, who might number from fifty to several hundred.[95] Confraternal dues varied, but an average seems to have been a sum approximating several days' wages of a working man.[96] Other costs included occasional alms for the poor, fines for missing confraternal events, and payments for the purchase of wax for devotional candles. As a result of such requirements, the very poor or destitute were largely unable to participate in the life of urban

[90] The cities include Nantes, whose population of 12,000 at the end of the fifteenth century contained 30 confraternities, and Dijon, with a similar population and number of confraternities. Ghent, with a population of 64,000, had 40. Florence, whose population shrank two-thirds from 110,000 to 37,000 in 1440, saw the number of its confraternities increase from 30 in 1325 to 52 in 1400. See Vincent, *Les Confréries médiévales*, 42–3 and Henderson, *Piety and Charity*, 39.

[91] Terpstra, *Lay Confraternities*, 83.

[92] Binz, "Les Confréries," *Le Mouvement confraternel*, 239. On confraternities devoted to St. Anne in Germany, see Angelika Dörfler-Dierken, *Vorreformatorische Bruderschaften der hl. Anna* (Heidelberg, 1992), *passim*.

[93] Barron, "Parish Fraternities," 28. The author cites parish figures for 1548 for St. Botolph Aldersgate and St. Margaret's at Westminster which numbered 1,100 and 2,500 communicants at that date respectively.

[94] De la Roncière, "Les Confréries à Florence," *Le Mouvement confraternel*, 299; Bossy, *Christianity*, 57–8. Cf. Le Bras, "Esquisse," *Etudes de sociologie religieuse*, 441.

[95] Vincent, *Les Confréries médiévales*, 54, 136.

[96] Binz, "Les Confréries," *Le Mouvement confraternel*, 250. Two days' wages of a workman plus the cost of one-half pound of wax for devotional candles was the entry fee for the fifteenth-century confraternity of Our Lady and the Blessed Sacrament in Liège. See David Henry Dietrich, "Brotherhood and Community on the Eve of the Reformation: Confraternities and Parish Life in Liège, 1450–1540." Ph.D. thesis, University of Michigan, 1982, 121. On the dues and death benefits for women and men confraternity members in Lübeck, see Monika Zmyslony, *Die Bruderschaften in Lübeck bis zur Reformation* (Kiel, 1977), 142, 221.

confraternities, at least as actual members.[97] These locally based confraternities generally attracted members from the working and middling ranks of urban society.[98]

Records from different sorts of confraternities suggest highly variable rates of participation among members. In one confraternity in thirteenth-century Brescia associated with the Franciscan Brothers, members attended mass together one Sunday a month, said two confessions, and sought to emulate the friars' fasts and charitable activities.[99] Although data are difficult to come by, attendance figures (generally for monthly meetings) suggest different levels of commitment. Officers were, not surprisingly, apt to attend more often than others. Figures for one flagellant confraternity in Renaissance Bologna showed that most members gathered for worship together at least once but more often twice a week. Other studies, such as Ronald Weissman's well-known study of another penitential confraternity in Florence, the Company of San Paolo, showed much lower figures.[100]

Preparing one's soul for the afterlife and caring for it after death were key goals of many late medieval devotional confraternities.[101] Historians studying this feature of confraternal life and devotions trace it to the growing importance of the idea of purgatory and to the belief that individuals were more likely to achieve salvation within a confraternal setting that offered a mutual "treasury of grace" made stronger by the presence of many members.[102]

Yet material forces such as basic demographic characteristics of towns and cities seem also to have played a part in the appeal of confraternities.[103] The dedication of much of their devotional life to commemorating the deaths of departed "brothers" and "sisters" suggests that confraternities filled a need in individuals' lives for community ties in the face of unpredictable mortality patterns and an absence of kin members to assist them.

Jacques Chiffoleau has made the most dramatic argument linking the growth of confraternal life to demographic conditions of late medieval towns and cities and, in particular, to the physical and psychological toll that high mortality and migration took on individuals. His study of the southern French city of Avignon

[97] Lester K. Little, *Liberty, Charity, Fraternity: Lay Religious Confraternities at Bergamo in the Age of the Commune* (Bergamo and Northampton, MA, 1988), 71–3.
[98] Vincent, *Les Confréries médiévales*, 185.   [99] Little, *Liberty*, 206.
[100] Weissman, *Ritual Brotherhood*, 109, 133–6. Terpstra, *Lay Confraternities*, 106–7, characterizes Weissman's attendance figures as "unusually low."
[101] Jacques Chiffoleau, "Sur l'usage obsessionel de la messe pour les morts à la fin du Moyen Age," in *Faire croire: modalités de la diffusion et de la réception des messages religieux du XIIe au XVe siècle* (Rome, 1981), 235–56.
[102] On the evolution of the idea of purgatory, see Jacques Le Goff, *La Naissance du purgatoire* (Paris, 1981).
[103] On the impact of demographic conditions on confraternal life, see Gervase Rosser, "Solidarité et changement social: les fraternités urbaines anglaises à la fin du Moyen Age," *Annales, ESC* 48, 5 (1993): 1129.

depicts urban dwellers who bear a striking resemblance to their anxious modern counterparts. Like other cities, the population of Avignon was composed of a large number of individuals who, having chosen to migrate to the city, found it cruelly lacking in several important respects. In their wills, many of them lamented being cut off from their ancestral roots in the countryside and from the consolation of burial among kin in their places of birth.

The contrast between migrants' real or imagined rural families and the ones they experienced in the city was sharp. Whereas rural families presented themselves in the migrants' minds as chains of kinship extending backwards in time, urban families seemed frail and transient. Urban dwellers seem to have had only a very short-term sense of their family's existence.[104] Migrants' wills expressed a longing for connection to kin both in daily life and in the afterlife, leading some to request burial in their places of birth and others simply to express longing for ancestors whom they had known or could only imagine.[105] According to Chiffoleau's analysis, it was hardly a surprise that city dwellers with few relatives nearby were especially motivated to join a confraternity to ensure themselves a proper Christian burial in the here-and-now and security for the care of their souls after death.[106]

Historians have also ascribed the appeal of parish fraternity membership in England in the fourteenth century to men's and women's concern for a proper burial, particularly in the wake of the mid-fourteenth-century epidemic of the Plague. Records of London parish fraternities that have survived from this period show that concern about the behavior of fraternity members at the death of one of their members was "dominant" in all extant fraternity regulations. Fraternity rules detailed formalities for the collection of the body if the person had died outside London, the saying of psalms and masses, and fulfilling requirements of attendance at the funeral. Rules prescribed the wearing of the fraternity's livery, financial penalties for nonattendance at members' funerals, and the provision of "a goodly number of candles and tapers around the corpse."[107]

Ravages of war also made confraternities an appealing source of social solidarity. In fifteenth-century Normandy, devastations of the Hundred Years' War drove thousands of refugees into the city of Rouen. Here, parishes most dominated by newcomers and refugees showed a particularly vibrant confraternal life. These temporary migrants apparently took their confraternal habits back to the countryside when they returned after the end of violence.

[104] Chiffoleau, "Sur l'usage," 252–4, and Jacques Chiffoleau, *La Comptabilité de l'au-delà: les hommes, la mort et la religion dans la région d'Avignon à la fin du Moyen Age (vers 1320–vers 1480)* (Rome, 1980), 71. Vincent, *Les Confréries médiévales*, 185, also links their emergence to the advent of the small family by the late thirteenth century.
[105] Chiffoleau, *La Comptabilité*, 180–1, 199–201.
[106] On the lack of family bonds in new areas of the cities, see de la Roncière, "Les Confréries à Florence," *Le Mouvement confraternel*, 305–6.
[107] Barron, "Parish Fraternities," in Barron and Harper-Bill, eds., *The Church*, 24–5.

Confraternities spread into rural areas surrounding the city after 1450 and the conclusion of peace.[108]

Individuals' attraction to confraternal life stemming from the absence of ties of solidarity with their families of origin or a sense of marginalization or isolation from one another in new and unfamiliar urban settings was thus magnified during mortality crises such as recurrent Plague epidemics beginning in the fourteenth century.[109] If individuals' fear of facing death and the afterlife without their blood kin was a primary spiritual cause of late-medieval confraternities' enormous popularity, the persistence of high urban mortality rates through the early modern period doubtless helped to maintain their appeal.[110]

Most studies of late-medieval devotional confraternities in northern and southern Europe show that women participated in them and that many confraternal associations were quite evenly balanced by gender.[111] In certain instances, this balance stemmed from the fact that husbands and wives joined the same confraternity together. Norman confraternities or "charities" contained married couples who sometimes joined with other members of their larger kin group.[112] In some German confraternities devoted to St. Anne, wives' membership seems to have come automatically when their husbands joined, with widows assuming "full" membership only after their husbands' death. In Münster, confraternity rules stipulated that whenever a female member died, a new one could be admitted along with her husband up to a total of seventy-two women.[113] Early fifteenth-century ordinances of the English guild of St. George in Norwich required that women, many of whom joined with their husbands, pay an entrance fee one-half as high as that required of men.[114] In others, however, men and

---

[108] Vincent, *Des Charités*, 74.

[109] Henderson, *Piety and Charity*, 71, notes the "rapid multiplication" of confraternities in the 150 years after the Black Death of the mid-fourteenth century.

[110] Chiffoleau, *La Comptabilité*, 91, argues, however, that the Black Death did not constitute a watershed in this regard.

[111] *Ibid.*, 277–8. Gender mixing was the norm in Switzerland, according to Binz, "Les Confréries," *Le Mouvement confraternel*, 247, 250. Banker, *Death*, 54, 59, 111, studying the Italian confraternity of San Bartolomeo, shows a balanced sex ratio from the 1260s to the early fourteenth century. Beginning in the early fourteenth century, however, both "praising" and "discipline" confraternities began to exclude women. Hanawalt, "Keepers," 25, found women in all but 5 of the 500-odd confraternities whose memberships were summarized in returns of 1389. When clergy members are excluded, women composed approximately 50 percent of the membership of those groups.

[112] Vincent, *Des Charités*, 207. She shows that individuals in couples constituted between 33 and 62 percent of members. On women joining as part of a couple, see also Remling, *Bruderschaften*, 96.

[113] Dörfler-Dierken, *Vorreformatorische Bruderschaften*, 34, 140. Quite exceptionally, women in this confraternity also served on the group's board and took on positions of management.

[114] Ben R. McRee, "Religious Gilds and Civic Order: The Case of Norwich in the Late Middle Ages," *Speculum* 67, 1 (1992): 80. McRee shows that local notables were required to pay higher fees than the regular members, who included a diverse group of craftsmen and more affluent merchants.

women joined as individuals.[115] In most parish fraternities in London, too, men and women could join as individuals as well as in couples and pay the same entrance fees. Women in the London associations were even named as founders of new groups alongside men, though women almost never served in leadership positions.[116] Confraternities in which women played the most active roles usually had strong bases in local neighborhoods.

In Italy, women were most numerous and active as members of devotional or charitable confraternities rather than penitential ones, especially after the late fourteenth century. While women were not necessarily excluded from all companies that practiced self-flagellation, in most instances they were mainly "auxiliary" members of them. Within penitential confraternities, women who were related to male members participated indirectly in the spiritual benefits conferred by their relative's membership and participation in rituals of self-mortification. In many parochial, sacramental confraternities, however, women enjoyed full membership, though no access to leadership positions.[117]

Joining a confraternity not only meant participating in a shared ritual life and gaining some entitlements to practical assistance in times of penury or death. It also meant agreeing to a code of conduct or set of behaviors towards other members. A membership document from the Gild of the Holy Trinity and St. Leonard in Lancaster attested to this group's concern with chastity and the marriage bond, noting that the "honour of the women of the gild was to be a matter of concern to all the brethren, who were enjoined not only to observe personal purity, but to refuse admission to their homes to those who were known to be adulterers."[118]

Like many confraternities on the Continent, urban parish fraternity regulations in England tried to ensure peace and harmony among their members at confraternal banquets and in daily life. They forbade lawsuits among members,

[115] Nicholas Morard, "Une Charité bien ordonnée: la confrérie du St-Esprit à Fribourg à la fin du Moyen Age (XIVe–XVe siècles)," in *Le Mouvement confraternel*, 278, shows husbands and wives entering devotional confraternities together. See also Vincent, *Les Confréries médiévales*, 57, and H. F. Westlake, *The Parish Gilds of Medieval England* (London, 1919), 23–4. Dietrich, however, found little evidence of husbands and wives joining the same confraternities. See "Brotherhood," 132, 163. He showed (193) that there were ties of blood linking together confraternity members, but noted that confraternities' "lines of spiritual kinship cut across the lines of blood kinship" (231).

[116] Barron, "Parish Fraternities," 31–2; Katherine L. French, " 'To Free Them from Binding': Women in the Late Medieval English Parish," *Journal of Interdisciplinary History* 27, 3 (Winter, 1997): 387–412.

[117] Henderson, *Piety and Charity*, 111; Giovanna Casagrande, "Confraternities and Lay Female Religiosity in Late Medieval and Renaissance Umbria," and Anna Esposito, "Men and Women in Roman Confraternities in the Fifteenth and Sixteenth Centuries: Roles, Functions, Expectations," in Nicholas Terpstra, ed., *The Politics of Ritual Kinship: Confraternities and Social Order in Early Modern Italy* (New York and Cambridge, 2000), 48–66, 82–97, respectively.

[118] Cited in Westlake, *The Parish Gilds*, 35. He notes that this clause seems to have been written before the composition of the company's ordinances in 1377, and was unusual.

refused to allow members to stand as guarantors of one another's debts, and excluded "quarrelsome" individuals from their midst. The lengths to which urban fraternities in Leicester, Norwich, London, and Canterbury sought to regulate their members' behavior may have stemmed from the fact that urban associations attracted wealthier members than did rural ones, sometimes including those who played a conspicuous role in town or city government. At their better moments, these sorts of men were quite conscious of the need for discretion and self-control in their behavior in order to preserve the group's reputation as well as their own.[119] Urban fraternities in England were also more likely than rural ones to contain clauses detailing the level of material assistance that members could expect in times of need. Whereas less than one-third of rural fraternities documented in a 1389 survey included such clauses, fully 55 percent of urban ones referred to this vital fraternal function.[120]

Confraternities also helped newcomers to the city become better integrated into urban life by linking them to other individuals for mutual assistance during life's most "critical situations."[121] Not all confraternities welcomed newcomers, however. Sometimes integration came from simply setting up a new group of one's own and then building one's personal network out from it. This was illustrated in the history of several Jewish confraternities in early modern Italy. Young unmarried Jewish men who migrated to Verona to serve as apprentices in local Jewish businesses found themselves excluded from the more prestigious Jewish confraternities already in existence there, and addressed this problem by simply forming their own. In the seventeenth century, another wave of Jewish migrants to Verona from the Sephardic community of Venice encountered the same sort of exclusion on the part of Verona's Jewish elite, but lost their marginal status in the city's Jewish community by gradually building up and dominating another confraternity.[122]

Studies of southern Europe, in particular, suggest that, by the fifteenth century, men in many cities and towns were increasingly attracted to the kinds of spiritual and social relations found within penitential confraternities. This evolution can be observed in the history of Bologna's confraternities, where many devotional (*laudesi*), literally "praising" groups originally included lower-class members and were quite balanced in the numbers of male and female members. Gradually,

---

[119] Ben R. McRee, "Religious Gilds and Regulation of Behavior in Late Medieval Towns," in Joel Rosenthal and Colin Richmond, eds., *People, Politics, and Community in the Later Middle Ages* (Gloucester and New York, 1987), 108–16. Remling, *Bruderschaften*, 268–77, describes the growing appeal of membership in Kitzingen's St. Anne confraternity among city councilors as well as merchants and wealthy craftsmen in the early sixteenth century.

[120] McRee, "Religious Gilds and Civic Order," *Speculum*, 75.

[121] Le Bras, "Esquisse," *Etudes de sociologie religieuse*, 423, for a discussion of the importance of urban confraternities for integrating newcomers to urban life.

[122] Elliott S. Horowitz, "Jewish Confraternities in Seventeenth-Century Verona: A Study in the Social History of Piety," Ph.D. thesis, Yale University, 1982, 116–19, 204–8.

however, many men left these more heterogeneous praising confraternities for those that were composed of men only.[123]

Thus, the more loosely knit, heterogeneous, and locally based sort of confraternal community contrasted sharply with the gender-restrictive, intensive, and inwardly focused mentality of the male penitential groups. Whereas the "praising" confraternity "was an ecumenical but comparatively passive sharing in the merits of the mendicant orders," the penitential model was "exclusive, secret, and demanding."[124] Moreover, many penitential confraternities of men required their members to take an oath of undivided allegiance which prohibited members from joining other groups.[125]

Nonetheless, these penitential brotherhoods sometimes served as the foundations for other social relations that resembled the sorts of "weak ties" so important to urban life. In late-medieval Florence, certain penitential confraternities provided networks of association for men of the city's patriciate, which themselves served as the foundation of civic republicanism. During the period of the Florentine Republic (roughly 1250–1500), members of these cross-neighborhood confraternal groups used their "ritual brotherhoods" to forge networks of acquaintanceship. Rather than reinforcing ties of neighborhood or parish, these confraternities did just the opposite, providing a means for patrician men to reach out beyond ties of family and neighborhood to construct broader bonds that helped to support a civic community. In this way, confraternal life contributed, at least for part of Florence's history, to inspiring certain mores and "habits of the heart" needed for a successful republican constitution to succeed.[126]

Urban confraternal life thus provided different sorts of opportunities to build networks of community that fulfilled the needs of different social groups: those composed of women and men that sought to enhance devotional life beyond regular practices of the parish; male groups that emulated the penitential piety of their mendicant mentors; and, finally, those which, while dedicated in principle to devotional solidarity, also encouraged bonds of civic republicanism.

Although Le Bras viewed confraternities as "artificial families," the large size of some urban confraternities, which numbered in the hundreds or thousands of members, suggests that it is wise not to take the analogy too literally. Maurice Agulhon's notion of confraternities as constituting a sort of artificial "extended family" seems more accurate.[127] As Catherine Vincent argued: "There was

---

[123] Banker, *Death*, 149; Terpstra, *Lay Confraternities*, 116–25, on the newer "Observant" model of confraternal life and the gradual exclusion of women from it.
[124] Terpstra, *Lay Confraternities*, 141.   [125] Weissman, *Ritual Brotherhood*, 97–8.
[126] *Ibid.*, 61–3, 198, shows that confraternities were run along republican models until the sixteenth century, when more hierarchical relationships began to prevail. On links between confraternal ties and civic organization, see: Nicholas Terpstra, "Confraternal Prison Charity and Political Consolidation in Sixteenth-Century Bologna," *Journal of Modern History* 66, 2 (June, 1994): 217–48, and McRee, "Religious Gilds and Civic Order," *Speculum*, 69–97.
[127] Agulhon, *La Sociabilité*, 211.

no substitution of one structure for another, but rather a prolongation of one into the other... Generally speaking, the confraternal movement was not built on the ruins of family bonds; better, it was nourished by them without ever totally eclipsing them."[128] For those who had kin in the city, confraternity membership served less as a substitute than as a complement for these ties.[129] Among individuals or couples literally without kin in the city, however, the extended kinship network that confraternities supplied might well have provided the principal persons who mourned their passing.

John Henderson's depiction of burial rituals in late-medieval Florence nicely illustrates how confraternal rituals based upon individuals' ties of solidarity with spiritual "sisters" and "brothers" could complement the presence of blood relatives. In sickness, he shows, the confraternities helped to provide medical assistance and priestly ministrations. In the event of death of a poor member, the confraternity helped with funeral expenses and supplied objects for a proper burial: "cushions for the corpse's head, the pall, and the bier." While female relatives of the deceased cleansed and dressed the body, performing "intimate" tasks of death and burial, confraternity members gathered to carry out more public rituals of mourning. These extended spiritual kin, in Bourdieu's terms, helped to fulfill obligations of both "practical" and "official" kinship.

Although sumptuary legislation in many cities controlled the lavishness of material displays permitted at funerals, confraternities supplied a large and comforting number of "brothers" and "sisters" to bear witness to the extensiveness of the individual's spiritual kin. Similarly, just as their choice of final resting place in the confraternal tomb could confirm their identity as members, bequests of the deceased to the company in the form of masses and prayers to be said for the care of their souls conveyed piety and hope of salvation.[130]

The differences between Chiffoleau's and Weissman's views of confraternities and of the cities in which they grew are noteworthy. Weissman's portrait of Florence shows a city composed of tightly knit neighborhoods filled with dense networks of kinship. This contrasts sharply with Chiffoleau's vision of towns and cities as places filled with individuals or couples in need of artificial kin networks to help them through "critical life situations." These divergent visions may stem from differences in patterns of rural-to-urban migration between the cities and towns of southern France and central Italy which the two authors studied. The more likely source of the difference lies, however, in the two historians' emphasis on the experience of different social groups. Because it focused on urban patricians, Weissman's study emphasized these men's extensive kin networks present in the city. Chiffoleau's portrait, on the other hand, captured more accurately the family and community lives of the common people.

---

[128] Vincent, *Les Confréries médiévales*, 61–2.
[129] Agulhon, *La Sociabilité*, 211. Cf. Heers, *Le Clan familial*, 259–61.
[130] Henderson, *Piety and Charity*, 157–60.

The importance of artificial families of spiritual kin in late-medieval and Renaissance Europe varied according to members' level of piety, wealth, and the presence of kin in the city, among other things. Those from wealthy and powerful families who might belong to several confraternities did not especially need material support from any of them. For wealthy members, these associations supplied the business contacts, the "weak ties" on which they could build profitable personal networks. For artisans or small merchants who constituted the backbone of confraternal membership in many cities, however, "confraternal membership . . . gave cooperative access to the spiritual resources that [the wealthy] enjoyed by virtue of . . . personal wealth and status: a confessor, indulgences, an honorable funeral, and interment in mendicant robes."[131] The same could be said of the differences between merchants and artisans in late-medieval London. Whereas merchants were wealthy enough to endow private foundations or "chantries" that paid for masses to be said for their souls, the same was not true of artisans and people of the middling ranks for whom the benefits of fraternity membership made it "often the centre of their social and spiritual world."[132]

By the late fifteenth century, there was a new tone detectable in confraternal life. A comparison of late-fifteenth- with fourteenth-century records of some English fraternities, for example, suggests the declining importance of an earlier preoccupation with burial rituals and intercessory prayers for the souls of dead members, and a shift towards "conviviality, decent living, processions and the celebration of saints' days."[133] Indeed, it was the reputation of confraternities for these sorts of social activities that would eventually earn them the wrath of urban humanists and religious reformers such as Martin Luther. Their survival and even revival in many Catholic cities of the sixteenth and seventeenth centuries as more charitably oriented institutions, to be discussed in Chapter 4, would come in part as a response to these critiques.

European confraternal life illustrated a range of experience among different kinds of groups.[134] While all communities existed to support and extend the religious observance of their members, the social purposes of confraternities appear as no less important, helping individuals establish and maintain networks of friendship and mutuality in ways not permitted through family or kinship alone. In situations where ties of family and kinship overlapped at the neighborhood level, as in the case of Renaissance Florence, confraternities afforded men of the city's patrician class the opportunity to escape dense local kinship and patron–clientage relations and establish voluntary bonds of solidarity with those from other neighborhoods. In other settings where urban migration and daily life did not occur within dense networks of kin relations, confraternities,

[131] Terpstra, *Lay Confraternities*, 81.
[132] Barron, "Parish Fraternities," 30.   [133] *Ibid.*, 27–8.
[134] John Bossy, "Holiness and Society," *Past and Present*, no. 75 (May, 1977): 124.

as "artificial" groups of extended spiritual kin, helped members address their moral and physical vulnerabilities. While confraternal life varied across time, place, and social class, one of its main accomplishments was to help bring individuals together into sustained, face-to-face relationships of their own choosing and to imbue these relationships with moral significance. The importance of rural confraternities in areas where ties of extended kinship were not threatened is evidence that these organizations fulfilled a need for sociability that went beyond the merely practical.

This exploration of urban networks of association among men and women has revealed the variety of ways women and men responded to the demographic and social exigencies of urban life by using associational models adapted from the medieval Church. Although laypeople cannot be assumed to have shared the Church's official "line" on the superiority of spiritual over blood kinship, their widespread participation in communities based upon these invented ties nonetheless demonstrated a certain respect for it.

As noted, some forms of extrafamilial solidarity discussed here existed in the rural world. Yet, as is so often the case, social institutions and practices that seem quite "natural" in a rural setting often become more self-conscious and formalized in the urban "field of action." Patterns of association and community building in towns and cities often need to be more intentional to endure within the more fragmented social field that urban life represents.

It was Marc Bloch who suggested that European town dwellers had a special need to "flee from isolation," a need that encouraged their apparent genius for forming the sort of voluntary associations discussed in this chapter. Indeed, Bloch saw the fulfillment of this need as one of the keys to the "profound originality" of cities in medieval Europe.[135] Although some of these associations of individuals doubtless germinated in areas of Europe's vast rural world, they flourished most luxuriantly in an urban setting. As settlements increased in size, the kinds of relations on which this chapter has focused became increasingly vital since larger towns and cities usually meant higher mortality and a greater proportion of their populations who had migrated in from greater distances, often as single people.

Throughout the medieval period, the Church made successful efforts to adapt the "natural" solidarity of kin groups to its larger community-building goals. Doubtless, as Jack Goody suggested, the weakening of solidarities of blood kinship helped the Church to become rich by convincing wealthy laymen to leave property that could have gone to relatives to the Church.[136] On the other hand, the Church's efforts to construct ties of community among unrelated

---

[135] M. Fougères [Marc Bloch], "Entr'aide et piété: les associations urbaines au moyen âge," *Annales d'histoire sociale* 5 (1944): 101–2.

[136] Jack Goody, *The Development of the Family and Marriage in Europe* (New York and Cambridge, 1983), 83–102.

individuals, thereby contributing to the establishment of peace among them, was arguably as critical to the Church's survival as its acquisition of great wealth.

But perhaps the most momentous, long-term result of the Church's efforts to shape family relations of the laity was its growing success in establishing the legitimacy of its vision of the family and its transformative intervention into the larger social world. While the early medieval Church's contempt of the carnal bases of blood kinship had become muted and softened by the thirteenth century, as exemplified in the work of Aquinas, the Church's teachings concerning the Christian family as a community, the ethical superiority of ties of spiritual kinship, and the need to extend the spirit of ties as intimate and "natural" as those between mother and child more broadly within the larger community, represented only several of many elements of the Church's powerful alternative system for thinking about family–community relations.

Among European urban dwellers, patrician men probably offered the stiffest resistance to the Church's vision of the family as a small, sacramentally based community of individuals with permeable boundaries. In contrast, this model resonated more deeply among the common people of Europe's towns and cities. Not the least of the sources of appeal of a Christianized model of the family was the wealth of extrafamilial models of association that church organizations suggested – ones that helped individuals and small families survive. As the discussions of the beguine movement and confraternal life have suggested, men and women of urban Europe seized upon models that had evolved within the Church itself, adapted them to their own uses, and put them to work to address perennial problems of urban living.

In the following chapter, we consider fundamental features of the Church's notion of charity, the elaboration of formal systems of relief for urban families and households in medieval and early modern Europe, and the articulation of a "civic" model of solidarity. We shall see the important ways that religious and civic programs for the relief of the poor reinforced one another, and helped in the construction of larger urban communities. The chapter also discusses the gradual decay of older forms of community building discussed here, and the rise of newer visions of community solidarity among humanists and early Protestant Reformers. An examination of some of the cities most affected by Reformed Protestantism will permit an analysis of the interesting tensions that arose between those who sought to build civic bonds of community versus those who defended a "confessional" model.

3   Charity, poor relief, and the family in religious and civic communities

In his study of European welfare states, Abram de Swaan proposes an analytical model to explain the long-term history of poor relief. He suggests that since the Middle Ages, provisions that successive generations of Europeans made for the poor served as a "collective good" for the village, town, region or, eventually, the nation that established them. "Charity," he argued, "was a form of altruistic behavior par excellence: the sacrificing of money or goods for the sake of others; moreover, it was a form of action that profited not only the receivers, but also the collectivity of possessors as a whole."[1] Viewing clergy as "charitable entrepreneurs," de Swaan suggests that poor relief programs helped regulate labor markets, dampened the likelihood of rebellion by the poor, and generally spread risks of dislocation and social catastrophe across a collectivity of individuals. Charity or poor relief programs thus served as a kind of insurance mechanism helping to protect increasingly larger groups of people. The history he traces followed a set of successive equilibrium states at different levels of population aggregation. Poor relief first existed at the level of locality or parish. When the equilibrium between needs for assistance and localities' ability to meet them broke down, the stage was set for the regionalization of poor relief, and by the nineteenth century, for the creation of national-level systems.[2]

One of de Swaan's most important insights is his observation of the close association that existed between provisions for poor relief and the building of communities. He suggests that Europeans did not somehow form communities and then, once they were established, go about the task of distributing various sorts of benefits. Rather, people created and maintained bonds of community in large part by entitling those who were or became members to those benefits. Providing relief to the poor thus proved essential to the formation of communities themselves.[3]

De Swaan identifies three characteristics of the poor as particularly important in legitimizing their entitlements to community assistance: "disability,"

---

[1] Abram de Swaan, *In Care of the State: Health Care, Education and Welfare in Europe and in the USA in the Modern Era* (New York, 1988), 23.
[2] *Ibid.*, 28–30.   [3] *Ibid.*, 6, 27.

"proximity," and "docility."[4] Interestingly, his focus on these features of poor people distinguishes his study from a generation of studies of poor relief in early modern Europe. In the last thirty years or so, social historians, many of them influenced by the work of Michel Foucault or repelled by an earlier self-congratulatory historiography on charitable institutions, have been more likely to focus on the vagrant or itinerant poor. Their work, as well as some of de Swaan's statements, highlights fear of disorder from the unruly poor rather than their docility as a cause of poor relief assistance.

Scholarship highlighting the repressiveness of policy towards beggars and vagrants in late medieval and early modern Europe has been useful in reinforcing a critical truth about the process of community building. As one historian so aptly put it, constructing "brotherhood" very often involves a simultaneous notion of "otherhood."[5] Imagining, building, and maintaining relationships of community have nearly always involved more or less conscious concerns over just where membership boundaries lie and who will be excluded from them.

However, this recent historiography on poor relief seems to have judged the efficacy of poor relief policies and organizations by their treatment of the poorest of the poor, those who enjoyed the fewest entitlements to assistance: the "sturdy beggars" and the homeless vagrants who haunted the countryside and towns of Europe in years of high prices, war, or general social disruption. Focusing on government-sponsored policy towards these poorest of the poor necessarily leads to a grim assessment of the generosity or effectiveness of poor relief, since policy was often designed mainly to expel or repress rather than to assist them.[6]

Historical studies focusing on the wandering poor can help illuminate only a small, if dramatic, part of a wider story of poor relief, however. They are not able to shed much light on the causes or consequences of efforts directed to the more docile poor, from whom religious and civic authorities had little to fear. Although it is unwise to dwell too much on distinctions among categories of the poor, since individuals could easily slide among them, it is clear that, from medieval times onwards, Europeans made key distinctions between the poor whom they knew and those who were strangers. The familiar poor were known

---

[4] *Ibid.*, 16–17.

[5] John Bossy, "Holiness and Society," *Past and Present*, no. 75 (May, 1977), 121, citing Benjamin Nelson, *The Idea of Usury*, 2nd edn. (London and Chicago, 1969).

[6] For gloomy assessments of assistance to the poor see: Michel Foucault, *Madness and Civilization: A History of Insanity in the Age of Reason*, trans. Richard Howard (New York, 1965), 38–64; Olwen Hufton, *The Poor of Eighteenth-Century France 1750–1789* (Oxford, 1974); Catharina Lis and Hugo Soly, *Poverty and Capitalism in Pre-industrial Europe* (Atlantic Highlands, NJ, 1979); Robert Jütte, *Poverty and Deviance in Early Modern Europe* (New York and Cambridge, 1994). For a critique of this trend in the history of poor relief, see Joel F. Harrington, "Escape from the Great Confinement: The Genealogy of the German Workhouse," *Journal of Modern History* 71, 2 (June, 1999): 308–45.

under a variety of labels including the "shamefaced poor," referring to those who were too ashamed to ask publicly for assistance; or the "residential" or "house poor," who were generally those most likely to be identified as "deserving."[7] Paying more attention to these sorts of people, and to programs devised to assist them, suggests a rather different set of conclusions about the effects of assistance to the poor.

Those who have been known over the centuries as the "respectable" or "deserving" poor sometimes enjoyed fairly dependable entitlements to small amounts of assistance from urban "collectivities" which helped them, their households, and often their wider kin to deal more effectively with "critical life situations" than they would otherwise have been able to do. The very modest kinds of financial assistance that civic governments tried to extend to the house poor, or that many confraternities provided to their own members in times of sickness or death, were in no way designed to constitute a household's or individual's budget. It is therefore not surprising that nearly all calculations of the value of money or assistance in kind given even to the domiciled poor have revealed their complete inadequacy to support individuals or families beyond a day or two.[8]

But this strictly quantitative approach to assessing the effects of assistance underestimates the importance of these resources to tactics of survival, especially among the "respectable" poor. Those who had various entitlements to assistance benefited by the restriction of programs to themselves and their households. While accepting assistance was a source of humiliation to most, being part of a network of regular charitable assistance also lent a bit of stability to the life of the poor. Those who received them could often parlay such entitlements to negotiate others. Indeed, the respectability attached to some forms of assistance often proved both cause and effect of the domiciled poor's integration into larger networks of association and patronage that they might tap during times of need. Being part of a network or, better yet, several networks of assistance that conferred legitimate entitlements to help from those whom one knew or with whom there was only a "weak" link of association is what often separated the house poor from the completely destitute.

This chapter first examines some of the fundamental features of urban systems of poor relief, showing the important participation of lay people and lay authorities in charitable, civic efforts since the Middle Ages. It considers both the Church's doctrine and lay understandings of charitable and civic values, and the central place of assistance and poor relief to communities based on them. It tries to show that far from being considered the exclusive province

---

[7] Linda Martz, *Poverty and Welfare in Habsburg Spain: The Example of Toledo* (Cambridge, 1983), 202, concerning aid to the "shamefaced poor."

[8] For calculations of these sums, see Bronislaw Geremek, *The Margins of Society in Late Medieval Paris*, trans. Jean Birrell (New York and Cambridge, 1987); Jütte, *Poverty*, 45–61.

of the Church, assistance to the poor has involved the participation of laymen and -women as well as collaboration between church and civic authorities since the Middle Ages, particularly as it was extended to urban families considered to be among the "respectable poor."

The discussion then turns to the community-building projects of the Protestant Reformation, showing how Reformation authorities, both clerical and lay, used assistance to households and families to establish new "confessional" communities. While most studies of "confessionalization" have emphasized its importance to the process of territorial state building in early modern Europe, the term is used here to explore the forging of confessional communities in several towns and cities deeply affected by the Reformed Protestantism.

The Reformation case is particularly interesting because it exposes tensions that could arise between competing models of community and their accompanying practices of assistance to poor families; for example between those who defended an older "civic" model of community according to which all of the house poor enjoyed certain entitlements to assistance, and those who wanted to create a more intensive, tightly knit community of individuals and families whose entitlements were based more on belief and behavior than residential status. As we shall see, tensions between confessional and civic models of community evolved particularly in a number of sixteenth-century cities where Calvinism rose to dominance during what Heinz Schilling termed the "Second Reformation."[9]

The bonds of "charity"

As described in medieval church teaching, charity referred to spiritual bonds of Christian love between people, especially those who lived in face-to-face relation to one another. Charitable behavior could take on many forms. Several examples considered in Chapter 2, such as creating bonds of godparenthood and co-parenthood with others, contracting a marriage, or even priests' and lay authorities' efforts to help control interfamilial violence, could exemplify charitable behavior in action.

Contrary to modern understanding which sometimes conceives of charitable behavior as based upon "impulse," charity in medieval terms was a duty or an obligation. One's will and not one's emotions was the seat of this obligation.[10]

---

[9] Heinz Schilling, ed., *Die reformierte Konfessionalisierung in Deutschland: das Problem der "Zweiten Reformation"* (Gütersloh, 1986).

[10] Brian Tierney, *Medieval Poor Law: A Sketch of Canonical Theory and its Application in England* (Berkeley, 1959), 38. Colin Jones' notion of a charitable "imperative" captures this point. See "Introduction: The Charitable Imperative," in Jones, *The Charitable Imperative: Hospitals and Nursing in Ancien Regime and Revolutionary France* (London and New York, 1989), 1–2. Contrast Anne E. C. McCants' discussion of the charitable "impulse" in *Civic Charity in a Golden Age: Orphan Care in Early Modern Amsterdam* (Urbana, IL, 1997), 3, 10, 14.

Here, the Church itself was supposed to serve as an example. Many church fathers believed in the poor's right or entitlement to assistance from its wealth, even though this right was not juridically enforceable. Advocating the poor's entitlements to assistance doubtless helped to reinforce the legitimacy of the Church's property-holding by suggesting that it served as steward of wealth for the larger community.[11] Thus, "when the bishop helped the poor from ecclesiastical revenues, it was precisely public assistance that he was administering."[12]

In laying out the obligations of the laity, the influential writings of St. Ambrose, the busy fourth-century bishop of Milan, used the image of concentric rings of obligation spreading out from the self. Obligations to others extended to parents, children, other household members, and then to strangers, in that order.[13] Under this enduring view, the family became the original seat of bonds of charity. Yet, as the examples of Saint Elizabeth and others illustrated, while charity was to originate within the family, it was to end well beyond its borders. The emphasis in the expression "charity begins at home" was on the "begin" as much as the "home." As medieval canonists articulated it, charity was supposed to inform face-to-face bonds between particular individuals, providing the grounds and moral legitimacy for relations of reciprocity between giver and receiver.[14]

As John Bossy pointed out, medieval canonists made a clear distinction between charity and alms. Charity could be expressed in alms but was not synonymous with almsgiving. Practices of charity ideally involved ongoing bonds between individuals, whereas the distribution of alms sometimes involved obligations that were a bit more abstract since the recipient might be a complete stranger. Indeed, giving alms was often prescribed as a penance. Therefore, while almsgiving could constitute an act of charity, it was not necessarily its ideal expression.[15] The difference between the concepts of *caritas* and *misericordia* captured this distinction rather well. Whereas *caritas* emphasized an obligation to assist those with whom one was in close relation, *misericordia* emphasized assistance to the poor and needy in general.[16] It was perhaps the spirit of *misericordia* which led most directly to gifts to the needy whom one did not know.

---

[11] Miri Rubin, *Charity and Community in Medieval Cambridge* (New York and Cambridge, 1987), 62.

[12] Tierney, *Medieval Poor Law*, 44.

[13] *Ibid.*, 52, 57, 119. Tierney notes thirteenth-century canonists' relative lack of attention to the treatment of vagrants. See also James William Brodman, *Charity and Welfare: Hospitals and the Poor in Medieval Catalonia* (Philadelphia, 1998), 136–7.

[14] Philip Gavitt emphasizes the reciprocity involved in late medieval charity in *Charity and Children in Renaissance Florence: The Ospedale degli Innocenti, 1410–1536* (Ann Arbor, 1990), 55.

[15] John Bossy, *Christianity in the West: 1400–1700* (New York, 1985), 144.

[16] Nicolas Terpstra, *Lay Confraternities and Civic Religion in Renaissance Bologna* (New York and Cambridge, 1995), 75.

Canonists believed that certain expressions of charity were more meritorious than others and that some persons were more deserving than others, especially in the case of planned gifts or institutional endowments.[17] Canonists' studies of charity therefore devoted some thought to the relative merits of giving to different sorts of people.[18] The Church's main intellectuals writing on the subject had a very clear sense of the existence of the "false poor" and the need to distinguish among varying levels of obligation and merit in dispensing what resources one had.[19] Although concepts of "deserving" and "undeserving" poor may not have been fully articulated until the sixteenth and seventeenth centuries, distinctions about the relative strength of charitable obligations to the poor who were the subjects of those obligations constituted part of what Michel Mollat termed the "Poor Man's Theology" as early as the twelfth century.[20] While distributions to the assembled poor made at medieval monastic gates or hospitals did not discriminate between deserving and undeserving poor, this was not true of parish-level distributions, which involved the increasing collaboration or even the leadership of the laity.

Medieval views of charity and almsgiving seem to have shared several features of the "gift" relationship that Marcel Mauss outlined in his classic work on the subject. Here, he examined the belief widespread in many societies that gifts have a power beyond their material uses because they bear the spirit of the giver. Indeed, in medieval society, expressions of charity were powerful because they were thought to bear the spirit of God as well as that of the giver. Another similarity between the gift relations Mauss described and medieval ideals of charity was that these gift or charity relations existed among people who participated in an ongoing, reciprocal, face-to-face relationship with one another.[21] Thus, families of blood and spiritual kin could be considered as the original charitable organizations because they epitomized the face-to-face relationship and ideals of reciprocity central to the concept. The family member who gave to another on one day might be the receiver the next.

Mauss' work also suggested another feature of gift-giving quite relevant to an understanding of medieval Christian models of charity. Among various systems of gift-giving that underlay bonds of reciprocity in the societies he studied, he described one system called "potlatch," which was an aggressive, competitive system of gift exchange in which the giver of more elaborate gifts used them

---

[17] Tierney, *Medieval Poor Law*, 62.
[18] Rubin, *Charity*, 69. The obligation to give alms varied with the closeness of the giver's relationship to the receiver, the virtue of the recipient, and whether the recipient could work.
[19] Brodman, *Charity and Welfare*, 26–7, 136–7.
[20] Michel Mollat, *The Poor in the Middle Ages: An Essay in Social History*, trans. Arthur Goldhammer (New Haven, CT and London, 1986), 102; Rubin, *Charity*, 59.
[21] Marcel Mauss, *The Gift: The Form and Reason for Exchange in Archaic Societies*, trans. W. D. Halls (London and New York, 1990), 5, 10–13.

to dominate the other.[22] Mauss' analysis of the potlatch system shows that reciprocity does not necessarily mean equality, but mainly connection.

Several preliminary conclusions can be drawn from this brief view of church teaching. Charity was an obligation based on love of God and neighbor. It was not based in the emotions, though compassion could help to stimulate expressions of charity. Charity should be expressed by general behavior as well as by gifts. Medieval notions of charity emphasized reciprocal face-to-face relations between giver and receiver. Thus, charity as understood by the medieval Church and perhaps even by the laity actually bore little resemblance to what is now called "altruism." Altruistic acts as they are generally viewed in today's world seem to be considered meritorious to the extent that they are both spontaneous and disinterested, involving giving to persons or organizations from which one wants or expects nothing in return. There is no duty to perform altruistic acts nor are they ideally based on any sort of ongoing relationship with others. Indeed, any resemblance of the altruistic act to one based on reciprocity contaminates it and reduces its merit.[23]

Medieval and early modern European men and women would most likely have been puzzled by this modern notion of altruism. For them, giving alms to a stranger might have occasionally been thoroughly spontaneous but, as has been suggested, giving alms to strangers was hardly the only or the main model of charitable behavior. The fact that a bond between a rich giver and poor recipient of alms involved reciprocity, with the poor man praying for the wealthy man's soul, would have increased rather than diminished the moral value of the alms since practices of charity were supposed to connect individuals together.

The point here is that face-to-face relations and reciprocity were key to establishing and maintaining relationships based on ideals of charity. In instances where these elements were lacking between giver and receiver, other sorts of values that motivated the givers were likely to spring up to complement or perhaps even supplant them. These might include such values as "civism" or a concern for the "common good," values which, as Peter Brown noted, were precisely those against which the early Church had mobilized, preferring to found its communities on values of charity instead.

The conflict between charitable and civic values during the waning years of the Roman Empire became less obvious, however, with the revival of urban life in the twelfth and thirteenth centuries. Indeed, efforts of church and municipal authorities to involve lay people in charitable endeavors would eventually lead to the co-existence or sometimes even the fusion of these two ideals, especially in

---

[22] *Ibid.*, 6–7.

[23] On Mauss, and the related emergence of concepts of pure self-interest and altruism in western society, see Jonathan Parry, "The Gift, the Indian Gift and the 'Indian Gift,'" *Man* (n.s.) 21, 3 (1986): 468–9. On the theoretical contributions of Mauss and others, see Natalie Zemon Davis, *The Gift in Sixteenth-Century France* (Madison, 2000), 4–8.

the large cities of the Italian peninsula. Here, the complementarity of charitable and civic ideals of community would come to be expressed in what some scholastics called *caritas patriae*.[24]

Although some studies of charity and poor relief in Europe over the *longue durée* view the main plot as a shift in responsibility from "church" to "state," other authors quite rightly suggest that the notion of "laicization" is a more appropriate term. For example, in his classic article on the inspiration and significance of Charles V's 1531 effort to standardize poor relief in the Holy Roman Empire, Pierre Bonenfant criticized Henri Pirenne's belief that the emperor's legislation should best be seen as an expression of Renaissance secularism. Noting the long-standing importance of lay participation in poor relief efforts in Hainaut and Brabant, Bonenfant argued that Ypres' new poor law of 1525 hardly represented the triumph of secularism, drawing an important distinction between laicization and secularization.[25] More recently, Brian Pullan put it this way:

> Secularization suggests a move toward worldly concerns: perhaps toward a pompous and materialistic piety, perhaps toward activities whose avowed purpose was to benefit society rather than the soul. Laicization may well refer to something almost opposite, that is, to a fuller participation of the laity in religious life, and the breaking down of barriers between the world and those who are out of it.[26]

Far from infusing a wholly secular mentality into organizations for the provision of the poor, laicization often served mainly as a means to draw more of the laity into practical efforts to build and maintain networks of community based on charitable religious ideals.[27]

Studies of charitable activities and community building in medieval towns and cities suggest that laicization is an appropriate descriptor, and that lay participation in these organizations did not necessarily mean the intrusion of a mentality wholly different from that of the clergy with whom members of the laity often worked. Lay involvement in urban systems of charity and poor relief did, however, raise the likelihood that values of particular concern to the laity, such as the survival of local families, would inform practices of charity.

As early as the twelfth century, laymen and -women in towns and cities were becoming actively engaged in organized charitable activities that went far

---

[24] John Henderson, *Piety and Charity in Late Medieval Florence* (Oxford and New York, 1994), 354–5.

[25] Pierre Bonenfant, "Les Origines et le caractère de la réforme de la bienfaisance publique aux Pays-Bas sous le règne de Charles-Quint," *Annales de la Société belge d'histoire des hôpitaux* 3 (1965): 124–5.

[26] Brian S. Pullan, "The Scuole Grandi of Venice: Some Further Thoughts," in *Poverty and Charity: Europe, Italy, Venice, 1400–1700* (Aldershot, 1994 [1990]), 289–90; Brodman, *Charity and Welfare*, 132.

[27] Sheila D. Muller, *Charity in the Dutch Republic: Pictures of Rich and Poor for Charitable Institutions* (Ann Arbor, 1985), 53.

beyond acts of almsgiving. A number of urban confraternities reached beyond their memberships to practice a kind of outward-looking charity or *misericordia* that extended to the larger urban community. In southern France, lay brotherhoods became responsible for the maintenance of bridges so indispensable to pilgrims and other travelers. Other confraternities extended their concern for Christian burial to the urban poor, often seeing to it that the poor were buried on hospital grounds.[28]

Small hospitals or hospices for the care of the poor, sick, or disabled containing only a few beds became favorite objects of lay endowments, and sometimes served as old-age refuges for the individuals who had endowed them. Municipal governments sometimes founded hospitals and almshouses for the care of the local poor. In thirteenth-century Wisbech, near Cambridge, local government authorities set aside cottages and five acres of land for the care of the local poor. In Cambridge, a market town of approximately 3,500 inhabitants, hospitals, almshouses, and chantries founded after the middle of the thirteenth century were almost all of lay origin, though some hospitals were founded and maintained in collaboration with municipal governments.[29] The founding and administration of such hospitals could remain an entirely lay affair. However, establishing a chapel in the hospital required the permission of the bishop, leading in some instances to the establishment of episcopal patronage. The hospital of Wisbech, which had developed from an earlier grant for the care of the local poor, passed from the patronage of the bishop to the control of the king after the devastations of the Plague in the fourteenth century.[30] This kind of transfer of control often happened to hospitals founded by individual laymen. In medieval Catalonia, for example, there were many instances in which families that had founded such institutions became unable to maintain them. As a result, these small hospitals often passed into the hands of church authorities or, after 1300, increasingly to municipal authorities.[31]

It was the engagement of the laity and in particular of urban patriciates in the life of hospitals in the Low Countries that led Pierre Bonenfant to refer to the "communalization" of the hospitals. In Brussels, Ypres, and Ghent, municipal leaders not only contributed to these institutions, but also became engaged in the administration of their day-to-day affairs.[32] In Frankfurt am Main, lay confraternities played a critical role in creating and administering hospitals for the sick, poor, and the elderly, working closely with the city council. They oversaw and, after 1430, approved all admissions to its principal institution for

---

[28] Mollat, *The Poor*, 92–3, 145.   [29] Rubin, *Charity*, 138–9.

[30] *Ibid.*, 138.   [31] Brodman, *Charity and Welfare*, 48.

[32] Pierre Bonenfant, "Les Hôpitaux en Belgique au Moyen Age," *Annales de la Société belge d'histoire des hôpitaux* 3 (1965): 31; Carter Lindberg, *Beyond Charity: Reformation Initiatives for the Poor* (Minneapolis, 1993), 52.

the care of citizens and longtime residents, the Heilig Geist Spital, which was first mentioned in the records in 1267.[33]

Once hospitals and almshouses had emerged as viable institutions for the relief of the sick and the poor, it was not surprising that they assumed the aspect of a religious community, given the presence of chapels and religious services in them and the ubiquity and prestige of monastic communities as models for corporate living. Yet towns whose governments were involved in the founding of these institutions often fought hard to retain lay control over hospital administrations. A 1311 Papal Bull of Clement V recognized the purely lay aspects of hospital administration and stated that the office of hospital administrator could not be considered an ecclesiastical benefice.[34]

Besides helping to care for the poor and dependent, small medieval hospitals also assisted families and the larger urban community by attracting lay boarders, lodgers, or retirees. Convents and monasteries also received individuals as lodgers on a variety of negotiated terms. In some instances hospitals received residents who chose them as places of retirement. "Corrodarians" was the name given to lay persons who chose to enter the hospital community on special terms, granting those organizations rights to their property in exchange for a secure residence. One such thirteenth-century agreement, which granted eight acres of land to the Hospital of St. John the Evangelist in Cambridge, entitled the pensioner to food at the hospital's "brethren table" for as long as he stayed, and permission to leave the hospital in secular garb to attend to his business.[35] These sorts of arrangements whereby individuals entered the hospital or monastic community instead of being cared for by their households or extended kin were entirely consistent with earlier medieval practices such as oblation, in which parents "donated" young children to be raised within monastic communities with the goal of eventual full membership there.[36]

The gradual establishment of stronger parish institutions in many towns and cities of northern Europe during the twelfth and thirteenth centuries also expanded the laity's involvement in charitable endeavors and the influence of their apparent preferences for assistance to families of the local poor. In parts of northern Europe as well as Spain, lay officials working in concert with episcopal authority used the parish community to distribute relief in the form of bread, pennies, shoes, and meat on feast days or even at regular weekly intervals. The

---

[33] Werner Moritz, *Die bürgerlichen Fürsorgeanstalten der Reichsstadt Frankfurt a.M. im späten Mittelalter* (Frankfurt am Main, 1981), 34–54. Brodman, *Charity and Welfare*, 137, notes that municipal councils in fourteenth-century Barcelona and Valencia also endowed hospitals.

[34] *Ibid.*, 134.

[35] Rubin, *Charity*, 172. The temporary nature of this particular agreement made it atypical.

[36] John Boswell, *The Kindness of Strangers: The Abandonment of Children in Western Europe from Late Antiquity to the Renaissance* (New York, 1988), 228–55, 296–321.

establishment of parish "poor tables," which collected and distributed money for the local poor, oftentimes involved the participation of town aldermen who contributed city funds to them and became increasingly involved in overseeing and participating in their work.[37] By the fourteenth century, municipal governments in many areas were exercising "quality control" over these organizations, inspecting their records and their operations.[38] Prominent lay inhabitants under the supervision of parish clergy helped to distribute funds to a stable list of recipients in regular fashion as well as to residents who were assisted only occasionally. In thirteenth-century Spain, the diocese of Valencia, as well as other areas, had its own "fathers of the poor" who were elected within the parishes to distribute money regularly and make home visits to the local poor.[39] The thirteenth century also witnessed the beginnings of a parish-based system of poor relief for the inhabitants of Brussels as well as the establishment of institutions for the aid of pilgrims. In many areas of thirteenth-century Aragon, newly developing parish organizations focused increasingly on the needs of the resident poor while the cathedral chapters were more preoccupied with the itinerant and pilgrim.[40]

By the fourteenth century, the inadequacy of ecclesiastical efforts to address the needs of the poor had become increasingly obvious, lending even greater urgency to lay participation.[41] A Bull of Pope Nicholas IV in 1448 formally acknowledged the laity's importance to organized charity and poor relief by recognizing the right of secular urban authorities to name temporal administrators of all poor relief institutions.[42]

Even on the issue of begging and assistance to those of the poor who were not native to towns where they sought aid, clergy and laity seem often to have been in broad agreement. Strict laws seeking to regulate begging emerged in Paris as early as the fourteenth century, at the same time as the bishop was complaining about the proliferation of beggars there. The relatively new phenomenon of high numbers of beggars competing for assistance helped to inspire the founding of the hospice and orphanage of the St. Esprit.[43] Legislation designed to restrict begging severely, often targeting non-natives, was established in Barcelona (1322), Leiden (1397, 1446, and 1459), Utrecht (1313), Bruges (1496), Brussels (1422, 1423, and 1433), and other cities, usually with little opposition from clergy, local or otherwise.[44]

[37] Mollat, *The Poor*, 274.   [38] *Ibid.*, 276.   [39] *Ibid.*, 139–40.
[40] Brodman, *Charity and Welfare*, 18–19.   [41] Geremek, *The Margins*, 167.
[42] Pierre Bonenfant, "Aperçu sur l'histoire de l'Assistance publique de Bruxelles," *Annales de la Société belge d'histoire des hôpitaux* 3 (1965): 47.
[43] Geremek, *The Margins*, 35.
[44] Bonenfant, "Les Origines," 132. Charles H. Parker, *The Reformation of Community: Social Welfare and Calvinist Charity in Holland, 1572–1620* (Cambridge, 1998), 87, cites legislation against begging by "foreigners" (meaning nonresidents) in Haarlem (1390), Amsterdam (1413), and Gouda (1488). See also Brodman, *Charity and Welfare*, 141.

Evidence thus suggests that laypeople and municipal authorities of towns and cities of medieval Europe became directly involved in relief to the local poor from very early on. Through the foundation of hospitals, and involvement in certain charitable confraternities and newly evolving parish organizations, laymen and -women became engaged in charitable relationships with people they knew. Moreover, it is clear that these activities went well beyond the "indiscriminate" almsgiving that has been viewed as the epitome of medieval practices of charity. Lay engagement arguably placed more emphasis on relieving the families of local poor, but this sort of choice did not necessarily violate the sort of charitable ideals advocated by the Church.

Families and poor relief in civic communities

The widespread involvement of lay organizations and urban governments in charitable and poor relief activities in the later medieval period is especially well documented for the large cities of Italy. In Florence, the confraternity of Orsanmichele became the largest charitable confraternity of the city during the fourteenth century, and the association that effectively organized poor relief to all of the city's residents. During its early years in the thirteenth century, the organization assisted the "voluntary poor" including members of mendicant orders. By the fourteenth century, however, the Orsanmichele's mission gradually shifted from a concern with the *miserabiles* towards the *famiglia povera*, the poor nuclear family whose members were particularly in need during a period of rapid inflation and declining standards of living for the city's working class.[45]

With a membership of several thousand in the early fourteenth century, the Orsanmichele gradually became an extremely wealthy organization as a result of the number of legacies it received during the city's Plague epidemic of the mid-fourteenth century. Confraternity members, so-called "worthy men," discovered and carried out assistance to respectable families of the city, including those burdened with children, as well as "biblical" categories of the poor, including widows, the orphans, the sick, and disabled. In crises like the Plague epidemic of 1347–8, the Orsanmichele probably assisted, in one way or another, one-quarter of the city's population of approximately 100,000 persons. In more normal times, the company devoted the lion's share of its budget to a much smaller number of the residential poor.[46]

Although the Orsanmichele's cash distributions to many of the city's poor families were small – often sufficient only for several days – individuals or families that had been formally registered and vetted could build upon their inclusion in the Orsanmichele's network of assistance by gaining access to other forms of aid, both formal and informal, such as hospital institutions or less formal

[45] Henderson, *Piety and Charity*, 243.   [46] *Ibid.*, 257, 262–3.

networks of patronage. Far from being a stigma, enrollment in the registers of the Orsanmichele, reserved as it was for the respectable of the city, reinforced a certain sense of legitimate entitlement to assistance from this and other sources. From origins in the voluntary association of the devotional confraternity, men of the Orsanmichele, working with city government, constructed a civic system of household-based assistance to the local poor. They built the system upon a set of ethics that combined clerical admonitions of charity with lay civic values that placed high premium on defending family, household, and domestic life.[47]

In the wake of the demographic catastrophe visited upon Florence by the Plague of 1347–8, the Orsanmichele had the opportunity to reveal its family-oriented, civic character in yet another way, by devoting increasing attention to the needs of poor women who lacked dowries to marry. Far from lying within a sphere of private family life or affairs, the morals and marital status of Florence's poor women were an eminently public concern to city fathers and members of the confraternity. By dowering poor young women of the city and its surrounding area, the Orsanmichele answered the requirements of both charity and the "common good." Indeed, in the years 1317–21, as many as 20 percent of marriages celebrated in the city, many involving couples from the surrounding countryside, may have been the direct result of assistance conferred on meritorious young women by the Orsanmichele. In the years following, some of these same couples continued to receive assistance through the company's regular focus on household relief.[48]

Civic forms of poor relief often grew quite naturally out of older efforts that had previously included only those individuals who were members of the parochial or confraternal community. While the charitable mission of fourteenth-century Venetian confraternities was largely limited to aid among its own members, the fact that many confraternal companies or *scuole* drew members from the whole city and across occupational lines meant that, while appearing inward-looking on the surface, charitable bonds solidified among themselves affected social relations in the whole city.[49] The fact that between the fourteenth and fifteenth centuries many Venetians gradually shifted their charitable bequests away from parish endowments and towards citywide endeavors, such as the Hospital of San Lazzaro, was both cause and effect of this development. The city's confraternities, which were growing in number and power during these years, became increasingly effective bearers of a "civic religion."[50]

---

[47] *Ibid.*, 271.   [48] *Ibid.*, 317–24.

[49] Dennis Romano, "Charity and Community in Early Renaissance Venice," *Journal of Urban History* 11, 1 (1984): 73.

[50] *Ibid.*, 66–73; Pullan, "The Scuole Grandi," 287. He notes: "The Scuole Grandi [those with the wealthiest members] represented a civic religion if by civic we mean 'citywide'."

The passage of endowed organizations from expressions of private or individual charity into institutions for the protection of the respectable families of the entire community could happen almost imperceptibly. The history of the Orbatello, Florence's home for widows and their children, provided an example of how some of the social consequences of the city's marriage system – one linking young women to older men – were dealt with in a civically minded institutional setting. Born of a patrician's will in 1370, taken over by the commune and directed by a church rector, the Orbatello housed some 100 widows, selected from poor and respectable families of the city and surrounding countryside who dwelt with their children in the individual apartments of the home. From its origins until the mid-sixteenth century, the Orbatello served as a haven for the kind of "respectable" poor so important to the work of the Orsanmichele.

Richard Trexler noted in his study of the Orbatello that the institution was filled with "segments" of viable families that remained after the death of a household's main wage earner. However, the Orbatello permitted adult women of the home to reconstruct their families in several ways.[51] Inmates gradually used their influence to introduce relatives into the apartments they occupied or into neighboring houses. Moreover, given the overall respectability of the establishment, widowed residents were able to see to it that their daughters' virtue remained intact during their residence there. Finally, given the dowries that daughters of the house received as part of their benefits, the young women of the Orsanmichele were very often able to make honorable marriages and begin the task of rebuilding the sort of families upon which the civic order depended.[52]

Florence's new foundling home, the Ospedale degli Innocenti, opened in 1419, sought to preserve the integrity and honor of families in a rather different way, by assisting mothers or parents who were unable or unwilling to take care of their infants. The organization was a typically civic kind of institution funded through the largesse of the city's silk guild, as well as a major donation from one of the city's patrician families and funding from the commune itself. The hospital's architecture displayed domestic as well as institutional elements, even though the residential population in the fifteenth century could total more than 100 persons including a number of dependents of the organization who were neither infants nor children. Like other urban residential organizations that

---

[51] Richard C. Trexler, "A Widows' Asylum of the Renaissance: The Orbatello of Florence," in *Power and Dependence in Renaissance Florence*, vol. II, *The Women of Renaissance Florence* (Binghamton, NY, 1993), 66–93. Trexler suggests certain lapses from habits of universal respectability, however. See 85, fn. 9 concerning the toleration of prostitution within its walls.

[52] The Parte Guelfa was the source of these dowries. See Trexler, "Widows," in *Women of Renaissance Florence*, 80.

sought to assist families that could not care for all their members, the Innocenti combined values that were at once religious, civic, and familial.[53]

A cynic might have noted that at the time of its founding and for nearly a generation thereafter, a majority of the infants received at the Innocenti were the illegitimate children of the city's civic elite, the fruit of sexual relations between them and slave women employed in some patrician Florentine households of the time.[54] Over time, however, the foundling hospital became a familiar institution which the working classes of the city began to use as "temporary and respite care" when they were experiencing illness or other "critical life situations."[55] The extremely high mortality of infants and children of the institution ensured that the temporary absence of infants from their mothers' care was frequently permanent. The foundlings' high mortality rate did nothing, however, to delegitimize or sully the hospital's reputation. Indeed, the Innocenti was widely viewed as a great civic institution of the commune, one that would be widely imitated in the cities of Europe in centuries to come.

By the fifteenth century, conditions of declining international commerce encouraged Florence's civic elites to work towards the protection of "good" families that had fallen on hard times. Given the oligarchic structure of many city governments, these sorts of efforts sometimes overlapped with or were seized upon temporarily by governments eager to use confraternal resources to distribute patronage of their own, as in the case of Florence's Compagnia de' Buonomini di San Martino (Company of the Good Men of Saint Martin) founded in 1442. Like some other confraternities in Italian cities of the fifteenth century, the Buonomini took as their principal mission the provision of assistance to the "shamefaced poor." With efforts such as these, organizations for the relief of the poor risked mutating imperceptibly into institutions for the care of those people of particular concern to the wealthy.[56]

Yet despite the respectability that often went along with receiving assistance as a family of the honorable, domiciled poor, evidence from the Buonomini's records suggests that the shamefaced poor were not limited to de-classed members of the urban elite. People of middling rank or artisan status, particularly men, sometimes felt shame at asking for assistance, even that which was rendered in the home.[57] Thus, outdoor assistance to the shamefaced poor in some

---

[53] Gavitt, *Charity and Children*, 143, 168, notes that the internal order of hospitals combined the features of various sorts of medieval *familiae*, including "the cloister, the political arena, and the family, if not in equal measure, at least with equal respect."

[54] *Ibid.*, 207.   [55] *Ibid.*, 204.

[56] Richard C. Trexler, "Charity and the Defense of Urban Elites in the Italian Communes," in Frederic Cople Jaher, ed., *The Rich, the Well Born, and the Powerful: Elites and Upper Classes in History* (Urbana, IL, 1973), 85, 102.

[57] Amleto Spicciani, "The 'Poveri Vergognosi' in Fifteenth-Century Florence: The First 30 Years' Activity of the Buonomini di S. Martino," in Thomas Riis, ed., *Aspects of Poverty in Early Modern Europe* (Alphen aan den Rijn, 1981), 154.

cities extended into the middling or even lower ranks of the city. In other areas, however, many of the working poor apparently did not consider begging as inherently dishonorable, but rather saw it as a familiar complement to other efforts to earn a living.[58]

A growing focus on assisting families of the local poor did not mean that efforts for the assistance of the itinerant and homeless disappeared, however. In the fourteenth century, the republican government of Florence worked hand-in-hand with the Orsanmichele during times of famine to distribute food to the destitute. Indeed, the Orsanmichele became a "semiofficial" agency after the fourteenth-century Plague epidemics, the communal government being attracted by the fraternity's enormous wealth.[59] In Italian towns and cities of the fifteenth and sixteenth centuries, at the same time that confraternal companies sought out and ministered to the shamefaced poor either alone or in cooperation with civic governments, those same governments maintained efforts for assisting the indigent through distributions of bread as well as through hospices and hospitals. On another front, civic governments in Italy became innovators in the area of social assistance by conferring retirement pensions on the "civil servants" who worked for them. They granted these benefits based upon an "associative or corporative" ethic of assistance that recognized pensioners essentially as belonging to the family of the commune's lords.

Some inhabitants of the large cities of Renaissance Italy doubtless continued to share a vision of civic community that included all citizens. However, by the fifteenth century there were signs in some places of an increasing specialization of institutions for different categories of the poor, and a sense that even the wealthiest families were sometimes faced with problems of poverty and dependency that required them to build and maintain charitable civic institutions for use mainly by their own kin and poor clients.[60]

By the sixteenth century, urban governments throughout Europe had a long experience of developing programs for the care of "their" poor, involving the participation of laity and clergy alike. However, during the sixteenth century, many towns and cities were deeply affected by population increases caused by in-migration from the countryside, and catastrophic poverty brought on by warfare, food shortages, and epidemics. Scholarship on changes in systems of assistance to the poor during the sixteenth century

---

[58] Jean-Pierre Gutton, *La Société et les pauvres: l'exemple de la généralité de Lyon, 1534–1789* (Paris, 1971), 161.

[59] Trexler, "Charity," in *The Rich*, 92–3.

[60] *Ibid.*, 82. Venice's fifteenth-century patriciate survived, in part, through a "welfare state for hard-pressed nobles," who received assistance in the form of political offices. See Stanley Chojnacki, "Political Adulthood in Fifteenth-Century Venice," *American Historical Review* 91, 4 (1986): 797.

has emphasized how similarly authorities in Protestant and Catholic areas reacted to these social dislocations by developing institutions for specific groups
of the poor, consolidating or rationalizing entire systems, and in many instances implementing policies to repress or expel non-native beggars and
vagrants.[61]

From another direction, historians of the Protestant and Catholic Reformations have used the concept of "confessionalization" to interpret the process
in which three major religious confessions – Lutheran, Calvinist, and Roman Catholic – spread through Europe during the sixteenth and seventeenth
centuries.[62] Confessionalization involved the establishment of theologically
well-defined churches with doctrines and prescribed norms of belief and behavior that clergy tried to teach more systematically to the laity than had been
attempted in earlier ages.[63] One of the primary goals of confessionalization
was to create a homogeneous religious community, ideally by persuasion but if
necessary by fiat, or by the emigration and expulsion of certain individuals.[64] In
Protestant areas, doctrines and behaviors were often enforced by new or newly
laicized organizations such as Reformed churches' "consistories" – local governing bodies composed mainly of laymen – or in many Lutheran areas by
church courts, both of which were designed to oversee the behavior of church
members or even the wider urban community.

Confessional and civic communities in the Protestant Reformation

The confessionalization process was particularly important in urban centers,
which served as incubators and sometimes as showcases for new forms of
confessional community. Urban dwellers were among the first to experience
intensifying forms of "social regulation," in which secular and religious authorities attempted to exert greater control over both domestic and public life.
These kinds of social regulation were among the most important results of
confessionalization, serving as harbingers of more aggressive forms of "social

---

[61] Natalie Zemon Davis, "Poor Relief, Humanism, and Heresy," in *Society and Culture in Early Modern France* (Stanford, 1975), 17–64; Jütte, *Poverty*; Lis and Soly, *Poverty and Capitalism*.
[62] Wolfgang Reinhard, "Reformation, Counter-Reformation, and the Early Modern State: A Re-assessment," *Catholic Historical Review* 75, 3 (1989): 383–404. He dates this process from the 1520s until the late seventeenth century and the Revocation of the Edict of Nantes. Others use the term to focus on the period after about 1550. For the most recent discussion of the work of Reinhard, Heinz Schilling, and others on confessionalization, see Joel F. Harrington and Helmut Walser Smith, "Confessionalization, Community, and State Building in Germany, 1555–1870," *Journal of Modern History* 69, 1 (March, 1997): 81–8.
[63] Reinhard, "Reformation," 390.   [64] *Ibid.*, 393.

discipline" that early modern territorial rulers gradually imposed upon their subjects in efforts to build up state institutions.[65]

Although early modern heads of state were doubtless innovative when it came to building new judicial or political means for regulating the lives of their subjects more closely, the spirit that informed the intensifying regulation of the urban social order was hardly new to the sixteenth and seventeenth centuries. Nor was it necessarily inspired by secular models. As Erasmus asked in an oft-cited letter of 14 August 1519: "What, else, I ask you, is a city than a great monastery?"[66]

The Reformation critique of religious subcommunities

At the heart of the early Reformation's message lay a scathing critique of con-fraternities that had at one time seemed to exemplify the piety and face-to-face charitable relationships lying at the heart of Christian models of community. Yet Martin Luther was only one among many critics of these organizations. For him, the first sin lay in their participation in a flawed theology based on the notion of a "treasury of grace," according to which the devotions and prayers of one's confraternal brothers helped each member to achieve salvation. Luther, in contrast, promulgated a doctrine of salvation "by faith alone," which re-jected the belief that good works performed either individually or collectively could lead to salvation. He and other reformers viewed confraternities as self-regarding subcommunities whose members sought special spiritual benefits for themselves alone.[67]

Ironically, at the same time as reformers were criticizing late medieval con-fraternities' preoccupation with masses for the souls of their dead, there was an apparent decline in this aspect of confraternal life in some areas and an in-crease in the importance of banquets and processions celebrating saints' days.[68] By the sixteenth century, clerical as well as lay observers of confraternities in many cities shared Luther's disgust at exaggerated forms of such conviviality,

---

[65] On social regulation and social discipline, see Heinz Schilling, "Confessional Europe," in Thomas A. Brady, Jr., Heiko A. Oberman, and James D. Tracy, eds., *Handbook of European History, 1400–1600: Late Middle Ages, Renaissance and Reformation* (Leiden and New York, 1995), vol. II, 652–9; Timothy G. Fehler, *Poor Relief and Protestantism: The Evolution of Social Welfare in Sixteenth-Century Emden* (Aldershot, Hants and Brookfield, VT, 1999), 260–70.

[66] Letter to Paul Volz of 14 August 1518, quoted in Lee Palmer Wandel, *Always among Us: Images of the Poor in Zwingli's Zurich* (New York and Cambridge, 1990), 14.

[67] Martin Luther, "The Blessed Sacrament of the Holy and True Body of Christ and the Brother-hoods (1519)," in Carter Lindberg, ed., *The European Reformations Sourcebook* (Oxford, 2000), 71–2. See also Steven E. Ozment, *The Reformation in the Cities: The Appeal of Protestantism to Sixteenth-Century Germany and Switzerland* (New Haven, CT and London, 1975), 84–5.

[68] Caroline M. Barron, "The Parish Fraternities of Medieval London," in Barron and Christopher Harper-Bill, eds., *The Church in Pre-Reformation Society: Essays in Honour of F. R. H. Du Boulay* (Suffolk, 1985), 27–8.

especially the riotous banqueting that took place on the occasion of many groups' annual feasts.[69] These activities appeared especially wasteful in the terrible economic times that visited many cities and towns in the sixteenth century.

A growing tone of hierarchy and paternalism had also begun to emerge in practices of the larger, wealthier confraternities, obscuring the idea of frater- nity that such organizations were intended to exemplify.[70] Such changes were obvious in the ways these organizations viewed their charitable outreach to the poor. Even those confraternities that continued to bring together rich and poor men as members in the same organization and to practice good works for the poor had in many instances become internally divided along class lines. Within many of Venice's Scuole Grandi, for example, poorer members had become essentially the charitable agents of the rich, taking what the wealthier members contributed and dispensing it to the poor on their behalf.[71] Whatever direct con- tact the wealthy members had once had with the poor who received assistance from them had almost completely disappeared.

In this historical context, many humanist scholars including Luther stressed the need to recapture a purer Pauline sense of charity to the living, one that was encouraged as well by the rediscovery of patristic writings about the charitable relationship.[72] Reformers were not especially concerned that wealthy confra- ternities neglected the thousands of foreign beggars who flocked to cities for relief, but that they apparently felt little brotherhood for those poor to whom they had stronger obligations – those who resided in the same town and whom they passed on the street every day – those who had strong claims to assistance on the basis of their common membership in the civic community. The goal of reclaiming a spirit of more authentic charity therefore began to focus, as it had in some Italian cities much earlier, upon the plight of the domiciled or house poor who had some resources but lived "on the borderline of self-sufficiency."[73] While problems of begging and vagrancy loomed large as policy questions for

---

[69] Brian S. Pullan, *Rich and Poor in Renaissance Venice: The Social Institutions of a Catholic State, to 1620* (Cambridge, MA, 1971), 126, cites a 1543 decree by Venice's Council of Ten forbidding the city's elite confraternities' ostentatious banqueting on the same grounds as Luther's earlier critique – because money so spent could better be devoted to the care of the poor.

[70] Nicholas Terpstra, "Kinship Translated: 'Confraternite Maggiori' and Political Apprenticeship in Early Modern Italy," in Danilo Zardin, ed., *Corpi, "fraternità," mestieri nella storia della società europea* (Rome, 1998).

[71] Pullan, *Rich and Poor*, 87–98.   [72] *Ibid.*, 224–38.

[73] On the house poor and the "worthy poor" in early Reformation plans for urban poor relief, see Carter Lindberg, *Beyond Charity: Reformation Initiatives for the Poor* (Minneapolis, 1993), 119, 144; William J. Wright, "A Closer Look at House Poor Relief through the Common Chest and Indigence in Sixteenth Century Hesse," *Archiv für Reformationsgeschichte* 70 (1979): 228; Wandel, *Always among Us*, 128, 151; Robert W. Scribner, "Mobility: Voluntary or Enforced? Vagrants in Württemberg in the Sixteenth Century," in Gerhard Jaritz and Albert Müller, eds., *Migration in der Feudalgesellschaft* (Frankfurt and New York, 1988), 84.

urban magistrates, the task of building new confessional communities suggested
to reformers a more urgent need to reaffirm bonds with those in need who had
the strongest entitlements to assistance from their neighbors on both charitable
and civic grounds.[74] Christian humanists as well as reformers of the 1520s and
1530s thus sought to reengage lay efforts to relieve the poor "as much to respect
a tradition of lay involvement as to bring about a revival of practical Christianity
among laymen."[75]

Assistance to the local poor was entirely consistent with long-standing church
teachings about charity that emphasized its practice within ongoing face-to-face
relationships between giver and receiver. It was also easier to screen domiciled
recipients of assistance to be sure of their conformity to emerging confessional
beliefs or increasingly explicit civic norms of behavior. Zurich's new Poor Law
of 1520 suggests that *caritas* was to be exercised within the limits of the community defined by a set of norms including "dress, demeanor, [and] behavior."[76]
Furthermore, the domiciled poor were also more likely to express the gratitude
appropriate to the receiver, thus exhibiting the kind of "docility" important to
de Swaan's portrait of those poor most entitled to assistance. Moreover, to the
extent that the house poor who received assistance from civic or confessional
sources were composed of "honest families" whose poverty resulted from ac-
cidents and circumstances not under their control, the social distance between
givers and receivers might not be very great. Nor were distinctions between
boundaries of civic and confessional communities notable during the earliest
days of the Protestant Reform movement, when Luther put forward his version
of the idea of combining urban poor relief funds in one "common chest."[77]

The desire to ensure that confessional and civic community boundaries coincided seems to have been more urgent in the vision of reformers such as Zwingli
in Zurich or Bucer in Strasbourg, who hoped to integrate confessional bonds
with those of urban citizenship.[78] Indeed, their efforts to integrate bonds of both
sorts of community helped to revive older civic traditions by overlaying onto

---

[74] Wandel, *Always among Us*, 13.   [75] Muller, *Charity in the Dutch Republic*, 61.

[76] Wandel, *Always among Us*, 132, 162. For an enumeration of the "pious, respectable poor
citizens" entitled to poor relief in the reformed city of Zurich, see Ulrich Zwingli's "Ordinance
and Articles Touching Almsgiving," in F. R. Salter, ed., *Some Early Tracts on Poor Relief*
(London, 1926), 101.

[77] For the text of the 1523 Ordinance for a "common chest" in the town of Leisnig, which bore
the direct influence of Luther's thinking, see "Ordinance of a Common Chest: Preface," Martin
Luther, *Luther's Works*, ed. Jaroslav Jan Pelikan (Philadelphia, 1962), vol. XL, *The Christian in
Society, II*. Here, he noted: "Now there is no greater service of God than Christian love which
helps and serves the needy, as Christ himself will judge and testify at the Last Day . . . This is why
the possessions of the church were formerly called *bona ecclesiae*, that is, common property, a
common chest . . . ," 172–3.

[78] Bernd Moeller argues that this view of Luther's exploded the "bonds of the old urban com-
munity." See: *Imperial Cities and the Reformation*, ed. and trans. H. C. Erik Midelfort and
Mark U. Edwards, Jr. (Philadelphia, 1972), 73–4. Cf. Thomas Brady, *Ruling Class, Regime and
Reformation in Strasbourg, 1520–1555* (Leiden, 1978), 3–19.

them a newer confessional model.[79] Despite reformers' differences of opinion about how exactly to organize urban assistance to the house poor, the 1520s and 1530s witnessed the growth of reinvigorated systems of assistance to the local poor throughout the Holy Roman Empire and beyond that were both cause and effect of city populations' sense of themselves as civic and/or confessional entities.

Poor relief and the boundaries of civic and confessional communities

Tensions over boundaries of civic and confessional communities grew more obvious in towns and cities where the Calvinist confession won over sizable portions of city populations. Here, churches of the Reformed faith confronted the obvious fact that boundaries of confessional and civic communities often did not coincide. The problem had to do in part with how restrictively sixteenth-century Calvinists defined their confessional community. Anyone could attend services in the Reformed Church, but only those who in the view of the Church's leadership had demonstrated their worthiness to participate in the sacrament of communion were considered full members.[80] Although Calvinist authorities hoped to expand their "household of faith" to include a large proportion of local civic communities, their restrictive theological and behavior requirements for joining the Church made this goal difficult to achieve. The experience of Calvinist churches during the late sixteenth and seventeenth centuries suggests that only a minority of any town's population where Reformed churches survived was likely to display the religious commitment and behavior required for full membership.

Struggles over how to make poor relief arrangements for members of confessional and civic communities became vastly more complicated in Calvinist than Lutheran or Catholic areas because of the problematic relationship which emerging Reformed churches bore to the states or cities in which they developed. While Calvinism was granted the status of "public" church in a number of localities, enjoying the support of local magistrates, in others it failed to gain the kind of monopoly status that Lutheran or Catholic churches earned in many territorial states and towns of the Empire.[81]

Studies of those areas most touched by the growth of Calvinism in the late sixteenth century suggest that, as elsewhere, there was no single way that church leaders organized poor relief. However, it is clear that in a number of places,

---

[79] Moeller, *Imperial Cities*, 69.
[80] Parker, *The Reformation*, 18, notes that, after 1572, Calvinists in Holland had a "eucharistic conception of Christian community."
[81] In 1572, the States of Holland and Zeeland made the Reformed faith the "privileged," but not formally established, church of the provinces.

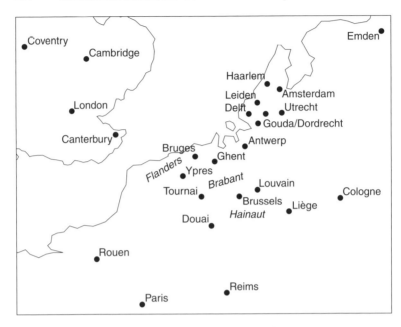

Map 2 Northern cities and towns in Reformation Europe

tensions developed between a desire to shape a spiritually restrictive confessional community and urban government officials' oft-competing desire to use poor relief resources to bind together the larger civic community. In the presence of such tensions, the solution that Calvinist authorities sought was usually freedom to organize poor relief within their confessional community without the intrusion of municipal authorities. In the southern French Calvinist stronghold of Nîmes, for example, Reformed congregations were content to be allowed to limit their poor relief activities to church members, being careful not to give money from legacies, church collections, or alms boxes to Catholic residents of the town, war refugees, or travelers.[82]

   This sort of arrangement also worked in certain towns of Holland. In Amsterdam and Dordrecht, where civic authorities were sympathetic to the Calvinist movement, municipal governments granted Calvinist officials a high degree of autonomy in organizing relief to the poor. These governments even allowed the Calvinist Church to organize assistance to the local poor who were not members of the congregation. In Leiden and Gouda, where town regents were hostile to the growth of a restrictive confessional church, however, Calvinist deacons directly in charge of distributing assistance were subject to more

[82] Raymond A. Mentzer, Jr., "Organizational Endeavour and Charitable Impulse in Sixteenth-Century France: The Case of Protestant Nîmes," *French History* 5, 1 (1991): 7–17.

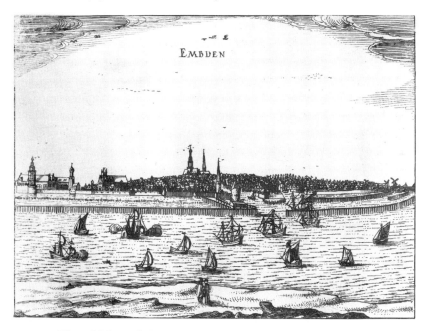

Plate 6 View of Emden, from Petrus Bertius, *Commentariorum rerum Germanicarum* (Amsterdam, 1616).

municipal control. The accommodation between regents and Calvinist churches in Haarlem and Delft lay between these two ends of the spectrum. In Haarlem, Calvinist deacons were allowed to minister to the poor of the congregation without municipal authority interference. In Delft, regents required Calvinist deacons to care for all of the city's poor, at least until 1614.[83]

The development of poor relief in the Calvinist East Frisian city of Emden illustrated many of the problems that the Calvinist movement encountered in adapting older forms of poor relief to its own confessional purposes. Like the domiciled urban poor in much of Europe, Emden's poor were assisted by income from endowments that pious laymen had willed over the years to various foundations for their care. In this tradition, a 1529 Church Ordinance in Emden set up a special administration for the support of the "house poor," and required inhabitants to contribute to their support (see Plate 6).[84]

With the success of the Calvinist movement in Emden during the 1560s and 1570s, church leaders advocated simply combining offices of church deacon and overseer of the town's poor. Tensions persisted, however, between the older poor relief system that combined Catholic piety and concern for the "civic"

[83] Parker, *The Reformation*, 90–6, 116–22.   [84] Fehler, *Poor Relief*, 41–55, 79.

poor and the Calvinist system that was designed essentially to bind together a newly emerging confessional community. Since the town still contained a large number of poor Catholics even as the Calvinist Church rose in status, what was one to do with them?

To address this problem, Emden's Calvinist leaders created a new way to raise money for their deacons to distribute exclusively to the poor of the Calvinist congregation so that the latter would not be forced to beg. They called it their "Becken" diaconate, so named for the collection plate passed around in Sunday services for this purpose. In this way, the Church raised monies for the congregation's poor while leaving funds from older endowments for the support of the "civic" poor without regard to church affiliation. Calvinists established this new source of poor assistance to allay any possible criticism from outside the Church that it was not taking care of its own poor.[85] In the competitive world of confessional rivalries, the charge of failing to support "one's own poor" was a serious one.

In 1577, the decision of the States of Holland to grant Dutch municipalities jurisdiction over poor relief unleashed a conflict between militant Calvinist leaders and Leiden's regents, who preferred a civic to a more strictly confessional Calvinist Church. The city government's willingness to protect the Reformed Church's monopoly of religious authority did not mean that it was willing to relinquish control of the city's poor relief funds, which Calvinist reformers had succeeded in placing under the control of church deacons.

In the ensuing power struggle, Calvinist leaders both lay and clerical succeeded in blocking magistrates' efforts to nominate church deacons who would serve as overseers of all the city's poor, claiming the right to assist the poor members of the Church unfettered by the meddling of city authorities. The powerful pastor Pieter Cornelisz asked the key question: "how could the community of Christ not be permitted to take care of its weakest members?"[86] Enforcing the right to assist their own poor without interference emerged as an important goal for confessional leaders whose religious communities did not enjoy the full support of local governments.

Divisions between Leiden's magistrates and the city's militant Calvinist leaders stemmed from the different communities that each was trying to serve as well as from variant understandings of the Calvinist Church's "public" or official status. In Leiden's magistrates' minds, the Calvinist Church's public status, which included the payment of ministers' salaries from the municipal budget, suggested to them that all members of the civic community should be welcome

---

[85] *Ibid.*, 122–30, 164–77. Keeping assistance for the congregation's poor separate from funds for the rest of the town poor became too difficult to manage, however, so the two funds were merged in 1578.

[86] Cited in Christine Kooi, *Liberty and Religion: Church and State in Leiden's Reformation, 1572–1620* (Leiden and Boston, 2000), 47.

as full members of the Church. Nothing could have been further from church leaders' view, however. In their minds, there was no conflict between the Calvinist Church being at the same time "public" and restricted in its membership. For them, the reason that the magistrates had recognized theirs as the official Church was not because it accepted all persons as members, but because it was the true Church.[87]

Nonetheless, Leiden's magistrates remained suspicious of the work of Calvinist consistories and of the home visits that Calvinist pastors organized in large part to discover evidence of religious heterodoxy. Magistrates here and in other Dutch cities hoped that the Calvinist Church could assume the same status of the Reformed Church of Zurich, where church consistories were unneeded because boundaries of confessional and civic communities were the same.

From the point of view of Calvinist leaders in Holland and elsewhere, it was not that they were hostile to ideals of civic community out of principle. Rather, it was the sheer empirical fact of the minoritarian status of Reformed churches in many areas that made their leaders generally more suspicious of secular authority than Lutherans or Catholics of the period.[88] Indeed, in Emden, which had historically been ruled by the Counts of East Frisia, the growth of Calvinism strengthened an urban civic movement by encouraging the emergence of a more vigorous city council.[89] On the basis of a newfound sense of unity reinforced by the Calvinist confessional movement, the council created new sorts of civic institutions affecting the lives of the poor, including a new Police Ordinance of 1545 that discouraged begging, banned foreign beggars, and revised town guild regulations to direct expenditures away from guild feasts and towards the care of the poor.[90] In the 1550s and 1560s, the in-migration of thousands of Calvinist refugees to Emden from towns with long communal traditions such as Bruges, Antwerp, Brussels, and Amsterdam strengthened the population's civic consciousness even further, leading eventually to the town's successful 1595 revolt against its Lutheran count and resulting in the granting of "public" status to the Calvinist Church there.[91]

The possibility of a highly compatible relationship between the civic and confessional aspirations of Reformed Protestants was also illustrated in the history of special institutions that granted distinctive entitlements to families of citizens. These sorts of collective institutions, designed to assist families through

---

[87] *Ibid.*, 7–10, 199–200.
[88] Parker, *The Reformation*, 106–11, contrasts tensions between Calvinist and civic authorities in Holland with the cooperative spirit that reigned between Catholics and Protestants, clergy and laity, in the city of Lyon when the reforms of the Aumône-Générale occurred in the 1530s.
[89] Heinz Schilling, "Calvinism and Urban Republicanism," in *Civic Calvinism in Northwestern Germany and the Netherlands: Sixteenth to Nineteenth Centuries* (Kirksville, MO, 1991), 21–8.
[90] Fehler, *Poor Relief*, 86–93, 262–3. The author also discusses the council's efforts to create a grain reserve during the economic crisis of the 1550s (147–53).
[91] *Ibid.*, 111–18, 224–5.

"critical life situations," maintained networks of solidarity by creating bridges across social class boundaries, particularly between a civic elite and families of the city's respectable middling ranks who were experiencing temporary difficulties. The work of Amsterdam's municipal orphanage (Burgerweeshuis) exemplified these multiple goals. Born originally from the bequest of a pious Catholic laywoman in 1523, the institution nonetheless had a clear civic character, admitting only children of citizens. With the conversion of the city to Reformed Protestantism after 1579, aid was narrowed further to provide only for children of Calvinist citizens. The link between citizenship and entitlement to have one's children received into the Burgerweeshuis was clear in the fact that the city devoted approximately one-quarter of the funds it received from those purchasing citizenship to it.[92] It was the middling ranks of the city's population who benefited most from its services, relying on it to support their children in the event of both parents' death. The Burgerweeshuis, like other charitable institutions, "was supposed to pick up exactly where the family – made frail by the vagaries of mortality – had left off."[93]

Members of Amsterdam's elite directed the orphanage's operations and contributed to its coffers.[94] Although day-to-day administration was left to paid staff, regentesses of this and many other residential institutions for the local poor in Holland played a significant role in their operations, suggesting a Protestant version of the earlier Catholic practices of maternalism, or "public motherhood" (see Plate 7).[95]

Although sources on the Burgerweeshuis' Reformation days lack detail, data from a later period suggest that children who had lost their biological parents and entered the orphanage were not entirely bereft of extended kin. Aunts, uncles, step-parents and older siblings living locally abounded, but in many instances they clearly preferred that children enter the orphanage rather than taking them in themselves. The pervasiveness of a small, nuclear family household system in Holland may have encouraged kin's reluctance to take in dependent children.[96] However, it is also likely that the presence of a well-funded, respectable orphanage limited to citizens' children must have enhanced its appeal. Indeed, the children's extended kin probably viewed their young relatives' entry into the institution as the fulfillment of a legitimate and thoroughly honorable entitlement.[97]

In the eyes of some, Amsterdam's Burgerweeshuis might not qualify as a charitable or even a "poor relief" institution given the restrictions on the children it received. In many ways, it looked more like a collective mutual insurance

---

[92] McCants, *Civic Charity*, 19, 25–6.   [93] *Ibid.*, 148.

[94] For a discussion of these institutions and the portraits of men and women who directed them, see Muller, *Charity in the Dutch Republic*.

[95] McCants, *Civic Charity*, 41, 90.   [96] *Ibid.*, 32–3.

[97] *Ibid.*, 33. The author suggests that in earlier times, kin may have been somewhat more willing to take in dependent children, but there is no evidence of this.

Plate 7 Jacob A. Backer, *Regentesses of the Burgerweeshuis, Amsterdam,*
1633.

system formed against risks of death among the city's citizens. However, those
who supported it believed that it expressed a combination of charitable and
lay civic values as they were evolving in early modern Europe. Citizens of
Amsterdam, like those in many other towns and cities, were simply experiencing
and reinforcing bonds of community with those who evoked their deepest sense
of affinity and obligation. Amsterdam's leaders created a separate institution
for children of noncitizens where conditions were less desirable, based upon the
widely shared notion that children of citizens' families were entitled to better
treatment than children of the destitute because of their citizen status.[98] The
concern of Amsterdam's ruling elite to govern the Burgerweeshuis suggested
their own sense of the importance of the orphanage as a symbol of a bond that
linked them to less prosperous members of the civic community.[99] It was thus
both symbolically and practically a vehicle for perpetuating it.

[98] *Ibid.*, 147–50, discusses differences between the diets of children in the Burgerweeshuis and
the poor children of other orphanages in the city.
[99] *Ibid.*, 28, 104, 112.

However, other trends in the history of Calvinism conspired to exert pressure on compatibilities between civic and confessional aspirations for community. The growth of large groups of refugees and exiles across Europe in the course of the sixteenth century helped to expose even further the latent tensions between civic and confessional notions of community in some areas. Calvinist authorities in towns receiving such refugees often tried to address increasing demands on poor relief resources by making use of solidarities of birthplace as well as confession to raise money for the relief of poor exiles. Beginning in the 1540s, Genevan authorities attempted to make various exile subcommunities – Italians, English, and Germans – care for themselves, with the many French exiles being relatively well provided for in legacies left for this purpose.[100] Although they organized assistance for the domiciled poor according to neighborhood, Emden's Calvinist officials aided the many exiles from Flanders and Brabant by assessing wealthy exiles from these areas for various levels of "voluntary" contributions for the assistance of their "brothers" from the same regions.[101]

Like all systems of poor relief, however, this one ran into occasional snags. In the case of one Emden couple consisting of a husband from the Dutch congregation and his Walloon wife, the couple's will became the object of dispute. The will, which was to be executed upon the death of the first spouse, made a provision of 50 guilders for the benefit of poor exiles. Although the written will provided only for Dutch exiles, the surviving husband protested that the Walloon congregation of which his wife had been a member had been omitted by mistake. The ensuing conflict between Dutch and Walloon congregations over the legacy was handed over to church deacons who eventually ruled in favor of accepting the testament at face value, thereby denying the claims of the Walloon congregation. These kinds of conflicts among co-religionists over scarce poor relief resources led Emden's Calvinist officials gradually to merge funds for foreign exiles so that meritorious refugees from whatever region were eligible to receive them.[102]

Conflicts between those who, like the magistrates of Leiden, favored a civic church to bind together all members of the local community and those who propounded a confessional community based on a restrictive church assumed larger dimensions in the face of the exile experience. Against "Libertines" in the

[100] Jeannine E. Olson, *Calvin and Social Welfare: Deacons and the* Bourse française (Selinsgrove, PA, 1989), 24–5, 37–49; Olson, *One Ministry, Many Roles: Deacons and Deaconesses through the Centuries* (St. Louis, 1992), 117–18.
[101] Numerous Protestant refugees from the mountains of southern France flooded into Nîmes in the 1580s, where they initially enjoyed the same entitlements to assistance as the local Protestant poor. A rapid increase in their numbers, however, led to efforts to keep them out. See Mentzer, "Organizational Endeavour," *French History*, 14–15.
[102] Fehler, *Poor Relief*, 230–2, 277–80. Andrew Pettegree notes that exiles themselves supported the policy of organizing poor assistance by nationality groups. See *Emden and the Dutch Revolt: Exile and the Development of Reformed Protestantism* (Oxford and New York, 1992), 152–3.

northern Netherlands, those who favored a Reformed church system in which all residents would be welcomed as full members, more radical Calvinists emphasized the stronger bonds they felt with their confessional "brothers" and "sisters" from other lands. This disagreement had very practical consequences in the two groups' differing responses to the in-migration of exiles from the south to the northern provinces. Whereas Libertine regents in towns such as Utrecht viewed refugees with great suspicion, and proved reluctant to confer on them rights to civic forms of assistance, militant Calvinist leaders considered the refugees' status as suffering members of the confessional community as legitimate and sufficient grounds of entitlement to that confessional community's resources.[103]

It was clear, especially in the Netherlands, that a vision of community that was essentially civic in nature could conflict with a newer vision of a confessional community bound together not mainly by common space or history, but by belief and behavior that now transcended local or even international boundaries. Thus, in places such as Holland, the opposition between a civic model of community bolstered by a latitudinarian approach to membership in the church community came into conflict with increasingly well-organized confessions of international scope, leading to ever sharper tensions between "a communal, particularistic model of religious community against the agents of divisiveness and supralocal integration."[104] Especially when threatened by one another, members of all three emerging major confessions were apt to feel a greater sense of solidarity with their real or "imagined" community of co-religionists than with actual neighbors of other faiths with whom they may have experienced face-to-face conflict. This development was ironic, of course, given the importance that humanists and early reformers had paid to the requirement of assisting the local poor.

Community and constraint: exacting contributions for the poor

Creating confessional or civic communities required members and authorities to assist those who by their residency or beliefs, or both, had established an entitlement to it. As noted in the discussion of Emden's system for the relief of poor exiles, new confessional systems of poor relief sometimes involved extreme pressure or outright constraint on church members to provide assistance to other members in need. With the frequent cooperation of government

---

[103] Benjamin Kaplan, "Dutch Particularism and the Calvinist Quest for 'Holy Uniformity'," *Archiv für Reformationsgeschichte* 82 (1991), 250, shows the same distinction between militant Calvinist and "Libertine" behavior among earlier civil authorities in Geneva.

[104] *Ibid.*, 254. The Synod of Emden in 1571 declared "Dutch Calvinism part of an international movement by signing the French confession of faith and adopting the Genevan and Heidelberg Catechisms as instructional material" (251).

authorities, Calvinist consistories sometimes required church members to fulfill their charitable obligations by simply assessing their households a certain amount on the basis of their wealth for contributions to their poor co-religionists.

During the Calvinist ascendancy in Nîmes, church authorities raised poor relief funds by assessing church members' wealth by household, and then adding in calculations of the wealth of the Catholic bishop, the cathedral chapter, and monastic foundations that remained in the town during the Protestant ascendancy. Calvinist leaders saw no conflict between using such methods to fulfill obligations of charity during the crisis years of the late 1580s and early 1590s. In addition to making careful assessments and lists of the poor by name, Nîmes' Calvinist consistory matched names on the list of the poor with wealthy families of the town so the poor could receive their benefits in the form of bread or money directly from the wealthier household that the consistory had chosen.[105] Such a system, the consistory believed, preserved important elements of an individual, face-to-face relationship while raising pressure on church members to contribute to the care of the local poor.[106]

The use of constraint was not limited, however, to those seeking to build confessional communities. In 1551 and 1555, Leiden's regents "levied a tax on all householders and authorized a special city-wide collection for the residential poor." Since this collection did not yield enough contributions, the regents decided to redirect part of their municipal excise taxes for poor relief.[107]

These poor taxes were not restricted to Protestant areas, though the renewed Counter-Reformation emphasis on the voluntary quality of charitable giving made some authorities in Catholic areas shrink from instituting regular obligatory taxes for the local poor.[108] Civic authorities in Venice engaged in this sort of policy several times during the sixteenth century. Taxation on wealthier citizens during the famine of 1528–9 came on the basis of assessments on the value of homes owned or rents paid. The clergy played several roles in the crisis, the most important of which was to persuade the noncompliant by reading their names aloud from parish pulpits at High Mass during feast days.[109] Government authorities elsewhere in Venice's dominions used the same tactics.

---

[105] Mentzer, "Organizational Endeavour," 25. Some of these pairings were not well received by the donors, who refused to assist the poor whom they had been assigned. It is doubtful that charitable contributions passed directly from donor to recipient.

[106] *Ibid.*, 21–3. This distribution assisted on average about 5 percent of the Calvinist population of some 10,000 persons, particularly solitary women (35 percent of the total of persons assisted), solitary women with children (11 percent), and children (19 percent).

[107] Parker, *The Reformation*, 88.

[108] Colin Jones, "Introduction: The Charitable Imperative," in *Charitable Imperative*, 4–5.

[109] Pullan, *Rich and Poor*, 247. The author suggests that this was a "species of formal disgrace which few would care to face with equanimity." The clergy played a similar role in urging the success of Lille's Bourse Commune in the 1520s. See Robert S. Duplessis, *Lille and the Dutch Revolt: Urban Stability in an Era of Revolution, 1500–1582* (New York and Cambridge, 1991), 143.

In 1539, faced with famine and epidemic, the city council of Brescia required all citizens to contribute to the creation of a fund for the relief of the local poor while reminding them of the sanctifying effects of almsgiving.[110]

In 1545, the Venetian city council required parish clergy to urge their congregations to higher levels of giving during another crisis, setting up a system for collecting the money and distributing it. While the voluntary nature of almsgiving was important in principle, the Venetian government felt entirely justified, and the clergy along with it, in bringing continuous moral pressure on citizens to give. Magistrates worked on other fronts as well, for example requiring notaries to inform their clients of the vast opportunities for almsgiving when making out their wills.[111]

Another epidemic of the Plague in 1575–7 helped to revive Venice's quite democratic poor tax, which was once again levied on renters and householders according to the value of the rents paid or real estate they owned. While the poorest were exempt from the levy, those living in the city's almshouses – but who owned homes of value – were assessed. During this epidemic, parish priests and their lay deputies once again collected the tax. However, this time only one-half of the money raised in each parish was kept there, with the rest going to a central fund to be distributed equitably across the different districts of the city.[112] Conditions in the city were so severe in 1576 that a second round of the tax was levied in mid-August of the same year. City officials mobilized clergy not only to collect taxes but to urge increased almsgiving during times of civic catastrophe.[113]

Lyon's mid-sixteenth-century civic relief fund, the Aumône-Générale, which was supported by a cross-section of Protestant and Catholic leaders as well as laymen, was funded at least in part by taxes. After its reorganization in 1544, one of the main tasks of the Aumône's board of directors was to oversee the collection of the city's poor tax, which was designed to aid the domiciled poor in their own homes. Like Emden's tax, Lyon's had a "voluntary" element. Various affluent groups of the city such as communities of foreign merchants were asked how much they would like to contribute. If the board considered the sum appropriate, it accepted the contribution. However, the board reserved the prerogative of suggesting a higher sum if it felt that the proposed contributions were too low, or if the demands on the institution were outstripping its resources. Some of Lyon's citizens chose the option of feeding several of the poor in lieu

---

[110] Pullan, *Rich and Poor*, 277–8. Objections of certain representatives of the mendicant orders against the right of officials to exact these payments met with resistance from other clerical as well as lay opinion.

[111] *Ibid.*, 296–8. At least one official of the newer Jesuit order supported these kinds of policies, introduced by Venice's poor law during the later famine of 1559–60.

[112] *Ibid.*, 319–20. A tax of this sort was levied a second time during the disaster.

[113] *Ibid.*, 247, 278, 298, 319–20.

of cash payments to the poor relief fund whose levies reached as far down the social ladder as the ranks of the city's artisan class.

Obligatory taxes for the local poor were also levied elsewhere in the Lyon region. In 1573, while expelling poor strangers from the town, the municipal councilors of Villefranche assigned the local poor to various households to be cared for during a time of food shortage. If and when those of the poor who had been assigned died, the city government found a new set of dependents for the wealthy to house. Those inhabitants who did not wish to lodge the poor in their own houses were allowed to send food to them in the local hospice.[114]

An obligation to pay for the relief of the resident poor also underlay England's Poor Law legislation of the late sixteenth and early seventeenth century, which differed from practices on the Continent mainly by its ubiquity within England as a whole and the ability of local officials to exact conformity to its terms even in normal times. Interestingly, part of the success of the English Poor Law stemmed from the fact that confessional and "civic" community boundaries overlapped, with the parish becoming a unit of local government as well as church life.[115] As historians of the English system have noted, the compulsory "rates" paid for the domiciled poor under terms of that society's poor law were in themselves nothing new. Those living in English parishes were used to being required to pay for church upkeep, street cleaning, and other civic requirements. Paying for the poor was merely an additional demand fortified, as in cities of the Continent, by the obligations of combined membership in both confessional and civic communities. Levying rates for the care of the local poor was simply "one further expression of the responsible local community fulfilling its obligations."[116]

Extracting payments from community members for the care of "their poor" was never easy, even among those who shared confessional loyalties during times of their greatest militancy. Nonetheless, concerns to fulfill entitlements to assistance of the confessional and/or civic poor figured importantly in the forging of confessional communities and the maintenance of civic ones during the troubled years of the sixteenth century.

---

[114] Gutton, *La Société*, 255–61, 276–7, 301. Maureen Flynn, *Sacred Charity: Confraternities and Social Welfare in Spain, 1400–1700* (Basingstoke, 1989), 81–2, notes this same practice in sixteenth-century Spain, though it is not clear whether the level of constraint on people was as high.

[115] Lynn Botelho, "Aged and Impotent: Parish Relief of the Aged Poor in Early Modern Suffolk," in Martin Daunton, ed., *Charity, Self-Interest and Welfare in the English Past* (New York, 1996), 92.

[116] Paul Slack, *Poverty and Policy in Tudor and Stuart England* (London and New York, 1988), 131. However, the enactment of a Poor Law in Scotland in 1574 in emulation of English legislation of 1572 proved highly contentious. See Michael Lynch, "The Reformation in Edinburgh: The Growth and Growing Pains of Urban Protestantism," in Jim Obelkevich, Lyndal Roper, and Raphael Samuel, eds., *Disciplines of Faith: Studies in Religion, Politics, and Patriarchy* (London and New York, 1987), 292–3.

So much has justly been written about the harshness of sixteenth- and early-seventeenth-century policies towards the mobile and vagrant poor that it is difficult to imagine different groups and their leaders battling one another for the right to assist "their" poor unimpeded. The focus of these struggles was the domiciled local or respectable poor: those people known in the locality and who therefore had strong claims to charitable help from both religious and secular sources.

An examination of the important conflicts over poor relief arrangements during the Calvinist Reformation suggests the tensions that could erupt when proponents of different sorts of communities were competing for people's hearts and minds. It also suggests the continuing centrality of poor relief systems to European community-building projects. The community-building efforts that emerged during the sixteenth century sparked a renewed focus on the household and family as objects of relief and central institutions for the building of confessional and civic communities. The following chapter therefore examines in more detail ways that religious and civic authorities intervened in the lives of individuals and families in support of their community-building goals, and the larger impacts of the growth of new confessions on individuals and their families.

4 Individuals, families, and communities in urban Europe of the Protestant and Catholic Reformations

This chapter broadens the discussion of individual, family, and community re- lationships by examining the many ways that domestic life and the family roles individuals played affected the building of civic and confessional communi- ties in Protestant and Catholic areas of the sixteenth and seventeenth centuries. The analysis takes place against the background of important developments in the early modern urban economy, particularly the increased gendering of wage work and the relative decline in the status of women workers in labor markets as work communities of men gained greater authority. A growing emphasis on the importance of married women's work in the home lent urgency to the need that civic leaders and Protestant reformers felt to regulate relations within the family as they affected both domestic relations and the building of new confessional communities. In Catholic Europe, where church policy made it increasingly difficult for women religious to lead lives outside formal and increasingly en- closed communities, women nonetheless sought to use their family-based ex- periences and authority to maintain a place for themselves in the public life of civil society.

Although some historians have emphasized the patriarchal aspects of many forms of civic and religious community building during the sixteenth and seventeenth centuries, the discussion will suggest that the evidence is not so clear. As we shall see, organizations in Protestant Europe that inter- vened into domestic life were not resolutely committed to the enforcement of patriarchal authority in the household. Nor was the rising importance attributed to women's domestic presence a simple matter of consigning women to an increasingly private household. The construction of confes- sional or civic communities, which frequently involved the infusion of highly charged religious beliefs or standards of behavior into household and family life, far from reaffirming traditional hierarchies of age or gender, sometimes provided subordinate individuals with means to enhance their authority in the home or establish identities in these new communities of belief and behavior.

136

Women and men in the early modern urban economy

Sixteenth-century cities offer evidence of the kind of declining fortunes of women workers identified with "phase three" of Jeremy Goldberg's model of urban development discussed in Chapter 1.[1] In sixteenth-century episodes illustrative of Goldberg's "phase three," workingmen or artisan-merchants who were organized into guilds sometimes succeeded in restricting women's access to the kinds of industrial work that provided relatively high wages. In Leiden, the gradual organization of occupations central to the woolen trade, such as weaving or fulling, into formal "crafts" communities led directly to the exclusion of single women from membership in them. Such crafts restrictions allowed married women to participate in the more lucrative branches of woolen production in partnership with their husbands. If working on their own account, however, women were restricted to those occupations not controlled by workingmen's guilds. The lack of crafts restrictions on such occupations as cloth selling meant that women were often found among the city's drapers.[2]

In many cities where workingmen's guilds had the power to control access to specific occupations, economic downturns and the glutting of labor markets also led to growing competition between male and female workers. Declining standards of living for some workingmen could result from the reorganization of whole industries along capitalist lines, for example when merchant-capitalists who controlled the distribution and sale of manufactured textiles grew more powerful at the expense of spinners and weavers engaged in production.[3] The over-supply of labor in many towns and cities of the sixteenth century could also lead to a breakdown in the upward mobility of journeymen into the ranks of masters, which resulted in the formation of guilds of journeymen who would most likely never achieve master status. Here, competition for employment with women could become especially fierce, targeting not only single women but also widows of guild members as well.[4]

Although there had been attempts to drive women out of a number of crafts in the fifteenth century in such cities as Augsburg and Frankfurt, the competition became even greater in the sixteenth and seventeenth centuries. In these towns, gender-based conflicts could take place on several fronts: over such things as limiting the continued participation of masters' widows in the trades; exercising tighter scrutiny over the morals of members' wives in order to find reasons for

---

[1] See above, pages 54–5.
[2] Martha C. Howell, "Women, the Family Economy, and the Structures of Market Production in Cities of Northern Europe during the Late Middle Ages," in Barbara A. Hanawalt, ed., *Women and Work in Preindustrial Europe* (Bloomington, 1986), 204–5.
[3] For a discussion of this trend in one south German town in the seventeenth century, see Christopher R. Friedrichs, *Urban Society in an Age of War: Nördlingen, 1580–1720* (Princeton, 1979), 270–87.
[4] Merry E. Wiesner, *Working Women in Renaissance Germany* (New Brunswick, NJ, 1986), 164–6.

their exclusion; controlling the number of female workers whom masters could employ; and eventually excluding women from certain tasks or shops simply because they were women.[5]

Pressures to marginalize working women in important export trades appeared beginning in the late sixteenth century in Geneva, where the manufacture of luxury silk cloth employed many women. Gradually, guild rules reduced the participation of young women in the trade. In 1595, regulations first affected the number of female orphans whom masters could train. Then, after 1606, widows of men who had engaged in the ribbon trade, or *passementerie*, but who subsequently married men outside the trade were prohibited from teaching it to daughters born of their second marriages. By 1657, these kinds of women were restricted from teaching the trade even to daughters of their first marriages. The exclusion of women, even wives and daughters of masters, from the skilled jobs in watchmaking – Geneva's newer export trade – was even more wideranging. On the other hand, Genevan rules regarding citizenship continued to protect the commercial interests of wives and daughters of citizens. When the city began to prohibit all noncitizens from owning commercial businesses, women who were considered citizens continued to engage in smaller commercial enterprises while often figuring as important investors in larger ones.[6]

In late medieval Europe, widows of guild workers had usually been allowed to continue to operate shops that they had previously run in partnership with their husbands for several years after their husbands' deaths. By the sixteenth century, however, the trend in many cities was to shorten this time period significantly. In one incident from seventeenth-century Frankfurt am Main, a widow's petition to city authorities to be allowed to continue running the family stonemasonry business met the opposition of other employers and workers. Their counter-petition was unusual only in its encyclopedic quality, seemingly appealing to every single argument ever made to justify the exclusion of women from a craft or profession. In response to the widow's petition, the stonemasons' reply noted that: "it was now the practice in Frankfurt and elsewhere that widows were allowed to work only four weeks after their husband's death." There could be no special consideration for her, since "other widows would want the same rights." Since the deceased husband had been among the wealthiest stonemasons in the town and was therefore disliked: "If his widow continued the shop, there would be many disputes between her and the other masters." Moreover, the

---

[5] Merry E. Wiesner, "Spinsters and Seamstresses: Women in Cloth and Clothing Production," in Margaret W. Ferguson, Maureen Quilligan, and Nancy J. Vickers, eds., *Rewriting the Renaissance: The Discourses of Sexual Difference in Early Modern Europe* (Chicago and London, 1986), 194–5. On widows' entitlements in Seville, see Mary Elizabeth Perry, *Gender and Disorder in Early Modern Seville* (Princeton, 1990), 17.

[6] E. William Monter, "Women in Calvinist Geneva (1550–1800)," *Signs*, 6, 2 (1980): 202–3. The movement to exclude women from this trade occurred in the late seventeenth century.

petitioners knew for a fact that the widow's dead husband personally opposed widows working for longer than four weeks after the demise of their husbands. Then, too, "she could not control the journeymen, who might marry and have children; but if they were accused of bad work, they might leave their wives and children, who would then need public support." Finally, "because she could not control the journeymen, they would want to work in her shop and not for the other masters." In response, and after consultation with the city council of Strasbourg, Frankfurt's own city council denied the widow's request, which she had couched in the name of Christian charity.[7]

Guild organizations in Cologne differed substantially in function and power from organizations of the same name in many other cities. Here, guilds seemed to be designed less to protect the entitlements of communities of crafts workers than the interests of wealthy "artisan-merchants." Despite the lesser power of organized groups of male workers in Cologne, over time the same process of exclusion of women took place, leading to their concentration in the manufacture of needles and belts, baking, beer brewing, and silken embroidery.[8] As in other towns and cities, this sort of transformation concentrated women in pursuits that were small in scale, relatively unprofitable, and undercapitalized.

Although the examples discussed thus far have emphasized the complicity of civic governments and men's guilds in limiting women's access to better-paid occupations, there were also places in which political authorities consciously reduced men's guild power and in so doing expanded women's employment opportunities, if not their economic standing relative to men. The rise of the Medicis in sixteenth-century Florence brought to power men who sought to stimulate economic growth in the Tuscan capital in part by reducing the power of the city's guilds. Under pressure from the Medicean ducal government, sixteenth-century guilds such as those of the linen workers gradually lost the ability to exclude women from their ranks. Rather, they sought to temper competition from female workers in their craft by lobbying the city government to exact from them the same small fee that male workers were required to pay to their guild.[9]

The opening up of whole new industries in southern Europe sometimes expanded wage-work opportunities for women, but without having much impact on the relative fortunes of men and women. The growth of the silk industry in late-sixteenth- and seventeenth-century Tuscany boosted the wage employment of women both in the countryside, where women oversaw the feeding and raising of silkworms, and in the city, where women spun and wove silk

---

[7] Wiesner, "Spinsters," in Ferguson *et al.*, eds., *Rewriting the Renaissance*, 195–6.
[8] Howell, "Women, the Family Economy," in Hanawalt, ed., *Women and Work*, 213.
[9] Judith C. Brown, "A Woman's Place was in the Home: Women's Work in Renaissance Tuscany," in Ferguson *et al.*, eds., *Rewriting the Renaissance*, 212–13.

fabric. Other changes intervened at the same time, however, to bolster the economic position of male workers. As women moved into the silk industry in large numbers, Florentine men entered the newer, better-paid consumer luxury trades including the production of ceramics, books, jewelry and furniture. They also occupied the most highly paid, skilled positions in silk weaving.[10]

The power of men's guilds to effect changes in the working lives of women should not be exaggerated, however. The examples from Italy and several cases from northern European cities are a reminder that although women were often severely disadvantaged by their lack of membership in officially recognized work communities, by the sixteenth century many workingmen's guilds were not sufficiently powerful to protect their members from either cyclical economic downturns or the more formidable and systemic threat that a shift of power from producers to merchant-capitalists represented.

Moreover, though guilds or workingmen or artisan-merchants could act to restrict women's access to work, urban crafts and guild organizations usually included only a minority of male workers. Thus, comparing the fortunes of male guild workers – those most likely to have accumulated capital and to have skills – with women workers biases the terms of the comparison towards men with the greatest power in urban labor markets. Finally, revisionist work on urban guilds in some areas suggests that crafts guilds often wielded a kind of power that was more symbolic and ceremonial than economic. Guild authority frequently served less to regulate urban labor markets and more to fulfill the need of urban governing classes for public displays that legitimized their own power.[11] Nonetheless, the fact remains that women workers in many areas of sixteenth- and seventeenth-century Europe seem to have experienced a relative decline in their access to better-paid jobs in the urban economy.

Households and the urban social order

Periods when women were losing the competition for jobs in more lucrative sectors of urban economies and were faced with declining wages and unemployment often coincided with the times when urban authorities expressed increasing alarm at growing numbers of "unattached," "independent," or "masterless" women in their midst. These were doubtless the same periods in which fears of "masterless" men, and social policies designed to deal with them, were at their highest pitch.[12] However, urban authorities faced rather different sorts of problems from "masterless" women and men who migrated in to the

---

[10] Judith C. Brown and Jordan Goodman, "Women and Industry in Florence," *Journal of Economic History* 40, 1 (1980): 73–80.

[11] Heather Swanson, "The Illusion of Economic Structure: Craft Guilds in Late Medieval English Towns," *Past and Present*, no. 121 (November, 1988): 29–48.

[12] A. L. Beier, *Masterless Men: The Vagrancy Problem in England, 1560–1640* (New York and London, 1985), *passim.*

city or attempted to stay there when their work opportunities were declining. During periods when women's job opportunities were narrowing, city fathers had reason to fear that single women who remained, especially those with no family or friends to take them in or assist them, might turn to prostitution, with all its attendant sources of disorder, to help tide them over.[13]

City authorities as early as the medieval period had often countered their fears of urban disorder with legislation. For example, concerns about high levels of in-migration of women and fears of urban disorder led city governments in Tuscan towns to enact policies against prostitution and sodomy as early as the thirteenth century.[14] Against the background of declining industrial crafts employment for women in fifteenth-century York and other English cities, authorities there met the perceived risk of increased prostitution with the kind of legislation that would be repeated in other cities. A 1492 ordinance in the town of Coventry, for example, ordered that single working women under age 50 desist from living on their own and place themselves in service.[15] Encouraging social order through the enforcement of adults' living arrangements was easier said than done, however. Coventry's law met with the active opposition of the town's "honest women," not all of whom were married, which led to several important revisions in the decree. First, authorities were forced to lower the age requirement to 40. Then they agreed not to prohibit an unmarried woman from living in her own rooms. Rather, she was required to let rooms from an "honest person," one who would "be responsible for her conduct." Women violating these compromises were, however, liable to imprisonment or expulsion.[16]

Similar sorts of regulations affecting the lives of independent working women arose sometimes from the needs of male household heads who wished to employ and house their female employees on their own terms. In sixteenth-century Augsburg, master weavers complained to the city administration that their livelihoods were being threatened. Women spinners who had formerly worked for them and dwelt under their roofs now chose to work for themselves and live with other families. The city council there duly countered with legislation forbidding all unmarried women, whether citizens or not, from living independently.[17]

---

[13] Maryanne Kowaleski has suggested that prostitutes in fourteenth-century Exeter had no family resident in the town. See "Women's Work in a Market Town: Exeter in the Late Fourteenth Century," in Hanawalt, ed., *Women and Work*, 154.

[14] Carol Lansing, "Gender and Civic Authority: Sexual Control in a Medieval Italian Town," *Journal of Social History* 31, 1 (November, 1997): 33–59.

[15] This 1492 legislation, found in M. D. Harris, ed., *Coventry Leet Book*, 544, is cited in P. J. P. Goldberg, *Women, Work, and Life Cycle in a Medieval Economy: Women in York and Yorkshire c. 1300–1520* (Oxford, 1992), 155.

[16] Christine Peters, "Single Women in Early Modern England: Attitudes and Expectations," *Continuity and Change* 12, 3 (1997): 329. She notes that the prescribed "honest person" did not have to be male.

[17] Wiesner, "Spinsters," in Ferguson *et al.*, eds., *Rewriting the Renaissance*, 200–1. The author adds, however, "these [ordinances] were probably just as ineffective as earlier laws."

Although women were clearly not the main or only individuals whose "masterless" presence aroused concern and inspired laws designed to "settle" them, the presence of unattached women and the official concern at the possible consequences of a decline in their work opportunities signaled a special sort of trouble, and an emerging set of family-centered solutions. As early as the fourteenth century, a variety of texts evinced the growing appeal of what Felicity Riddy has termed a "bourgeois ethos" centering on the household. City authorities and clergy alike expressed this ethos in various texts and laws, both designed to address perceived breakdowns of the urban social order by exposing its dependency upon stability in the residential family. This ethos identified the household as center of "production and trade" involving family members and resident servants.[18] Women, or more precisely, wives played an important role in this ethos, which identified the urban bourgeois household as key to maintaining order in the city. Specifically, married women who supervised young female servants within the household were believed to serve as important models of the conduct that leaders hoped those new to the city would learn. Indeed, in this ethos, mistresses of households provided the single most important teachers of codes of orderly urban conduct for migrant women, thus helping to integrate the young and restless into the urban labor market and the larger society.[19]

While the origins of this bourgeois ethos are obscure, it is clear that its appeal extended well beyond the time of its first appearance, reappearing with downturns in urban business cycles. As Riddy notes: clerical and lay authorities were apt to preach "domesticity as 'natural' for women precisely during a period when young girls migrating to the towns as unskilled labor and contracting marriages away from parental oversight, or not marrying at all, were seen to pose threats of various kinds to bourgeois interests."[20] When the influx of "masterless" men and women was most obvious or threatening, the integration of single women into solid and reliable urban households appeared most urgent.[21]

One sixteenth-century version of this bourgeois ethos elaborated more deeply on the proper division of labor within the household, highlighting differences between the work roles of men and women. It was the man's duty "to get, to trauaille abroad, to defende; the wife, to saue that which is gotten, to tarrie at home to distribute that which commeth of the husbandes labor ... and to keepe

---

[18] Felicity Riddy, "Mother Knows Best: Reading Social Change in a Courtesy Text," *Speculum* 71, 1 (1996): 67–8.

[19] *Ibid.*, 83–5.   [20] *Ibid.*, 72–3.

[21] Michael Roberts, "Women and Work in Sixteenth-Century English Towns," in Penelope J. Corfield and Derek Keene, eds., *Work in Towns, 850–1850* (Leicester and New York, 1990), 88. The emergence of the household as an agency of "social control" is suggested by the changing language of ordinances of Douai in the fifteenth century. See Ellen E. Kittell and Kurt Queller, "'Whether Man or Woman': Gender Inclusivity in the Town Ordinances of Medieval Douai," *Journal of Medieval and Early Modern Studies* 30, 1 (Winter, 2000): 84–6.

all at home neat and cleane."[22] Women's work *producing* goods or wealth was characteristically missing from an emerging prescriptive literature, even though married women of the middling ranks of urban society typically engaged in spinning or other productive tasks at home, and were accustomed to dividing their time between house and the world outside.

The search for a kind of urban peace and integration based upon domestic ideals directed especially towards women was perpetually challenged, however, by the continuing effects of demographic and economic systems that required the circulation of servants and other single workers in and out of the city. In the sixteenth as in the fourteenth century, the streets, neighborhoods, and marketplaces of towns in northern and southern Europe teemed with women going about their business chatting, hawking their wares, doing errands, or taking breaks from their work tasks. Thus, the reappearance of the desire to build urban communities on the basis of orderly women and households was more a function of the "social imaginary," than a reflection of the quotidian realities of urban life. As Michael Roberts observed: "[t]he woman's 'domestic' position in the household had to be emphasized, at just the time that female economic activity of all kinds appeared to be spilling over into the streets and lanes as never before."[23]

The growth of patriarchal tendencies in the economic and social regulations under discussion here was filled with certain ambiguities and contradictions, however. Protecting the livelihoods of male-headed households was all well and good, but dispossessing single women or widows of their livelihoods, especially when these same women were long-term residents or even citizens, with entitlements to remain in the city, had important implications for social order as well. Despite the support of urban political authorities for many efforts by groups of workingmen to limit women's access to well-paid wage labor, city fathers were also keenly aware of the economic, social, and moral problems that could result from increasing levels of poverty and unemployment among women.[24] As we have seen, women who were shut out of opportunities in crafts work were not only more liable to engage in prostitution, they were also more likely to become financially dependent upon assistance from city coffers given their low wages even in good times. Indeed, the exclusion of women from higher-paid industrial work helped explain the feminization of poverty in many towns and cities of the early modern period. Households headed by women, mainly widows, could account for up to 25 percent of the total in early modern German cities and were among the likeliest to require charitable assistance.[25]

---

[22] A mid-sixteenth-century text by Sir Thomas Smith, quoted in Roberts, "Women," in Corfield and Keene, eds., *Work in Towns*, 89–90.

[23] *Ibid.*, 94–5.

[24] Natalie Zemon Davis, "Women in the Crafts in Sixteenth-Century Lyon," in Hanawalt, ed., *Women and Work*, 185–6.

[25] Wiesner, *Working Women*, 4–5.

In sixteenth-century Lyon, silk merchants faced with declining livelihoods from their trade sought to solve their problem by restricting competition. To protect the livelihoods of men in the craft, they pressed the city's governors to eliminate female apprentices from the trade unless their families were linked to the industry. However, the reaction of the council was not automatic, and the merchants in question had to keep up the pressure over a number of years. The final exclusion of women from skilled jobs in the silk industry required another century or so, and resulted not from efforts to restrict competition, but rather from larger-scale capitalist production, which required increasingly large sums to set up viable workshops.[26]

A consideration of the working lives of urban women in the sixteenth and seventeenth centuries suggests that increasing restrictions on women's labor in many crafts was real, and that women's exclusion from them led to a relative decline in women's standing in the world of paid industrial work outside the home. Conversely, there is some evidence that in towns or within occupational groups where household forms of production persisted and where wives worked in trades or businesses alongside their husbands, they continued to enjoy a relatively high work status.[27] This suggests that the early modern period may have witnessed an increasing gulf between the relative economic statuses of single and married women of the middling and lower classes. Whereas single women working on their own account may have enjoyed relatively more physical and legal autonomy, women's gradual exclusion from higher-paid crafts work may have made marriage, purely in financial terms, a more attractive proposition than remaining single.

An emphasis on the importance of married women's domestic work and the household itself, in terms of a bourgeois ethos emerging as early as the fourteenth century, appeared once again in the sixteenth century in association with civic and confessional values of Protestant reformers, and later with the increasing value placed on family relations by a reformed Catholic Church during the seventeenth century.[28]

Family foundations of confessional communities

Although views of the household as an important building block for the construction of urban communities were a familiar part of European urban and civic traditions by the sixteenth century, the activities of city governments and

[26] Davis, "Women in the Crafts," in Hanawalt, ed., *Women and Work*, 188.

[27] Martha C. Howell, "Citizenship and Gender: Women's Political Status in Northern Medieval Cities," in Mary Erler and Maryanne Kowaleski, eds., *Women and Power in the Middle Ages* (Athens, GA, 1988), 201–2.

[28] Jean-Louis Flandrin, *Families in Former Times: Kinship, Household, and Sexuality* (New York and Cambridge, 1979), 156–66.

certain religious bodies in this latter period revealed a rising ambition on the part of civic and religious leaders to shape the domestic lives of city dwellers. Although such intervention was not new, evidence suggests that the domestic and public behavior of ordinary citizens during this time became subject to increased scrutiny as confessional and civic authorities worked to teach and enforce standards of acceptable behavior.

Confessional and civic bodies of the period seem to have wished to inculcate the sort of peaceful behavior that late medieval confraternal groups required of their members, but with an increasing emphasis on individuals in their families and neighborhoods. Like many late medieval confraternities, the Church, consistory, and civic marriage courts that were instituted during the Reformation set themselves the task of overseeing the behavior of those whom they considered members. In the course of their duties, Calvinist consistories, civic courts in Lutheran areas, and church courts in England dealt with those sins of "aversion" that had long threatened ties of charity and sociability within families and neighborhoods. In addition, their increasing concern for domestic life led authorities to focus on at least public manifestations of sins of "concupiscence" that threatened family life and the larger civic and confessional order that was built upon it.[29] Although all areas touched by the Protestant Reformation experienced the growth of new courts regulating marriage, regions marked by the Calvinist brand of Reformed Protestantism seem to have been particularly affected by new agencies that sought to reform morals within the families of believers, and sometimes in the larger civic community as well.[30]

The Reformation in the imperial city of Augsburg brought with it the establishment in the 1530s of two lay institutions with jurisdiction over marriage and family life. These included the "Discipline Lords," who had the power to levy fines, imprisonment, and banishment for transgressions including violent behavior, fornication, and adultery; and the Marriage Court which adjudicated disputes over promises of marriage, the loss of virginity, child support, and divorce.[31] Although the Discipline Lords had the power of banishment and imprisonment, they, like members of the Marriage Court, carried out their mission mainly through admonition. In their goal of teaching proper behavior they had few guides in medieval canon law. While it did focus on marriage, canon law had no real interest in nor remedy for the sort of "disorderly marriages" that the Discipline Lords confronted daily. The new organizations therefore

[29] John Bossy, *Christianity in the West, 1400–1700* (New York and Oxford, 1985), 35, discusses this distinction between sins of the spirit and sins of the flesh, the former (including pride, envy, and anger) being particularly destructive of bonds of community.

[30] Lyndal Roper, *The Holy Household: Women and Morals in Reformation Augsburg* (Oxford and New York, 1989), 16–17.

[31] *Ibid.*, 61–9.

had to draw on a mixed repertoire of confessional piety, common sense, and their members' civic values to address the multiple domestic problems they faced.[32]

City fathers sitting on the Marriage Court sought to reinforce Augsburg's families using the values identified with the households of respectable guild members, including the subordination of wives to husbands and children to parents. They tried, for example, to enforce a family ethic that emphasized the virtue of gaining parental permission for marriage. However, their role was also to limit excesses of domestic discipline. The Marriage Court did not challenge husbands' right to "discipline" their wives, but prohibited excessive violence and affirmed that what went on within the household was very much the business of authorities now eager to enforce both civic and Lutheran confessional values.[33]

There were broad similarities between the concerns of Augsburg's Marriage Court and those of Calvinist consistories elsewhere. In their earliest years, the clergy and lay church officers who composed these local church bodies were mainly concerned to enforce Calvinist religious tenets while eradicating other loyalties, whether Catholic or Lutheran. But beyond trying to inculcate and enforce the theological teachings and rules of their newly emerging confession, Calvinist consistories were also presented with a variety of domestic and community issues for their resolution, ranging from ruling on the validity of certain promises of marriage, to resolving problems between wives and husbands, parents and children, households and neighbors.

Calvinist authorities in Nîmes' consistory were initially concerned mainly with extirpating lingering Catholic practices, regulating sexual behavior, resolving questions relating to marriage vows, and resolving disputes among members of the confessional community. On the issue of marriage, the consistory here was particularly eager to ensure that parental consent for marriage was given for women under 25 and men under 30.[34] It also used church members to effect mutual reconciliation among quarreling neighbors. As in Augsburg, minor sins such as card-playing and dancing brought on a "tongue-lashing." More serious

[32] Martin Ingram makes the same point about the work of the church courts in England in a slightly later period. See *Church Courts, Sex and Marriage in England, 1570–1640* (New York and Cambridge, 1987), 142.

[33] Roper, *Holy Household*, 169–71.

[34] Legislation requiring parental consent for marriage was a product of the Reformation in many areas, though the age of majority varied. See J. Estèbe and B. Vogler, "La Genèse d'une société protestante: étude comparée de quelques registres consistoriaux languedociens et palatins vers 1600," *Annales, ESC* 31, 2 (1976): 376; Thomas M. Safley, "Civic Morality and the Domestic Economy," in R. Po-Chia Hsia, ed., *The German People and the Reformation* (Ithaca, NY, 1988), 176; Manon van der Heijden, "Secular and Ecclesiastical Marriage Control: Rotterdam, 1550–1700," in Anton Schuurman and Pieter Spierenburg, eds., *Private Domain, Public Inquiry: Families and Lifestyles in the Netherlands and Europe, 1550 to the Present* (Hilversum, 1996), 42, fn. 15.

offenses led to the consistory's censure, their requirement of public penance, or finally excommunication for fornication, apostasy, and "other outrageous acts."[35]

In Calvinist Geneva, the supervision of community and family life required the consistory to become involved in a similar variety of problems that were either referred to them by neighbors or ferreted out by deacons or other officials of church and civic community. Errors that included deviations from Calvinist practice, lack of respect for secular officials, conflicts between neighbors, or adulterous behavior that had become public knowledge, all qualified as fit subjects for consideration by church consistories. Unlike secular courts, which could and did mete out mutilation and capital punishments, the consistory mainly cajoled and admonished the errant, giving severe tongue lashings for recidivists and reserving their harshest penalty of excommunication for the most intransigent.[36]

The population of Geneva was subjected to a high level of scrutiny in the 1560s, when an estimated 7 percent of the city's population was called in annually by the consistory to answer charges. Excommunication took place in over half of the cases it heard: an atypically high figure when compared to consistories in other areas. However, excommunication, which meant the exclusion of the offender from communion, was nearly always temporary. Those willing to express penitence publicly in church were readmitted to the confessional community. The admonitions of the Genevan Consistory, which Robert Kingdon has described as a "remarkably intrusive institution" on matters related to marital discord, seem to have had some effect, however, since recidivism rates here were quite low.[37]

There has been some disagreement on how and whether Calvinist consistories were more active than other local judicial or police institutions in intervening into domestic life. In his comparative study of Catholic and Calvinist areas of the Rhineland Palatinate, Joel Harrington found that, while there was little difference between the two areas in the proclivity of civil magistrates to intervene in family matters, Calvinist consistories engaged more actively in regulating

---

[35] Raymond A. Mentzer, Jr., "*Disciplina nervus ecclesiae*: The Calvinist Reform of Morals at Nîmes," *Sixteenth Century Journal* 18, 1 (1987): 111.

[36] Robert M. Kingdon notes that earlier published studies on the consistory of Geneva focused on exceptional and notorious cases. A more systematic sample yields a portrait of the Geneva consistory from the 1530s to 1560s as mainly a "compulsory counseling service" (8). See Kingdon, "Calvin and the Family: The Work of the Consistory of Geneva," *Pacific Theological Review* 17 (1984): 5–18. See also E. William Monter, "The Consistory of Geneva, 1559–1569," *Bibliothèque d'humanisme et Renaissance* 38, 3 (1976): 467–84. Monter, cited in Mentzer, Jr., "*Disciplina*," 112, estimated that at least 1 in 12 adults in Geneva, or 300 per annum were excommunicated, though nearly all of these were temporary. Ingram saw little "counseling" in the English church court setting. See *Church Courts*, 188.

[37] Robert M. Kingdon, *Adultery and Divorce in Calvin's Geneva* (Cambridge, MA, 1995), 180.

domestic life. Indeed, he notes that at least one consistory there brought a "striking sophistication in its approach to marital strife."[38]

It does not seem that overworked consistory members, the majority of whom were generally laymen, aggressively searched out matters to consider, however.[39] In most cases, consistories summoned church members to appear before them only when neighbors became aware of domestic troubles, scandal had become public knowledge, or persistent rumors reached the ears of the consistory, whose members routinely made home visits to members of their congregations. Similarly, though conversations between the consistory and church members who had been summoned before them were themselves private, punishments that they meted out were frequently public, whether between individual men and women, among neighbors, or before entire congregations.

Calvinist consistories' emphasis on public expressions of penitence and atonement seems rather consistent across time and space, especially in cases where those who had been excommunicated were requesting reintegration into the community. Thus, one woman whom the Nîmes consistory had excommunicated and who requested that she be allowed to participate in a ceremony of penitence at a 5 a.m. Sunday religious service rather than the 9 a.m. service was denied her request.[40] On the other hand, though Calvinist consistories saw themselves as fully entitled to summon individuals or couples to answer for domestic behavior that violated confessional norms against fornication or adultery, there were certain areas of privacy that interested them relatively little. From all accounts, an appearance before a Calvinist consistory was relatively unlikely to probe the inner workings of individuals' private consciences, and more apt to concentrate on the need for individuals to modify their behavior towards family members or neighbors. Consistories' concern to modify domestic behavior that sometimes literally spilled out into public, or that had obvious negative public consequences, thus contrasted sharply with the intense probing of individual conscience and private penitential regime that increasingly prevailed in the Catholic confessional of the sixteenth and seventeenth centuries.[41]

---

[38] Joel F. Harrington, *Reordering Marriage and Society in Reformation Germany* (New York and Cambridge, 1995), 263. Harrington is more skeptical about the definitive nature of the behavioral changes that consistories were able to effect, noting (though not statistically) that many couples were recidivists, especially those in which domestic violence was the cause of their original summoning.

[39] Harrington suggests that the aggressiveness of Calvinist consistories has been exaggerated. He cites their hesitancy to intervene into household affairs unless constrained by the need to suppress what were public scandals. *Ibid.*, 249–51.

[40] Mentzer, Jr., "*Disciplina*," 112.

[41] *Ibid.*, 113–14. See also his reference to a judicial official summoned before the consistory to answer charges of sexual misconduct. Having gone through one appearance before the consistory, he refused to return for a second, expressing his preference for auricular confession over the pastor's "harsh admonitions" (95). Roper, *Holy Household*, makes the same distinction, 64–5.

Although Calvinist consistories could in principle order disciplinary measures only for church members, in many instances they attempted to exert control over the larger urban community, for example by trying to urge magistrates to enforce restrictions on activities during the Sabbath.[42] Moreover, in areas where the Calvinist Church had some claims to public support, those of the "house poor" who received assistance from church coffers were expected to conform to behavioral norms of congregation members. As in many cities of Holland, in Nîmes the Calvinist consistory supervised distributions of bread to all of the town's resident poor, not just members of the Church. Along with their bread, the poor received a "strong dose of moral guidance and social discipline."[43]

Interestingly, though consistorial regulation in Nîmes and other Calvinist cities often met with grumbling and only grudging compliance among people on the margins of Calvinist congregations, the poor did not necessarily reject the principle of church discipline itself. Indeed, in Emden, some of those receiving poor relief from the Calvinist congregation actually criticized the Church's consistory because of its relative laxity when compared to more exacting standards of conduct required by the rival Anabaptist congregation![44]

Resistance to efforts to correct behavior resulted from causes ranging from apathy and religious heterodoxy to anger at the violation of personal dignity that an appearance before a consistory could entail. In areas of the Empire where Calvinism was instituted or recently reinstituted, as was the case with the Rhineland Palatinate after 1584, lingering Lutheran sympathies among the common people led to the heckling of Calvinist preachers during sermons, general rowdiness during worship, and a widespread failure to attend the growing number of required prayer and catechetical meetings that took place outside regular worship times.[45] Huguenots of Languedoc, for their part, had notions of personal honor that meant that consistories often had to summon individuals several times in order to exact their appearance. A certain lay skepticism over the authority of the entire consistorial system, with its lay elders, encouraged reluctant Calvinists here to resist the consistory's efforts to regulate relations inside the family and wider urban community.[46]

---

[42] Heinz Schilling notes important variations in the level of power of different consistories to intervene in the families of those who were not church members. See Schilling, "Reform and Supervision of Family Life in Germany and the Netherlands," in Raymond A. Mentzer, Jr., ed., *Sin and the Calvinists: Morals Control and the Consistory in the Reformed Tradition* (Kirksville, MO, 1994), 15–61.

[43] Raymond A. Menzter, Jr., "Organizational Endeavour and Charitable Impulse in Sixteenth-Century France: The Case of Protestant Nîmes," *French History* 5, 1 (1991): 1–29.

[44] Andrew Pettegree, *Emden and the Dutch Revolt: Exile and the Development of Reformed Protestantism* (Oxford and New York, 1992), 236.

[45] Estèbe and Vogler, "La Genèse d'une société protestante," 371–2.

[46] *Ibid.*, 385.

Men at the top of the social hierarchy were particularly difficult to bring to order. In Calvinist Scotland, the Presbyterian kirk sessions (the equivalent of continental consistories) encountered little resistance to their authority of the kind found in the Palatinate. Yet even they found it difficult to exert their authority over powerful men, particularly in matters of sexual promiscuity that had led to public scandal. Kirk sessions were prepared to adjust the requirement of public penance into penalties more in keeping with the gentry's need to save face in the community. One 1585 case of fornication called forth a punishment rather different from the sort imposed upon the lowly. Confessing his sin to the kirk session, the Provost of Elgin nonetheless argued that "repentance consistit not in the external gestoir of the bodie ... but in the hart." Despite this astonishing theology, he was allowed to contribute to the repair of a church window instead of making a public penitential appearance.[47]

Although consistories and church courts were not able to enforce compliance in the same way as secular courts, and were hardly able to enforce it at all on the geographically mobile, the threat or reality of excommunication from Calvinist congregations apparently meant a great deal to the more residentially stable householders and church members. For the less committed, the power of consistories or church courts might affect one's entitlements to assistance. Thus, both the workings of poor relief systems targeting the house poor and the relatively widespread acceptance of church discipline suggest that those who wished to be members of the confessional community or to remain within boundaries of the civic one gradually accepted a tighter scrutiny of their domestic lives. Indeed, many had little choice if they wished to remain within town walls.

Individual, family, and community power in the Protestant Reformation

Considered in different times and places, and from multiple points of view, the activities of Reformation-era confessional bodies and lay magistratures seem alternatively to have signaled the increasing authority of communities over families, of parents over their adult children, and individuals over their own lives and consciences when it came to marriage.

Noting the "unresolved tension" that characterized these competing and mutually contradictory impacts of the Protestant Reformation on relationships

---

[47] Rosalind Mitchison and Leah Leneman, *Sexuality and Social Control: Scotland 1660–1780* (Oxford and New York, 1989), 74–5, 237. Ingram, *Church Courts*, 336, suggests that English ecclesiastical courts believed that "it was not necessarily in the interests of public order to expose leading citizens to shame and humiliation," and sometimes permitted punishments to be paid in cash.

linking individuals, families and their wider communities, Thomas Safley has provided an interesting example of their interaction.[48] He shows how the city councils in a number of free imperial cities, which had long enjoyed relatively high levels of autonomy, sought to gain even greater control over laws regulating marriage in order to preserve the integrity of the civic community as a whole. Magistrates exercised their authority over marriage in a number of ways. In Strasbourg, the council made laws prohibiting the marriages of servants who in their judgment had inadequate funds to support a viable household. Conversely, like authorities in many late medieval cities, they tried to encourage marriages among the city's citizen families, and dowered poor respectable girls who would otherwise have been unable to marry. Strasbourg officials also extended the historic practice of its guilds in overseeing marriages of their members, requiring all young couples of the town to make available to them clauses of their marriage contracts.

City magistrates here also tried to control the impact that new Lutheran-inspired laws permitting divorce had on families and the larger civic community. While laws permitting divorce were thought to be desirable in allowing individuals to end unhappy unions, this aspect of the city's new confession threatened the elaborate property settlements of Strasbourg's wealthier families. The council therefore adopted new laws affecting divorce proceedings that empowered it to divide up spouses' community property according to its own estimation of the guilty party in the dispute. Parents reacted to this legislation by sharply reducing the proportion of brides' and grooms' property assigned to "community property" status in the marriage contract. Instead, they increased the proportion of family property that would remain under the control of their own child so that brides and grooms now became "trustees" of property they acquired from their families of birth.

In this instance, a law that increased the power of community officials over family matters led to the defensive reaction of parents, who became increasingly concerned to protect the property interests of both their adult children and the larger family group. Yet such legislation and the parental reaction to it also enhanced brides' and grooms' individual control over a larger proportion of the property each brought to the marriage. Finally, to make things even more complicated, at the same time as the Strasbourg City Council was enforcing civic patriarchal controls over marriage, divorce laws represented at least in principle an increasing civic and confessional accommodation to men's and women's individual consciences in choosing whether to maintain the marriage bonds they had contracted. For although consistories and secular courts in all Protestant areas worked hard to discourage divorce, and studies show that it was

[48] Safley, "Civic Morality," in Hsia, ed., *The German People*, 180–1, 189.

extremely rare during the sixteenth and seventeenth centuries, the principle of divorce was nevertheless admitted.[49]

Interestingly, while the tendency has been to see confessional and secular manifestations of patriarchal power emerging during the Reformation era as mutually reinforcing, here the patriarchal power that civic officials wielded was not always coordinated with literal patriarchal authority within the family. In Strasbourg, the interests of city "fathers" eager to assert the legitimacy of civic control over marriage relations were not necessarily synonymous with their own interests as fathers of actual households and families.

A variety of beliefs and practices also kept the Discipline Lords and Marriage Court of Augsburg from becoming consistent defenders of a patriarchal status quo. As in most areas affected by Reformation-era Marriage Courts, adultery on the part of husbands was treated with much the same seriousness as adultery on the part of the wife.[50] Moreover, the courts' sheer ability to intervene in domestic life often had different effects from a simple validation or reinforcement of patriarchal authority within the household. Although authorities tried to serve as mediators in many disputes between husbands and wives, the official status of the Discipline Lords and Marriage Court made their intervention quite different from the informal intervention of neighbors. As Lyndal Roper has observed: "The household became a sphere of public-official concern; quarrels were breaches of the civic peace; and husbands had to justify their beatings of their wives, explaining their exercise of authority."[51]

Lest consistories or discipline courts be seen as nothing more than vehicles of social control by powerful elites, it is clear that Augsburgers with marital problems also sought out the courts for their own reasons, not simply to end abusive relationships. Since grounds for divorce in the city included only adultery and desertion, the fact that men and women brought cases of physical abuse before the Marriage Court suggested that they sought to use the new institution mainly to change their spouses' behavior. In many instances, those who brought cases before the Marriage Court were trying to use its authority and sanctions mainly as a means of "redrawing" their marital relationship.[52] Far from rejecting the legitimacy of the regulation afforded by these new institutions, the people of the city seem to have found them sometimes useful as means for resolving family problems.

---

[49] *Ibid.*, 177–81, 189. He notes (182) that Zurich was an exception on this score, with 207 cases of divorce being brought in 1525–31.

[50] The suspension of the sexual double standard was identified with the most militant days of the Reformation in Geneva 1560s and 1570s. See Monter, "Women in Calvinist Geneva," *Signs*, 192.

[51] Roper, *Holy Household*, 193, 205. Roper suggests how "fragile" patriarchal authority seemed to be.

[52] *Ibid.*, 170.

Similarly, though Protestant consistories were hardly progressive in the modern sense of equalizing relations between children and their parents, or wives and husbands, evidence suggests that in addition to supporting the entitlement of parents to be apprised of the marriages of their children, consistorial officials also made efforts to curb excesses of paternal authority when fathers or parents refused permission for their children to marry. Rotterdam's consistory even arrogated to itself the right to grant permission for minors to marry in situations where it believed that parents were unreasonably withholding their consent.[53]

Evidence thus suggests contradictory conclusions about the impact of Reformation-era consistories and church courts on the individual, family, and community relationship. On the one hand, courts and consistories sought to reinforce the power of community authority, whether confessional or civic, over marriage and family life. They often sought to maintain the patriarchal status quo involving the power of husbands over wives and parents over children. Yet they also enforced limits on that authority. In matters of divorce, these organizations seem to have enhanced (albeit reluctantly) the power of individual young men and women over marriage arrangements.

The practices of church courts, civic courts, and consistories can alternatively be seen as essentially repressive institutions for the imposition of confessional and civic values that may well have been foreign to the households of the poor and marginal. On the other hand, sources show that urban dwellers, sometimes the most subordinate, often tried to use them to help resolve problems within their households and extended families.

In the face of such different possible interpretations of the main effects of Protestant confessional development on individual, family, and community relations in urban Europe in the sixteenth century, several things seem clear. Efforts to build civic and confessional communities drew upon older traditions of urban regulation and an ethos linking the household and family to the security of the urban social order. The decline in women's relative position in urban labor markets helped reinforce the new emphasis placed upon their domestic roles. Finally, the addition of newer visions of confessional communities gave new life to the belief that authorities outside the family had not only the right but the obligation to intervene and regulate domestic life.

The notion that civic communities were practically and morally founded upon well-ordered households and families emerged with new vigor in the sixteenth

---

[53] Van der Heijden, "Secular and Ecclesiastical Marriage Control," 56; Harrington, *Reordering Marriage*, 199, which disputes Lawrence Stone's and Steven Ozment's characterization of this period as entailing the growth of patriarchy in both legislation and practice. Mitchison and Leneman, *Sexuality*, 94–5, cite a number of cases in which kirk sessions approved a marriage when they believed paternal objections unreasonable. From the other direction, Mentzer cites a case in which a young woman's obstinate refusal to marry a man of her father's choosing resulted in her excommunication. See *"Disciplina,"* 100. Balancing the claims of individuals and family authority was the task of English Church courts. See Ingram, *Church Courts*, 211.

century in part because of its compatibility with religious ideals associated with the Protestant Reformation, including the abolition of clerical celibacy and corresponding advocacy of marriage, and a new emphasis on the household as a locus of worship and prayers.[54] As Lyndal Roper demonstrated, the notion of a "holy household" was also inspired by a "guild" mentality, emphasizing the subordination of wives to husbands and women's devotion to domestic work that was strongly differentiated from the work of their husbands.[55]

It should be noted, however, that much of the emphasis that religious and lay authorities increasingly placed on married women's place within the home seems to have been less concerned with consigning women to a private sphere removed from public life than to ensuring their workfulness in the household. In the course of his own homely musings about women and marriage, Martin Luther contrasted the workfulness of married women with the idleness he imagined among the celibate and cloistered. Moreover, as in the past, Protestant confessional leaders emphasized that married women's obligations extended to the communities beyond their households. Luther followed his argument that "a woman is not created to be a virgin, but to conceive and bear children" by his reflection that "if a girl must do something she dislikes and that gives her no joy, it is better that she do it in the estate of marriage, where she at least serves her fellow man, that is, her husband, children, servants, and neighbors."[56] The household thus appeared ideally as the main but not the sole focus of married women's work, backed up by the knowledge that work responsibilities often spilled beyond the domestic sphere and extended into the life of the Church and larger community.[57] It is therefore not surprising that conversions to Protestantism among urban women in sixteenth-century France included many of the

---

[54] Steven E. Ozment, *When Fathers Ruled: Family Life in Reformation Europe* (Cambridge, MA, 1983); Merry Wiesner, "Women's Response to the Reformation," in Hsia, ed., *The German People*, 148–71; Scott Hendrix, "Luther on Marriage," *Lutheran Quarterly* 14, 3 (2000): 335–50.

[55] On the convergence of pro-family and pro-household values from a variety of social classes and values during the sixteenth century, see Heide Wunder, "Gender Norms and their Enforcement in Early Modern Germany," in Lynn Abrams and Elizabeth Harvey, eds., *Gender Relations in German History: Power, Agency and Experience from the Sixteenth to the Twentieth Century* (Durham, NC, 1997), 43–6.

[56] On the Protestant rehabilitation of marriage and rejection of clerical celibacy, see Ozment, *When Fathers Ruled*, 1–25. Luther's pronouncement cited here is found on 17, fn. 74. Cf. Allison P. Coudert, "The Myth of the Improved Status of Protestant Women: The Case of the Witchcraze," in Jean R. Brink, Allison P. Coudert, and Mary Anne Horowitz, eds., *Politics of Gender in Early Modern Europe* (Kirksville, MO, 1989), 61–89, which emphasizes the misogynistic and patriarchal features of Protestant social ideology.

[57] Even sixteenth-century Spanish prescriptive literature for pious wives, which could not have drawn the same distinction as Luther between lives of women religious and married women, emphasized the virtues of married women's work in the domestic sphere more than the woman's "seclusion." See Carmen Sarasúa, "The Role of the State in Shaping Women's and Men's Entrance into the Labour Market: Spain in the Eighteenth and Nineteenth Centuries," *Continuity and Change* 12, 3 (1997): 352–3, 355. On the tension between the rhetoric of enclosure and the reality of women's lives in family and the streets, see Perry, *Gender*, 6, 13, 68, 179.

middling ranks who had work-related identities independent of their husbands' occupations and spent much of their days engaged in productive activities outside their own homes.[58]

Of course, neither the ideal nor the reality of women's "workfulness" in the home was limited to Protestant towns and cities of the sixteenth century. A case study of the families of Nantes' notarial bourgeoisie in the seventeenth century shows the central importance of the values of *bon mesnagement* (good order, or good management). The increasingly self-conscious "family values" of the French urban bourgeoisie, like those of Augsburg's guild members, suggested that women and men both gained status in family and larger community through their obedience to ideals of *bon mesnagement*, which dictated that married women as well as men be hard-working. Although married women of this milieu generally employed female servants, they themselves worked long hours both within the household and outside it as well, often supervising agricultural tasks such as grape harvests in family landholdings near the city. They also participated in their husbands' notarial work in the absence of a paid clerk, and sometimes spun flax to earn cash for household expenses. Men's and women's work was highly differentiated, yet domestic ideals of *bon mesnagement* applied to both genders.[59]

The community lives of lay women: early modern "maternalism" and outreach to the poor

Girls' early training in the importance of work within the home was an important source of their later identity in the more public world of the city. As in Protestant cities such as Amsterdam where women played important public "maternalist" roles in assistance to the young, religious revival in Catholic Europe of the sixteenth and early seventeenth centuries renewed earlier maternalist traditions of service to the poor. The confessionalization of Catholic Europe led to a growing participation of women in outreach to the poor in both civic and confessional organizations, helping to ensure their presence in a number of community-building projects of the period.

Although all confessional groups of the sixteenth and seventeenth centuries used poor relief to invent or reinvent networks of familiarity between rich and poor that were viewed as essential to the construction of solid communities, there seem to have been some differences between Protestant and Catholic

---

[58] Natalie Zemon Davis, "City Women and Religious Change," in *Society and Culture in Early Modern France* (Stanford, 1975), 80–1.

[59] Julie Hardwick, *The Practice of Patriarchy: Gender and the Politics of Household Authority in Early Modern France* (University Park, PA, 1998), 84–100. For a discussion of these same domestic ideals, see Robert Jütte, "Household and Family Life in Late Sixteenth-Century Cologne: The Weinsberg Family," *Sixteenth Century Journal* 17, 2 (Summer, 1986): 165–82.

areas. As the discussion in Chapter 3 suggested, Protestant leaders seem to have focused almost exclusively on the "house poor" or the "respectable poor." Married women of the urban bourgeoisie were central to these kinds of efforts, particularly involving children.

In keeping with earlier traditions, however, poor relief programs of the towns and cities of Catholic Europe during the sixteenth and seventeenth centuries continued to target the marginal poor while also paying new attention to the civic poor as well. There was some division of labor here by gender, however, with men being more likely to participate in activities involving educational or training programs with the "able-bodied poor," while women carried out missions especially to the house poor and the sick.[60]

Like Protestant women, Catholic laywomen of the upper and middling ranks brought their organizational skills as well as their religious commitments to bear on the creation of confessional residential institutions that brought them face-to-face with the poor. Indeed, the institutionalization of the poor in controlled residential environments proved to be especially critical in bringing these women face-to-face with the marginal poor whom they hoped to convert, catechize, and care for.

The Catholic Reformation's goal of rebuilding its own confessional community by encouraging face-to-face charitable relations between rich and poor helped reinforce the appeal of institutions where this sort of contact could take place. The idea of "enclosing" the poor and helping to transform them into productive subjects was inspired by new Dutch institutions such as the workhouse. However, the proliferation of large residential institutions such as the general hospital was more characteristic of Catholic than Protestant cities.[61] Indeed, these large residential institutions represented the most ambitious expression of an effort to inculcate new religious values among the poor, within the "total discipline of a closed institution." With their conventual atmosphere, the hospitals provided one of the settings for implementing a new form of confessional charity "whose highest ideals lay in self-sanctification through heroic personal service to the poor, rather than in the acquisition of merit through casual or impersonal almsgiving."[62]

Although arguments defending the forced institutionalization of the vagrant poor were primarily economic in the period up to the 1640s, resonating with

---

[60] Elizabeth Rapley, *The Dévotes: Women and Church in Seventeenth-Century France* (Montreal and Buffalo, 1990), 77.

[61] On the Dutch influence on ideas of enclosing the poor, see Jean-Pierre Gutton, *La Société et les pauvres: l'exemple de la généralité de Lyon, 1534–1789* (Paris, 1971), 325, 338, 378.

[62] Brian S. Pullan, "The Counter-Reformation, Medical Care and Poor Relief," in Ole Peter Grell and Andrew Cunningham with Jon Arrizabalaga, eds., *Health Care and Poor Relief in Counter-Reformation Europe* (London and New York, 1999), 27. Pullan identifies catechetical training, proof of attendance at mass, or attendance at schools of Christian doctrine as the preferred forms of evidence the poor could furnish of their religious conformity.

the goal of "social control," after this date the defense of residential institutions such as the general hospitals was waged mainly on moral grounds by some of the most militant lay spokesmen for reformed Catholic values. Members of the Company of the Holy Sacrament, a secret male organization devoted to the conversion or reconversion of the poor, pressed hard for and participated actively in the establishment of general hospitals in France, for example. A Royal Edict of 1656 establishing the General Hospital in Paris bore the imprint of the Company's ideology which focused, among other missions, on the need to "save the poor who were living together out of wedlock, [living] nearly always in ignorance of religion, disdain for the sacraments, and in continuous habits of all sorts of vices."[63]

Members of the Company also believed that the religious conversion of the poor was critical for another more practical reason involving relations between rich and poor. The poor, once converted, would be more likely than the "dishonorable" poor to arouse the sympathy of charitably minded people who would find them meritorious enough to assist. Without this conversion, life for the dishonorable poor on the margins of society, filled as it was with so many elements of disorder, would continue to alienate all but the most charitably minded Counter-Reformation militants.[64]

In a number of cities, upper- and middle-class women became involved in charitable work within the general hospitals or older hôtels-Dieu. In Lyon, upper-class women organized themselves into charitable confraternities such as the Société des dames hospitalières, who visited the poor and sick in the Hôtel-Dieu, bringing material and spiritual aid and enjoying wide leeway in their interactions with the personnel of the establishment.[65] Alternatively, new confraternities of wealthy laywomen sometimes created their own hospitals or hospices for the reformation of penitent prostitutes or for orphans. In these sorts of institutions, women enforced a sense of their own "maternal" authority over inmates. Laywomen who worked to reform the morals of prostitutes placed in the hospice of the Madeleines in Grenoble were strict in dealing with their charges, seeing themselves as "perfect mothers to the poor."[66]

The latter years of the seventeenth century were difficult ones economically for many parts of France, including the city of Grenoble which was much affected by two wars fought against the neighboring Kingdom of Savoy. These years witnessed a growth in women's involvement with the local or parish poor and with further institutional developments. The donations of five women, and the support of other city residents, led to the initiation in 1676 of the city's

---

[63] The Edict of 1656 creating the General Hospital of Paris, cited in Gutton, *La Société*, 325–6.
[64] Gutton, *La Société*, 326.
[65] *Ibid.*, 371–2. This society had originated in the city in the sixteenth century.
[66] Kathryn Norberg, *Rich and Poor in Grenoble, 1600–1814* (Berkeley, 1985), 26. Brothers of the Company of the Holy Sacrament, likewise, viewed themselves as "fathers of the poor" (64).

small Hospital of the Providence.[67] Women of Grenoble who made wills also left traces of their connections with confraternal organizations by favoring local religious houses that had confraternities open to women. Clearly, many women who participated in charitable outreach to the poor sought out these confraternal organizations for a level of spiritual engagement not possible in their parish churches.[68] Similarly, upper-class women in Spain were also involved in trying to establish face-to-face relationships with poor women. In Seville, a group of them worked to create new institutions such as small hospitals, often set up in the homes of wealthy donors.[69] To be sure, these female institution builders maintained their authority on the bases of their own wealth and social power, which enhanced their "maternal" power over the dependents who dwelt in these residential institutions.

The seventeenth century also witnessed the growth of new confraternal organizations of wealthy women, such as the French Dames de la miséricorde or Dames de la charité, who visited the sick in hospitals or in their homes.[70] Inspired by the work of Vincent de Paul, these organizations had originally been conceived as confraternities of laywomen who would visit the poor in their own homes. The original model envisaged rural women of modest means constituting the principal members of this new sort of outward-looking confraternity. However, amidst the militant outreach and missionary efforts of the Catholic Reformation, the appeal of this charitable model quickly spread to urban areas, where it aroused the support of upper-class and bourgeois women.

The involvement of upper-class women in the Dames de la charité was both devotional and charitable. In the region of Franche-Comté, the Dames de la charité who visited the poor in their homes were mainly involved in distributing food.[71] In Paris, where the women of the court nobility rapidly flocked to join the Dames de la charité, the high status of the members created an insuperable barrier to establishing face-to-face relations with the local house poor. How could high-born women be expected to enter the homes of the poor, however respectable, to establish the face-to-face contacts between rich and poor required to build a reformed Catholic community?

As noted in Chapter 3, the wealthy confraternities of men in Venice had faced the same dilemma. Members of the Scuole Grandi had gotten used to delegating charitable visits to the civic poor to poorer members of the company

---

[67] Norberg, *Rich and Poor*, 83.   [68] *Ibid.*, 252.   [69] Perry, *Gender*, 24.

[70] The confraternity of the Dames de la charité was founded in 1617 by Vincent de Paul, with its first local organization in Châtillon-les-Dombes in the Lyonnais. See Colin Jones, "Hospitals in Seventeenth-Century France," in *The Charitable Imperative: Hospitals and Nursing in Ancien Regime and Revolutionary France* (London and New York, 1989), 38. A Paris group was founded in 1634.

[71] Hazel Mills, "La Charité est une mère: Catholic Women and Poor Relief in France, 1690–1850," in Hugh Cunningham and Joanna Innes, eds., *Charity, Philanthropy, and Reform: From the 1690s to 1850* (New York, 1998), 171–2.

who acted as their agents. Members of male confraternities in Spain had also faced this dilemma but in a slightly different way. Here, upper-class men often arrived at the homes of the poor with a retinue of their retainers.[72] For their part, members of the Dames de la charité in Paris tried to resolve the problem in the same way, by turning over the responsibility of home visits to their servants, a solution that nonetheless violated the "heroic" charitable ideals that Vincent and his collaborators were advocating.

Difficulties that upper-class women encountered in carrying out home visits to the poor or their sheer reluctance to do so helped inspire the founding of the Filles de la charité in 1633 by Vincent and several of his female collaborators, including Louise de Marillac.[73] Local associations of these single women of modest means that were organized to carry out charitable work among the poor were initially linked tightly to the Dames de la charité, but gradually grew increasingly independent of them.

The Filles de la charité were organized into simple associations or "congregations" of women who, like earlier beguines or women penitents living in "open" monasteries, did not require solemn perpetual vows and were therefore exempt from the requirement of strict cloister.[74] Members wore identifiable somber dress and sometimes chose to live in residential communities, generally becoming involved in parish-level charitable activities such as caring for the sick, making medicines, and giving religious counsel.[75] The Filles were gradually recruited into the care of the poor in small as well as larger general hospitals, a development that nonetheless also ran counter to Vincent's original desire to minister to the poor in their own homes.[76]

Contact between the upper-class Dames de la charité and the Filles de la charité, who increasingly did the actual work of caring for the poor, persisted in hospital institutions where the Filles served as nurses and in the provision of outdoor aid to the parish poor in their homes. Although the Filles became

---

[72] Linda Martz, *Poverty and Welfare in Habsburg Spain: The Example of Toledo* (New York and Cambridge, 1983), 29.

[73] Colin Jones, "Vincent de Paul, Louise de Marillac, and the Revival of Nursing in the Seventeenth Century," in *The Charitable Imperative*, 89–121.

[74] Rapley, *The Dévotes*, 83, 187, on the peasant and artisanal backgrounds of the Filles de la charité. The Filles were placed under the ultimate authority of Vincent de Paul's Mission Fathers rather than bishops. Patricia Ranft, *Women and the Religious Life in Premodern Europe* (New York, 1996), 121, notes that the Filles were treated like "diocesan confraternities" rather than religious orders in order to avoid strict cloister.

[75] Rapley, *The Dévotes*, 87–8.

[76] Its leader wrote: "What will become of the work of the Dames de la Charité . . . if their patients are forced to go to the hospital? . . . the worthy poor will be deprived of the help that they receive from prepared food and remedies, and the little bit of money that they get now will no longer be available for their needs." Quoted in Rapley, *The Dévotes*, 90. On the role of the Filles in parish-based charitable programs, see Josseline Guyader, "Bureau et maisons de charité: l'assistance à domicile aux 'pauvres malades' dans le cadre des paroisses toulousaines (1687–1797)," *Revue d'histoire de l'Eglise de France* 80, 205 (July–December, 1994): 217–47.

increasingly autonomous from local groups of Dames de la charité, gaining the right to sign their own contracts for their services, for example, they continued to interact with the socially prominent women who engaged in voluntary hospital work and sometimes supervised Filles who had contracted with various parishes to visit the poor in their homes.

The failure of many upper-class women to become true foot soldiers in charitable outreach to the poor in their homes, and the growth of more professional efforts to do so by women of the lower classes, did not mean that women's participation in poor relief became completely professionalized. In many cities, women of the middling ranks of society did participate in outdoor relief to the "respectable" poor in their parishes either through new parish confraternities or through regular administrative organs of the parish itself.

Parish confraternities grew more popular and active in Paris as well as provincial cities such as Lyon during the second half of the seventeenth century, involving laywomen in the instruction and catechization of the local poor. During their home visits, they inquired about the moral life of adults and children and about children's attendance at religious instruction and first communion, making careful notes of their conversations in registers of the parish companies.[77] These notes and other records from urban parishes during the seventeenth century provide a glimpse into the multifaceted relationships between women's charitable activities, their intervention into the homes of the poor, and the process of confessional community building in a large city.

Although they never served as full churchwardens or members of parish vestries, seventeenth- and eighteenth-century women played a critical part in the public organizational life of urban parishes. By the early eighteenth century, the most religiously rigorous parishes in Paris – those identified with the Jansenist movement – were also those most likely to have women treasurers, who often wielded administrative authority over most of the parish's poor relief funds and through their offices gained seats *ex officio* in parishes' *assemblées de charité*.

Churchwardens or *commissaires des pauvres* had the authority to make decisions about the distribution of alms and other kinds of assistance to the local domiciled poor, and to decide, for example, which poor young women of the parish might receive contributions towards their dowry. Female church treasurers also assisted poor women by writing letters on their behalf to government authorities. Through these offices, urban women of the middling ranks also figured importantly in maintaining neighborhood networks of assistance. Their focus on the local respectable poor led them into ongoing relations with a network of elderly women and widows with small children whose homes they visited and whom they supplied with assistance in the form of sewing supplies

---

[77] Gutton, *La Société*, 375–7.

and cash alms.[78] The facts that the parish officer was herself of middling rank and the poor she assisted were chosen from among the respectable poor made these home visits and face-to-face contacts more manageable.

Although the sort of spiritual education that women activists of the Parisian parishes meted out to the house poor of their neighborhoods was probably more muted than the religious admonitions to prostitutes or other social outcasts living in the general hospitals of late-sixteenth- and early-seventeenth-century France, women in charge of eighteenth-century Parisian parish funds were not above excluding women from assistance who failed to conform to their ideals of proper mothering or housekeeping.[79]

Women of the urban middling classes were also attracted to religious service as members of female "third orders," which enjoyed a renewal during the Catholic Reformation. A crisis of membership in these sorts of organizations threatened, however, when papal policy sought to enforce strict cloister for women religious of all kinds, including members of third orders. Following the Council of Trent (1545–63), the Church issued two constitutions, in 1566 and 1568, in which Pope Pius V ordered monasteries to observe the strict isolation of their members from the outside world, and all laywomen members of third orders to accept strict cloister or disband. Over time, the papacy mitigated the effects of these rulings on men by allowing new orders such as the Jesuits to live in regular communities while pursuing activities in the world. The same was not generally the case for women religious.[80] However, this ruling's enforcement depended entirely on the disposition of bishops and archbishops. Whereas in France the rule of strict cloister seems to have been well enforced, it was not the case in the Spanish Netherlands or Italy, where nuns pursuing an "active" vocation continued to be tolerated or even encouraged in some dioceses.[81]

In parts of southern Europe, groups of pious laywomen known as *beatas* sought to pursue an active vocation in the world by avoiding solemn vows. They lived alone, with their families, or in small residential communities, often serving as nurses for the sick and poor. Like late medieval beguines, they were usually recognizable by their somber garb. Their charitable work was generally integrated into the life of local parish churches, and seems to have been appreciated by urban governments. Compared to other single women, *beatas* in Seville,

---

[78] David Garrioch, *The Formation of the Parisian Bourgeoisie, 1690–1830* (Cambridge, MA, 1996), 51–2, 97.

[79] *Ibid.*, 51.

[80] Rapley, *The Dévotes*, 26. Third orders consisted of laymen and -women who took simple, private vows of poverty and chastity and devotion to good works while remaining in the secular world. In Italy, third orders of women and Ursulines do not seem to have suffered the same level of pressure for strict enclosure as documented for France. See Gabriella Zarri, "Gender, Religious Institutions and Social Discipline: The Reform of the Regulars," in Judith C. Brown and Robert C. Davis, eds., *Gender and Society in Renaissance Italy* (London and New York, 1998), 211–12.

[81] Rapley, *The Dévotes*, 41.

for example, seem to have enjoyed a great deal of physical autonomy, circulating rather freely in the city's streets. Given the strict enclosure of Seville's nuns, *beatas* carried out nearly all of the charitable activities that women with formal religious identities could perform. In recompense, the municipal government awarded them pensions for their work.[82] Although information on the number of *beatas* in early modern Spanish towns is lacking, one estimate suggests that as many as 30 percent of adult women in some sixteenth- and seventeenth-century towns identified themselves as such.[83]

Like late medieval beguines, *beatas* and other women seeking to live on the boundary between secular and religious worlds seem to have enjoyed greater acceptance in Mediterranean Europe than women religious farther north who tried to pursue "active" vocations. As noted, the attitude and support of individual bishops and archbishops was critical. The well-known archbishop of Milan, Carlo Borromeo, who served from 1560–84, protected the nonenclosed female members of the Company of St. Ursula's right to circulate freely in the city because of the important place they occupied in his plans to catechize children in schools of the Christian doctrine.[84]

Even in cities where there was widespread support of *beatas'* work, this support had its eventual limits. Spanish church authorities seem to have tolerated *beatas'* active vocations only until some of them began exhibiting a penchant for an ecstatic, sometimes mystical, piety and a desire to lead their own religious movements. By the seventeenth century, many *beatas* there were forced into strict enclosure, leading almost inevitably to the inability of their communities to support themselves financially. Indeed, amidst the increasingly difficult conditions of Spain in the seventeenth century, *beatas* were numbered among the recipients rather than the providers of assistance to the poor.[85]

In France, the presence of *filles seculières* in the street often created public disturbances, with children following and mocking them. Certain municipal authorities feared the growth of these groups because of the threat that their religious vocations might represent to the civic community. To the extent that church authorities were increasingly likely to require nonprofessed women to accept cloistering, the civic community would be faced by the presence of

---

[82] Perry, *Gender*, 25.

[83] Ranft, *Women and the Religious Life*, 108. Olwen Hufton notes the presence of *beatas* in southern France in the eighteenth century. See "Women without Men: Widows and Spinsters in Britain and France in the Eighteenth Century," in Jan Bremmer and Lourens van den Bosch, eds., *Between Poverty and the Pyre: Moments in the History of Widowhood* (London and New York, 1995), 129–30.

[84] Ruth P. Liebowitz, "Virgins in the Service of Christ," in Rosemary Ruether and Eleanor McLaughlin, eds., *Women of Spirit: Female Leadership in the Jewish and Christian Traditions* (New York, 1979), 143. This order was, however, gradually transformed into the professed and cloistered order of Ursuline nuns.

[85] Perry, *Gender*, 97–113, 153, 172.

additional religious houses claiming ever more urban space. Moreover, if such women's religious communities failed financially, their members might fall into financial dependency upon city coffers.[86]

Suspicion of societies or congregations of women religious seeking active lives in the city while avoiding enclosure was not limited to church or lay authorities or mocking children, however.[87] Women who took simple private religious vows could create problems for their parents and extended families by interfering with the kind of increasingly conscious "family strategies" that historians have seen emerging in the sixteenth and seventeenth centuries.[88]

Upper-class parents generally favored strict enclosure for their daughters entering religious life because of the potential dishonor or even physical danger that might result if daughters or other female kin joined groups that allowed them to appear in city streets.[89] Moreover, the ambiguous legal status of women who were neither fully lay nor fully religious in terms of the Tridentine Church went right to the heart of the long-standing relationship between the family strategies of wealthy patricians and the Church. Although women who took solemn, perpetual vows generally had no claims on inheritance once their vows were formalized, after they had experienced "legal death" it was not clear exactly what claims men and women taking only simple vows might have on family wealth if they decided to resume their life in society.[90] The potential for conflict between parents and children seeking to join nonenclosed orders was also increased by the fact that sixteenth- and seventeenth-century civil legislation and jurisprudence in many areas was tending to expand paternal authority.[91]

Individual lives in communities and families during the Catholic Reformation

It was not only parents of the upper classes who sometimes sought to "solve" family problems by disposing of unwanted daughters within the walls of enclosed religious communities. Laywomen of the upper classes also used them

---

[86] Rapley, *The Dévotes*, 113–14.

[87] Liebowitz, "Virgins," in Ruether and McLaughlin, eds., *Women of Spirit*, 135, notes the use of these terms to distinguish newer groups of active, religious women from older regular orders of professed nuns.

[88] Natalie Davis, "Ghosts, Kin, and Progeny: Some Features of Family Life in Early Modern France," *Daedalus* 106, 2 (Summer, 1977): 87–92.

[89] Liebowitz, "Virgins," in Ruether and McLaughlin, eds., *Women of Spirit*, 140. Rapley, *The Dévotes*, 59, shows that it was not until they rejected their active outreach to children of the poor and accepted strict enclosure that Ursulines in France began to enjoy the patronage of the French court and nobility, who would agree to confide their daughters only to a religious order so regulated.

[90] *Ibid.*, 38–9, 55, 116.

[91] Sarah Hanley, "Family and State in Early Modern France: The Marriage Pact," in Marilyn J. Boxer and Jean H. Quataert, eds., *Connecting Spheres: Women in the Western World, 1500 to the Present* (New York, 1987), 53–63.

Plate 8   Pietro Longhi (1702–1785), *Visit to the Convent.*

as places of refuge where they sometimes developed new individual identities that could either complement or even compete with their identities as family members. In some cities of southern Europe where wealthy women were particularly disadvantaged by patrilineal systems of inheritance, widows often used convents as places of residence. Convents in Italy, in particular, attracted wealthy widows who sometimes preferred living there as a nonprofessed nun to other residential alternatives available to them, such as living in a separate apartment of the house belonging to their deceased husband's lineage or living alone in a separate dwelling (see Plate 8).

The life of one such wealthy widow in sixteenth-century Milan illustrated how women's individual, family, and community identities could evolve over their life course, and how they sought to circumvent some of the institutional realities of conventual life. By 1535, Ludovica Torelli, a young childless widow, had already survived two husbands. In that year, she helped to found a new convent of San Paolo or "Angelics" in Milan, a house of 100 nuns and other pious widows like herself. Using her high social status and standing in clerical circles, she obtained special papal exemption from enclosure for the nuns and nonprofessed women of the convent who wished to undertake missionary work among prostitutes, and lead devotional reading groups for the urban laity.

In the will prepared for her in 1541, Torelli made her "new family" – the convent of San Paolo – her principal heir while granting smaller gifts to nuns of the convent.[92] A second will she made in 1546 made minor adjustments to the document but preserved her choice of burial place inside the nuns' church, rejecting the option of burial in a chapel that her family had endowed in the local Dominican monastery. This will stayed in effect until 1552, when a papal decree ordered that all nonprofessed women within the convent either leave or accept strict enclosure and take solemn vows.

Rather than accept a condition that would have prevented her from carrying out an active mission in the city, Torelli left the convent she had helped to found and entered a local convent for "fallen women" as a resident. This departure occasioned significant changes in her new will, which now named "the poor" as her principal heir and included legacies for masses for the souls of her parents and her two husbands. The loss of her "new family" at San Paolo seems to have rekindled her sense of identification with both her natal and marital kin. This was not the end of Torelli's story, however, for in 1559 she once again pursued her desire for an "active" vocation, and founded a school for girls that was exempt from cloistering, and which she now designated as principal heir of her estate.

In contrast to Torelli's decision, other widows of San Paolo did accept the Church's requirement of strict cloister. Yet their histories and wills also reflected the competing pulls of conventual and family loyalties in their decisions regarding legacies to children and convent. The strength of women's adopted identities was evidenced in the fact that most of them advantaged institutions where they intended to live out their days over the children whom they had left on the outside.[93]

These stresses and strains in women's identities were not all-or-nothing affairs pitting loyalty to family versus loyalty to their adoptive communities. Nor did entry into religious life necessarily mean that one was cut off entirely from one's family. The story of Camilla Rossermini, a Pisan girl born in 1608, illustrated the ironic fact that entry into a religious community could strengthen an individual's sense of identification with her extended family.

Born five months after the death of her father, Rossermini was given as an infant into the legal control of the city's Magistracy, which appointed a paternal uncle as her guardian, the mother remarrying several months thereafter. Meanwhile the young child was placed in the convent of San Matteo in the care of a paternal aunt. Here, Camilla found herself in a community filled with her paternal kin. Over time, she turned against the mother who had "abandoned"

---

[92] This locution came from a later chronicle of her life, not from Torelli herself. See P. Renée Baernstein, "In Widow's Habit: Women between Convent and Family in Sixteenth-Century Milan," *Sixteenth Century Journal* 25, 4 (1994): 796.
[93] *Ibid.*, 800–1.

her as a young child, and as an 11-year-old, refused her mother's request to return to her home after the mother had been widowed for a third time.

Interestingly, like the civic courts and consistories of Protestant Europe, the Pisan Magistracy tried to negotiate among the competing desires of family members. When Camilla's mother tried to reclaim her, the magistrates allowed the 12-year-old girl to defend her wish to remain in the convent in a formal audience. Camilla's testimony before them revealed that she felt "safe" in the convent, that she had been well taken care of and received an education there, and had come to identify with the extended family and community she found within its walls.[94] After the death of her mother, who excluded her from receiving any portion of her sizable dowry, Camilla left the convent and was married to her paternal cousin, the match having probably been engineered by the paternal kin from within the convent walls.

In a conventual setting that was socially the opposite of Rossermini's situation, a seventeenth-century convent of poor Clares from quite modest backgrounds on the outskirts of Florence, even Tridentine rules of strict cloister did not inhibit one member from maintaining links with her well-known father. Fearing that he would be unable to find husbands for his two illegitimate daughters, Virginia and Livia, Galileo had received special dispensation to place them in the convent at ages 13 and 12, though they had to wait until reaching the canonical age of 16 to take their formal vows. Not only did Galileo's elder daughter maintain an intensive correspondence with her father until her death at age 34, through these letters she also played an important filial role despite the cloister. Gifts, advice, gossip, and information flowed freely back and forth between father and daughter, showing the penetrability of cloister walls even within one of the strictest and most austere of conventual orders.[95]

Ironically, the growth of more strictly enclosed convents under Tridentine reforms often made it more difficult for parents to use them to dispose of unwanted daughters in the course of implementing family "strategies" to plan for the future of their children.[96] For militant confessional leaders, the goal of building a renewed Catholic community led reformers to fight against some of the worst abuses of families' "forced monacation" of young people, and work arduously to repair the lax morality of many religious communities.[97] In

---

[94] Giulia Calvi, "Reconstructing the Family: Widowhood and Remarriage in Tuscany in the Early Modern Period," in Trevor Dean and K. J. P. Lowe, eds., *Marriage in Italy, 1300–1650* (Cambridge, 1998), 287–8.

[95] Dava Sobel, *Galileo's Daughter: A Historical Memoir of Science, Faith, and Love* (New York, 1999), 45, 60, 81–2, 116–17.

[96] For a critical discussion of this concept, see: Pier Paolo Viazzo and Katherine A. Lynch, "Anthropology, Family History, and the Concept of Strategy," *International Review of Social History* 47 (2002): 423–52.

[97] Zarri, "Gender," in Brown and Davis, eds., *Gender and Society*, 197–8. Part of the impetus for the "reform of the regulars" was to address Lutheran attacks on the moral corruption of monastic communities, both male and female.

the widely translated and distributed text, *Il Sommario della santa Scrittura e l'ordinario dei cristiani* first published in the 1530s, for example, the authors denounced families that pressured young people to enter religious orders with no real sense of vocation.

Moreover, the reluctance of some patrician women to obey their parents' designs of placing them in religious orders stemmed not only from the lack of an important sense of "vocation," but also from an unwillingness to accept the sort of austere discipline increasingly required of Counter-Reformation convents.[98] Evidence from Vatican sources suggests that young women and men whose parents had placed them in convents at early ages and pressured them to take solemn vows were able to seek redress against their families by successfully renouncing their vows and in some instances gaining even their "annulment," which permitted them to marry.[99]

Rebellion against the forced monacation that awaited girls born to wealthy Catholic families trying to preserve their wealth also came in the form of publications authored by women who were most involved. Arcangela Tarabotti, a Venetian woman of a non-noble family of "respectable means," had been forced into the convent of Saint Anna di Castello at age 13 and took her vows at 16. In her several publications denouncing the fate of young women forced into religious orders, Tarabotti lashed out against the "tyranny" of paternal authority, the Venetian government, and the Church which allowed it to happen. Part of her denunciation of Venetian conditions rested upon her argument that women in France, Germany, and northern Europe as a whole enjoyed an autonomy and access to public life that put Venice to shame.[100]

In other cases, tensions between young adults and their families came from exactly the opposite direction, when young people sought to forge new identities for themselves by joining the newer, militant religious orders against their parents' wishes. In such cases, when young people insisted on joining religious orders out of a sense of deep individual vocation typical of the early years of the Catholic Reformation, even the wealthiest, most patriarchal fathers were not always able to bring their children under control.

Conflicts often arose over issues of majority. In France, for example, while church rules prohibited young people from taking solemn vows before age 16, the age of majority in civil law was set at 25, leaving a period of 9 years when the

---

[98] Virginia Cox, "The Single Self: Feminist Thought and the Marriage Market in Early Modern Venice," *Renaissance Quarterly* 48, 3 (1995): 535–43.

[99] Zarri, "Gender," in Brown and Davis, eds., *Gender and Society*, 196–7.

[100] Cox, "Single Self," 539. At this moment, women in France were denouncing the "tyranny" and "slavery" of French marriage legislation. See Sarah Hanley, "Social Sites of Political Practice in France: Lawsuits, Civil Rights, and the Separation of Powers in Domestic and State Government, 1500–1800," *American Historical Review* 102, 1 (February, 1997): 36–40.

young person's status appeared ambiguous, at least until civil courts ruled that 16 was the age of consent to religious vows only with parental permission. This legislation notwithstanding, the ages between 16 and 25 constituted a period in which young adults' level of autonomy could be highly contested, sometimes pitting them and the religious orders they wished to join against angry parents and magistrates.[101]

Parents often pursued minor children under the law using the fiction that they had been seduced, lured, or even kidnapped into religious orders, seeking redress under the same laws that enabled parents to seek the annulment of marriages between minors to which they had not consented. In a letter to his 19-year-old son who, knowing the long reach of the French law, had run away to join the Jesuit order in the Kingdom of Savoy in 1583, Guichard Coton expressed the sense of authority mixed with impotence which such conflicts inevitably aroused. He wrote:

Are these, my son, the promises that you made so many times to obey me, to serve me, to lighten the burden of my old age, according to God's commandment? Do you wish instead to make your mother and me die of melancholy? Far from prolonging our days, do you wish to shorten them? What have I done to you that has displeased you? Have I ever refused you any thing that you have wished from me? And is this my recompense? Am I a heretic, or a wicked man? Are we scandalous persons, to oblige you to separate yourself from us? Are you of age to make a choice against our will? And is there a human or divine law that permits a child to dispose of himself at the age of nineteen? Do you prefer to serve strangers and teach children in a secondary school instead of living with your parents? Don't you think about how much you are offending God in causing us this displeasure, and how much you should fear his punishment? No, my son, I cannot believe that you persist in this disobedience. I beg you and command you to leave those who have suborned you and return instantly to my side. I will listen to your reasons and tell you mine. If you do not do this, I [will] protest your ingratitude before God and before men: I will have you constrained by justice, and I will exhaust my wealth to have punished those who have seduced you and who prevent you from obeying a father who loves you tenderly.[102]

The son replied to his father's letter in terms that proclaimed his allegiance to his adoptive community, terms that evoked the kind of identity that confessional communities sought to inspire among their members: "I cannot resist the voice of God...without a culpable ingratitude, and without rendering myself unworthy of the good education that you have given me." Rather than assuaging his father's anger, the son's response inspired the elder Coton to pursue his fight with Jesuit authorities directly rather than trying to persuade his son.[103] The father made good on his threats, launching appeals to the duke of Savoy and the

---

[101] Barbara B. Diefendorf, "Give Us Back Our Children: Patriarchal Authority and Parental Consent to Religious Vocations in Early Counter-Reformation France," *Journal of Modern History* 68, 2 (June 1996): 273.

[102] *Ibid.*, 265–6. Cited with permission.   [103] *Ibid.*, 266.

governor of Milan through the queen mother of France, Catherine de Medici, that were, however, without success.

Although this sort of father–son confrontation may have been more muted when it occurred between parents and their daughters, there is no doubt that the desire of some young women to join militant religious orders also created the same sort of family drama. Daughters' decisions to enter the most ascetic women's religious orders such as the Carmelites often caused even more consternation than sons' entry into religious orders because of daughters' greater removal from their parents that certain convents required. A daughter's choice to enter one of the highly ascetic orders sometimes represented a life-threatening decision given the harshness of the daily life and discipline. In entering these orders voluntarily, sons and daughters were renouncing the values and way of life of their family in favor of new individual identities within monastic communities.[104]

In France at least, the kinds of family conflicts that pitted Guichard Coton against his son seem to have been more likely to occur in the late sixteenth and early seventeenth centuries, when the Catholic Reformation was enjoying its greatest success among the kingdom's ruling elite. With the passage of time and a certain waning of the fervor of initial waves of reform, a number of newer religious houses fell on financial and even spiritual hard times, leading to a growing number of "failed vocations" and the renunciation of solemn vows. And, just as family patriarchs and civil authorities had feared, renunciations of solemn vows did wreak havoc on carefully crafted inheritance plans, as those individuals reestablished their claims and sought shares of the wealth they had previously renounced.[105]

This discussion has tried to show that the confessionalization projects taking place in Europe in the sixteenth and seventeenth centuries had important effects on domestic life and were, in turn, shaped by the needs that individuals felt to express both individual and family identities. Church authorities in Protestant areas were especially eager to create and maintain new agencies for the confessionalization of domestic life, reinvigorating an older tradition that had linked the security of the civic community to its constituent households.

Although some historians have viewed the Catholic Church's policy of "enclosure" of women religious as a simple exaggeration of the "enclosure" of laywomen in exclusively domestic roles, this discussion has suggested that the impact of the Catholic Reformation on urban women was as complex and multifaceted as that of the Reformation on Protestant women. Catholic Church legislation was doubtless increasingly patriarchal in its emphasis on the "enclosure" of women religious. However, the increasing attention paid to conscience and belief as well as behavior so important to these confessional

---

[104] *Ibid.*, 283.   [105] *Ibid.*, 307.

movements also suggests a strengthening of individuals' sense of personal identity that could spark resistance to the countervailing growth of paternal and community power over the individual. Moreover, though the latter part of the chapter focused mainly on women, it is clear that women and men affected by the confessionalization processes in Protestant and Catholic Europe used their domestic identities as fathers or mothers – whether real or fictive – in organized community-building activities that shaped and enlarged the sphere of civil society.

5   Constructing an "imagined community":
    poor relief and the family during the
    French Revolution

The founding of the French nation during the revolutionary years 1789 to 1794 provides an opportunity to examine the place of poor relief and the family in efforts to create what Benedict Anderson famously called an "imagined community."[1] Constructing national communities arguably involves challenges far greater than the kinds explored in earlier chapters. Most of the communities observed up to this point were based on face-to-face relations and networks of acquaintanceship, at least among community leaders. Yet we have already seen evidence of larger communities such as certain confraternities in Renaissance Italian cities, or entire civic communities. Moreover, the confessionalization process of the sixteenth and seventeenth centuries had already led to the formation of communities of co-religionists that were arguably more "imagined" than real well before the founding of modern nation-states. Without minimizing differences that questions of scale introduce, this chapter explores French revolutionary efforts to create a nation against the background of earlier traditions of European community building.

By the end of the Old Regime, those who sought to reform government and society on the basis of their dream of a "nation" would sharply distinguish between a model of poor relief they identified with Church and State, and their own.[2] Their criticism centered mainly on the Church for a failure to use its vast wealth for the care of the poor, what they saw as the clergy's favoritism towards the "shamefaced poor," and the exclusionary patron–client relationships it suggested, and on the large hospitals – mainly Counter-Reformation era "general hospitals" – that housed many of the poor. These hospitals became hated symbols of inefficient management, clerical patronage, and idleness, all of which violated basic tenets of a competing model of poor relief that critics hoped would reflect a renewal of civic ideals. Progressive critics of the system of poor relief prevailing in the eighteenth century as well as revolutionary leaders from the early days of the Revolution to the fall of Robespierre advocated a

---

[1] Benedict Anderson, *Imagined Communities: Reflections on the Origin and Spread of Nationalism*, rev. edn. (London and New York, 1991).
[2] On the growth of the idea of the nation, see David A. Bell, *The Cult of the Nation in France: Inventing Nationalism, 1680–1800* (Cambridge, MA, 2001).

reinvented civic model of poor assistance. They advocated policies to reinvigorate the notion of the community's obligation to the poor, prevent rather than repress mendicity, and, most importantly, build the nation's poor relief system on the distribution of benefits to "deserving" individuals, their households, and their families.

The fact that revolutionary leaders from 1789 to 1794 seem to have shared the fundamental features of a civic vision of poor relief has led historians to emphasize the internal consistency of poor relief policy through these years. According to this analysis, the poor relief system that emerged by summer 1794 was more or less what earlier reformers or revolutionaries working in 1789–90 had envisioned.

Recently, however, Catherine Duprat has challenged this line of argument, bringing into sharper focus some of the differences of social identity and goals between earlier and later revolutionaries with regard to the relief of the poor. Whereas Old Regime progressives and members of the National Constituent Assembly who worked on the problem of poor relief shared an upper-class "philanthropic" attitude, Jacobin leadership of the Revolution's Year II (22 September 1793 – 21 September 1794) saw things differently. They sought to use poor relief much more consciously to create ties of "fraternal solidarity" within the nation, and to involve citizens as a whole in the task of relieving their "poor brothers."[3]

It is also clear that whereas the revolutionary rationale for assistance to the poor began with a fundamental civic notion of individual citizens' entitlements to assistance and the nation's obligation to fulfill it, by the time of the First Republic, Jacobin policies became more preoccupied with the nation's need for very specific sorts of expressions of solidarity and community-mindedness. Under the Jacobin leadership, the nation's need for men to serve in the nation's armies would lead to a complex, confusing penumbra of entitlements to assistance for a growing number of categories of kin of soldiers, or "defenders of the fatherland" as well as some important departures from earlier civic traditions of poor relief.

During the Year II, Jacobin discourse concerning poor relief shifted as well. Whereas earlier revolutionary discussions emphasized citizens' entitlement to assistance as one of numerous individual "rights," Jacobin leaders gradually came to view these entitlements more in the aggregate and to emphasize the national community's obligation to fulfill them as a means for building and maintaining bonds of "fraternity."[4]

---

[3] Catherine Duprat, *"Pour l'amour de l'humanité": le temps des philanthropes. la philanthropie parisienne des Lumières à la monarchie de juillet* (Paris, 1993), 332.

[4] Jean-Pierre Gross, *Fair Shares for All: Jacobin Egalitarianism in Practice* (New York and Cambridge, 1997), 203, argues that "Jacobin egalitarianism followed a course which was destined to complement, rather than undermine, the liberal, individualist programme of the Revolution."

As we shall see, in cities such as Paris, with a long history of institutions for the care of the domiciled poor, the Revolution gave new impetus to civic-minded sorts of poor relief. However, vast areas of the nation, particularly rural ones, would continue to suffer from a dearth of institutional infrastructure for the relief of the poor, even the most respectable. By 1793, with counter-revolution flaring up in many areas of the nation, representatives of the Convention dispatched to the provinces to help raise armies and repress rebellion often took it upon themselves to use the appropriation of resources for the poor to deliver lessons in revolutionary civism as they saw it. While these lessons were sometimes benign, in other cases representatives would engage in highly coercive efforts to repress the uncivic "egoism" of the wealthy, confiscating property and levying "taxes" for assistance to the local poor.

The re-emergence of a "civic" vision of poor relief

In the waning years of the Old Regime, criticism of the Monarchy and Church's combined inability to address problems of poverty satisfactorily helped to fuel the national movement for reform of both institutions. Like other issues, debates on the poor began to be waged on a national level, in the case of the poor focusing largely on those who were the most obvious and most threatening to the social order – the vagrants and beggars who were the scourge of countryside and city especially during years of economic crisis. Emerging "enlightened" opinion, while dealing with this element of the poor, gradually became more interested in discussing means of prevention than repression, and focusing on ways to help the poor in their homes. Even the royal government became convinced of the desirability of home-based assistance and tried to pass legislation in 1764 that, while repressing vagrancy and begging, would have entitled the resident poor to outdoor relief from local *bureaux d'aumônes* (alms bureaus) that it hoped to encourage throughout the kingdom. It was thwarted in this reform effort, however, by the Parlement of Paris, which was concerned both with jurisdictional questions and the repressive features of the proposed anti-begging elements of the Edict.[5]

Evidence of the terrible state of France's poor, and declining levels of charitable giving to traditional organs of poor relief in the waning years of the Old Regime lend support to Alexis de Tocqueville's portrait of Old Regime France as a society where rich were alienated from poor and the rural poor, in particular, were left to fend for themselves.[6] While bad faith on the part of the

---

[5] Thomas McStay Adams, *Bureaucrats and Beggars: French Social Policy in the Age of the Enlightenment* (New York, 1990), 52–68.

[6] Alexis de Tocqueville, *The Old Regime and the French Revolution*, trans. Stuart Gilbert (Garden City, NY, 1955), Part I, ch. 12 (120–37); Colin Jones, *Charity and Bienfaisance: The Treatment of the Poor in the Montpellier Region, 1740–1815* (New York and Cambridge, 1983), 39; Cissie Fairchilds, *Poverty and Charity in Aix-en-Provence, 1640–1789* (Baltimore, 1976), 154–8.

wealthy may have been part of the problem, it was also clear that progressive, "philanthropic" opinion emerging in the late eighteenth century was hostile less to the poor than to existing institutional solutions to helping them. Centuries of founding and donating to hospitals where many of the poor were received created institutions that had become inefficient in both their inherent inadequacies and their uneven distribution throughout the kingdom. Wealthier areas of the kingdom that seemed to need them least had the most. By the end of the Old Regime, a number of hospitals simply could not fulfill their intended mission of helping the poor because their endowments had shrunk.[7] The more recently founded general hospitals, which had figured so importantly as locuses of outreach to the poor during the Catholic Reformation, were now accused of being poorly administered bastions of religious clientelism that encouraged that most uncivic of vices – idleness.

The waning appeal of the general hospital was reflected in the declining number of testamentary contributions to them, especially by middle- and upper-middle-class donors.[8] Some historians, most notably Michel Vovelle, attribute this trend to the "de-christianization" process associated with the Enlightenment and the corresponding decline in Catholic belief and piety.[9] On the other hand, evidence suggests that a decline in testamentary contributions to general hospitals and other religious institutions may have signaled less a rejection of religious or even charitable ideals, than a shift in the laity's taste for forms of donation more consonant with changing religious sensibilities and civic aspirations. From the early 1740s to the mid-1780s, for example, charitable donations to Montpellier's general hospital and Hôtel-Dieu declined significantly. However, contributions to poor relief institutions that assisted the "parish poor" in their own homes and were less identified with Counter-Reformation institutions increased in favor.[10]

Well into the early years of the Revolution, appeals for voluntary contributions for the poor continued to be framed in a combined language of Christian charity and a newer language of philanthropy. Many members of clergy and laity alike saw little inherent conflict between obligations to the poor based

---

[7] Muriel Jeorger, "La Structure hospitalière de la France sous l'Ancien Régime," *Annales, ESC* 32, 5 (1977): 1025–51. On the viability of eighteenth-century hospitals, see Jean Imbert, "Les Institutions sociales à la veille de La Révolution," in Comité d'histoire de la sécurité sociale, *La Protection sociale sous la Révolution française*, ed. Jean Imbert (Paris, 1990), 39–41; Daniel Hickey, *Local Hospitals in Ancien Régime France: Rationalization, Resistance, Renewal, 1530–1789* (Montreal and Kingston, 1997), 197, 206.

[8] Jones, *Charity*, 89. Jean Imbert, *Le Droit hospitalier de l'Ancien Régime* (Paris, 1993), 255–6.

[9] Michel Vovelle, *Piété baroque et déchristianisation en Provence à XVIIIe siècle: les attitudes devant la mort d'après les clauses des testaments* (Paris, 1973).

[10] Jones, *Charity*, 90, 132; Olwen Hufton, *The Poor of Eighteenth-Century France, 1750–1789* (Oxford, 1974), 159–66. Robert M. Schwartz, *Policing the Poor in Eighteenth-Century France* (Chapel Hill, 1988), 65, 116, who notes urban officials' long-standing preference for outdoor relief.

upon Christian charitable principles and those based on secular values of philanthropy. As in the case of urban "civic religion" of the great towns and cities of Renaissance Italy, there seemed to be little conflict between admonitions of solidarity based on the two different but compatible ideals.

By the middle of the eighteenth century, however, there were signs of growing tension between the older "heroic" Counter-Reformation ideal of charity, which had sought to reach out to the most marginal members of society within highly controlled environments such as general hospitals, and newer ideals of assistance to the poor based on the obligation to fellow citizens as well as a larger love for "humanity."[11]

Programs for urban poor relief that emerged in the eighteenth century, while sometimes dressed in new ideological garb, were not themselves new. Certain cities, especially in the south, witnessed a revival of Christian confraternal life among members of the working and lower-middle classes. Civic-minded confraternities such as the Freemasons who espoused newer philanthropic ideals also grew in popularity, particularly among men of the bourgeoisie and nobility. Like earlier Catholic confraternities in their times of greatest outreach, some Masonic groups extended the bonds of "fraternal" solidarity beyond the boundaries of their lodge to serve the needs of the local poor in the name of a common humanity.[12]

In an influential 1788 pamphlet, one of the most eloquent proponents of a civic approach to assistance criticized older practices of "indoor relief" in general hospitals while advocating relief of the poor in their homes. Like other civic-minded progressives, Angot des Rotours argued that the incarceration of paupers encouraged laziness and would lead to an increase in their numbers. Furthermore, hospitals privileged their inmates while neglecting large numbers of the poor outside their walls. In contrast, Angot argued that assistance to households presented several advantages. The first was financial. Based on his study of English data and contemporary information from French philanthropic societies, he showed that assisting households burdened with dependents, whether small children or the elderly, was significantly less expensive than maintaining dependents in large institutional settings.[13]

Angot also made important claims about the moral preferability of "outdoor" relief. By assisting individuals in their households, he argued, authorities strengthened natural bonds of solidarity within the family and re-knit bonds between needy individuals and their surrounding community. Outdoor relief also

---

[11] Duprat, *Le Temps*, xvii, discusses the second generation of philosophes as harbingers of this distinction.

[12] *Ibid.*, 49–52; Jones, *Charity*, 91–2; Margaret C. Jacob, *Living the Enlightenment: Freemasonry and Politics in Eighteenth-Century Europe* (New York and Oxford, 1991), 210–12; Marcel David, *Fraternité et Révolution française, 1789–1799* (Paris, 1987), 88–90, 99.

[13] Angot des Rotours, *Notice des principaux règlements publiés en Angleterre concernant les pauvres* (London and Paris, 1788), 39, 43.

took advantage of what we might call household-level "economies of scale," but without incurring the huge costs of housing large numbers of the poor in general hospitals:

the wood that you distribute to the old man serves to warm his children and grand-children ... it creates light for all of them; he shares his food with them ... all the children of a widow burdened with a family share the enjoyment of the assistance ... In assisting the head of the family, you often prevent all the individuals who compose it from being reduced to begging.[14]

Furthermore, outdoor relief reinforced bonds within the family. By assisting the elderly in their homes:

you will maintain this sacred flame of filial love that your hospitals would have quickly extinguished by accustoming children to isolate themselves from their parents[.] Parents, in turn, will preserve the hope of being assisted in their old age by those to whom they gave birth; and this hope will contribute more to the progress of arts and industry because it will encourage fathers to procure for their children the talents which make them as useful to their families as to the fatherland.[15]

In generous ecumenical terms, Angot also reconciled his essentially civic model of assistance with the older tradition of Counter-Reformation piety, at one point identifying Vincent de Paul, France's greatest Counter-Reformation saint, as a "philanthropist"![16]

All commentators realized that outdoor assistance to families would not suffice as the sole means of aid to the poor. Hospitals for the poor and sick would have to be maintained if only because large numbers of people, especially the itinerant poor and those who had recently migrated to the cities, often lacked kin, neighbors, or friends who could care for them. Nonetheless, the most progressive advocates of a civic model of poor relief argued that newer hospitals should aim to capture the small scale and "feel" of domestic life.[17]

Two voluntary associations founded in the late eighteenth century exemplified this family-oriented civic approach to poor assistance: the Parisian Philanthropic Society (Société philanthropique) and the Society for Maternal Charity (Société de charité maternelle), which had chapters in Paris, Lyon, and other provincial cities. While the Society for Maternal Charity, which was organized and run by upper-class women, was more apt than its brother organization to use an older language of charity to describe its efforts, both organizations concurred in their commitment to outdoor relief. Both associations also devoted their attention to the residential poor, focusing on "respectable" families of the

---

[14] *Ibid.*, 50–1.   [15] *Ibid.*, 46–7.   [16] *Ibid.*, 50–1.

[17] Pierre-Samuel Dupont de Nemours, *Idées sur les secours à donner aux pauvres mendiants* (Paris, 1988 [1786]), 19–22, 32–3. Imbert, "Les Institutions sociales," in *La Protection sociale*, 42; Imbert, *Le Droit*, 83–4, 156.

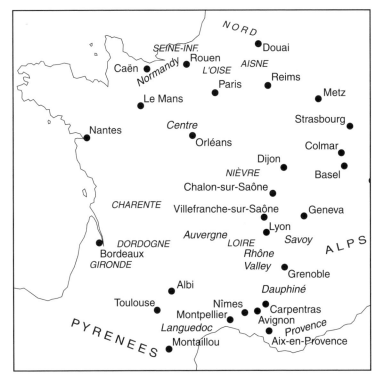

Map 3 France in the late eighteenth century

working class.[18] Finally, both organizations sought to reaffirm family bonds for the betterment of the larger civic community.

The precise origins of the Philanthropic Society, founded in 1780, are somewhat obscure, but evidence suggests that from its documentable beginnings it attracted members from the liberal elements of the court nobility, *magistrature*, and finance. The society was held together by networks of male friendship born in the Masonic movement in the capital and adjacent provinces. The publicity that its efforts enjoyed from such influential periodicals as the *Journal de Paris* during the waning years of the Old Regime attracted contributions to its efforts from nonmembers as well as members.

Despite the presence of many Masons in its leadership and within its ranks, the Philanthropic Society's own manifestos proclaimed its freedom from any sectarianism or "superstition" (read militant Catholicism) as well as the desire to make itself an entirely "public" organization. A 1787 manifesto referred

---

[18] Duprat, *Le Temps*, 65–80.

neither to the virtue of charity, the Church, nor the King, citing only the work of St. Vincent de Paul as a model, whom it identified as "hero of patriotism and religion." The participation of high church leaders, including several archbishops, demonstrated that values of the Society were entirely compatible with late-eighteenth century ideals of Christian charity.

Importantly, the Society sought to aid categories of poor whom it believed were neglected by existing systems of assistance in the capital. It reserved its funds for the elderly, the blind, and gradually, for women in childbirth and families burdened with children. The Society aided the latter through cash assistance or sometimes by helping them pay wages for wet nurses. The Philanthropic Society required that the poor whom it assisted be resident in the capital for at least three years and produce evidence of good conduct.[19]

The Philanthropic Society's family-oriented work was seconded at the very end of the Old Regime by the Society for Maternal Charity, which was founded in May 1788, and whose work focused exclusively on women in childbirth and mothers and children during the first years of the child's life. Its principal goal was to convince women to breastfeed their children, and thereby to achieve the larger civic goal of stemming the growing numbers of infants abandoned to the Paris Foundling Home, who numbered approximately 5,000–7,000 annually in the 1780s. It accomplished this by providing funds for home delivery of the child and a monthly pension to the mother during the first two years of the child's life. Women accepted as clients of the Society were obligated to be legitimately married and to accept the visits of members of the Society for Maternal Charity in their homes for the duration of their pension.[20]

Judging by the prestige of their membership and the growth of their financial resources and clientele, the Philanthropic Society and the Society for Maternal Charity enjoyed some success in the last years of the Old Regime. From 1785 to 1787, the number of "virtuous citizens" in the capital whom the Philanthropic Society assisted grew from 374 to 1,043 and then increased again in 1788 to 1,507 people based on a sum of 112,000 livres collected. The Society for Maternal Charity's budget grew from 26,627 livres for eight months in 1788 to 77,192 livres in 1789. In 1788, 152 mothers and 160 children received assistance, with the number growing to 588 mothers and 565 children in 1789.[21]

Both the Philanthropic Society and the Society for Maternal Charity epitomized ideals of civic-mindedness and philanthropy in several ways. Both organizations focused on the "respectable" poor; they sought to assist them in their own homes; and they undertook their efforts with some sense that they were thereby contributing to larger civic goals of reinforcing bonds between mother and child, advocating marriage, and creating the conditions for the preservation

---

[19] *Ibid.*, 72–3.   [20] *Ibid.*, 76.   [21] *Ibid.*, 70, 80.

of children's and women's lives. They also used a system of subscriptions and donations from living persons rather than testamentary bequests.

These societies also demonstrated innovative features identified with the growth of the "public sphere" by the use of the print media to publicize their work and proclaim their principles to a larger public. The two societies' coffers grew rapidly, if only for a relatively short time, suggesting the desire of many to be publicly identified with their efforts.[22]

National opinion on assistance to the poor

An examination of the grievance lists (*cahiers de doléances*) prepared for the 1789 meeting of the Estates-General suggests that concern about problems related to poor relief extended beyond those writing about the issue for publication, working within the royal government, or attempting to assist the civic poor through philanthropic organizations. Grassroots opinion gleaned from parish lists, and opinion gathered at meetings of regional assemblies of the nobility and Third Estate expressed a belief in the obligation of the state or the "nation" to assist traditional categories of the "deserving" poor, and the desirability of locally elected municipal officials serving on hospital boards and as administrators of local charity. In contrast, opinion seemed hostile to the participation of royal officials, parlements, and high clergy in the day-to-day running of institutions for the care of the poor.[23]

A broader, systematic sample of the parish cahiers and the General Cahiers of the Nobility and Third Estate reflects some differences of opinion among peasants, bourgeois, and nobles. Fifteen and 25 percent of the General Cahiers of the Nobility and the Third Estate, respectively, mentioned the problem of the kingdom's poor at least once, with many lists of both orders supporting the establishment of the kind of local *bureaux* or *caisses de charité* that philanthropic leaders advocated. Opinion suggested that funding for these bureaus should come from church resources and to a lesser extent from monies raised by

---

[22] On the development of the "public sphere," see: Jürgen Habermas, *The Structural Transformation of the Public Sphere: An Inquiry into a Category of Bourgeois Society*, trans. Thomas Burger (Cambridge, MA, 1991 [1962]); Margaret C. Jacob, "The Enlightenment Redefined: The Formation of Modern Civil Society," *Social Research* 58, 2 (Summer, 1991): 475–95; Keith Michael Baker, "Defining the Public Sphere in Eighteenth-Century France: Variations on a Theme by Habermas," in Craig Calhoun, ed., *Habermas and the Public Sphere* (Cambridge, MA, 1992), 181–211; Dena Goodman, "Public Sphere and Private Life: Toward a Synthesis of Current Historiographical Approaches to the Old Regime," *History and Theory* 31, 1 (1992): 1–20.

[23] Louis Trenard, "L'Idéologie révolutionnaire et ses incidences," in *La Protection sociale*, ed. Imbert, 118–34, bases his discussion on the sample of cahiers included in the first six volumes of the *Archives parlementaires*, ed. Jérôme Mavidal and E. Laurent (Paris, 1862–1875) (hereafter *AP*), critiqued in Gilbert Shapiro and John Markoff, *Revolutionary Demands: A Content Analysis of the Cahiers de Doléances of 1789* (Stanford, 1998), 117–18.

fines. In almost all instances, cahiers that expressed an opinion on who should administer such institutions identified provincial governments or provincial estates. Those that urged the establishment of workshops for the unemployed (*ateliers de charité*) also advocated municipal or provincial control over their administration.[24]

The General Cahiers of the Third Estate and of the Nobility also distinguished sharply between policies towards the poor and policy towards beggars, or at least beggars who were not local. While attitudes towards the local or domiciled poor expressed in the grievance lists were generally sympathetic, attitudes towards beggars, and the *dépôts de mendicité* that were designed to imprison wandering beggars, were quite negative. Most General Cahiers that mentioned the issue urged the government to forbid begging when it was associated with outsiders, reiterating the long-standing notion that parishes were responsible only for their "own" poor.

Thirty percent of parish cahiers, which generally reflected peasant opinion, contained at least one grievance related to public welfare issues, with 15.2 percent of them expressing a grievance on the poor specifically.[25] Calls for assistance to different categories of the poor such as children or orphans were outnumbered by grievances that were more concerned with who, exactly, should pay for their care. Parish cahiers frequently identified the Church's wealth as the proper source of funds for poor relief, and identified the community or locality as responsible for maintaining its own poor.

The General Cahiers of the Third Estate and of the Nobility concerning the Church expressed distrust of the regular clergy, and urged the expropriation of church wealth as the major source of assistance for the poor. The General Cahiers' view of the tithe argued for it to be used as "originally" intended – to pay a decent salary to the local clergy member, maintain church buildings, and care for the local poor. Opinion expressed here also favored local or regional authorities as administrators of funds for the poor.

Shapiro and Markoff's systematic sample of the *cahiers de doléances* thus reveals interest in problems of the poor, as well as support for the use of church property and tithes to assist them. There are hints that authors of the cahiers who expressed concern for public welfare issues were willing to accept some central state intervention in hospital administration, but seemed committed both to the responsibility of localities to care for "their" poor and the consequent necessity

---

[24] On the ateliers, see, most recently, William Olejniczak, "Working the Body of the Poor: The Ateliers de Charité in Late Eighteenth-Century France," *Journal of Social History* 24, 1 (1990): 87–107.

[25] Shapiro and Markoff, *Revolutionary Demands*, 263–4, discuss the distribution of parish grievances regarding public welfare. Duprat, *Le Temps*, 292–3, argues that questions of assistance were "primordial" in "urban cahiers."

for provincial or even local administration. It is difficult to gauge whether there was consensus on how the Estates-General should reform policies towards the poor, since only a minority of parish or General Cahiers expressed opinions on this matter.[26] From the data available, however, it seems that on the eve of the meeting of the Estates-General in May 1789, many French subjects, from the nobility to the peasantry, were agreed on the need to reinvent local responsibility for the residential poor, hand more authority over the administration of poor relief to local or provincial administration, and devote church resources to them.[27]

In his discussion of a sample of the cahiers, Louis Trenard has argued that "the part of the grievance lists devoted to questions of assistance was limited and unoriginal." The first of these characterizations may well have been true, but the second seems technically true but substantively false. Against the background of a century of royal policy that had focused mainly on the vagrant and the marginal poor, and the failure of local and regional institutions to effectively relieve growing numbers of the poor, both itinerant and residentially stable, these opinions seem quite innovative. The fact that many cahiers expressed a desire to renew or reinvigorate older obligations to assist "their" poor seems, in fact, quite revolutionary.

Legislating a civic vision of poor relief

Almost from the time of the proclamation of a National Constituent Assembly in June 1789, the sovereignty and the legitimacy of the "nation" as a community-in-the-making was evidenced by the new Assembly's role in seeking and distributing assistance to the poor. One sign of the Assembly's growing legitimacy was the haste with which hopeful citizens now sent their appeals for aid to representatives of the nation. In response, the Assembly reinforced its legitimacy by using some of its resources to grant assistance to meritorious citizens. These grants often occurred in public flourishes of largesse that enhanced the Assembly's status as representative of the new nation in matters of poor relief.[28]

Just as important was the way the National Assembly sought to integrate into its proceedings the face-to-face relationships that had been so critical to older traditions of charity and civic poor relief. It did this by admitting citizens onto the floor of the Assembly, including those who came to make donations to the "nation," in many instances for the relief of the poor. Public gift-giving

---

[26] Jean-Charles Sournia, *La Médecine révolutionnaire (1789–1799)* (Paris, 1989), 66–7.

[27] Trenard, "L'Idéologie révolutionnaire," in *La Protection sociale*, ed. Imbert, 129–31.

[28] Ferdinand Dreyfus, *L'Assistance sous la Législative et la Convention (1791–1795)* (Geneva, 1978 [1905]), 20.

Plate 9 "Dons Patriotiques" ("Patriotic gifts" to the nation), 7 September 1789 [Versailles].

to the nation provided newly entitled citizens the opportunity to express both their sense of belonging to the national community and their sense of solidarity with the nation's poor (see Plate 9). In the event memorialized in this plate, the women presenting the gift to the National Assembly were a delegation of "wives and daughters" of artists, whose spokesman read a speech on their behalf requesting that all "true friends of the fatherland be given the possibility of offering voluntary contributions" to help pay the nation's debts.[29]

The popularity of this form of revolutionary ritual, which provided moments of high drama on the floor of the National Assembly, suggests that for many men and women the nation really was becoming their community, since some "fraternal" gifts to the nation doubtless replaced contributions to local charities.[30] Far from being the product of the early "honeymoon" period in the life of the National Assembly, these rituals of patriotic gift-giving to the

---

[29] *AP* 8: 591, meeting of 7 September 1789. This event was memorialized visually in several versions. For another depiction, see Joan B. Landes, *Visualizing the Nation: Gender, Representation, and Revolution in Eighteenth-Century France* (Ithaca, NY and London, 2001), 92, 94. References to such presentations during the terms of the National Constituent Assembly, Legislative Assembly and Convention abound in volumes of the *AP*.

[30] Duprat, *Le Temps*, 342–4.

nation through its representatives continued throughout the life of successive revolutionary assemblies right up to the fall of Robespierre in summer 1794.[31]

By the end of 1789, opinion in the capital grew increasingly favorable to establishing a committee to serve as the National Assembly's agent in receiving donations for the poor. Over time, however, a committee of philanthropically minded representatives in the National Assembly who were experts on the topic of poor relief proposed to define its task more broadly. Its self-appropriated role would be to advise the Assembly on the best way to establish a national system for the relief of the poor. The final name of the National Assembly's committee, the Committee on Mendicity (Comité de mendicité), emphasized only one narrow focus of what would become the group's wide-ranging effort to design a system of poor relief consistent with the civic values of those who were constructing the nation.

Philanthropic ideas and policy models of the sort that the Philanthropic Society and the Society for Maternal Charity espoused shaped the work of the Committee from its first sitting in February 1790 until the end of this Assembly's tenure in September 1791. The presence of such ideas in their discussions came about quite naturally because of the participation of philanthropically minded notables in powerful positions of the committee structure itself. Indeed, many committees of the Constituent Assembly such as the Committee on Mendicity functioned essentially like voluntary associations of the Old Regime, being composed of networks of men who knew one another as the result of their research, personal engagement, and lobbying on behalf of programs to reform poor relief within the kingdom.[32] The difference was that these men now used their expertise to affect national policy directly through their work in committees of the National Assembly. In this way, the momentum of revolutionary change blurred the line between the sphere of civil society, in which voluntary associations for the relief of the poor had previously operated, and the newly emerging life of the nation.

Under the forceful leadership of the redoubtable duc de Liancourt, a noted Old Regime philanthropist, the Committee on Mendicity's debates, its seven major reports, and many shorter ones laid down the terms within which national-level policy discussions on poor relief would be waged.[33] Throughout its work, which involved the collection of national data on the poor, the investigation of the nation's hospital infrastructure, and finally the creation of a system of

---

[31] On the involvement of members of the Jacobin clubs in charitable and "humanitarian" contributions in the first several years of the Revolution, see Michael L. Kennedy, *The Jacobin Clubs in the French Revolution: The First Years* (Princeton, 1982), 123–8.

[32] Duprat, *Le Temps*, 127, 145.

[33] Liancourt adopted the title duc de la Rochefoucauld-Liancourt after the assassination of his cousin, the duc de la Rochefoucauld, in 1792. The latter was also known as a prominent Old Regime philanthropist.

assistance, the Committee demonstrated its commitment to the civic values and corresponding family-based relief policies that Old Regime reformers had advocated for the nation's respectable poor.

One of the key theoretical and practical questions the Committee on Mendicity had to answer was a contentious one – to whom did the poor belong?[34] What were the grounds of their entitlements to assistance, and what forms should that assistance take? In its meeting of 14 May 1790, committee member Thouret's lengthy report cited the traditional principle of local responsibility for the poor that had been so evident in many of the *cahiers de doléances*. Rather than building on this older ground of entitlement, however, Thouret emphasized how much the principle had decayed over time, focusing on the growth of a more recent set of policies by which the royal government had insinuated itself, often reluctantly, into problems of poor relief at the national level. This royal intervention, Thouret suggested, had occurred because of the Church's "abandonment" of the poor.[35]

Thouret outlined for the Committee a system of assistance that he believed was as economical as it would be if municipalities or districts were funding it, but that incorporated this newer notion of central state responsibility in the domain of public assistance. The choice, he argued, was between a system that relied essentially on local taxes and indirect taxes authorized by the royal government versus one that used real "public" monies – that is, direct tax money levied by the central government – to assist the poor.

That the nation bore principal responsibility seemed obvious to Liancourt. He asked: *"Do the poor belong to the municipalities or to the government? No one could fail to believe the latter, since they constitute an integral part of the nation."* Since the poor were part of the nation, funding for their needs, he argued, should logically flow from the nation's funds.[36] The practical and symbolic advantages of funding poor relief from "public" funds distributed through the departmental and district levels, Liancourt argued, would make this part of government more consistent with the rest of the emerging administrative system and avoid the sort of interparish feuding which the Committee associated with the administration of the English Poor Law.

In a critical respect, Liancourt's model incorporated the long-standing tradition of community responsibility for its own poor. The difference was that the community-in-the-making was now a national one. As members of the

[34] See *Procès-verbaux et rapports du Comité de mendicité de la Constituante, 1790–1791*, ed. Camille Bloch and Alexandre Tuetey (Paris, 1911) (hereafter *PV*), Introduction, x. Duprat, *Le Temps*, 294–319, recounts the history of the Committee on Mendicity and offers her interpretation of its work. See also Trenard, "L'Idéologie," in *La Protection sociale*, ed. Imbert, 138–58.
[35] *PV*, 10–13.
[36] "Réponse à la question proposée par le Comité par M. Thouret," meeting of 14 July 1790. *PV*, 40–1.

new National Assembly, Liancourt and other members of the Committee on Mendicity simply had a clearer vision of this "imagined" community than the authors of many of the *cahiers de doléances* who continued to associate their community with their locality or region.[37]

In substituting the nation for the Church or King as protector of the entitlements of the poor, the Committee on Mendicity at least discursively buttressed the legitimacy of the National Assembly's claims on the Church's financial resources, as it freely acknowledged. Since the goods of the clergy "belonged" to the poor, the National Assembly seizure of the Church's wealth would "claim and thereby sanctify and legitimate operations carried out on the goods of the clergy." The Committee's focus on church property as the source of funding for a new system of national poor relief, and its rejection of the idea of local taxes for the poor, also stemmed from its judgment that the resulting low cost of poor relief would help to endear the new regime to the nation's taxpayers.[38] At their meeting of 12 May 1790, the Committee voted unanimously for the principle of a common fund based on public monies for the relief of the nation's poor.

Nevertheless, the Committee on Mendicity had to accommodate itself to older traditions while trying to resolve the problem of *where* the poor were to receive the nation's funds. It was over this question that the Committee established, and the Assembly ratified, the idea of one's legal residence for purposes of relief – one's *domicile de secours*. Although the citizen's entitlement to assistance was national in principle, its effective exercise was to be local in fact. While the poor belonged to the nation, their entitlements to assistance were to be fulfilled principally in the place where, by the fact of their birth or "industrious habits," they had "earned" their right to it. Establishing this principle, which was entirely in keeping with older civic traditions, became necessary as the result of the Committee's experience in setting up government workshops to put men to work building roads or repairing infrastructure in areas hard hit by unemployment. Experience showed that the establishment of such programs inevitably encouraged many men to migrate away from their places of residence to take advantage of the programs.[39]

The Committee on Mendicity also recommended repressive policies towards those begging away from their *domicile de secours*. There was, of course, no contradiction in civic tradition between sympathy for the residential poor or the resident beggar who was occasionally found to be begging, and repressiveness

---

[37] On the Committee on Mendicity's vision of a "national community," see William J. Olejniczak, "Change, Continuity, and the French Revolution: Elite Discourse on Mendicity, 1750–1815," in David G. Troyansky, Alfred Cismaru, and Norwood Andrews, Jr., eds., *The French Revolution in Culture and Society* (New York, 1991), 140.

[38] Annexe to meeting of 26 February 1790. *PV*, 4.

[39] Discussions of the residency issues are contained in the Committee's meetings in July, August, and October–November, 1790. *PV*, 102, 121–4, 137.

towards the "professional" beggar or vagrant. Thus, in good civic tradition, the Committee denounced begging in its effort to distinguish those citizens who were and were not entitled to assistance. Their repeated requests for the expulsion of foreign beggars with no *domicile de secours* was part of their attempt to erect a kind of entitlement "wall" around the nation, but this met with little success. An expulsion order voted by the National Assembly failed to prevent their circulation.[40]

The Committee was at a relative disadvantage compared to earlier civic leaders whose restrictive notions of citizenship had provided a way of limiting assistance to the local poor. Now, the Committee on Mendicity had to grapple with the implications of their much enlarged notion of citizenship and the rights that accompanied it. Liancourt voiced some uncertainty about the legal and moral ramifications of the concept of a *domicile de secours* and policies for arresting beggars. He and other Committee members clearly also had second thoughts about the repressive elements of the relief system they were shaping. Liancourt presented a number of these issues to the Committee in November 1790:

1. Aren't individual liberty and rights of man injured by outlawing begging?
2. On what principle should we found the principle that a municipality, district, département, should take care of its poor, and consequently, that the poor who need assistance must remain in their municipality, district or département?
3. What distinction should be made between policing domiciled and vagrant beggars?[41]

Although these sorts of doubts remained, the Committee did ratify the idea of the *domicile de secours*. The Committee and the Assembly also reformed older practices, for example by broadening entitlements to all citizens of the nation and reducing the number of years one had to be resident in a specific locale to receive assistance.

The Committee's preference for outdoor relief as the centerpiece of a national system of assistance emerged early in its deliberation. They favored it "as much as possible, so as to stimulate work, maintain natural and social affections, encourage morality, and make [assistance] as economical as possible."[42] Committee members used English and French data to show that outdoor relief

---

[40] Meeting of 26 May 1790, Annexe to meeting of 28 June 1790, and meeting of 5 July 1790. *PV*, 54, 92–4. On efforts to repress begging during the revolution, see Alan Forrest, *The French Revolution and the Poor* (New York, 1981), 87–95.

[41] Annexe to meeting of 17 November 1790. *PV*, 190.

[42] Annexe to meeting of 26 February 1790. *PV*, 2. La Rochefoucauld-Liancourt brought a copy of Angot des Rotours' text to the meeting of 30 April 1790. *PV*, 23–4. Arguments in favor of outdoor relief also figured prominently in the meeting of 11 June 1790, 74, and 27 August 1790, 121–2. Calculations of the lower costs of outdoor relief, based on data from the Philanthropic Society of Paris and of Orléans, appear in the "Cinquième Rapport du Comité de mendicité. Estimation des fonds à accorder au département des secours publics, par M. de la Rochefoucauld-Liancourt." *PV*, 472–4, 500–4.

cost substantially less than maintaining the poor in large institutions. Committee member Thouret compared figures on the annual costs of assisting people from the General Hospital of Rouen and the Philanthropic Societies in Paris and Orléans, showing that whereas Rouen's hospital paid 120 livres per head, the Philanthropic Society paid 105 and 74 livres in the two cities respectively.[43]

Liancourt noted that beyond virtues of economy, outdoor relief helped the poor by encouraging broader social ties in the form of assistance from family, neighbors, and friends.[44] Thouret echoed Angot's and Dupont de Nemours' belief that outdoor relief encouraged "natural affections" both within the family, and between households and their community, while reinforcing ideals of household independence:

> when we help the poor as much as possible in his own home, he is left with a thousand small ways of helping himself, which form many resources that he would be obliged to renounce by being transported into a hospital, where one takes on the obligation of overseeing his complete upkeep, thereby relieving him in this way of caring [for himself].[45]

Liancourt's belief that kin should be the main source of support for their members was so strong that he wished to repeal citizenship rights in instances where "ungrateful children" with sufficient means failed to assist their aged parents. In such situations, outdoor relief to poor households would permit needy individuals to seek assistance from other quarters: "If...an elderly or sick person cannot find the consolation and care that the well-meaning law wishes to procure for him within his family, he should be free to seek them elsewhere, to find children among his friends, relatives, or neighbors by [being provided with] aid from public welfare (*'bienfaisance publique'*)."[46]

Consistent with their own philanthropic views, members of the Committee on Mendicity did not wish the state to have a monopoly on assistance to the poor, only the major role. Constructing a system of outdoor relief for the most deserving of the nation's poor in no way precluded the assistance of kin or the intervention of voluntary associations of individuals who, like Committee members, were inspired by a concern for human welfare. Indeed, the Committee

---

[43] Annexe to the meeting of 11 June 1790. *PV*, 73–4. The Philanthropic Society of Paris, noting how expensive the capital was, had expended from 70–100 livres per person annually among its clients in the years 1781 to 1790. The Society had assisted 824 people in 1787, 1,507 in 1788, 1,200 in 1789, and 1,204 in 1790.

[44] "Quatrième rapport du Comité de mendicité. Secours à donner à la classe indigente dans les différents âges et dans les différentes circonstances de la vie, par M. de la Rochefoucauld-Liancourt," read to the Committee on 1 December 1790, *PV*, 202, quoted on 395–6.

[45] See Thouret's speech in the meeting of 14 June 1790. *PV*, 88.

[46] "Quatrième rapport du Comité de mendicité. Secours à donner à la classe indigente dans les différents âges et dans les diférentes circonstances de la vie, par M. de la Rochefoucauld-Liancourt." *PV*, 421.

believed that "benevolent" persons and organizations could play a key role in making systems of outdoor relief more effective.

In the Committee on Mendicity's first general report on the new public assistance system-in-the-making, Liancourt confirmed the importance of voluntary associations of benevolent persons:

the field of benevolence [*bienfaisance*] will always remain open to individuals and associations who would like to increase the well-being of the poor of whatever class or region by supplementary assistance. Legislation should authorize and even encourage this generous liberality which can only grow under the new Constitution, since in every time and among all peoples, [love of] humanity is an inseparable companion of liberty.[47]

The appeal of voluntary associations lay in their ability to provide outdoor relief relatively inexpensively while encouraging family ties as well as solidarity beyond the household.

The National Assembly therefore looked favorably upon efforts to keep poor respectable families together. To this end, the National Assembly and its Committee on Mendicity voted to extend support to the Society for Maternal Charity, which continued to operate in the capital. As the result of a request from the National Assembly, which granted the Society 1,000 livres from each drawing of the National Lottery, the Committee heard two reports on the organization in June and July 1790, received copies of its rules, and prepared a report on it that quoted liberally from those rules.[48]

The report gave an overview of this "maternalist" organization, which was administered by ladies ("benefactresses") who met at the office of the Paris Foundling Home, with members having responsibility for different neighborhoods of the capital. Although, as noted, benefactresses or deputies of the organization were recruited from among the court nobility, those who did the actual

---

[47] "Premier rapport du Comité de mendicité. Exposé des principes généraux qui ont dirigé son travail, par M. de la Rochefoucauld-Liancourt, présenté à l'Assemblée Constituante par La Rochefoucault-Liancourt, dans la séance du 12 juin 1790." *PV*, 333. On the Philanthropic Society of Lyon, see Jean-Pierre Gutton, "L'Action sociale dans le département du Rhône (1789–1796)," in *La Protection sociale*, ed. Imbert, 285. The Philanthropic Society of Orléans spent over 74 livres per person annually, but the average was probably less, since children required only half this sum, and women assisted in childbirth were aided only temporarily. See: "Cinquième rapport du Comité de mendicité. Estimation des fonds à accorder au département des secours publics, par M. de la Rochefoucauld-Liancourt." *PV*, 500.

[48] Meetings of 18 June 1790, 5 July 1790, and Annexe to the latter. *PV* 89, 94–6. The rules were sent and acknowledged in the meeting of 31 July 1790 (105). The Society's text: "Mémoire sur la Charité maternelle, donné par les dames de cette Société," is contained in the "Rapport sur l'établissement de la Charité maternelle de Paris par le Comité de mendicité." *PV*, 693–703, dating from 21 January 1791. The "Mémoire sur la Charité maternelle" is undated, but contains financial data up to early July 1790, suggesting that it was composed shortly before being sent to the Committee. See also: "Rapport fait au nom du Comité de mendicité. Des visites faites dans divers hôpitaux, hospices et maisons de charité de Paris, par M. de la Rochefoucault-Liancourt, député du département de l'Oise." *PV*, 594–5.

in-home visits to mothers during and after their pregnancies were more likely to be the wives of high *fonctionnaires*, including Mmes. Dupont de Nemours and Lavoisier.[49]

Potential clients came to the attention of the Society via local clergy or personal networks of acquaintanceship. Having gathered information on the women, members proposed them for support to the larger administrative group, which approved or rejected each candidate. To be eligible for support, women had to be poor, domiciled in Paris for at least one year, able to produce a marriage certificate, and of good reputation as attested by their clergyman, neighbors, and landlord.

The Society for Maternal Charity expressed its commitment to civic goals by its attempts to serve all areas of the capital equally. Rather than adopting children and their mothers one by one, the Society established a kind of "cohort" organization by area of the city. Each time the Society succeeded in raising 12,000 livres, it divided the money into sixty parts of 192 livres (totaling 11,520 livres, adding another 480 for twin births) and allocated these places to different parts of the city "in the proportion which has been judged most appropriate given the spatial extent and number of poor."[50]

The Society concentrated on several groups of children and their mothers who were facing the kinds of "critical life situations" endemic to urban working-class life. Women who were widowed during pregnancy or whose husbands had been crippled were objects of the Society's special interest. Some women and their children were eligible simply because their households had too many children for parents to support, the Society's memoir noting its assistance to households with five or six children. One sample of families whom the Society aided in the 1780s showed that a wide variety of working-class male occupations was represented among the families assisted, who had on average 4.3 children.[51] Even women who had been abandoned by their husbands were eligible as long as the wife's "bad behavior" was not deemed responsible for the abandonment.[52]

By assisting married women of good character, the Society hoped to provide other poor women with models of maternal virtue worthy of emulation: "In protecting childhood, [the Society] wishes to reinforce family ties, attach mothers

[49] Stuart Woolf, "The Société de Charité Maternelle, 1788–1815," in Jonathan Barry and Colin Jones, eds., *Medicine and Charity before the Welfare State* (London and New York, 1991), 102–3.

[50] "Mémoire sur la Charité maternelle," *PV*, 696; Woolf, "*Société*," 106, notes that the neediest parts of the capital including the St. Antoine and St. Marceau areas received larger numbers of grants than others.

[51] Woolf, "*Société*," 106.

[52] "Mémoire sur la Charité maternelle," *PV*, 697. The Society also noted that the support of the Société philanthropique and the queen were going to enable them to extend a third year of support to all sixth-born children with young brothers and sisters as well as all orphans and twins who were being nursed by their mothers.

to their duties, require them to remain at home and thereby protect them from disorder and from begging, which is grounds for absolute exclusion."[53] Giving her child to a wet nurse without the Society's permission was also grounds for excluding a mother from assistance.

Mothers who were accepted received a total of 192 livres divided over the two years of their pension: 18 livres at the time of delivery, a layette for the baby worth 20 livres, 8 livres a month from birth to one year, and 4 livres a month from one to two years, as well as clothing worth 10 livres.[54] The Society knew from experience that this monthly payment was an absolute minimum. When they paid only 3 livres a month, they found that a number of mothers took their infants surreptitiously to a wet nurse or "perhaps" even to the Foundling Home.[55] Their records showed that between May 1788 and December 1790, the Society helped 991 children and spent over 147,000 livres, with administrative expenses totaling only 5,500 livres.[56] Given the large number of children and the fact that on average the support of each child cost 135–140 livres for a full term, the Society calculated that an annual budget of 300,000 livres would be barely sufficient for its work.

The Society for Maternal Charity sought to enhance child health, domestic virtue, and the life of the larger society by lowering infant, child, and maternal mortality. The Society's memoir noted that though it had assisted almost 1,000 mothers since its inception, it had lost only 2 to death in childbirth. Among children assisted, only about a fifth had died, a figure they contrasted with the high mortality of children brought to the Foundling Home.[57] The benefits of the Society for Maternal Charity were not limited to the domestic sphere, however. Its work helped to instill families with civic virtues, bringing "a love of order, of work and of duty as well as the unity of households into the interior of families. It restores to the state precious mothers and a prodigious number of children."

In its complimentary commentary on the Society and its memoir, the Committee on Mendicity approved an annual "subscription" of 15,000 livres to the organization, which the Committee hoped would be able to stand on its own feet financially. Yet, it noted that current conditions – including the flight of many wealthy citizens from the capital and the climate of financial insecurity – did not bode well for the kind of voluntary, individual-level support on which the Society depended. Nonetheless, the Committee's report suggested

---

[53] "Mémoire sur la Charité maternelle," *PV*, 698.

[54] *Ibid.*, 695. Mothers received a double benefit in the case of twins.   [55] *Ibid.*, 700–1.

[56] A report to Marie-Antoinette about the Society stated that 1,500 mothers had been rejected in the first eight months of the Society's work in the capital. See Woolf, "*Société*," 106.

[57] *Ibid.*, 107, notes that infant mortality among children assisted totaled about 20 percent while the rate for Paris foundlings was two-thirds.

that the Society for Maternal Charity was exactly the kind of association that merited emulation in other towns, given that it "complements and . . . perfects public benevolence, which, to be just, must be submitted to exact and almost severe law."[58]

While the Committee on Mendicity believed strongly in the complementarity of government assistance and assistance through voluntary associations, the complementarity was based on the premise that voluntary associations would receive most of their funding from sources outside the government. Thus, in November 1790, while applauding the efforts of the "brother" society of the Society for Maternal Charity, the Philanthropic Society, it responded negatively to the latter's requests for funds. Financial constraints were part of the Committee's problem. The other part was principled:

Doubtless, philanthropic societies need to be encouraged and supported. They spread individual charity with rare care, intelligence and virtue, and none has fulfilled this duty as completely as the Parisian society. Moreover, these societies greatly economize public funds; they inspire individual benevolence without which public welfare can only be incomplete.

However, Liancourt added:

This sort of association must [be able to] exist on its own, or it is no longer a charitable, voluntary organization.

Liancourt reminded the Philanthropic Society's members that the Society for Maternal Charity received public funding regularly, but that no such funding had ever been designated for the Philanthropic Society, not even from the king. He, the authors noted, had never supported the Society with *public* funding. The assistance the king had given was "in his own and private name, as a friend of humanity."[59]

From its beginnings in Autumn 1791, the new Legislative Assembly's committee charged with assisting the poor demonstrated the same interest as the Committee on Mendicity in maintaining a distinction between different groups of the poor, while emphasizing the legitimacy of the respectable poor's entitlements to assistance. At one of the first meetings of the as-yet-unnamed committee, a member objected to a motion that the committee retain the name "Committee on Mendicity" or choose the title of "Welfare Committee" (Comité de bienfaisance) and devote part of its attention to problems of hospitals and prisons. He proposed instead what would become the committee's eventual name, the Committee on Public Assistance (Comité des secours publics), in the following terms:

[58] "Mémoire sur la Charité maternelle," *PV*, 701–2.
[59] Meeting of 1 November 1790. *PV*, 165–6.

I believe that giving assistance to those who truly have need of it is just, especially on the part of the nation. I therefore request that this committee be called Committee on Public Assistance, but I request that we separate everything related to prisons or jails from its functions so that we do not... degrade the lower classes by entrusting the care of the unfortunate and the criminal to the same persons.[60]

Like the Committee on Mendicity before it, the Legislative Assembly's Committee on Public Assistance was concerned with begging and its prevention, and yet, like its predecessor, its focus remained mainly with the respectable poor, who were brought to their attention by administrative and governing bodies, voluntary organizations, and individual correspondence.

In contrast to the programmatic innovations that the Committee on Mendicity outlined, at least on paper, records of the Legislative Assembly's Committee on Public Assistance convey a sense of immobility and frustration. First, as "new" men, members of the Committee simply had to familiarize themselves with the particulars of the work of the Committee on Mendicity, which seems to have taken up a great deal of its time. Furthermore, they were plagued by the fact that many of the nation's newly formed départements had still not furnished information that was needed to guide the distribution of public funds for poor relief in a rational and equitable manner.[61]

During the one year of the Legislative Assembly's existence, its Committee on Public Assistance seems to have devoted most of its meeting time to requests for assistance from individuals, from deputies attempting to get assistance for their constituents, and from municipalities. It was not able to fulfill all of these appeals, and the grounds of their approval or disapproval are difficult to disentangle, as are their decisions to return certain requests to the district or departmental level. The Committee on Public Assistance's willingness to dispense its resources in an ad hoc manner doubtless violated the intent of the Committee on Mendicity, whose main goal had been to develop a fair system of assistance for the national community via the creation of local public assistance bureaus (*agences de secours*) funded primarily with funds from the state's treasury.

In another sense, however, the Legislative Assembly's Committee on Public Assistance's work disbursing funds to individuals, which doubtless distracted

---

[60] Deputy Garran de Coulon, speaking in the meeting of the Legislative Assembly of 14 October 1791, cited in Dreyfus, *L'Assistance*, 10; Michel Bouchet, *L'Assistance publique en France pendant la Révolution* (Paris, 1908), 281–2.

[61] Archives nationales (hereafter AN), Procès-verbaux of the Comité de Secours publics of the Legislative Assembly, Paris, AF II*39. Concerns about gathering data were expressed in the Committee's meetings of 30 November and 5 December 1791. By early 1792, the Committee still had not discussed basic principles of a new assistance system, and decided to cancel meetings for a week to delve more deeply into the Committee on Mendicity's work. See minutes of meeting of 9 January 1792. On the annoyance with the need to address individual petitions, see minutes of the meeting of 23 January 1792. Bouchet cites a number of these cases in his discussion of the committee. See Bouchet, *L'Assistance publique*, 282–7.

them from policy-making tasks, should not be discounted entirely. Fulfilling such appeals and responding to individual letters, as well as government and administrative entities, constituted part of the task of confirming the political and moral legitimacy of the evolving revolutionary regime. By distributing hundreds of thousands of livres in small sums to the many named individuals who appealed to them for relief, the Committee on Public Assistance of the Legislative Assembly demonstrated their preference for outdoor relief to all sorts of virtuous citizens fallen on "hard times." Acceding to such requests, or if necessary, channeling them back through layers of a new revolutionary government, was not simply a distraction from the Committee's "real" mandate to make policy. Fulfilling many of these requests was one way to demonstrate that the nation truly constituted a community responsible for its worthy poor.

By early 1792, the Committee on Public Assistance put the finishing touches on plans for a nationwide system of poor relief, whose main features the Committee on Mendicity had already outlined, one based on the distribution of funds from the central government through départements, districts, and cantons. As several commentators have noted, however, the Legislative Assembly's preoccupation with growing internal dissension made it difficult for the Committee on Public Assistance to get the Assembly's ear. Even when it had finally completed its task of developing and proposing specifics of a national public assistance system, the Committee had to try repeatedly to present this information to the Assembly as a whole.[62]

The Committee's major report, which Representative Bernard presented to the Legislative Assembly on 13 June 1792, differed little from the Committee on Mendicity's vision. It continued to rely principally on outdoor relief as its main tool, supporting the need for voluntary efforts to complement state-financed assistance.[63] Before the disbanding of the Legislative Assembly, the Committee on Public Assistance suggested that the eighty-three départements of the nation should be granted "the ability to regulate by themselves the specific mode of execution" of a general law on public assistance.[64]

Building a national community of individuals and families

In contrast to the lack of interest in matters relating to poor relief expressed by members of the Legislative Assembly in spring and summer 1792 when Representative Bernard read his report to the relatively uninterested members of the Legislative Assembly, members of the Convention, especially those most closely affiliated with the Montagnard group of the Jacobin Party, placed assistance to the worthy poor at the top of their agenda.

[62] Bouchet, *L'Assistance publique*, 280.   [63] *AP* 45: 137–58; Dreyfus, *L'Assistance*, 21–33.
[64] Procès-verbaux of the Comité de Secours publics of the Legislative Assembly, AN AF II*39, meeting of 18 August 1792; Dreyfus, *L'Assistance*, 31–3.

The needs of families came to the Convention's attention most aggressively in the form of requests from Paris "sections," where many men were volunteering to fight the foreign enemy. As the Paris sections began to raise money to equip "their" soldiers for foreign wars, a number of them raised the specter of dependency that many families would face once volunteers left for the front.[65]

Beginning with a law of 26–7 November 1792 granting assistance to family members dependent upon the labor of departed volunteers for their survival, legislation for soldiers' families gradually expanded. In proposing legislation for these families, Representative Maignet, a member of the Convention's Committee on Public Assistance, defended the entitlements of dependents of volunteers to annual pensions. The law conferred pensions of 40 livres per child under age 8, 25 livres for children from 8–12, 40 livres for parents aged 60 to 69, 60 livres for parents over the age of 70, and 60 livres for wives. Maignet maintained that these pensions were only for family members who were utterly dependent upon the financial support of the volunteer, those who had a kind of "direct natural right" to the product of the man's work. Thus, in his initial presentation, wives' claims were conditional upon illness or other circumstances that would prohibit them from earning a living. This qualification disappeared from the final wording of the law, however.[66]

By a law of 4–5 May 1793, the Convention expanded these entitlements in two ways, extending them to nearly all men under arms and to a growing number of categories of soldiers' relatives. The law granted the right of assistance to needy ascendant kin and to brothers and sisters who were orphans and judged by their sections or municipalities "not to have sufficient means to subsist."[67]

Reports of the failure of authorities to carry out these laws for the relief of volunteers' families reached the Convention in short order, however, forwarded to members by individuals in their electoral districts, by revolutionary clubs and associations, and by section leaders or petitioners who came to the floor of the Convention itself. The société populaire of Cambrai brought its complaints to the Convention's representatives-on-mission to the Army of the North. A petition from the société populaire of Rieux complained that military officials were not furnishing documentation verifying volunteers' presence in the ranks that their relatives needed to prove eligibility and receive their money.[68]

---

[65] "Adresse de la section du Pont-Neuf," *AP* 60: 471, meeting of 23 March 1793. An increasing proportion of citizen-soldiers were married men. See: Isser Woloch, "War-widows Pensions: Social Policy in Revolutionary and Napoleonic France," *Societas* 6, 4 (1976): 238–9.

[66] *AP* 53: 595–6, meeting of 26 November 1792. The text of the law is also contained in Camille Bloch, ed., *L'Assistance publique: instruction, recueil de textes et notes* (Paris, 1909), Doc. 95, "Décret sur les secours à accorder aux pères, mères et enfants des citoyens-soldats volontaires, qui sont dans le besoin," of 26–7 November 1792, 85–6.

[67] *AP* 64: 124–6, meeting of 5 May 1793.

[68] *AP* 65: 651, meeting of 31 May 1793; *AP* 67: 11, meeting of 20 June 1793; *AP* 73: 476, meeting of 7 September 1793. Other complaints from families not receiving their benefits are contained in *AP* 73: 533, meeting of 8 September 1793.

The Convention responded by allowing departmental authorities to pay families of deserving soldiers from taxes collected in 1791 and 1792, requiring them to furnish the central government with lists of names and documentation needed for the families to prove their eligibility, promising to reimburse the départements out of the fund of 12 million livres allocated to fulfill terms of the laws of 26 November 1792 and 4 May 1793.[69] The complaint of one woman to the Convention during summer 1793 expressed the terms of the assistance "contract" which family members of volunteers understood now to exist between the nation and themselves:

the petitioner, Citizens, is the spouse of Charles-Louis Pagnot, sergeant of a battalion . . . currently serving with the army in the Vendée.

Burdened with four children of whom the eldest is only four years old, her husband whose patriotic zeal is excessive, does not fear risking his life for the service of the Republic and was one of the first to depart. At the time of his departure, the section of Arcis where he is domiciled . . . promised the petitioner to take care of her children and to give her all that was granted by the law.

The petitioner went to her section to claim her payment, without success. They told her that the section is poor and that they could not give her the assistance she needs.

In response, the Convention ordered its executive committee to report to it about the execution of the law of 4 May 1793.[70]

These assurances were not sufficient however, and it was clear that stronger measures were needed. In mid-September 1793, Representative Jeanbon Saint-André noted on the floor of the Convention that the promise of assistance to the "widows, wives and children" of volunteers was still not being fulfilled. The causes, in his judgment, included the lack of civism and the "bad faith" of members of the administration, particularly those at the departmental level, as well as the burden of paperwork requirements for proving eligibility. His solution was to make municipal authorities responsible for receiving and distributing funds supplied from the Minister of the Interior, who was voted another 5 million livres for this purpose.[71] But by January 1794, the Convention was still being "besieged" by reports of the nonpayment of assistance to soldiers' families.[72]

Given the lack of funding coming to families of volunteers, new voluntary associations took up some of the slack. "Patriotic donations" flowed from

---

[69] *AP* 69: 146, meeting of 18 July 1793.
[70] *AP* 73: 533, meeting of 8 September 1793. The Minister of the Interior assured the Convention of his efforts to carry out the two laws on aid to volunteers in the session of 13 September 1793, *AP* 74: 41.
[71] *AP* 74: 212–13, meeting of 15 September 1793.
[72] *AP* 83: 52–3, meeting of 17 nîvose II (6 January 1794). In the session of 20 January 1794, learning that the Ministry of Interior had exhausted its funds for this project, the Convention voted another 10 million livres for it on the urging of Couthon speaking for the Committee of Public Safety. *AP* 83: 504.

organizations such as the *sociétés populaires* to the worthy poor of their communities. These organizations acted not only to assist families of the "deserving poor" of their area who had sent volunteers to the army, but also kept pressure on the Convention to fulfill the entitlements it had pledged – often through example:

> The *Société républicaine et montagnarde* of Mont-de-Marsan, département of Landes, touched by the needs of parents of defenders of the fatherland whose [military] leaders neglect to send certificates attesting to the presence of volunteers and sailors in their ranks, decided to distribute to these parents patriotic gifts from members of the Society in the amount of 9,618 livres.[73]

Further discussion suggested that "red tape" was an important reason for the lack of execution of the laws. The Convention therefore enacted more legislation extending benefits to military replacements and setting up an administrative process that they hoped would streamline the provision of benefits to families of soldiers.[74]

Although the urgency of assistance to families of volunteers was paramount in the minds of members of the Convention almost from the beginning of its existence, the need for a system of assistance to *all* deserving citizens also claimed representatives' attention during the Year II. In an address to the Convention on 19 March 1793, Representative Bo, speaking for the Convention's Committee on Public Assistance, laid down some of the principal features of the general system of assistance that the Committee was planning.[75] He called particular attention to the need to care for infants and their mothers, noting the infant mortality rate of 250 per 1,000 then prevailing, and decrying the loss of these citizens to the fatherland. Assistance in the home would, he argued, encourage maternal breastfeeding and discourage the sending of infants to mercenary wet nurses.

Just as important to Bo and the Convention was the need to ensure that all assistance to the poor would come from a common fund ("d'un centre commun"), one whose organization would eventually lead to the suppression of the assets of all hospitals, charity bureaus, and other foundations for the poor of the nation. The distribution of benefits through different layers of government

---

[73] *AP* 82: 53, meeting of 21 December 1793.

[74] In his speech outlining the new measures, Collot d'Herbois, speaking for the Committee of Public Safety, noted that the Ministry of the Interior had 100 clerks working on the correspondence relative to assistance to families of volunteers. *AP* 129, meeting of 12 pluviôse II (31 January 1794), 281–2.

[75] Jean-Paul Bertaud notes that this speech was delivered in the midst of the Convention's consideration of a new "Declaration of the Rights of Man," whose Article 21 stated that the right of citizens to assistance was a "sacred debt." See Bertaud, "La Crise sociale (septembre, 1792–juillet 1796)," in *La Protection*, ed. Imbert, 214, and "La Révolution et la politique sociale en faveur des militaires," *Revue du Nord* 75, 299 (January–March, 1993): 181–91.

would, he argued, obviate the need for a face-to-face relation between individual donors and recipients, thus allowing the citizen to "make his fate depend on no one by placing it under the guardianship of all." Those who wished to contribute to the poor could do so through a new assistance bureau to be established in each canton and run by unpaid officials, which would disburse funds raised nationally and locally. Indeed, the system that Bo outlined even required localities to supplement the funds they received from the central government by 20 percent, thus encouraging concern for the poor among their neighbors.[76]

The project for a national system of outdoor relief was presented to the Convention on 26 June 1793 by Representative Maignet for the Committee on Public Assistance, which outlined the Committee's plan for assistance to poor families through provisions for children and the elderly (see Plate 10).[77] Maignet's long speech introducing the legislative proposal revealed the sort of individual, family, and community model that the Committee hoped to foster. In it, Maignet rehearsed the failings of Royalty and Church under the Old Regime, lamenting the inadequacy of assistance to poor families. Through its defense of paternal power, Maignet argued, the royal government had allowed fathers to abuse their authority while failing to protect the state's interest in the well-being of families. Under the Old Regime, "The interest of the state was what was considered the least; one never dreamed that the first of civic virtues was to contribute to making the society of which one was a member eternal." What was more:

Laws that were always in contradiction with those of nature placed power in the hands of the father to render marriages impossible by letting him have the freedom to dispose of almost all of his goods in favor of one child and to reduce the others to a state of distress that made them renounce marriage so that they would not pass on their poverty to their posterity. As if that wasn't enough, other similarly barbaric laws left him the power to prolong the single status of other children on whom he had not succeeded in imposing permanent celibacy. Paternal power poorly understood served as a pretext to these abuses. One feigned not to know that children belong more to the Republic than to their father.[78]

In contrast, new legislation on assistance to poor families would regenerate the nation through its encouragement of marriage and reproduction, leading to the formation of virtuous republican families centered in the household.

---

[76] Bo's report and the project are contained in *AP* 60: 322–8, meeting of 19 March 1793. Bertaud, "La Crise sociale," 214–18 suggests that at the time of Bo's speech, word of counter-revolutionary activity in the Vendée lent urgency to the task of finally institutionalizing a national assistance program.

[77] Bertaud, "La Crise sociale," 219–26, notes that this report occurred less than a month after the fall of the Girondins that followed sans-culotte uprisings in late May and early June.

[78] See Maignet's speech in *AP* 67: 476–96, meeting of 26 June 1793.

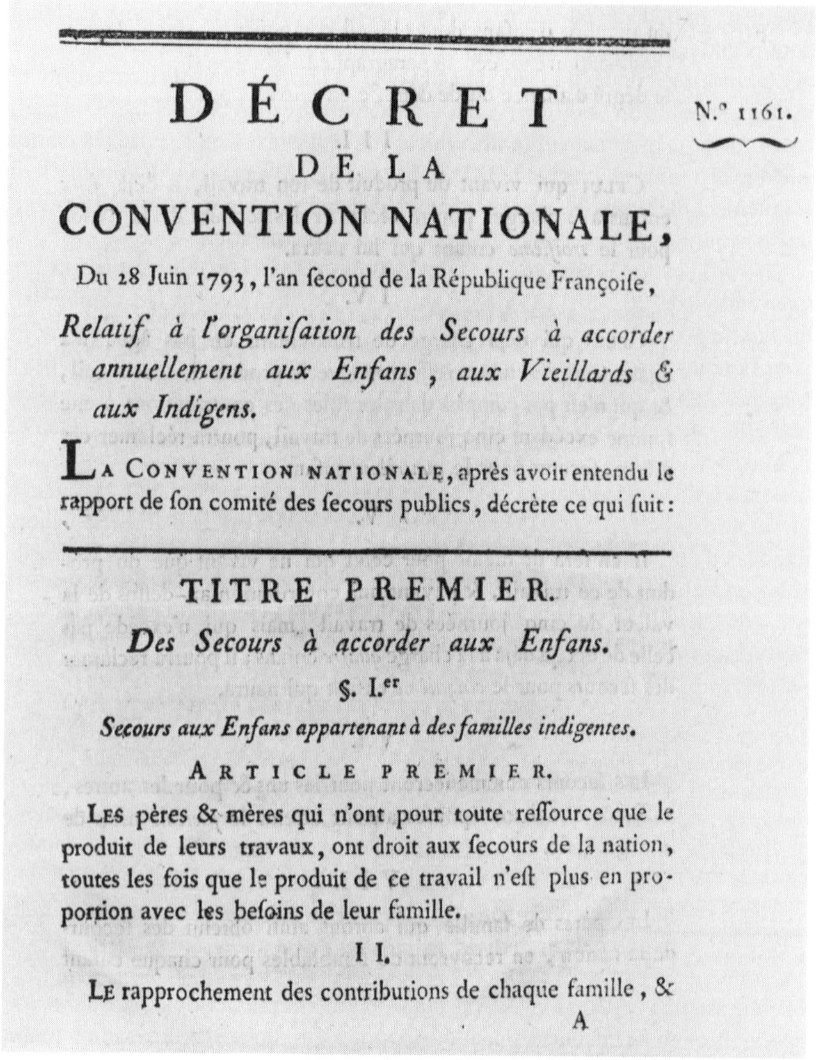

DÉCRET

N.º 1161.

DE LA

CONVENTION NATIONALE,

Du 28 Juin 1793, l'an fecond de la République Françoife,

Relatif à l'organifation des Secours à accorder annuellement aux Enfans, aux Vieillards & aux Indigens.

LA CONVENTION NATIONALE, après avoir entendu le rapport de fon comité des fecours publics, décrète ce qui fuit :

TITRE PREMIER.

Des Secours à accorder aux Enfans.

§. I.er

Secours aux Enfans appartenant à des familles indigentes.

ARTICLE PREMIER.

LES pères & mères qui n'ont pour toute reffource que le produit de leurs travaux, ont droit aux fecours de la nation, toutes les fois que le produit de ce travail n'eft plus en proportion avec les befoins de leur famille.

I I.

LE rapprochement des contributions de chaque famille, &

A

Plate 10 *Décret de la Convention nationale relatif à l'organisation des Secours à accorder annuellement aux Enfans, aux Vieillards & aux Indigens* (Decree of the National Convention regarding poor relief), 28 June 1793.

Maignet noted that the poor were members of the "grande famille" of the "nation" and, like all citizens, gained membership in this extended family on the basis of a sacred contract between themselves and the nation. Of course, this contract prohibited the nation from contributing to the poor any more than what was "strictly necessary" for their survival, and required that poor citizens first seek assistance from their own family.[79] Nonetheless, in the case of poor children, the nation had to step in to replace those parents who were unable to take care of them. Indeed, the nation's provision of care served as a kind of "perfect adoption" of needy children.

Maignet's use of the metaphor of adoption was more than a simple rhetorical flourish. Nowhere was an emerging Jacobin vision of the republican family better illustrated than by the reality and metaphor of adoption. Although the adoption of children had never entirely disappeared from France, it remained relatively marginal, at least in its legal form, from the medieval period until philanthropically minded advocates for its legalization introduced the theme for public discussion at the end of the eighteenth century.[80]

In January 1793, the Convention itself became a parent when it officially "adopted" Suzanne Lepeletier, the daughter of a republican martyr assassinated as a result of his vote for the execution of Louis XVI. During the Year II, numerous Jacobin clubs throughout the nation emulated the Convention's gesture by adopting local children, particularly foundlings or those in need. Adopting a poor infant or foundling, whom the Convention would rename "natural children of the fatherland" or simply "children of the fatherland" by a decree of 4 July 1793, represented an acceptable act of face-to-face "philanthropy." Assisting poor children through adoption brought the spirit of national solidarity into the homes of citizens in a very practical way. As a recent commentator has suggested: "the incorporation of a stranger into one's family through adoption became a metaphor for the incorporation of the individual into the nation."[81] Citizens' willingness to adopt a child demonstrated the infusion of civic solidarity into the family, thus furthering the Jacobins' goal of integrating individuals and their families more closely into the larger national community they were working to create.

The June 1793 poor relief legislation that Maignet introduced required that mothers whose households were receiving assistance breastfeed their infants. For Maignet, the mother who breastfed her infant served as the moral center of the republican household. Quoting from Rousseau, he deduced how the reinforcement of bonds of sentiment between mother and infant within households of the poor who received pensions from the nation would rekindle bonds of

---

[79] *Ibid.*, 476, 478, 480, 489.

[80] Jean-Pierre Gutton, *Histoire de l'adoption en France* (Paris, 1993), 99–100, 104–6, discusses the Committee on Mendicity's preparation of a project of a law on adoption. Kristin E. Gager, *Blood Ties and Fictive Ties: Adoption and Family Life in Early Modern France* (Princeton, 1996), shows that adoption continued to exist in France from the Middle Ages onward, despite the lack of legal provisions for it in customary law.

[81] Eric Andrew Goodheart, "Adoption in the Discourses of the French Revolution" (Ph.D. dissertation, Harvard University, 1997), 24, 36. On the rich as the putative "adoptive brothers" of the poor, see Gross, *Fair Shares*, 32.

love among other members of the household and further the goal of building "public virtues."[82]

Maignet strongly advocated outdoor assistance, particularly concerning needy children. Terms he used to address problems of the elderly were quite similar, though here Maignet toned down his anti-institutional rhetoric, allowing the elderly poor to receive pensions in local "hospices," which were to be constructed in each arrondissement. The continuing desire to assist the young and the old within the home was clear, however. As in municipal policies of the distant and recent past, legislators trusted that conferring secure entitlements to outdoor assistance on France's vulnerable citizens would encourage "relatives, friends" or even "strangers" to receive aged pensioners into their own homes, since they would be able to "profit by the assistance given to each of them."[83]

Maignet's speech suggested that households to be relieved under the Convention's plan had to be "respectable," consisting either of wives living with their husbands or widows with children. Yet the law also made illegitimate children and their mothers eligible for assistance. In a departure from older civic traditions, Conventionnels seemed to be breaking down historic boundaries between the respectable and dishonorable poor.

What the Convention did, however, was even more innovative. As leaders of the national community, the revolutionary body tried to raise the status of illegitimate children and their mothers by the act of conferring on them entitlements to assistance from the nation. The historic linkage between respectability and eligibility for assistance from the community was thus maintained by the fact that the law expanded the boundaries of respectability itself. The Convention sought to do this through a variety of means, including the already-mentioned transformation of bastards into "children of the fatherland" ("enfants de la patrie"), and laws equalizing the inheritance rights of illegitimate and legitimate children retroactive to 14 July 1789.[84]

The practical results of provisions designed specifically for volunteers' families and those for families of the poor are difficult to discern. One assessment suggests that the law of 28 June 1793 was enforced at least in some areas.[85] However, in the Rouen region, for example, the district government noted that one year after the enactment of the law of 28 June 1793, none of the

[82] *AP* 67: 484. In "extremely rare" cases, women would be released from this duty on the basis of the opinion of a public health officer, to be appointed to each assistance bureau in her canton.
[83] *Ibid.*, 612–19, meeting of 28 June 1793. The citation is from Art. 14.
[84] See the classic discussion of the Convention's decree of 4 June 1793 and the law of 12 brumaire II (2 November 1793) in Crane Brinton, *French Revolutionary Legislation on Illegitimacy, 1789–1804* (Cambridge, MA, 1936), 23–41; Marcel Garaud, *La Révolution française et la famille* (Paris, 1978); James F. Traer, *Marriage and the Family in Eighteenth-Century France* (Ithaca, NY and London, 1980), 156–65.
[85] Bouchet, *L'Assistance publique*, 445–6.

41,000 livres allocated had been distributed among the three main categories of indigent families, foundlings, and the aged because two-thirds of the municipalities of the area had failed to furnish the district with lists of names of their eligible poor.[86]

Sectional assistance to families of the Parisian poor

In Paris, where local welfare committees of the Year II were relatively well organized, pro-revolutionary, and highly motivated, national legislation on behalf of the poor probably enjoyed as much enforcement as was possible given the difficulties that the central government encountered in distributing funds. A decree of 13 pluviôse II (1 February 1794) ordered the distribution of 10 million livres to all communes of the nation to fund groups entitled by the legislation of 28 June 1793. It was rigorously fulfilled in the capital, which received 250,000 livres of the funds.

The work of the Paris sections' welfare commissioners was critical in enabling citizens of Paris to receive the benefits of new entitlements that the Convention was busy bestowing, helping residents establish their entitlement status with birth certificates or even tax records. These local officials also actively publicized laws on poor relief through the use of street criers.[87] Welfare commissioners of the Paris sections were also willing to sidestep some terms of the law of 28 June 1793, opting for a "flexible" needs-based system of assistance to the domiciled poor, often distributing bread, rice, and other assistance in kind rather than the monetary pensions ordered by the legislation.

The forty-eight sections of Paris had to wrest control over poor relief funds from the control of parishes and a city-wide Welfare Commission (Commission de bienfaisance), which the Municipality had authorized to receive and oversee the distribution of poor relief in the capital since May 1791. By 1792–3, the Municipal Commission had a fund yielding 300,000 to 400,000 livres of income annually, which was distributed to parish poor relief commissions for assistance to approximately 100,000 indigents, or one in six residents of the capital.[88]

This system did not satisfy sectional leaders of Paris, however, who gradually claimed their right to direct poor relief efforts, arguing that they had been

[86] Yannick Marec, "L'Action sociale dans la région rouennaise (1792–1795)," in *La Protection sociale*, ed. Imbert, 294.

[87] Isser Woloch, "From Charity to Welfare in Revolutionary Paris," *Journal of Modern History* 58, 4 (December 1986): 799–800. For the text of the decree, see "Décret qui ordonne la répartition d'un secours de dix millions dans toutes les communes de la République," 13 pluviôse II (1 February, 1794), in Bloch, ed., *L'Assistance publique*, Doc. 171, 133–4.

[88] Bouchet, *L'Assistance publique*, 559.

aiding the poor and building new bonds of "fraternal" solidarity long before the Municipality set up its Commission.[89] Section leaders claimed that sections, not parishes, now provided the normal setting of community life in the capital. Citizens saw one another in section meetings; they were censused and documented for military service in their sections. Sections also had the advantage of being smaller than parishes, so that sectional welfare committees could know "their" poor personally and serve their needs more effectively than parish authorities.[90]

In a petition to the Convention dated 11 November 1792, sectional welfare commissioners claimed the right of each section to elect a commission to "regulate, divide up and distribute" assistance to its poor. By a decree of 28 March 1793, the Convention concurred, and established a new organization, the Central Welfare Commission (Commission centrale de bienfaisance) composed of one representative from each of the capital's forty-eight sections who had been elected in a meeting of the general assembly of his section by majority voice. This group was given jurisdiction over financial resources to be granted to the residential poor of the capital, excluding those in hospitals.

Section leaders' desire to observe and know "their" poor, and to break down the secrecy they believed had surrounded relations between the Municipal Commission and the parish committees was powerful. Parish officials' practice of distributing assistance discreetly to the "shamefaced poor" appeared particularly antithetical to the fraternal and egalitarian spirit of the outdoor relief system the Convention was designing for the nation. Section officials' requirement that the local poor state their need for financial assistance publicly stemmed partly from their own need to meet standards of public accountability. However, they also sought to establish a new attitude towards assistance reflecting the idea that assistance was a "right" ensured by the nation and carried out by its local agents.

Section leaders' success in seizing the right to control poor relief funds gave new life to a centuries-old civic tradition, but with a more democratic twist. Whereas the leadership of the capital's earlier Municipal Commission had been filled with notables and men of the upper bourgeoisie, the transfer of power to the sections themselves represented a democratization of the assistance project. The newly empowered assistance committees of the sections were composed of men of much more modest means.[91]

---

[89] Section de la Fontaine Grenelle, "Pétition à l'Assemblée nationale," cited in Bouchet, *L'Assistance publique*, 563. The document dates from 1792, but the specific date is not indicated.
[90] Bouchet, *L'Assistance publique*, 567, citing "Section des Enfants-Rouges, Extrait des procès-verbaux des assemblées générales" (n.d.). The battle between the Municipal Commission and the section leaders is detailed in Dreyfus, *L'Assistance*, 120–35.
[91] Duprat, *Le Temps*, 173.

Nonetheless, as Isser Woloch has clearly shown, the outdoor relief system that the Parisian sections organized and ran was quite tame and even conservative in its essential features.[92] The section's welfare committees (comités de bienfaisance) consisted of 16–24 commissioners administering relief at the section level, who were conscientious local residents, many of them retired, who were members of the "sans-culotte bourgeoisie" that included master artisans, tradesmen, and small merchants.[93]

Meetings of the welfare committees of the Paris sections avoided the Convention's harsh republican rhetoric in the Year II, its officials apparently succeeding in their efforts to avoid making outdoor relief contingent upon individuals' republican credentials. Sectional welfare commissioners seem to have held to the belief that they should distribute assistance to deserving individuals and families of nearly any description as long as they were officially domiciled in the section.

Like nearly all urban poor relief systems in the European past that emphasized assistance to the deserving poor in their homes, urban women were critical to the sections' local missions. Despite appearing only as "adjuncts" to section commissioners in official records, women proved especially important in providing assistance in kind to pregnant and lactating women as well as to widows. Indeed, sectional leaders were quick to point out the many attributes that uniquely qualified women to participate in relieving the poor, including their "sensibility" to the sufferings of the poor and their "stoicism" in the face of misfortune.[94]

Besides distributing funds raised at the national level to households of the capital's poor, sectional welfare commissions also tried to raise voluntary donations to their efforts using a combination of Christian and secular imperatives. Appeals for contributions were apparently most successful when donations remained within the section itself, representing "a tangible form of localized fraternity." During the Year II, the forty-eight sectional welfare committees of the capital distributed nearly one million livres of assistance, of which less than half came from the Central Commission. The rest came from gifts, subscriptions, and door-to-door collections in various neighborhoods.[95]

The Convention's willingness to transfer authority over poor relief in the capital to the sections came as the result of grassroots pressure on it to do so, and represented an important episode in the larger story of the way issues of poor relief grew in importance after the Revolution of 10 August 1792. Viewed against the longer background of European community-building projects, it illustrates very well Sandra Cavallo's innovative analysis of the close relationship

[92] Woloch, "From Charity," 779–812; Bouchet, *L'Assistance publique*, 556–75.
[93] Woloch, "From Charity," 789.   [94] *Ibid.*, 795.
[95] *Ibid.*, 802, 812; Duprat, *Le Temps*, 171.

that exists between shifts in political power and different sorts of poor relief regimes.[96] In the case of the French Revolution, the transition from a philanthropic civic vision of poor relief to a more egalitarian one involved the rise to authority of many relatively "new" men, some of modest means, who translated their vision of a more democratic national community into the systems of poor relief they were able to seize. As we have seen, the actual day-to-day functioning of poor relief under sectional control did not look much different from civic systems of relief in earlier periods, the major difference lying in the apparent absence of clerical involvement once sectional welfare commissioners took over. The broad continuities in the way the Parisian outdoor relief system functioned are noteworthy as well. Despite the coming to power of new men with more radical ideas of what the national community should look like, their actions with regard to poor relief showed quite clearly that they grasped the essential link between community building and the provision of assistance to the respectable poor.

Poor relief initiatives of representatives-on-mission

The emergence of new sectional welfare organizations in the capital was critical in helping Parisians realize some of the basic goals of poor relief legislation for families. In many areas of the nation, however, the lack of organizations for the relief of even the local poor helped contribute to the drama of visits by certain of the Convention's representatives-on-mission during the Year II.

In some of these areas that had long lacked organized efforts for the poor, representatives-on-mission from the Convention had a benign influence, working to try to allay peasants' fears of food shortages by helping to establish collective grain storage facilities, for example.[97] In other cases, where they found severe extremes of wealth and poverty and few efforts to implement the Convention's legislation on assistance to families of soldiers or to poor families in general, representatives who had been sent into the provinces mainly to suppress counter-revolution or raise troops took it upon themselves to teach the inhabitants new lessons about the nation's obligations to its poor.

In rituals consisting of a mixture of redistributive justice and punishment for the rich and "egoists," representatives-on-mission and revolutionary armies that helped them often oversaw the seizure of property and the imposition of "revolutionary taxes" from the "wealthy" who lay in their paths. In a burlesque

[96] Sandra Cavallo, *Charity and Power in Early Modern Italy: Benefactors and Their Motives in Turin, 1541–1789* (New York and Cambridge, 1995). Cavallo details the competing models of poor relief associated with civic and absolutist governance.
[97] Gross, *Fair Shares*, 85.

of the act of almsgiving, and in clear violation of national policy largely designed to extinguish face-to-face relations between giver and receiver, representatives could insist that the transfer of resources from rich to the deserving poor of their neighborhood be effected in face-to-face ceremonies.[98]

In the Nièvre, Representative-on-Mission Fouché, whose sympathies lay with the radical Hébertiste wing of sans-culotte opinion, devoted particular attention to legislation affecting soldiers' families. During his mission there in the summer and early autumn of 1793, Fouché ordered the creation of the office of commissioners, named by districts, to help municipalities establish lists of those who were entitled to assistance under terms of revolutionary legislation. By late October, even he was still waiting for information from some quarters. He therefore instructed both district and local government authorities that if he did not receive the required data within two weeks, he would levy a tax on their own property and have it distributed to local families of volunteers in need.[99]

The rapid succession of laws regulating assistance to the poor in general, and to needy families of volunteers in particular, that flowed out of the Convention during the Year II could confound even the most pro-revolutionary officials, who were often confused about the precise grounds of people's entitlements. Officials in the Nièvre, who were justifiably terrified by Fouché's presence there, were, like officials in many areas, confused over whether *all* families of soldiers were entitled to benefits conferred by laws of November 1792 and May 1793 or just the certifiably indigent ones.[100]

Along with Representatives Collot d'Herbois and Albitte, Fouché was involved in similar activities in the Lyon area, where the goal in this recently defeated counter-revolutionary city was to benefit all of the poor, not just the families of volunteers. They decreed there on 24 brumaire II (14 November 1793) that:

All infirm, aged, orphan, indigent citizens will be housed, fed and clothed at the expense of the rich of their respective cantons. All signs of poverty will be destroyed. Begging and laziness will be similarly outlawed: all beggars and loafers will be incarcerated. Able-bodied citizens will be supplied with work and things necessary for the exercise of their occupation or industry. To this end, constituted authorities, along with *comités de surveillance*, will raise a revolutionary tax on the rich proportional to their fortune

---

[98] Dreyfus, *L'Assistance*, 94–5; Bouchet, *L'Assistance publique*, 401–3. On the participation of the armées révolutionnaires in these efforts, see Richard Cobb, *Les Armées révolutionnaires: instrument de la Terreur dans les départements, avril 1793 – floréal An II* (Paris, 1963), vol. II, 548–51.

[99] Guy Thuillier, "L'Action sociale dans le Nivernais (1789–1797)," in *La Protection sociale*, ed. Imbert, 301–4. He notes that Fouché's policies, which favored "patriots," left a terrible legacy, and gave a bad name to the policy of outdoor relief.

[100] *Ibid.*, 302.

and their lack of civism. Those who do not obey these financial requisitions assigned to them will be recognized as suspects. The goods of those recognized as suspects, which can be considered only dangerous in their hands, will be sequestered until peace comes; and only that which is strictly necessary for their family will be left to them.[101]

The terms of this decree spread well beyond the Lyon region, however. On 3 frimaire II (23 November 1793), the Commune of Paris applauded the spirit of the decree and sent it to the capital's own Central Welfare Commission "to direct it in its work."[102]

The lack of local assistance agencies in many parts of rural France, decried since the waning years of the Old Regime, remained a problem for the Convention and for its representatives-on-mission. Many therefore tried to work with sociétés populaires or sociétés philanthropiques, some of which they themselves had ordered into existence and whose political orthodoxy they believed they could trust.[103] While sometimes devoted mainly to rooting out real and imagined political suspects, sociétés populaires also served more down-to-earth civic functions that included lobbying for or distributing assistance to the poor.[104] In the département of the Loire, which was subject to the influence of another much-feared representative-on-mission, Claude Javogues, local sociétés populaires lobbied authorities to provide employment for the local poor, and tried to remove the stigma of poverty by urging members to reveal their need of assistance to other members without shame.[105]

The experience of Representative-on-Mission Roux-Fazillac in the départements of the Dordogne and Charente was also instructive in this regard. Seeing that the laws of 28 June and 15–18 October 1793 – which provided home assistance to the poor and repressed mendicity, respectively – were not being fulfilled, Roux called together a member of each district administration and revolutionary committee on 19 frimaire II (9 December 1793) admonishing them to work together to set up a local system of public assistance to carry out terms of the laws. He ordered the directory of each district to name a commissioner for each canton who would be responsible "for stimulating the zeal and activity of the municipalities to accelerate nominations of members

[101] Arrêté of Albitte, Fouché, and Collot d'Herbois, 24 brumaire II (14 November 1793), cited in Bouchet, *L'Assistance publique*, 402–3. Part of this text is also cited in Thuillier, "L'Action sociale," in *La Protection sociale*, ed. Imbert, 303.

[102] Bouchet, *L'Assistance publique*, 403, 405–7; Gross, *Fair Shares*, 115–21.

[103] On Fouché's use of these organizations in the Allier, see Elizabeth Liris, "On rougit ici d'être riche," *Annales historiques de la Révolution française*, no. 300 (April–June, 1995): 295–301.

[104] Colin Lucas, *The Structure of the Terror: The Example of Javogues and the Loire* (Oxford, 1973), 114–16. Cobb argues that sociétés populaires in many areas were largely removed from national-level debates, and had very local, non-ideological matters on their minds. See *Les Armées*, vol. II, 631.

[105] Lucas, *The Structure*, 116.

to compose the assistance bureaus."[106] Since he suspected that officials of these new agencies might lack the republican zeal required to carry out the Convention's mandates, he placed them under the surveillance of the local sociétés populaires, which were generally bastions of Jacobin loyalty. As a final touch, he ordered that any citizen who failed to accept an appointment to such a post would "be judged heedless of the public good and as a result known as a 'suspect.'"

Roux also levied a poor tax of one million livres on the local rich to try to improve the situation of the local poor. Somewhat ironically, however, and in conformity with the idea of the nation's "common fund," the million livres that Roux raised through hard work and coercion was immediately seized by the Convention to be placed in the national treasury. Roux's response indicated both his understanding of the nation's needs and an insistence on the importance of bringing the solicitude of the nation to the poor of the provinces:

> Doubtless, you will not suffer the poor of this département to be disappointed in their hopes, and if the unity of the Republic requires that all its taxes be deposited in a common center, you will promptly assign funds for the execution of decrees relative to public assistance and to the extinction of mendicity [here] . . . The rich and uncivic will continue to bear the costs of all extraordinary expenses for the execution of salutary decrees on mendicity, public assistance and instruction. A million [livres] was imposed and collected for that: the sum will be doubled if necessary.[107]

Back in the département of the Loire, Representative Javogues' tasks centered on repressing counter-revolution in Lyon and addressing economic problems that plagued the region during autumn and winter 1793–4. Social provision was integral to the first goal. Javogues therefore forced districts of the Loire to distribute a "daily allowance" to families of men who had volunteered to suppress the federalist uprising in Lyon in August 1793, allocating 3 livres for each soldier's wife and 20 sous per child. He tried to continue this system even after the return of the soldiers following the successful repression of the revolt mainly through employment schemes in several key municipalities.[108]

More radical efforts to implement assistance to the poor of the Loire came when Javogues was able to impose a confiscatory revolutionary tax on the wealthy there.[109] By a decree of 26 nivôse II (26 December 1793), he ordered all municipalities of the département to compile two lists, one of the wealthy

---

[106] Bouchet, *L'Assistance publique*, 447–8; F.-A. Aulard, ed., *Recueil des actes du Comité de salut public* (Paris, 1895), vol. IX, 292, 478, 614.

[107] Bouchet, *L'Assistance publique*, 448–9. Summing up the example of Roux-Fazillac's mission, Bouchet notes dryly: "It was truly a great illusion to hope to stimulate the benevolent activity of citizens by terror."

[108] Lucas, *The Structure*, 279–80.

[109] *Ibid.*, 282–95. "Wealthy" meant fortunes of over 100,000 livres for married men and 50,000 for bachelors.

and the other of the indigent. However, he was able to actualize his plans for such a "taxe révolutionnaire" in only a small number of places where municipal authorities supported or, in some instances, suggested such a plan. In the one municipality where Javogues' tax was implemented, the initial sum of over 16,000,000 livres levied on the wealthy netted some 450,000 livres, of which only 70,000 went to the poor, with most of the rest being given to the district's expenditures for expanding the local arms industry.[110] Javogues' ambitious plan to transfer wealth from rich to poor foundered on a lack of cooperation from municipal authorities, gross overestimates of the wealth of the "rich," the fact that most of the wealth was in land not readily transferable to the poor, and, most importantly, the fact that, like all representatives-on-mission in the provinces, his presence was only temporary.

Other efforts to teach new lessons in solidarity and to repress habits of egoism were the result of the work of men who had been delegated authority by representatives-on-mission. These men – civil commissioners or sometimes officers of revolutionary armies – went to the trouble of organizing festivals in honor of the poor, or giving "civic" banquets funded by the local wealthy, which, in at least one case, featured the rich being required to serve the poor their meals.[111]

As recent scholarship on the Jacobins of the Year II has suggested, many Jacobin leaders were sincerely committed to building new universalistic forms of citizenship and concrete bonds of "fraternity" across the nation, which they saw as a "new moralized entity."[112] The kinds of confiscations discussed here founded, at least in some part, by the desire of representatives-on-mission and the commissioners whom they appointed to demonstrate, however crudely, the nation's willingness to enforce solidarity that would stretch across families, geographic communities, even regions. In dramas of expropriation and redistribution in the Year II, representatives-on-mission believed that they were acting in the name of their "imagined community." The problem was that, unlike those donating their resources to the nation on the floor of the National Assembly, many in the provinces either could not imagine, or had only contempt and fear for the community that Jacobin leaders were trying to build.

Later legislation by the Convention, especially the general welfare law of 22 floréal II (11 May 1794), tried to address poverty in the countryside very specifically. This law, passed at the height of the Terror, extended outdoor relief to rural artisans and the aged. It also established the "Great Welfare Ledger" (*Grand Livre de Bienfaisance*) that was designed to contain the names of all individuals newly honored by their entitlements to pensions from the nation.

---

[110] *Ibid.*, 292–3.   [111] Cobb, *Les Armeés*, vol. II, 624.

[112] Marcel David, *Fraternité et Révolution française, 1789–1799* (Paris, 1987); Gross, *Fair Shares*; Patrice Higonnet, *Goodness beyond Virtue: Jacobins during the French Revolution* (Cambridge, MA, 1998), 69, 146, 317–18.

The law of 22 floréal II was designed to spread ideals of outdoor relief that had flourished in towns and cities to the respectable poor of the countryside such as the disabled, who were poor through no fault of their own. Aged male peasants and rural artisans were granted the most lavish entitlements under the legislation, though widows and nursing mothers were also included.

The law of 22 floréal II seems to have succeeded better than previous legislation despite its requirement of numerous documents to establish entitlement, including baptismal records and doctors' records for the sick. Its effective implementation may have lain in the fact that it was restricted to a relatively small number (160,000) of beneficiaries nationally, and in many areas it was not implemented until the less disruptive period after Thermidor, Year II.[113]

Family and community under the Jacobin Republic

Although revolutionary legislation from the Committee on Mendicity through the Convention targeted the household as the privileged seat of assistance in its national-level civic vision, the advent of war and the need to ensure a continuous supply of soldiers for armies fighting enemies of the Revolution, both domestic and foreign, drew the Convention into granting entitlements to an increasingly wide circle of soldiers' extended kin who could claim dependency on his earnings.

Yet in most respects, leaders of the Revolution, from its earliest days through the First Republic, never seem to have felt particularly comfortable with the world of extended kinship in any other than metaphorical terms. As Lynn Hunt observed, there was a general "distrust of families" in revolutionary legislation affecting the family.[114] From the beginning of the Revolution, successive assemblies had passed laws to reduce patriarchal authority by abolishing primogeniture (*droit d'aînesse*) and the hated *lettres de cachet*, which real or fictive "fathers" such as the king had used to control subordinates (laws of 15–28 March 1790). They later lowered the age of majority for marriage of women and men to 21 and legalized divorce (25 September 1792).[115] Taken as a whole,

---

[113] Marec, "L'Action," in *La Protection sociale*, ed. Imbert, 294, notes that the success of the law of floréal varied widely among rural communes most affected. See also: Guy Thuillier, "L'Action sociale," in *La Protection sociale*, ed. Imbert, 303–4, who describes widespread compliance there, though the pensions were eventually paid in highly devalued assignats. See also Forrest, *The French Revolution*, 82–3.

[114] Lynn Hunt, *The Family Romance of the French Revolution* (Berkeley, 1992), 42, 65–7, and Hunt, "Male Virtue and Republican Motherhood," in Keith Michael Baker, ed., *The French Revolution and the Creation of Modern Political Culture*, vol. IV, *The Terror* (Oxford and New York, 1994), 199.

[115] On the thrust of legislation on the family, see André Burguière, "La Révolution française et la famille," *Annales, ESC* 46, 1 (1991): 151–68.

French revolutionary legislation seems to have wished to construct a family originating in a marital bond between two individuals who had chosen one another freely, one that was quite open to the invention of new ties of kinship not based on blood through the adoption of needy children. As illustrated in Maignet's speech on the welfare law of June 1793, the fundamental ties of blood that lay at the heart of the republican family were those of mother and infant, forming a bond that was eminently peace-loving and domesticated, and that could serve as the foundation of more extensive civic virtues on which the national community rested.[116] There was only one good "extended family" as far as Montagnards of the Year II were concerned, and that was the nation itself.

Thus, like medieval churchmen and generations of urban civic authorities before them, what revolutionary legislators and representatives-on-mission of the Convention feared were male-dominated kinship groups, or even entire villages or hamlets that were bound together by ties of blood and inward-looking loyalties, which could defeat the revolutionary project of building a nation held together by the participation of individuals and their families in larger civic goals.

Revolutionary policy of the Year II thus shared important features of a long-standing European tradition of civic poor relief that linked community membership to entitlements to assistance. As we have seen, revolutionaries favored assistance to individuals in their families. They saw poor relief as a means to strengthen both family bonds and networks of solidarity outside the family. While favoring voluntary giving, they did not hesitate to use coercion to force those with resources to contribute to the upkeep of the poor, though the levels of coercion they used went far beyond those we saw in earlier episodes of civic or confessional community building.

Attempts by Jacobin leaders to implement a civic system of poor relief for the nation were hampered not only by obvious material factors brought on by the pressing demands of war, but more importantly by inherent contradictions between their civic model of poor relief – doubtless inspired by their urban backgrounds and mentality – and their vision of the nation as the community they were seeking to build.[117] The civic model of poor relief that informed their efforts to assist poor families had been born, tested, and refined in Europe's towns and cities since the Middle Ages. Civic relief programs had flourished where entitlements to aid were limited, based on longtime residence or even

---

[116] On the Jacobins' vision of the republican family, see Gross, *Fair Shares*, 46–53; Higonnet, *Goodness*, 193–7, 334. On the role of women and the mother–child bond, see Hunt, *Family Romance*, 153–6; Mary Jacobus, "Incorruptible Milk: Breast-Feeding and the French Revolution," in Sara E. Melzer and Leslie W. Rabine, eds., *Rebel Daughters: Women and the French Revolution* (New York, 1992), 54–75; Landes, *Visualizing*, 98–9, 102.

[117] On the urban mentality of Jacobins, see Higonnet, *Goodness*, 104, 314.

local citizenship.[118] The construction of a national community was predicated, however, on dismantling precisely those traditions of localism and limited access to assistance resources that had helped make earlier civic models of poor relief possible. Once revolutionaries developed an aspiration for entitling citizens of a whole nation, they had launched into uncharted and perilous new territory.

[118] For a discussion of the difficult transition from local to national citizenship in another setting, see Maarten Prak, "Burghers into Citizens: Urban and National Citizenship in the Netherlands during the Revolutionary Era (*c.* 1800)," in Michael Hanagan and Charles Tilly, eds., *Extending Citizenship, Reconfiguring States* (Lanham, MD, 1999), 17–35.

Conclusion

The chapters of this study have explored what I see as fundamental features of western society, which began to develop together in medieval times, and evolved most fully in the material, organizational, and ideological conditions of urban life. I have tried to show that the demographic setting of towns and cities, with their relatively high levels of mortality and migration, tended to weaken extended family structures, especially among the middle and working classes, thereby making both individuals and smaller households vulnerable to poverty and social isolation.

Through a number of examples, I have suggested the critical importance of Abram de Swaan's insight into the close association in western history between community formation and the creation of entitlements to assistance. Community building came in many different forms, however. Many medieval and early modern confraternities afforded some measure of mutual protection for men and women of the lower and middling classes. At various times and places in their history, urban confraternities managed programs to care for the poor who were not actual members, but who numbered among the "house poor" or "respectable poor" of their city. In times of greatest religious militancy – through the preaching of mendicant orders in medieval cities or the admonitions of Counter-Reformation divines – confraternal associations also engaged in outreach efforts to the poorest of the poor in search of merit for the donor, solace for the receiver, or a bond between the two.

The Church was an important stimulus of a rich organizational life. Some of its most active agents worked to create networks of association based on ties of the "spirit" rather than those of blood. The Church itself created communities of men and women that exemplified this goal, providing specific models of association that the laity adapted for their own protection and edification. The sociability project of the Church, which also included efforts to control or re-channel violence among the powerful, was eminently practical, since keeping the peace and building social ties was critical to the survival of the Church as an organization. The Church's influence in creating a valuative and practical space lying outside the family encouraged the development of "civil society," relations, especially in cities and towns.

While the care of the poor was a central feature of this Christian community-building project beginning in the late-ancient period, organized assistance to the poor was not limited to this tradition. Perhaps inspired by ancient civic models of poor relief, urban notables from medieval times onward saw the organized relief of the poor as a key responsibility of urban governors. Lay efforts to provide for the domiciled poor went well beyond the random provision of alms. As we have seen, civic and Christian values often meshed and reinforced one another in the form of lay and clerical collaborations in the practice of "civic religion" and efforts for the "common good."

My analysis of voluntary associations and civic poor relief activities has thus argued against the convenient but false notion that at one time, the "Church" was responsible for relief of the poor until the "State" began to take it over. Rather, I have suggested that from the Middle Ages onward, religious and secular authorities at the local level worked with organized groups of laymen and -women to try to address problems of poverty. Disputes between "Church" and "State" about jurisdiction over hospital funds and management that grew in acrimony during the seventeenth and eighteenth centuries are worth noting. However, focusing upon institutions such as the Church and the State introduces unnecessary abstraction and neglects the obvious fact that decisions about poor relief policy and, more importantly, its implementation, generally remained the responsibility of local church and government authorities well into the twentieth century.

Understanding community-building activities and the place of poor relief in them requires us to understand the very fine line that existed between the world of voluntary associations and the world of local urban officials. This can be seen in ways civic leaders of Renaissance Italy often tried to control the activities and purse strings of certain confraternities lest they grow too wealthy or powerful, or even seized their financial resources to implement their own visions of "civic" relief. On the other hand, the same kinds of leaders sometimes gave confraternities the task of organizing relief for the civic poor. In the Reformation-era Netherlands, as we have seen, Calvinist organizations often tried to seize the right to aid their own poor as well as the poor of other confessional groups.

Not only did voluntary associations often take on tasks associated with the protection of civic communities. From the opposite point of view, civic communities also frequently took on the aspect of voluntary associations, as evidenced by requirements many of them imposed on new in-migrants who wished to "join," including taking oaths or providing proof of property ownership and "good character" as credentials for citizenship. The analysis has suggested, therefore, that the line between the worlds of voluntary and civic communities – or between the public realms of "civil society" and the political community – was often a fine one.

In exploring the life of civil society in European cities and towns, I have tried to show the presence of women as important participants in public life on a variety of fronts. The prominent role of women in the economic life of Europe's towns and cities through their labor in workshops, markets, and streets, and the need that so many of them faced to integrate wage-earning activities with obligations to family and household, left an indelible imprint on western society. Levels of women's labor force participation varied by place and time along with their relative standing in the skilled trades. Nonetheless, the widespread expectation that women of the lower and middling ranks would normally engage in economic activities beyond the boundaries of their own families sometime during their lifetimes provided an important foundation for women's presence in other arenas of public life.

The position of urban family life on the boundary of public and private also reinforced women's integration into the public life of civil society. Not only the physical and economic conditions of urban life, but families' dependency on extrafamilial sources of assistance meant that only the wealthiest families could preserve something of a "private" aspect to their domestic lives. Households that received relief from religious or civic sources were particularly likely to experience the intervention of outsiders into their midst. Intervention was not necessarily unwelcome or inimical to the interests of women, however. Social-historical research on men and women in European cities confirms this point by showing that women were particularly likely to build networks of association among their neighbors that could serve as a source of solidarity or even protection in times of domestic strife. Furthermore, it is clear that women and men alike were quite willing to appeal to courts, police, or other local authorities to help them control troublesome children or even spouses if they could. These kinds of evidence, in addition to cross-cultural research on the determinants of women's standing in society, suggest that the relative publicity of family life more likely than not improved women's lives.

Women's participation in the economic life of towns and cities, the liminal position of their families at the boundaries of public and private life, and the availability of Christian models of association open to both men and women helped to make women's participation in voluntary associations unsurprising in western Europe. Women's associational activities often centered upon the parish church but also included more elaborate residential communities such as beguinages and convents that allowed them to forge identities separate from households and kin. A religiously inspired model of "public motherhood" encouraged upper- and middle-class laywomen to project their identities and skills as mothers and managers of households into the public world to care for poor women and children, oftentimes in institutions of their own founding. All of these activities, I believe, gave women in European towns and cities a relatively high level of autonomy in their economic and associational lives in civil society. Like men, urban women developed habits of association that created not only informal bonds of solidarity but also formal organizations with important public purposes.

What has been the impact of changes such as industrialization, increased urbanization, or state political development on these fundamental patterns in the more recent past? First, there is the issue of continuities and change in the urban settings. It is true that the Industrial Revolution, which began in England during the latter part of the eighteenth century and spread to the Continent during the nineteenth, sparked the founding of new towns and the growth of many older ones to sizes well beyond those of most preindustrial cities. Basic demographic and economic forces fueling this growth were familiar ones, however. Migrants continued to come to towns and cities to find work, and as in the past, generally traveled rather short distances to do so. Permanent migration gradually became a more important component of total migration, though short-term, circular, and seasonal migration persisted, facilitated by the growth of railroad systems after the middle of the nineteenth century.[1] Until at least the middle of the nineteenth century, the mortality rates in most cities remained high relative to rates for rural places.

Even admitting that some fundamental demographic characteristics of cities persisted with the advent of industrialization, can we usefully compare the social worlds of large modern cities with those I have explored here? After all, many classic social investigations of modern cities, such as those of Henry Mayhew on London's poor, Friedrich Engels on workers in Britain's cities, or Villermé's investigations of workers' lives in industrial France, suggested the advent of an urban world filled with *new* forms of human suffering and class alienation.[2] Recent research on migration in England during the nineteenth century suggests that the largest cities may have attracted a disproportionate number of single migrants than smaller places, which in turn may have created greater difficulties in the process of integration into city life.[3] Police and social welfare records, especially in the larger places, suggest that lone migrants who lacked these connections continued to be overrepresented among those in urban jails and hospitals, just as they had in the past.[4] Furthermore, studies have also

---

[1] Leslie Page Moch, *Moving Europeans: Migration in Western Europe since 1650* (Bloomington, 1992), 112–47.

[2] Henry Mayhew, *London Labour and the London Poor: A Cyclopaedia of the Condition and Earnings of Those that will work, Those that cannot work, and Those that will not work*, 4 vols. (London, 1967); Friedrich Engels, *The Condition of the Working Class in England* (Oxford, 1993); Louis-René Villermé, *Tableau de l'état physique et moral des ouvriers employés les manufactures de coton, de laine et de soie*, 2 vols. (Paris, 1840).

[3] Colin Pooley and Jean Turnbull, *Migration and Mobility in Britain since the Eighteenth Century* (London, 1998), 113, 119.

[4] William H. Sewell, Jr., *Structure and Mobility: The Men and Women of Marseille, 1820–1870 Marseille* (New York, 1985).

suggested that many of the "respectable poor" followed the sort of survival strategies familiar to medieval and early modern Europe. Most tried to piece together different sorts of assistance from a variety of sources, including kin, neighbors, civic and religiously based poor relief agencies, and voluntary associations as well, such as British "friendly societies," French *compagnonnages*, or other kinds of mutual assistance groups.[5] By the nineteenth century, many societies for workers' mutual assistance had quite likely lost their religious character, but nonetheless maintained important "fraternal" values and language.

What of other fundamental features of towns and cities? Studies of women's work suggest that the Industrial Revolution introduced little that was new in the kinds of occupations women filled or in the continuing importance of women's dual responsibilities for work inside and outside their homes. Women worked in sectors of the economy where they had always been present in large numbers, including domestic service, textile production and dressmaking, the food trades, and prostitution.[6] Women continued to migrate to the city for work, and, like male migrants, increasingly chose to stay there. The exclusion of urban women from skilled trades continued to mark women's labor force participation in the nineteenth century. It is no accident that this later period also witnessed the reappearance of an ideology vaunting women's domestic roles – in the form of the modern idea of men's and women's "separate spheres."[7]

What was the impact of the industrialization process on urban households and families during the nineteenth century? Again, evidence suggests that basic household and family structures of urban industrial Europe did not change very much until the beginnings of the "demographic transition" in the 1870s and 1880s, when the spread of family limitation led to a decline in family sizes and a major compression of the time that women spent raising and caring for children. As in the medieval and early modern periods, urban households and families of the lower and middling ranks remained overwhelmingly nuclear in structure, but could also expand to take in migrants, usually temporarily, especially when newcomers could contribute wages to the household economy or provide key services such as child care – the specialty of grandmothers, in particular.[8] But, it was still generally the wealthier inhabitants of towns and

[5] William H. Sewell, Jr., *Work and Revolution in France: The Language of Labor from the Old Regime to 1848* (Cambridge, 1980), 168–87; David Garrioch and Michael Sonenscher, "*Compagnonnages*, Confraternities and Associations of Journeymen in Eighteenth-Century Paris," *European History Quarterly* 16, 1 (1986): 25–45.

[6] Louise Tilly and Joan Scott, *Women, Work and Family* (New York, 1978).

[7] On this topic see, most recently, Amanda Vickery, "Golden Age to Separate Spheres? A Review of the Categories and Chronology of English Women's History," *The Historical Journal* 36, 2 (1993): 383–414.

[8] Michael Anderson, *Family Structure in Nineteenth-Century Lancashire* (Cambridge, 1971).

cities who were most likely to take collateral kin into their households and structure their social worlds among dense networks of relatives.[9]

The explanation for this difference between working- and middle-class families of the nineteenth century was partly financial and partly demographic. Already at the end of the eighteenth century, mortality levels in some towns and cities had begun to decline, allowing their populations to grow as much by natural increase as in-migration. Not until the very end of the nineteenth century, however, did improvements in public health result in widespread and sustained declines in urban mortality rates in the very largest cities. This trend, when combined with high rates of permanent migration and rising standards of living for the urban lower classes, permitted the growth of working-class neighborhoods characterized by the sort of dense, multigenerational networks of kin captured in classic twentieth-century studies of working-class life such as Michael Young and Peter Willmott's *Family and Kinship in East London*.[10] Rising standards of living and declining mortality increased both the presence of working-class kin networks in the city and the ability of their members to help one another.

Studies of assistance to the nineteenth-century urban poor also echo findings about earlier periods. The modern poor consisted of the same categories of people as in the Middle Ages: lone women or couples overburdened with young children, and families whose breadwinner(s) was (were) unemployed or unable to work because of injury or age. Similarly, concern about the urban poor led to the creation of a variety of civic and religiously inspired organizations for their edification and care. As in the past, with the notable exception of England's national Poor Law, the vast majority of these programs were local in inspiration and scope, based on the participation of civic elites, and in some cases the collaboration of clergy.[11] Nineteenth-century programs for the poor, whether the product of voluntary association or government initiative, were also very much committed to distinguishing the "deserving" from the "undeserving" poor.

Although the process of secularization during the later eighteenth century had inspired a number of poor relief efforts that were philanthropically or civically minded, nineteenth-century religious revivals in both Protestant and Catholic areas reinvigorated earlier Christian models of assistance. As in the past, women were particularly likely to engage in religiously inspired associations in the city that represented "maternalist" efforts to improve the lives of poor women and

---

[9] Steven Ruggles, *Prolonged Connections: The Rise of the Extended Family in Nineteenth-Century England and America* (Madison, 1987).

[10] Michael Young and Peter Willmott, *Family and Kinship in East London* (Berkeley, 1992); see also Wally Seccombe, *Weathering the Storm: Working-Class Families from the Industrial Revolution to the Fertility Decline* (London and New York, 1993), 136–40.

[11] For a case study of the participation of civic elites in local poor relief efforts in one of France's most important industrial cities, see Timothy B. Smith, "Public Assistance and Labor Supply in Nineteenth-Century Lyon," *Journal of Modern History* 68, 1 (March, 1996): 1–30.

children.[12] As noted in the preface to this study, Catholic activists in France in the 1830s even reinvented the charitable lay confraternity in the form of voluntary groups such as the Society of Saint Vincent de Paul.[13]

The development of European welfare state policy beginning at the end of the nineteenth century should also be seen as a legacy of the patterns I have explored here. Like earlier efforts to build "civic" communities, the process of constructing welfare states has demonstrated the enduring link between community membership and assistance entitlements in the European setting, and the central place that assistance to individuals in their homes continues to occupy. As in the past, welfare state policies identify assistance to individuals and families as keys to maintaining bonds of national or even now supranational "solidarity."[14] Furthermore, as a number of studies have begun to emphasize, many of the models for welfare state policies – such things as family allowances or the insurance of working people against "critical life situations" – originated in the world of voluntary associations or even business enterprise, what some term the "private" sector of the economy, but what I see as part of civil society.[15]

Thus, I conclude that the patterns explored here have left a powerful legacy in European society despite the material revolutions caused by the processes of modern industrialization and urbanization. Indeed, by expanding the number and size of urban places as well as the proportion of people living in towns and cities, industrialization increased the importance of the interrelated patterns this work has explored.

Several observers have suggested that factors that have figured prominently in this study helped lay the groundwork for Europeans' efforts to build communities on an ever-increasing scale. This was certainly one of de Swaan's findings. Another recent scholar, viewing European developments from an Asian perspective, has emphasized Christianity's "relatively simple interpersonal ethic and its attack both on exclusive, wide-ranging kinship and on magical practices." Church organizations, including monastic communities and the larger diocesan and Vatican structures during the Middle Ages, he argues, prepared western society for the later acceptance of "the idea of the state." The

---

[12] Bonnie G. Smith, *Ladies of the Leisure Class: The Bourgeoises of Northern France in the Nineteenth Century* (Princeton, 1981), 136–49; Leonore Davidoff and Catherine Hall, *Family Fortunes: Men and Women of the English Middle Class, 1780–1850* (Chicago, 1987), 429–36.

[13] Katherine A. Lynch, *Family, Class, and Ideology in Early Industrial France: Social Policy and the Working-Class Family, 1825–1848* (Madison, 1988), 33–48.

[14] On the comparative history of European welfare states, see: Gøsta Esping-Andersen, "The Three Political Economies of the Welfare State," in Jon Eivind Kolberg, ed., *The Study of Welfare State Regimes* (Armonk, 1992), 92–123; Peter Baldwin, *The Politics of Social Solidarity: Class Bases of the European Welfare State, 1875–1975* (Cambridge, 1990); Ann Shola Orloff, *The Politics of Pensions: A Comparative Analysis of Britain, Canada, and the United States 1880–1940* (Madison, 1993).

[15] See, for example, Susan Pedersen, *Family, Dependence, and the Origins of the Welfare State: Britain and France, 1914–1945* (Cambridge, 1993), ch. 5.

Church was also responsible, as early as the Middle Ages, for causing "the *individual* to emerge from the coils of kin and clan in practice as well as in principle."[16]

By contrast, E. L. Jones has argued that Christianity's contribution to Europe's development was only indirect at best. He notes, rather, that the West was fortunate to have a religious tradition that constituted a binding thread within the society, yet did not itself create a single political entity, thriving instead along with political decentralization as European kingdoms developed.[17] More importantly for my analysis, however, is Jones' emphasis on what he sees as the unusual development of "public goods" in western Europe, especially those, such as the provision of assistance to the poor, which allowed groups to "counter disaster" and manage risks collectively. He points to regulations for protection against recurring disasters such as Plague, epidemics, and fire. More homely urban policies such as street paving or street cleaning represented "social precautions" or "social provisions" at the local level. Medieval and Renaissance civic republics, he argues, left a legacy of social regulation as a common heritage for later kingdoms and nation-states to exploit.[18]

Recent discussions of "social capital" also suggest that societies where different social classes of people have become adept at creating organized communities are richer in mutual trust, individuals' ability to see beyond interests of self, family, or clan to imagine a "common good," and habits of association I have been discussing.[19] Thus, in his study of the political implications of practices of civic community, Robert Putnam hypothesized an association between longstanding habits of civic association and levels of good government in different

---

[16] Satish Saberwal, *Roots of Crisis: Interpreting Contemporary Indian Society* (New Delhi and London, 1996), 55–6, 104, 110, 112. The author also suggests the importance of legal codes, courts of justice, and the rule of law as factors in reducing uncertainty and helping to encourage social and political integration in the West. I thank Jan Breman for this reference.

[17] E. L. Jones, *The European Miracle: Environments, Economies and Geopolitics in the History of Europe and Asia*, 2nd edn. (Cambridge, 1987), 111–12, 160–1.

[18] *Ibid.*, xii–xiii, xxx, 139, 145–8. For a recent debate on the efficacy of the English poor laws in insuring the welfare of the poor and contributing to England's modern economic development, see Peter M. Solar, "Poor Relief and English Economic Development before the Industrial Revolution," *Economic History Review* 48, 1 (1995): 1–22; Solar, "Poor Relief and English Economic Development: A Renewed Plea for Comparative History," *Economic History Review* 50, 2 (1997): 369–74; and Steve King, "Poor Relief and English Economic Development Reappraised," *Economic History Review* 50, 2 (1997): 360–78.

[19] Abram de Swaan, *In Care of the State: Health Care, Education and Welfare in Europe and the USA in the Modern Era* (New York, 1988), 22–3, terms these programs a "collective good." Marco van Leeuwen, "Logic of Charity: Poor Relief in Preindustrial Europe," *Journal of Interdisciplinary History* 24, 4 (Spring, 1994), 603, also sees the provision of relief to the poor as "social capital." He demonstrates the critical importance of charity to nineteenth-century urban populations in "Surviving with a Little Help: The Importance of Charity to the Poor of Amsterdam, 1800–50, in a Comparative Perspective," *Social History* 18, 3 (1993): 319–38. For a discussion of the concept, see James S. Coleman, "Social Capital in the Creation of Human Capital," *American Journal of Sociology* 94, Supplement S (1988): S95–S120.

regions of Italy. Those areas where there was a history of civic republicanism, he argued, were those where modern political integration was deepest.[20]

This research, in turn, has led several historians of the Renaissance to question both the depth of civic involvement in the cases Putnam used and the causal underpinnings of his argument. Gene Brucker suggests that, despite the existence of civic traditions, there was really no sphere of "civil society" in medieval or Renaissance Italy. He writes:

If the definition of *civil society* includes as a central feature "a complex tissue of voluntary associations which occupy a public space and have a public voice," then it is difficult to find evidence for this phenomenon in prerevolutionary Italy. The academies and fledgling masonic lodges that were formed in the eighteenth century did not have a political agenda.[21]

Edward Muir argues that habits of civic engagement in Renaissance Italy cannot have been that profound since many of the republics based on them collapsed. To explain what civil society development there was, he points to the impacts of "civic religion," judicial practice, and the "civilizing process" imposed on many areas of the peninsula by absolutist courts. Writing of differences between northern and southern Italy, he notes however, that:

Before the Catholic Reformation, the South also lacked the North's vibrant tradition of lay confraternities, which, by the fourteenth century, had become not only the principal source of public charity but also ... a training venue for participation in other kinds of cooperative organizations. It would hardly be an exaggeration to suggest that the lay confraternities provided the single most important lesson about cooperation of any Italian civic lesson.[22]

It is clear that the life of civil society is somehow key to social and political integration, but the question remains: how are we to define it? As noted in Chapter 5, well-known work on the history of the "public sphere" suggests that civil society was born in towns and cities of the seventeenth and eighteenth centuries among the middle and upper classes as evidenced in the emergence of voluntary associations such as academies and Masonic lodges, new patterns of sociability in coffeehouses and cafes, and new forms of writing and publishing.[23] Muir's comments suggest, and I have argued, however, that habits of association within the world of civil society long predated the Enlightenment and involved women and men from nearly all social groups above the poorest

---

[20] Robert D. Putnam, *Making Democracy Work: Civic Traditions in Modern Italy* (Princeton, 1993).

[21] Gene Brucker, "Civic Traditions in Premodern Italy," in Robert I. Rotberg, ed., *Patterns of Social Capital: Stability and Change in Historical Perspective* (Cambridge, 2001), 39.

[22] Edward Muir, "The Sources of Civil Society in Italy," in Rotberg, ed., *Patterns of Social Capital*, 53.

[23] See above, page 179, fn. 22.

of the poor. What was new to the seventeenth and eighteenth centuries was the increasingly secular and political tone of associational life.

Moreover, the fact that certain civic republics collapsed should not lead us to underestimate the importance of values that informed their founding and glory days. Forms of community life, like everything that is human, can lose their vitality when the vision on which they were originally based is lost, when the society in which they were born and thrived seeks new ways of achieving solidarity, and when leaders emerge to preach new ideas of community that capture the imaginations of others.

Despite their demise, even collapsed civic republics leave behind habits, collective memories, and expectations that may enjoy a revival in later periods and fuel future efforts to build new sorts of communities. My discussion of the French Revolution suggested as much, showing how a reinvention and new application of an older civic model of family and community helped to animate both the movement for reform and the path of the Revolution.

In conclusion, I have tried to show that community building in western society constitutes an extremely long-lived tradition and set of behaviors that began and flourished in specific sorts of demographic, economic, and religious environments. The persistence of fundamental features of these settings helped to perpetuate "habits of the heart" that informed the building of face-to-face networks of association as well as larger national communities.[24] Demographic, religious, and other cultural factors, such as views regarding the participation of women in the paid labor force, all contributed.

Sorting out which of these factors, if any, have been fundamental for the creation of viable communities in other societies and cultures will require comparative, cross-national scholarship over long historical periods that is beyond the abilities of one person. Only through such research, however, will we be able to see how individual – family – and – community relationships evolved in other parts of the world. If this study encourages research on the sorts of factors and interrelationships explored here, I will count my work a success.

---

[24] Robert N. Bellah *et al.*, *Habits of the Heart: Individualism and Commitment in American Life* (Berkeley, 1985).

Bibliography

Abrams, Philip. "Introduction." In Philip Abrams and E. A. Wrigley, eds., *Towns in Societies: Essays in Economic History and Historical Sociology*. New York and Cambridge, 1978.

Adams, Thomas M. *Bureaucrats and Beggars: French Social Policy in the Age of the Enlightenment*. New York, 1990.

Agulhon, Maurice. *La Sociabilité méridionale: confréries et associations dans la vie collective en Provence orientale à la fin du 18e siècle*. Aix-en-Provence, 1966.

Anderson, Benedict. *Imagined Communities: Reflections on the Origin and Spread of Nationalism*. Rev. edn. London and New York, 1991.

Anderson, Michael. *Family Structure in Nineteenth-Century Lancashire*. Cambridge, 1971.

Angot des Rotours, Noël François Mathieu. *Notice des principaux règlements publiés en Angleterre concernant les pauvres, à laquelle on a joint quelques réflexions qui peuvent la rendre utile aux Assemblées provinciales*. London and Paris, 1788.

Appleby, Joyce, Lynn Hunt, and Margaret Jacob. *Telling the Truth about History*. New York, 1994.

Archives nationales, Paris, AF II*39. Procès-verbaux of the Comité de Secours publics of the Legislative Assembly.

Ariès, Philippe and Georges Duby, eds. *The History of Private Life*. 5 vols. Cambridge, MA, 1987–1992.

Arru, Angiolina. "Serviteurs et servantes à Rome: différences de 'genre', Life Cycle et pouvoirs (1650–1860)." In Erik Aerts, Paul M. M. Klep, Jürgen Kocka, and Marinia Thorborg, eds., *Women in the Labour Force: Comparative Studies on Labour Market and Organization of Work since the 18th Century*. Proceedings of the Tenth International Economic History Conference, Leuven, August 1990, Session B-8.

Assier-Andrieu, Louis. "Le Play et la famille-souche des Pyrénées: politique, juridisme et science sociale." *Annales, ESC* 39, 3 (1984): 495–512.

Atkinson, Clarissa. *The Oldest Vocation: Christian Motherhood in the Middle Ages*. Ithaca, 1991.

Aulard, [François-Alphonse], ed. *Receuil des actes du Comité de salut public, avec la correspondance officielle des représentants en mission et le registre des représentants en mission et le registre du Conseil executif provisoire*. 28 vols. (Paris, 1889–)

Baernstein, P. Renée. "In Widow's Habit: Women between Convent and Family in Sixteenth-Century Milan." *Sixteenth Century Journal* 25, 4 (1994): 787–807.

Bailey, Mark. "Demographic Decline in Late Medieval England: Some Thoughts on Recent Research." *Economic History Review* 49, 1 (1996): 1–19.

Bairoch, Paul, Jean Batou, and Pierre Chèvre. *La Population des villes européennes: banque de données et analyse sommaire des résultats, 800–1850.* Geneva, 1988.

Baker, Keith Michael, ed. *The French Revolution and the Creation of Modern Political Culture.* 4 vols. Oxford and New York, 1987–94.

Baldwin, Peter. *The Politics of Social Solidarity: Class Bases of the European Welfare State, 1875–1975.* Cambridge, 1990.

Bankcr, James R. *Death in the Community: Memorialization and Confraternities in an Italian Commune in the Late Middle Ages.* Athens, GA, 1988.

Bardet, Jean-Pierre. *Rouen aux XVIIe et XVIIIe siècles: les mutations d'un espace social.* 2 vols. Paris, 1983.

Barron, Caroline M. "The Parish Fraternities of Medieval London." In Caroline M. Barron and Christopher Harper-Bill, eds., *The Church in Pre-Reformation Society: Essays in Honour of F. R. H. Du Boulay.* Suffolk, 1985.

Beier, A. L. *Masterless Men: The Vagrancy Problem in England 1560–1640.* New York and London, 1985.

Bell, David A. *The Cult of the Nation in France: Inventing Nationalism, 1680–1800.* Cambridge, MA, 2001.

Bellah, Robert N. *et al. Habits of the Heart: Individualism and Commitment in American Life.* Berkeley, 1985.

Benedict, Philip. "French Cities from the Sixteenth Century to the Revolution: An Overview." In Philip Benedict, ed., *Cities and Social Change in Early Modern France.* London and Boston, 1989.

 "Was the Eighteenth Century an Era of Urbanization in France?" *Journal of Interdisciplinary History* 21, 2 (1990): 179–215.

Benigno, Francesco. "The Southern Italian Family in the Early Modern Period: A Discussion of Co-residential Patterns." *Continuity and Change* 4, 1 (1989): 165–94.

Bennett, Judith M. "'History that Stands Still': Women's Work in the European Past." *Feminist Studies* 14, 2 (1988): 269–83.

Bennett, Judith M., Elizabeth A. Clark, Jean F. O'Barr, B. Anne Vilen, and Sarah Westphal-Wihl, eds. *Sisters and Workers in the Middle Ages.* Chicago and London, 1989.

Bertaud, Jean-Paul. "La Révolution et la politique sociale en faveur des militaires." *Revue du Nord* 75, 299 (January–March, 1993): 181–91.

Binz, Louis. "Les Confréries dans le diocèse de Genève à la fin du Moyen Age." In *Le Mouvement confraternel au Moyen Age: France, Italie, Suisse.* Geneva, 1987.

Bitel, Lisa M. "Women's Monastic Enclosures in Early Ireland: A Study of Female Spirituality and Male Monastic Mentalities." *Journal of Medieval History* 12, 1 (1986): 15–36.

Bloch, Camille, ed. *L'Assistance publique: instruction, recueil de textes et notes.* Paris, 1909. Doc. 95, "Décret sur les secours à accorder aux pères, mères et enfants des citoyens-soldats volontaires, qui sont dans le besoin," 26–7 November 1792, 85–6.

Bloch, Camille and Alexandre Tuetey, eds. *Procès-verbaux et rapports du Comité de mendicité de la Constituante, 1790–1791.* Paris, 1911.

Bloch, Marc. "A Contribution towards a Comparative History of European Societies."
    In Frederic C. Lane and Jelle C. Riemersma, eds., *Enterprise and Secular Change:
    Readings in Economic History*. Homewood, IL, 1953.
    Feudal Society. 2 vols., trans. L. A. Manyon. Chicago, 1961.
    The Historian's Craft, trans. Peter Putnam. New York, 1971; first published 1953.
Bonenfant, Pierre. "Aperçu sur l'histoire de l'Assistance publique de Bruxelles." *Annales
    de la Société belge d'histoire des hôpitaux* 3 (1965): 45–8.
    "Les Hôpitaux en Belgique au Moyen Age." *Annales de la Société belge d'histoire
    des hôpitaux* 3 (1965): 5–44.
    "Les Origines et le caractère de la réforme de la bienfaisance publique aux Pays-Bas
    sous le règne de Charles-Quint." *Annales de la Société belge d'histoire des hôpitaux*
    3 (1965): 115–47.
Bossy, John. *Christianity in the West, 1400–1700*. New York and Oxford, 1985.
    "Godparenthood: The Fortunes of a Social Institution in Early Modern Christianity."
    In Kaspar von Greyerz, ed., *Religion and Society in Early Modern Europe,
    1500–1800*. London, 1984.
    "Holiness and Society." *Past and Present*, no. 75 (1977): 119–37.
Boswell, John. *The Kindness of Strangers: The Abandonment of Children in Western
    Europe from Late Antiquity to the Renaissance*. New York, 1988.
Botelho, Lynn. "Aged and Impotent: Parish Relief of the Aged Poor in Early Modern
    Suffolk." In Martin Daunton, ed., *Charity, Self-Interest and Welfare in the English
    Past*. London, 1996.
Bouchet, Michel. *L'Assistance publique en France pendant la Révolution*. Paris,
    1908.
Boulton, Jeremy. *Neighbourhood and Society: A London Suburb in the Seventeenth
    Century*. New York and Cambridge, 1987.
Bourdelais, Patrice. "Choléra des villes et choléra des champs: faits et représentations."
    In Michel Pouvain, René Leboutte, Henriette Damas, and Eric Vilquin, eds.,
    Historiens et populations: Liber amicorum Etienne Hélin. Louvain-la-Neuve, 1991.
Bourdieu, Pierre. *Outline of a Theory of Practice*, trans. Richard Nice. Cambridge,
    1977.
Boxer, Marilyn J. and Jean H. Quataert, eds. *Connecting Spheres: Women in the Western
    World, 1500 to the Present*. New York, 1987.
Brady, Thomas A. *Ruling Class, Regime and Reformation in Strasbourg, 1520–1555*.
    Leiden, 1978.
Braudel, Fernand. *On History*, trans. Sarah Matthews. Chicago, 1980.
Brinton, Crane. *French Revolutionary Legislation on Illegitimacy, 1789–1804*.
    Cambridge, MA, 1936.
Brodman, James William. *Charity and Welfare: Hospitals and the Poor in Medieval
    Catalonia*. Philadelphia, 1998.
Brown, Judith C. and Robert C. Davis, eds. *Gender and Society in Renaissance Italy*.
    London and New York, 1998.
Brown, Judith C. and Jordan Goodman. "Women and Industry in Florence." *Journal of
    Economic History* 40, 1 (1980): 73–80.
Brown, Peter. "Late Antiquity." In Paul Veyne, ed., *The History of Private Life*, vol. I:
    From Pagan Rome to Byzantium. Cambridge, MA, 1987.
Burguière, André. "La Révolution française et la famille." *Annales, ESC* 46, 1 (1991):
    151–68.

Burguière, André. "Le Rituel du mariage en France: pratiques ecclésiastiques et pratiques populaires (XVIe–XVIIIe siècle)." *Annales, ESC* 33, 3 (1978): 637–49.

Bynum, Caroline Walker. "Did the Twelfth Century Discover the Individual?" In Bynum, *Jesus as Mother: Studies in the Spirituality of the High Middle Ages.* Berkeley, 1982.

"Women's Stories, Women's Symbols: A Critique of Victor Turner's Theory of Liminality." In Robert L. Moore and Frank E. Reynolds, eds., *Anthropology and the Study of Religion.* Chicago, 1984.

Calhoun, Craig. "History, Anthropology and the Study of Communities: Some Problems in Macfarlane's Proposal." *Social History* 3, 3 (1978): 363–73.

Calhoun, Craig, ed. *Habermas and the Public Sphere.* Cambridge, MA, 1992.

Calvi, Giulia. "Reconstructing the Family: Widowhood and Remarriage in Tuscany in the Early Modern Period." In Trevor Dean and K. J. P. Lowe, eds., *Marriage in Italy, 1300–1650.* Cambridge, 1998.

Cavallo, Sandra. *Charity and Power in Early Modern Italy: Benefactors and Their Motives in Turin, 1541–1789.* New York and Cambridge, 1995.

Chiffoleau, Jacques. *La Comptabilité de l'au-delà: les hommes, la mort et la religion dans la région d'Avignon à la fin du Moyen Age (vers 1320 – vers 1480).* Rome, 1980.

"Sur l'usage obsessionnel de la messe pour les morts à la fin du Moyen Age." In *Faire croire: modalités de la diffusion et de la réception des messages religieux du XIIe au XVe siècle.* Rome, 1981.

Chojnacki, Stanley. "Political Adulthood in Fifteenth-Century Venice." *American Historical Review* 91, 4 (1986): 791–810.

Women and Men in Renaissance Venice: Twelve Essays on Patrician Society. Baltimore and London, 2000.

Clark, Peter. "Migrants in the City: The Process of Social Adaptation in English Towns." In Peter Clark and David Souden, eds., *Migration and Society in Early Modern England.* London, 1987.

Cobb, Richard. *Les Armées révolutionnaires: instrument de la terreur dans les départements, avril 1793 – floréal An II.* 2 vols. Paris, 1961–3.

Cohn, Samuel Kline, Jr. *The Laboring Classes in Renaissance Florence.* New York, 1980.

Coleman, James S. "Social Capital in the Creation of Human Capital." *American Journal of Sociology* 94, Supplement S (1988): S95–S120.

Comité d'histoire de la sécurité sociale. *La Protection sociale sous la Révolution française*, ed. Jean Imbert. Paris, 1990.

Coudert, Allison P. "The Myth of the Improved Status of Protestant Women: The Case of the Witchcraze." In Jean R. Brink, Allison P. Coudert, and Mary Anne Horowitz, eds., *Politics of Gender in Early Modern Europe.* Kirksville, MO, 1989.

Cox, Virginia. "The Single Self: Feminist Thought and the Marriage Market in Early Modern Venice." *Renaissance Quarterly* 48, 3 (1995): 513–81.

Cressy, David. "Kinship and Kin Interaction in Early Modern England." *Past and Present*, no. 113 (November, 1986): 38–69.

Da Molin, Giovanna. "Family Forms and Domestic Service in Southern Italy from the Seventeenth to the Nineteenth Centuries." *Journal of Family History* 15, 4 (1990): 503–27.

David, Marcel. *Fraternité et Révolution française, 1789–1799.* Paris, 1987.

Davidoff, Leonore and Catherine Hall. *Family Fortunes: Men and Women of the English Middle Class, 1780–1850.* Chicago, 1987.

Davis, Natalie Zemon. *The Gift in Sixteenth-Century France*. Madison, 2000.
    Society and Culture in Early Modern France. Stanford, 1975.
    "Ghosts, Kin, and Progeny: Some Features of Family Life in Early Modern France."
    Daedalus 106, 2 (Summer, 1977): 87–114.
De la Roncière, Charles M. "Les Confréries à Florence et dans son contado." In *Le
    Mouvement confraternel au Moyen Age: France, Italie, Suisse*. Geneva, 1987.
De Swaan, Abram. In *Care of the State: Health Care, Education and Welfare in Europe
    and the USA in the Modern Era*. New York, 1988.
De Vries, Jan. *European Urbanization, 1500–1800*. Cambridge, MA, 1984.
Diefendorf, Barbara B. "Give Us Back Our Children: Patriarchal Authority and Parental
    Consent to Religious Vocations in Early Counter-Reformation France." *Journal of
    Modern History* 68, 2 (1996): 265–307.
Dietrich, David Henry. "Brotherhood and Community on the Eve of the Reformation:
    Confraternities and Parish Life in Liège, 1450–1540." Ph.D. thesis, University of
    Michigan, 1982, 121.
Dörfler-Dierken, Angelika. *Vorreformatorische Bruderschaften der hl. Anna*.
    Heidelberg, 1992.
Dreyfus, Ferdinand. *L'Assistance sous la Législative et la Convention (1791–1795)*.
    Geneva, 1978, first edn 1905.
Duby, Georges. *Medieval Marriage: Two Models from Twelfth-Century France*, trans.
    Elborg Forster. Baltimore and London, 1978.
    La Société aux XIe et XIIe siècles dans la région mâconnaise. Paris, 1953.
Duparc, Pierre. "Confréries du Saint-Esprit et communautées d'habitants au Moyen-
    Age." *Revue historique de droit français et étranger* 36 (1958): 349–67.
Duplessis, Robert S. *Lille and the Dutch Revolt: Urban Stability in an Era of Revolution,
    1500–1582*. New York and Cambridge, 1991.
Dupont de Nemours, Pierre-Samuel. *Idées sur les secours à donner aux pauvres men-
    diants*. Paris, 1988 [1786].
Duprat, Catherine. *'Pour l'amour de l'humanité': le temps des philanthropes. La
    Philanthropie parisienne des Lumières à la monarchie de Juillet*. Paris, 1993.
Dyer, Christopher. *Standards of Living in the Later Middle Ages: Social Change in
    England, c. 1200–1500*. New York and Cambridge, 1989.
Earle, Peter. "The Female Labour Market in London in the Late Seventeenth and Early
    Eighteenth Centuries." *Economic History Review* 42, 3 (1989): 328–53.
Elliott, Vivien Brodsky. "Single Women in the London Marriage Market: Age, Status
    and Mobility, 1598–1619." In R. B. Outhwaite, ed., *Marriage and Society: Studies
    in the Social History of Marriage*. New York, 1981.
Engels, Friedrich. *The Condition of the Working Class in England*. Oxford, 1993.
Eriksson, Ingrid and John Rogers. "Mobility in an Agrarian Community: Practical
    and Methodological Considerations." In Kurt Ågren *et al.*, eds., *Aristocrats,
    Farmers, Proletarians: Essays in Swedish Demographic History*. Stockholm,
    1973.
Espinas, G. "Les Guerres familiales dans la commune de Douai aux XIIIe et XIVe siècles:
    les trèves et les paix." *Nouvelle revue historique de droit français et étranger* (1899):
    415–73.
Esping-Andersen, Gøsta. "The Three Political Economies of the Welfare State." In Jon
    Eivind Kolberg, ed., *The Study of Welfare State Regimes*. New York, 1992.

Estèbe, J. and B. Vogler. "La Genèse d'une société protestante: étude comparée de quelques registres consistoriaux languedociens et palatins vers 1600." *Annales, ESC* 31, 2 (1976): 362–88.

Fairchilds, Cissie. *Poverty and Charity in Aix-en-Provence, 1640–1789*. Baltimore, 1976.

Farge, Arlette and Michel Foucault. *Le Désordre des familles: lettres de cachet des Archives de la Bastille au XVIIIe siècle*. Paris, 1982.

Farmer, Sharon. *Surviving Poverty in Medieval Paris: Gender, Ideology, and the Daily Lives of the Poor*. Ithaca and London, 2002.

Fasano-Guarini, E. "Politique et population dans l'histoire des villes italiennes aux XVI et XVIIe siècles." *Annales de démographie historique* (1982): 77–90.

Fauve-Chamoux, Antoinette. "Les Structures familiales au royaume des familles-souche: Esparros." *Annales, ESC* 39, 3 (1984): 513–28.

"Le Surplus urbain des femmes en France préindustrielle et le rôle de la domesticité." *Population* 53, 1–2 (1998): 359–78.

Fauve-Chamoux, Antoinette and Emiko Ochiai, eds. *House and the Stem Family in EurAsian Perspective*. Proceedings of the C18 Session, Twelfth International Economic History Congress, Kyoto, 1998.

Fehler, Timothy. *Poor Relief and Protestantism: The Evolution of Social Welfare in Sixteenth-Century Emden*. Aldershot, Hants and Brookfield, VT, 1999.

Ferguson, Margaret W., Maureen Quilligan, and Nancy J. Vickers, eds. *Rewriting the Renaissance: The Discourses of Sexual Difference in Early Modern Europe*. Chicago and London, 1986.

Fine, Agnès. *Parrains, marraines: la parenté spirituelle en Europe*. Paris, 1994.

Finlay, Roger. *Population and Metropolis: The Demography of London, 1580–1650*. New York and Cambridge, 1981.

Flandrin, Jean-Louis. *Families in Former Times: Kinship, Household, and Sexuality*. New York and Cambridge, 1979.

Flynn, Maureen. *Sacred Charity: Confraternities and Social Welfare in Spain, 1400–1700*. Basingstoke, 1989.

Fontaine, Laurence. "Droit et stratégies: la reproduction des systèmes familiaux dans la Haut-Dauphiné (XVIIe–XVIIIe siècles)." *Annales, ESC* 47, 6 (1992): 1259–77.

Forrest, Alan. *The French Revolution and the Poor*. New York, 1981.

Foucault, Michel. *Madness and Civilization: A History of Insanity in the Age of Reason*, trans. Richard Howard. New York, 1965.

Fougères, M. [Marc Bloch]. "Entr'aide et piété: les association urbaines au moyen âge." *Annales d'histoire sociale* 5 (1944): 100–6.

Fox, Edward Whiting. *History in Geographic Perspective: The Other France*. New York, 1971.

France. Commission d'histoire économique et sociale de la Révolution française. *L'Assistance publique: instruction, recueil de textes et notes*, ed. Camille Bloch. Paris, 1909.

François, Etienne, ed. *Immigration et société urbaine en Europe occidentale, XVIe–XXe siècle*. Paris, 1985.

French, Katherine L. "'To Free Them from Binding': Women in the Late Medieval English Parish." *Journal of Interdisciplinary History* 27, 3 (1997): 387–412.

Friedrichs, Christopher R. *Urban Society in an Age of War: Nördlingen, 1580–1720.* Princeton, 1979.

Froeschlé-Chopard, Marie-Hélène. "Pénitents et sociétés populaires du sud-ouest." *Annales historiques de la Révolution française,* no. 267 (January–March, 1987): 117–57.

Gager, Kristin E. *Blood Ties and Fictive Ties: Adoption and Family Life in Early Modern France.* Princeton, 1996.

Galley, Chris. "A Model of Early Modern Demography." *Economic History Review* 48, 3 (1995): 448–69.

Garaud, Marcel. *La Révolution française et la famille.* Paris, 1978.

Garrioch, David. *The Formation of the Parisian Bourgeoisie, 1690–1830.* Cambridge, MA, 1996.

   Neighbourhood and Community in Paris, 1740–1790. New York and Cambridge, 1986.

Garrioch, David and Michael Sonenscher. "*Compagnonnages,* Confraternities and Associations of Journeymen in Eighteenth-Century Paris." *European History Quarterly* 16, 1 (1986): 25–45.

Gauvard, Claude. "Violence citadine et réseaux de solidarité: l'exemple français aux XIVe et XVe siècles." *Annales, ESC* 48, 5 (1993): 1113–26.

Gavitt, Philip. *Charity and Children in Renaissance Florence: The Ospedale degli Innocenti, 1410–1536.* Ann Arbor, 1990.

Geremek, Bronislaw. *The Margins of Society in Late Medieval Paris,* trans. Jean Birrell. New York and Cambridge, 1987.

Gill, Katherine. "Open Monasteries for Women in Late Medieval and Early Modern Italy: Two Roman Examples." In Craig A. Monson, ed., *The Crannied Wall: Women, Religion, and the Arts in Early Modern Europe.* Ann Arbor, 1992.

   "*Scandala*: Controversies Concerning Clausura and Women's Religious Communities in Late Medieval Italy." In Scott L. Waugh and Peter D. Diehl, eds., *Christendom and its Discontents: Exclusion, Persecution, and Rebellion, 1000–1500.* Cambridge, 1996.

Goldberg, P. J. P. *Women, Work, and Life Cycle in a Medieval Economy: Women in York and Yorkshire c.1300–1520.* Oxford, 1992.

Goldstone, Jack A. "Gender, Work, and Culture: Why the Industrial Revolution Came Early to England but Late to China." *Sociological Perspectives* 39, 1 (1996): 1–22.

Goldthwaite, Richard A. "The Florentine Palace as Domestic Architecture." *American Historical Review* 77, 4 (1972): 977–1012.

Goodheart, Eric Andrew. "Adoption in the Discourses of the French Revolution." Ph.D. dissertation, Harvard University, 1997.

Goodman, Dena. "Public Sphere and Private Life: Toward a Synthesis of Current Historiographical Approaches to the Old Regime." *History and Theory* 31, 1 (1992): 1–20.

Goody, Jack. "Comparing Family Systems in Europe and Asia: Are there Different Sets of Rules?" *Population and Development Review* 22, 1 (March, 1996): 1–20.

   The Development of the Family and Marriage in Europe. New York and Cambridge, 1983.

   The Oriental, the Ancient and the Primitive: Systems of Marriage and the Family in the Pre-Industrial Societies of Eurasia. New York and Cambridge, 1990.

Goubert, Pierre. "Family and Province: A Contribution to the Knowledge of Family Structures in Early Modern France." *Journal of Family History* 2, 3 (1977): 179–95.

Granovetter, Mark S. "The Strength of Weak Ties." *American Journal of Sociology* 78, 6 (1973): 1360–80.

"The Strength of Weak Ties: A Network Theory Revisited." In Peter V. Marsden and Nan Lin, eds., *Social Structure and Network Analysis*. Beverly Hills, 1982.

Gross, Jean-Pierre. *Fair Shares for All: Jacobin Egalitarianism in Practice*. New York and Cambridge, 1997.

Gutton, Jean-Pierre. *Histoire de l'adoption en France*. Paris, 1993.

La Société et les pauvres: l'exemple de la généralité de Lyon, 1534–1789. Paris, 1971.

Guyader, Josseline. "Bureau et maisons de charité: l'assistance à domicile aux 'pauvres malades' dans le cadre des paroisses toulousaines (1687–1797)." *Revue d'histoire de l'Eglise de France* 80, 205 (1994): 217–47.

Haas, Louis. "Il Mio Buono Compare: Choosing Godparents and the Uses of Baptismal Kinship in Renaissance Florence." *Journal of Social History* 29, 2 (1995): 341–56.

Habermas, Jürgen. *The Structural Transformation of the Public Sphere: An Inquiry into a Category of Bourgeois Society*, trans. Thomas Burger. Cambridge, MA, 1991, c1962.

Hajnal, John. "European Marriage Patterns in Perspective." In D. V. Glass and D. E. C. Eversley, eds., *Population in History: Essays in Historical Demography*. Chicago, 1965.

"Two Kinds of Preindustrial Household Formation System." *Population and Development Review* 8, 3 (1982): 449–94.

Hanawalt, Barbara A. "Keepers of the Lights: Late Medieval English Parish Gilds." *Journal of Medieval and Renaissance Studies* 14, 1 (1984): 21–37.

ed. *Women and Work in Preindustrial Europe*. Bloomington, IN, 1986.

Hanley, Sarah. "Social Sites of Political Practice in France: Lawsuits, Civil Rights, and the Separation of Powers in Domestic and State Government, 1500–1800." *American Historical Review* 102, 1 (February, 1997): 27–52.

Hardwick, Julie. *The Practice of Patriarchy: Gender and the Politics of Household Authority in Early Modern France*. University Park, PA, 1998.

Harrington, Joel F. "Escape from the Great Confinement: The Genealogy of the German Workhouse." *Journal of Modern History* 71, 2 (1999): 308–45.

Reordering Marriage and Society in Reformation Germany. New York and Cambridge, 1995.

Harrington, Joel F. and Helmut Walser Smith. "Confessionalization, Community, and State Building in Germany, 1555–1870." *Journal of Modern History* 69, 1 (1997): 77–101.

Heers, Jacques. *Le Clan familial au Moyen Age: étude sur les structures politiques et sociaux des milieux urbains*. Paris, 1974.

Esclaves et domestiques au Moyen-Age dans le monde méditerranéen. Paris, 1981.

Henderson, John. *Piety and Charity in Late Medieval Florence*. Oxford and New York, 1994.

Henderson, John and Richard Wall, eds. *Poor Women and Children in the European Past*. London and New York, 1994.

Hendrix, Scott. "Luther on Marriage." *Lutheran Quarterly* 14, 3 (2000): 335–50.

Herlihy, David. "Family." *American Historical Review* 96, 1 (1991): 1–16.
  "Family Solidarity in Medieval Italian History." In David Herlihy, Robert S. Lopez,
    and Vsevolod Slessarev, eds., *Economy, Society and Government in Medieval Italy:
    Essays in Memory of Robert L. Reynolds*. Kent, OH, 1969.
  Medieval Households. Cambridge, MA, 1985.
Herlihy, David and Christiane Klapisch-Zuber. *Tuscans and their Families: A Study of
    the Florentine Catasto of 1427*. New Haven, 1985.
Hickey, Daniel. *Local Hospitals in Ancien Régime France: Rationalization, Resistance,
    Renewal, 1530–1789*. Montreal and Kingston, 1997.
Higonnet, Patrice. *Goodness beyond Virtue: Jacobins during the French Revolution*.
    Cambridge, MA, 1998.
Hilton, R. H. "Medieval Market Towns and Simple Commodity Production." *Past and
    Present*, no. 109 (1985): 3–23.
  "Small Town Society in England before the Black Death." *Past and Present*, no. 105
    (1984): 53–78.
Hochstadt, Steve. "Migration in Preindustrial Germany." *Central European History* 16,
    3 (1983): 195–224.
Hohenberg, Paul M. and Lynn Hollen Lees. *The Making of Urban Europe, 1000–1950*.
    London and Cambridge, MA, 1985.
Horowitz, Elliott S. "Jewish Confraternities in Seventeenth-Century Verona: A Study in
    the Social History of Piety." Ph.D. thesis, Yale University, 1982.
Hotz, Brigitte. *Beginen und willige Arme im spätmittelalterlichen Hildesheim*.
    Schriftenreihe des Stadtarchivs und der Stadtbibliothek Hildesheim, vol. XVII.
    Hildesheim, 1988.
Howell, Martha C. "Citizenship and Gender: Women's Political Status in Northern
    Medieval Cities." In Mary Erler and Maryanne Kowaleski, eds., *Women and Power
    in the Middle Ages*. Athens, GA, 1988.
Hsia, R. Po-Chia, ed. *The German People and the Reformation*. Ithaca, 1988.
Hufton, Olwen. *The Poor of Eighteenth-Century France, 1750–1789*. Oxford, 1974.
  "Women and the Family Economy in Eighteenth-Century France." *French Historical
    Studies* 9, 1 (1975): 1–22.
  "Women without Men: Widows and Spinsters in Britain and France in the Eighteenth
    Century." In Jan Bremmer and Lourens van den Bosch, eds., *Between Poverty and
    the Pyre: Moments in the History of Widowhood*. London and New York, 1995.
Hughes, Diane Owen. "Domestic Ideals and Social Behavior: Evidence from Medieval
    Genoa." In Charles E. Rosenberg, ed., *The Family in History*. Philadelphia, 1975.
  "Kinsmen and Neighbors in Medieval Genoa." In Harry A. Miskimin, David Herlihy,
    and Abraham L. Udovitch, eds., *The Medieval City*. New Haven, CT, 1977.
Hunt, Lynn. *The Family Romance of the French Revolution*. Berkeley, 1992.
Imbert, Jean. *Le Droit hospitalier de l'Ancien Régime*. Paris, 1993.
  ed. *La Protection sociale sous La Revolution française*. Paris, 1990.
Ingram, Martin. *Church Courts, Sex and Marriage in England, 1570–1640*. New York
    and Cambridge, 1987.
Jacob, Margaret C. "The Enlightenment Redefined: The Formation of Modern Civil
    Society." *Social Research* 58, 2 (Summer, 1991): 475–95.
  Living the Enlightenment: Freemasonry and Politics in Eighteenth-Century Europe.
    New York and Oxford, 1991.

Jacobus, Mary. "Incorruptible Milk: Breast-Feeding and the French Revolution." In Sara
E. Melzer and Leslie W. Rabine, eds., *Rebel Daughters: Women and the French
Revolution.* New York, 1992.

Jeorger, Muriel. "La Structure hospitalière de la France sous l'Ancien Régime." *Annales,
ESC* 32, 5 (1977): 1025–51.

Jones, Colin. *The Charitable Imperative: Hospitals and Nursing in Ancien Regime and
Revolutionary France.* London and New York, 1989.

*Charity and Bienfaisance: The Treatment of the Poor in the Montpellier Region,
1740–1815.* New York and Cambridge, 1982.

Jones, Colin and Michael Sonenscher. "The Social Functions of the Hospital in
Eighteenth-Century France: The Case of the Hôtel-Dieu of Nîmes." *French
Historical Studies* 13, 2 (Fall, 1983): 172–214.

Jones, E. L. *The European Miracle: Environments, Economies and Geopolitics in the
History of Europe and Asia.* 2nd edn. Cambridge, 1987.

Jussen, Bernhard. 'Le Parrainage à la fin du Moyen Age: savoir public, attentes
théologiques et usages sociaux.' *Annales, ESC* 47, 2 (1992): 467–502.

Jütte, Robert. "Household and Family Life in Late Sixteenth-Century Cologne: The
Weinsberg Family." *Sixteenth Century Journal* 17, 2 (Summer, 1986): 165–82.

Poverty and Deviance in Early Modern Europe. New York and Cambridge, 1994.

Kaplan, Benjamin. "Dutch Particularism and the Calvinist Quest for 'Holy Uniformity'."
Archiv für Reformationsgeschichte 82 (1991): 239–56.

Kennedy, Michael L. *The Jacobin Clubs in the French Revolution: The First Years.*
Princeton, 1982.

Kent, D. V. and F. W. Kent. *Neighbours and Neighbourhood in Renaissance Florence:
The District of the Red Lion in the Fifteenth Century.* Locust Valley, NY, 1982.

Kertzer, David. *Family Life in Central Italy, 1880–1910: Sharecropping, Wage Labor,
and Coresidence.* New Brunswick, 1984.

Kertzer, David I. and Caroline Brettell. "Advances in Italian and Iberian Family History."
Journal of Family History 12, 1–3 (1987): 87–120.

King, Steve. "Poor Relief and English Economic Development Reappraised." *Economic
History Review* 50, 2 (1997): 360–78.

Kingdon, Robert M. *Adultery and Divorce in Calvin's Geneva.* Cambridge, MA, 1995.

"Calvin and the Family: The Work of the Consistory of Geneva." *Pacific Theological
Review* 17 (1984): 5–18.

Kittell, Ellen E. "Testaments of Two Cities: A Comparative Analysis of the Wills of
Genoa and Douai." *European Review of History* 5, 1 (1998): 47–84.

Kittell, Ellen E. and Kurt Queller. "'Whether Man or Woman': Gender Inclusivity in
the Town Ordinances of Medieval Douai." *Journal of Medieval and Early Modern
Studies* 39, 1 (Winter, 2000): 63–100.

Kooi, Christine. *Liberty and Religion: Church and State in Leiden's Reformation,
1572–1620.* Leiden and Boston, 2000.

Koven, Seth and Sonya Michel, eds. *Mothers of a New World: Maternalist Politics and
the Origins of Welfare States.* New York, 1993.

Kowaleski, Maryanne. "The History of Urban Families in Medieval England." *Journal
of Medieval History* 14, 1 (1988): 47–64.

Kowaleski, Maryanne and Judith M. Bennett. "Crafts, Gilds, and Women in the Middle
Ages: Fifty Years after Marian K. Dale." In Judith M. Bennett, Elizabeth A. Clark,

Jean F. O'Barr, B. Anne Vilen, and Sarah Westphal-Wihl, eds., *Sisters and Workers in the Middle Ages*. Chicago, 1989.

Kumar, Krishan. "Civil Society: An Inquiry into the Usefulness of an Historical Term." *British Journal of Sociology* 44, 3 (1993): 375–95.

Kussmaul, A. S. "The Ambiguous Mobility of Farm Servants." *Economic History Review* 34, 2 (1981): 222–35.

Landers, John. *Death and the Metropolis: Studies in the Demographic History of London, 1670–1830*. New York and Cambridge, 1993.

Landes, David S. *The Wealth and Poverty of Nations: Why Some Nations are so Rich and Some so Poor*. New York, 1998.

Landes, Joan B. *Visualizing the Nation: Gender, Representation, and Revolution in Eighteenth-Century France*. Ithaca and London, 2001.

Lansing, Carol. "Gender and Civic Authority: Sexual Control in a Medieval Italian Town." *Journal of Social History* 31, 1 (November, 1997): 33–59.

Larochelle, Lucie. "L'Intégration des étrangers au sein de l'oligarchie d'Aix-en-Provence (1400–1535)." In *Les Sociétés urbaines en France méridionale et en péninsule ibérique au Moyen Age*. Actes du colloque de Pau, 21–23 septembre 1988. Paris, 1991.

Laslett, Peter. "Family, Kinship and Collectivity as Systems of Support in Pre-Industrial Europe: A Consideration of the 'Nuclear-Hardship' Hypothesis." *Continuity and Change* 3, 2 (1988): 153–75.

Family Life and Illicit Love in Earlier Generations: Essays in Historical Sociology. Cambridge and New York, 1977.

Laslett, Peter and Richard Wall, eds. *Household and Family in Past Time*. Cambridge, 1972.

Le Bras, Gabriel. "Esquisse d'une histoire des confréries." In Le Bras, *Etudes de sociologie religieuse*, vol. I. Paris, 1955.

Le Goff, Jacques. "L'Apogée de la France urbaine médiévale." In Georges Duby, ed., *Histoire de la France urbaine*, vol. II, *La Ville médiévale: des Carolingiens à la Renaissance*, eds. André Chédeville, Jacques Le Goff, and Jacques Rossiaud. Paris, 1980.

La Naissance du purgatoire. Paris, 1981.

"Ordres mendiants et urbanisation dans la France médiévale: l'état de la question." *Annales, ESC* 25, 4 (1970): 924–46.

Time, Work and Culture in the Middle Ages, trans. Arthur Goldhammer. Chicago, 1980.

Le Roy Ladurie, Emmanuel. *Montaillou: village occitan de 1294 à 1324*. Paris, 1975.

Les Paysans de Languedoc. 2 vols. Paris, 1966.

Lesthaeghe, Ronald. "On the Social Control of Human Reproduction." *Population and Development Review* 6, 4 (1980): 527–48.

Lestocquoy, Jean. *Aux origines de la bourgeoisie: Les Villes de Flandre et d'Italie sous le gouvernement des patriciens XIe–XVe siècles*. Paris, 1952.

Liebowitz, Ruth P. "Virgins in the Service of Christ." In Rosemary Ruether and Eleanor McLaughlin, eds., *Women of Spirit: Female Leadership in the Jewish and Christian Traditions*. New York, 1979.

Lindberg, Carter. *Beyond Charity: Reformation Initiatives for the Poor*. Minneapolis, 1993.

Lindberg, Carter, ed. *The European Reformations Sourcebook*. Oxford, 2000.

Liris, Elizabeth. "On rougit ici d'être riche." *Annales historiques de la Révolution française* no. 300 (April–June 1995): 295–301.

Lis, Catharina and Hugo Soly. *Disordered Lives: Eighteenth-Century Families and their Unruly Relatives*, trans. Alexander Brown. Cambridge, 1996.

Poverty and Capitalism in Pre-industrial Europe. Atlantic Highlands, NJ, 1979.

Little, Lester K. *Liberty, Charity, Fraternity: Lay Religious Confraternities at Bergamo in the Age of the Commune*. Bergamo and Northampton, MA, 1988.

Religious Poverty and the Profit Economy in Medieval Europe. Ithaca, 1978.

Lucas, Colin. *The Structure of the Terror: The Example of Javogues and the Loire*. London, 1973.

Luther's Works, ed. Jaroslav Jan Pelikan. Vol. XL. Philadelphia, 1962.

Lynch, Joseph H. *Godparents and Kinship in Early Medieval Europe*. Princeton, 1986.

Lynch, Katherine A. *Family, Class, and Ideology in Early Industrial France: Social Policy and the Working-Class Family, 1825–1848*. Madison, 1988.

"The European Marriage Pattern in the Cities: Variations on a Theme by Hajnal." *Journal of Family History* 16, 1 (1991): 79–96.

"The Family and the History of Public Life." *Journal of Interdisciplinary History* 24, 4 (1994): 665–84.

"Geographical Mobility and Urban Life: Comparative Perspectives on American and European Demographic Trends in the Past." In A. Bideau *et al.* eds., *Les Systèmes démographiques du passé*. Lyon, 1996.

Lynch, Michael. "The Reformation in Edinburgh: The Growth and Growing Pains of Urban Protestantism." In Jim Obelkevich, Lyndal Roper, and Raphael Samuel, eds., *Disciplines of Faith: Studies in Religion, Politics, and Patriarchy*. London and New York, 1987.

McCants, Anne E. C. *Civic Charity in a Golden Age: Orphan Care in Early Modern Amsterdam*. Urbana, IL, 1997.

McDonnell, Ernest W. *The Beguines and Beghards in Medieval Culture, with Special Emphasis on the Belgian Scene*. New Brunswick, NJ, 1954.

Macfarlane, Alan. *The Origins of English Individualism: The Family, Property, and Social Transition*. New York and Cambridge, 1978.

The Family Life of Ralph Josselin: An Essay in Historical Anthropology. New York and Cambridge, 1970.

McNamara, Jo Ann Kay. *Sisters in Arms: Catholic Nuns through Two Millennia*. Cambridge, MA, 1996.

McNeill, William H. "Migration Patterns and Infection in Traditional Societies." In N. F. Stanley and R. A. Joske, eds., *Changing Disease Patterns and Human Behaviour*. New York and London, 1980.

McRee, Ben R. "Religious Gilds and Civic Order: The Case of Norwich in the Late Middle Ages." *Speculum* 67, 1 (1992): 69–95.

"Religious Gilds and Regulation of Behavior in Late Medieval Towns." In Joel Rosenthal and Colin Richmond, eds., *People, Politics, and Community in the Later Middle Ages*. Gloucester and New York, 1987.

Martz, Linda. *Poverty and Welfare in Habsburg Spain: The Example of Toledo*. New York and Cambridge, 1983.

Mauss, Marcel. *The Gift: The Form and Reason for Exchange in Archaic Societies*, trans. W. D. Halls. London and New York, 1990.

Mayhew, Henry. *London Labour and the London Poor: A Cyclopaedia of the Condition and Earnings of Those that will work, Those that cannot work, and Those that will not work*. 4 vols. London, 1967.

Medick, Hans and David Warren Sabean. "Interest and Emotion in Family and Kinship Studies: A Critique of Social History and Anthropology." In Hans Medick and David Warren Sabean, eds., *Interest and Emotion: Essays on the Study of Family and Kinship*. New York and Cambridge, 1984.

Meeks, Wayne A. *The First Urban Christians: The Social World of the Apostle Paul*. New Haven, CT, 1983.

Mentzer, Raymond A., Jr. "*Disciplina nervus ecclesiae*: The Calvinist Reform of Morals at Nîmes." *Sixteenth Century Journal* 18, 1 (1987): 89–116.

"Organizational Endeavour and Charitable Impulse in Sixteenth-Century France: The Case of Protestant Nîmes." *French History* 5, 1 (1991): 1–29.

Mills, Hazel. "La charité est une mère: Catholic Women and Poor Relief in France, 1690–1850." In Hugh Cunningham and Joanna Innes, eds., *Charity, Philanthropy, and Reform: From the 1690s to 1850*. New York, 1998.

Mitchison, Rosalind and Leah Leneman. *Sexuality and Social Control, Scotland 1660–1780*. Oxford and New York, 1989.

Mitterauer, Michael. "Christianity and Endogamy." *Continuity and Change* 6, 3 (1991): 295–333.

Moch, Leslie Page. *Moving Europeans: Migration in Western Europe since 1650*. Bloomington, 1992.

Moeller, Bernd. *Imperial Cities and the Reformation*, ed. and trans. H. C. Erik Midelfort and Mark U. Edwards, Jr. Philadelphia, 1972.

Mollat, Michel. *The Poor in the Middle Ages: An Essay in Social History*, trans. Arthur Goldhammer. New Haven, CT and London, 1986.

Mols, Roger. *Introduction à la démographie des villes d'Europe du XIVe au XVIIIe siècle*. 3 vols. Louvain and Gembloux, 1954–6.

Monter, E. William. "The Consistory of Geneva, 1559–1569." *Bibliothèque d'humanisme et Renaissance* 38, 3 (1976): 467–84.

"Women in Calvinist Geneva (1550–1800)." *Signs* 6, 2 (1980): 189–209.

Morard, Nicholas. "Une Charité bien ordonnée: la confrérie du St-Esprit à Fribourg à la fin du Moyen Age (XIVe–XVe siècles)." In *Le Mouvement confraternel au Moyen Age: France, Italie, Suisse*. Geneva, 1987.

Moritz, Werner. *Die bürgerlichen Fürsorgeanstalten der Reichsstadt Frankfurt a.M. im späten Mittelalter*. Frankfurt am Main, 1981.

Muller, Sheila D. *Charity in the Dutch Republic: Pictures of Rich and Poor for Charitable Institutions*. Ann Arbor, 1985.

Nicholas, David. *The Domestic Life of a Medieval City: Women, Children, and the Family in Fourteenth-Century Ghent*. Lincoln, NE, 1985.

Nicholson, Linda. *Gender and History: The Limits of Social Theory in the Age of the Family*. New York, 1986.

Nimal, H. *Les Béguinages*. Nivelles, 1908.

Norberg, Kathryn. *Rich and Poor in Grenoble, 1600–1814*. Berkeley, 1985.

Nübel, Otto. *Mittelalterliche Beginen- und Sozialsiedlungen in den Niederlanden; ein Beitrag zur Vorgeschichte der Fuggerei*. Tübingen, 1970.

Oexle, Otto Gerhard. "Les Groupes sociaux du Moyen Age et les débuts de la sociologie contemporaine." *Annales, ESC* 47, 3 (1992): 751–65.

Olejniczak, William. "Change, Continuity, and the French Revolution: Elite Discourse on Mendicity, 1750–1815." In David G. Troyansky, Alfred Cismaru and Norwood Andrews, Jr., eds., *The French Revolution in Culture and Society*. New York, 1991.

"Working the Body of the Poor: The Ateliers de Charité in Late Eighteenth-Century France." *Journal of Social History* 24, 1 (1990): 87–107.

Olson, Jeannine E. *Calvin and Social Welfare: Deacons and the* Bourse française. Selinsgrove, PA, 1989.

One Ministry, Many Roles: Deacons and Deaconesses through the Centuries. St. Louis, 1992.

Orloff, Ann Shola. *The Politics of Pensions: A Comparative Analysis of Britain, Canada, and the United States 1880–1940*. Madison, 1993.

Ozment, Steven E. *The Reformation in the Cities: The Appeal of Protestantism to Sixteenth-Century Germany and Switzerland*. New Haven, CT, and London, 1975.

When Fathers Ruled: Family Life in Reformation Europe. Cambridge, MA, 1983.

Padgett, John F. and Christopher K. Ansell. "Robust Action and the Rise of the Medici, 1400–1434." *American Journal of Sociology* 98, 6 (1993): 1259–1319.

Pagels, Elaine. *Adam, Eve, and the Serpent*. New York, 1988.

Papi, Anna Benvenuti. "Mendicant Friars and Female Pinzochere in Tuscany: From Social Marginality to Models of Sanctity." In Daniel Bornstein and Roberto Rusconi, eds., *Women and Religion in Medieval and Renaissance Italy*, trans. Margery J. Schneider. Chicago and London, 1996.

Parker, Charles H. *The Reformation of Community: Social Welfare and Calvinist Charity in Holland, 1572–1620*. Cambridge, 1998.

Parry, Jonathan. "The Gift, the Indian Gift and the 'Indian Gift'." *Man* (New series) 21, 3 (1986): 453–73.

Pedersen, Susan. *Family, Dependence, and the Origins of the Welfare State: Britain and France, 1914–1945*. Cambridge, 1993.

Perrenoud, Alfred. "The Attenuation of Mortality Crises and the Decline of Mortality." In Roger Schofield, David Reher, and Alain Bideau, eds., *The Decline of Mortality in Europe*. Oxford, 1991.

"Croissance ou déclin? Les mécanismes du non-renouvellement des populations urbaines." *Histoire, economie et société* 4, 4 (1982): 581–601.

La Population de Genève du seizième au début du dix-neuvième siècle: étude démographique. Geneva, 1979.

Perry, Mary Elizabeth. *Gender and Disorder in Early Modern Seville*. Princeton, 1990.

Peters, Christine. "Single Women in Early Modern England: Attitudes and Expectations." *Continuity and Change* 12, 3 (1997): 325–45.

Pettegree, Andrew. *Emden and the Dutch Revolt: Exile and the Development of Reformed Protestantism*. Oxford and New York, 1992.

Phillips, Dayton. *Beguines in Medieval Strasburg: A Study of the Social Aspect of Beguine Life*. Ph.D. thesis, Stanford University, 1941.

Phillips, Roderick G. "Gender Solidarities in Late Eighteenth-Century Urban France: The Example of Rouen." *Histoire Sociale/Social History* 13, 26 (1980): 325–37.

"Tribunaux de famille et assemblées de famille à Rouen sous la Révolution." *Revue historique de droit français et étranger* 58, 1 (1980): 69–79.

Phythian-Adams, Charles. *Desolation of a City: Coventry and the Urban Crisis of the Late Middle Ages*. New York and Cambridge, 2002; first published 1979.

Pillorget, René. "Vocation religieuse et Etat en France aux XVIe et XVIIe siècles." In *La Vocation religieuse et sacerdotale en France: XVIIe–XIXe siècles*. Angers, 1979.

Planinc, Zdravko. "Family and Civil Society in Hegel's *Philosophy of Right*." *History of Political Thought* 12, 2 (1991): 305–15.

Pollock, Linda A. *Forgotten Children: Parent–Child Relations from 1500 to 1900*. New York and Cambridge, 1983.

Pooley, Colin and Jean Turnbull. *Migration and Mobility in Britain since the Eighteenth Century*. London, 1998.

Poussou, Jean-Pierre. *Bordeaux et le sud-ouest au XVIIIe siècle: croissance économique et attraction urbaine*. Paris, 1983.

Power, Eileen. *Medieval English Nunneries, c. 1275 to 1535*. New York, 1964.

Prak, Maarten. "Burghers into Citizens: Urban and National Citizenship in the Netherlands during the Revolutionary Era (*c.* 1800)." In Michael Hanagan and Charles Tilly, eds., *Extending Citizenship, Reconfiguring States*. Lanham, MD, 1999.

Pullan, Brian S. "The Counter-Reformation, Medical Care and Poor Relief." In Ole Peter Grell and Andrew Cunningham with Jon Arrizabalaga, eds., *Health Care and Poor Relief in Counter-Reformation Europe*. London and New York, 1999.

Rich and Poor in Renaissance Venice: The Social Institutions of a Catholic State, to 1620. Cambridge, MA, 1971.

"The Scuole Grandi of Venice: Some Further Thoughts." In *Poverty and Charity: Europe, Italy, Venice, 1400–1700*. Aldershot, Hampshire and Brookfield, VT, 1994; first published 1990.

Putnam, Robert D. *Making Democracy Work: Civic Traditions in Modern Italy*. Princeton, 1993.

Ranft, Patricia. *Women and the Religious Life in Premodern Europe*. New York, 1996.

Rapley, Elizabeth. *The Dévotes: Women and Church in Seventeenth-Century France*. Montreal and Buffalo, 1990.

Rappaport, Steve Lee. *Worlds within Worlds: Structures of Life in Sixteenth-Century London*. New York and Cambridge, 1989.

Reher, David Sven. "Family Ties in Western Europe: Persistent Contrasts." *Population and Development Review* 24, 2 (June, 1998): 203–34.

Reinhard, Wolfgang. "Reformation, Counter-Reformation, and the Early Modern State: A Reassessment." *Catholic Historical Review* 75, 3 (1989): 383–404.

Remling, Ludwig. *Bruderschaften in Franken: kirchen- und sozialgeschichtliche Untersuchungen zum spätmittelalterlichen und frühneuzeitlichen Bruderschaftswesen*. Würzburg, 1986.

Rettaroli, Rosella. "Age at Marriage in Nineteenth-Century Italy." *Journal of Family History* 15, 4 (1990): 409–25.

Riddy, Felicity. "Mother Knows Best: Reading Social Change in a Courtesy Text." *Speculum* 71, 1 (1996): 66–86.

Robert, Gaston. *Les Béguines de Reims et la maison de Ste-Agnès*. Reims, 1923.

Roberts, Michael. "Women and Work in Sixteenth-Century English Towns." In Penelope J. Corfield and Derek Keene, eds., *Work in Towns, 850–1850*. London and New York, 1990.

Romano, Dennis. "Charity and Community in Early Renaissance Venice." *Journal of Urban History* 11, 1 (1984): 63–82.

Roper, Lyndal. *The Holy Household: Women and Morals in Reformation Augsburg.* Oxford and New York, 1989.

Rosaldo, Michelle Z. "Women, Culture and Society: A Theoretical Overview." In Michelle Zimbalist Rosaldo, Louise Lamphere, and Joan Bamberger, *Woman, Culture, and Society.* Stanford, 1974.

Rosser, Gervase. "Solidarité et changement social: les fraternités urbaines anglaises à la fin du Moyen Age." *Annales, ESC* 48, 5 (1993): 1127–43.

Rossiaud, Jacques. "Crises et consolidations, 1330–1530." In Georges Duby, ed., *Histoire de la France urbaine*, vol. II, *La Ville médiévale: des Carolingiens à la Renaissance*, ed. André Chédeville, Jacques Le Goff, and Jacques Rossiaud. Paris, 1980.

Rotberg, Robert I., ed. *Patterns of Social Capital: Stability and Change in Historical Perspective.* Cambridge, 2001.

Rowland, Robert. "Sistemas matrimoniales en la Península Ibérica (siglos XVI–XIX): Una perspectiva regional." In Vicente Pérez-Moreda and David-Sven Reher, eds., *Demografía histórica en España.* Madrid, 1988.

Rubin, Miri. *Charity and Community in Medieval Cambridge.* New York and Cambridge, 1987.

Ruggles, Steven. *Prolonged Connections: The Rise of the Extended Family in Nineteenth-Century England and America.* Madison, 1987.

Sabean, David Warren. *Property, Production, and Family in Neckarhausen, 1700–1870.* New York and Cambridge, 1990.

Saberwal, Satish. *Roots of Crisis: Interpreting Contemporary Indian Society.* New Delhi and London, 1996.

Safley, Thomas M. "Civic Morality and the Domestic Economy." In R. Po-Chia Hsia, ed., *The German People and the Reformation.* Ithaca, NY, 1988.

Salter, Frank Reyner, ed. *Some Early Tracts on Poor Relief.* London, 1926.

Sanday, Peggy Reeves. *Female Power and Male Dominance: On the Origins of Sexual Inequality.* Cambridge and New York, 1981.

Sarasúa, Carmen. "The Role of the State in Shaping Women's and Men's Entrance into the Labour Market: Spain in the Eighteenth and Nineteenth Centuries." *Continuity and Change* 12, 3 (1997): 347–71.

Schilling, Heinz. *Civic Calvinism in Northwestern Germany and the Netherlands: Sixteenth to Nineteenth Centuries.* Kirksville, MO, 1991.

"Confessional Europe." In Thomas A. Brady, Jr., Heiko A. Oberman, and James D. Tracy, eds., *Handbook of European History, 1400–1600: Late Middle Ages, Renaissance and Reformation.* 2 vols. Leiden and New York, 1994–1995.

"Reform and Supervision of Family Life in Germany and the Netherlands." In Raymond A. Mentzer, ed., *Sin and the Calvinists: Morals Control and the Consistory in the Reformed Tradition.* Kirksville, MO, 1994.

Schilling, Heinz, ed. *Die reformierte Konfessionalisierung in Deutschland: das Problem der "Zweiten Reformation."* Gütersloh, 1986.

Schwartz, Robert M. *Policing the Poor in Eighteenth-Century France.* Chapel Hill, 1988.

Scribner, Robert W. "Mobility: Voluntary or Enforced? Vagrants in Württemberg in the Sixteenth Century." In Gerhard Jaritz and Albert Müller, eds., *Migration in der Feudalgesellschaft.* Frankfurt and New York, 1988.

Seccombe, Wally. *Weathering the Storm: Working-Class Families from the Industrial Revolution to the Fertility Decline.* London and New York, 1993.

Seligman, Adam B. *The Idea of Civil Society*. New York, 1992.

Sewell, William H., Jr. *Structure and Mobility: The Men and Women of Marseille, 1820–1870*. New York, 1985.

Work and Revolution in France: The Language of Labor from the Old Regime to 1848. Cambridge, 1980.

Shapiro, Gilbert and John Markoff. *Revolutionary Demands: A Content Analysis of the Cahiers de Doléances of 1789*. Stanford, 1998.

Sharlin, Allan. "Natural Decrease in Early Modern Cities: A Reconsideration." *Past and Present*, no. 79 (1978): 126–38.

"Debate: Natural Decrease in Early Modern Cities." *Past and Present*, no. 92 (1981): 169–80.

Sharpe, Pamela. "Literally Spinsters: A New Interpretation of Local Economy and Demography in Colyton in the Seventeenth and Eighteenth Centuries." *Economic History Review* 44, 1 (1991): 46–65.

Sheehan, Michael. "Sexuality, Marriage, Celibacy, and the Family in Central and Northern Italy: Christian Legal and Moral Guides in the Early Middle Ages." In David I. Kertzer and Richard P. Saller, eds., *The Family in Italy: From Antiquity to the Present*. New Haven, CT, 1991.

"The European Family and Canon Law." *Continuity and Change* 6, 3 (1991): 347–60.

Siddle, D. J. "Migration as a Strategy of Accumulation: Social and Economic Change in Eighteenth-Century Savoy." *Economic History Review* 50, 1 (1997): 1–20.

Simons, Walter. *Cities of Ladies: Beguine Communities in the Medieval Low Countries, 1200–1565*. Philadelphia, 2001.

"The Beguine Movement in the Southern Low Countries: A Reassessment." *Bulletin de l'Institut historique belge de Rome* 59 (1989): 63–105.

Sklar, Kathryn Kish. *Florence Kelley and the Nation's Work: The Rise of Women's Political Culture, 1830–1900*. New Haven, CT, 1995.

Slack, Paul. *Poverty and Policy in Tudor and Stuart England*. London and New York, 1988.

Smith, Bonnie G. *Ladies of the Leisure Class: The Bourgeoises of Northern France in the Nineteenth Century*. Princeton, 1981.

Smith, Richard M. "Marriage in Late Medieval Europe." In P. J. P. Goldberg, ed., *Woman is a Worthy Wight: Women in English Society c.1200–1500*. Wolfeboro Falls, NH, 1992.

"Some Reflections on the Evidence for the Origins of the 'European Marriage Pattern' in England." In Chris Harrison in association with Michael Anderson *et al.*, eds., *The Sociology of the Family: New Directions for Britain*. Keele, 1979.

Smith, Timothy B. "Public Assistance and Labor Supply in Nineteenth-Century Lyon." *Journal of Modern History* 68, 1 (March, 1996): 1–30.

Sobel, Dava. *Galileo's Daughter: A Historical Memoir of Science, Faith, and Love*. New York, 1999.

Solar, Peter M. "Poor Relief and English Economic Development: A Renewed Plea for Comparative History." *Economic History Review* 50, 2 (1997): 369–74.

"Poor Relief and English Economic Development before the Industrial Revolution." *Economic History Review* 48, 1 (1995): 1–22.

Sournia, Jean-Charles. *La Médecine révolutionnaire (1789–1799)*. Paris, 1989.

Southern, R. W. *Western Society and the Church in the Middle Ages*. London, 1970.

Spicciani, Amleto. "The 'Poveri Vergognosi' in Fifteenth-Century Florence: The First 30 Years' Activity of the Buonomini di S. Martino." In Thomas Riis, ed., *Aspects of Poverty in Early Modern Europe*. Alphen aan den Rijn, 1981.

Stone, Lawrence. *The Family, Sex and Marriage in England, 1500–1800*. New York, 1977.

Styles, Philip. "The Evolution of the Law of Settlement." *Studies in Seventeenth-Century West Midlands History* (Kineton, 1978): 175–204.

Swanson, Heather. "The Illusion of Economic Structure: Craft Guilds in Late Medieval English Towns." *Past and Present*, no. 121 (November, 1988): 29–48.

Taylor, Charles. "Modes of Civil Society." *Public Culture* 3, 1 (1990): 95–118.

Terpstra, Nicholas. "Confraternal Prison Charity and Political Consolidation in Sixteenth-Century Bologna." *Journal of Modern History* 66, 2 (1994): 217–48.

"Kinship Translated: 'Confraternite Maggiori' and Political Apprenticeship in Early Modern Italy." In Danilo Zardin, ed., *Corpi, "fraternità," mestieri nella storia della società europea*. Rome, 1998.

Lay Confraternities and Civic Religion in Renaissance Bologna. New York and Cambridge, 1995.

ed. *The Politics of Ritual Kinship: Confraternities and Social Order in Early Modern Italy*. New York and Cambridge, 2000.

Thrupp, Sylvia. *The Merchant Class of Medieval London, 1300–1500*. Chicago, 1948.

Tierney, Brian. *Medieval Poor Law: A Sketch of Canonical Theory and its Application to England*. Berkeley, 1959.

Tilly, Louise and Joan Scott. *Women, Work and Family*. New York, 1978.

Tocqueville, Alexis de. *The Old Regime and the French Revolution*, trans. Stuart Gilbert. Garden City, NY, 1955.

Tönnies, Ferdinand. *Community and Society (Gemeinschaft und Gesellschaft)*, ed. and trans. Charles P. Loomis. New Brunswick, NJ and Oxford, 1988, first edn. 1957.

Traer, James F. *Marriage and the Family in Eighteenth-Century France*. Ithaca and London, 1980.

Trexler, Richard C. "Charity and the Defense of Urban Elites in the Italian Communes." In Frederic Cople Jaher, ed., *The Rich, the Well Born, and the Powerful: Elites and Upper Classes in History*. Urbana, 1973.

"Le Célibat à la fin du Moyen Age: les religieuses de Florence." *Annales, ESC* 27, 6 (1972): 1329–50.

Power and Dependence in Renaissance Florence. 3 vols., vol. II, *The Women of Renaissance Florence*. Binghamton, NY, 1993.

Public Life in Renaissance Florence. Ithaca, NY, 1980.

Van der Heijden, Manon. "Secular and Ecclesiastical Marriage Control: Rotterdam, 1550–1700." In Anton Schuurman and Pieter Spierenburg, eds., *Private Domain, Public Inquiry: Families and Lifestyles in the Netherlands and Europe, 1550 to the Present*. Hilversum, 1996.

Van Leeuwen, Marco. "Logic of Charity: Poor Relief in Preindustrial Europe." *Journal of Interdisciplinary History* 24, 4 (Spring, 1994), 603.

Van der Woude, Ad, Akira Hayami, and Jan de Vries, eds. *Urbanization in History: A Process of Dynamic Interactions*. Oxford, 1990.

Van der Woude, A. M. "Population Developments in the Northern Netherlands (1500–1800) and the Validity of the 'Urban Graveyard' Effect." *Annales de démographie historique* (1982): 55–75.

Verdon, Michel. *Rethinking Households: An Atomistic Perspective on European Living Arrangements.* London and New York, 1998.

Viazzo, Pier Paolo. *Upland Communities: Environment, Population and Social Structure in the Alps since the Sixteenth Century.* New York and Cambridge, 1989.

Viazzo, Pier Paolo and Dionigi Albera. "The Peasant Family in Northern Italy, 1750–1930: A Reassessment." *Journal of Family History* 15, 4 (1990): 461–82.

Viazzo, Pier Paolo and Katherine A. Lynch. "Anthropology, Family History, and the Concept of Strategy." *International Review of Social History* 47 (2002): 423–52.

Vickery, Amanda. "Golden Age to Separate Spheres? A Review of the Categories and Chronology of English Women's History." *The Historical Journal* 36, 2 (1993): 383–414.

Villermé, Louis-René. *Tableau de l'état physique et moral des ouvriers employés dans les manufactures de coton, de laine et de soie.* 2 vols. Paris, 1840.

Vincent, Catherine. *Des Charités bien ordonnées: les confréries normandes de la fin du XIIIe siècle au début du XVIe siècle.* Paris, 1988.

Les Confréries médiévales dans le royaume de France, XIIIe–XVe siècle. Paris, 1994.

Vovelle, Michel. *De la cave au grenier: un itinéraire en Provence au XVIIIe siècle. De l'histoire sociale à l'histoire des mentalités.* Québec, 1980.

Piété baroque et déchristianisation en Provence au XVIIIe siècle: les attitudes devant la mort d'après les clauses des testaments. Paris, 1973.

Walker, Mack. *German Home Towns: Community, State, and General Estate, 1648–1871.* Ithaca, 1971.

Wall, Richard. "European Family and Household Systems." In Michel Pouvain, René Leboutte, Henriette Damas, and Eric Vilquin, eds., *Historiens et populations: liber amicorum Etienne Hélin.* Louvain-la-Neuve, 1991.

Walzer, Michael. "Citizenship." In Terence Ball, James Farr, and Russell L. Hanson, eds., *Political Innovation and Conceptual Change.* Cambridge and New York, 1989.

Wandel, Lee Palmer. *Always among Us: Images of the Poor in Zwingli's Zurich.* New York and Cambridge, 1990.

Weber, Max. *Economy and Society: An Outline of Interpretive Sociology,* ed. Guenther Roth and Claus Wittich. 2 vols. Berkeley, 1978.

The City, trans. and ed. Don Martindale and Gertrud Neuwirth. Glencoe, IL, 1958.

Weissman, Ronald F. E. *Ritual Brotherhood in Renaissance Florence.* New York, 1982.

Westlake, H. F. *The Parish Gilds of Medieval England.* London, 1919.

Wiesner, Merry E. *Working Women in Renaissance Germany.* New Brunswick, NJ, 1986.

Wilts, Andreas. *Beginen im Bodenseeraum.* Sigmaringen, 1994.

Wolff, Philippe. *Commerces et marchands de Toulouse (vers 1350–vers 1450).* Paris, 1954.

Woloch, Isser. "From Charity to Welfare in Revolutionary Paris." *Journal of Modern History* 58, 4 (1986): 779–812.

"War-widows Pensions: Social Policy in Revolutionary and Napoleonic France," *Societas* 6, 4 (1976): 235–54.

Woolf, Stuart. "The Société de Charité Maternelle, 1788–1815." In Jonathan Barry and Colin Jones, eds., *Medicine and Charity before the Welfare State*. London and New York, 1991.

Wright, William J. "A Closer Look at House Poor Relief through the Common Chest and Indigence in Sixteenth-Century Hesse." *Archiv für Reformationsgeschichte* 70 (1979): 225–37.

Wrigley, E. A. and R. S. Schofield. *The Population History of England, 1541–1871: A Reconstruction*. Cambridge, MA, 1981.

Wunder, Heide. "Gender Norms and their Enforcement in Early Modern Germany." In Lynn Abrams and Elizabeth Harvey, eds., *Gender Relations in German History: Power, Agency and Experience from the Sixteenth to the Twentieth Century*. Durham, NC, 1997.

Wytsman, Klemens. *Des Béguinages en Belgique*. Gand, 1862.

Young, Michael and Peter Willmott. *Family and Kinship in East London*. Berkeley, 1992.

Zink, Anne. *L'Héritier de la maison: géographie coutumière du sud-ouest de la France sous l'Ancien Régime*. Paris, 1993.

Zmyslony, Monika. *Die Bruderschaften in Lübeck bis zur Reformation*. Kiel, 1977.

Index of placenames

Aix-en-Provence, 37
Albi, 42
Amsterdam, 124, 127, 128–129, 155
Antwerp, 127
Anvers, 80
Aragon, 113
Augsburg, 137, 141, 145–146, 152, 155
Auvergne, 89
Avignon, 93

Barcelona, 113
Basel, 58
Bologna, 92, 97
Bordeaux, 38
Brabant, 73, 110, 130
Brescia, 93, 133
Bristol, 56
Bruges, 113, 127
Brussels, 85, 111, 113, 127

Cambridge, 111, 112
Canterbury, 97
Carpentras, 58, 59
Catalonia, 111
Chalon-sur-Sâone, 42
Charente (French département), 206
Cologne, 80, 85, 139
Coventry, 141

Dauphiné, 36, 89
Delft, 125
Dordogne (French département), 206
Dordrecht, 124
Douai, 51–52, 73, 74

Emden, 125–126, 127, 130, 131, 133, 149
England, 27, 29, 38, 39, 45, 52, 53, 55, 76, 94, 96, 100, 215
Europe:
  eastern, 3, 38

northern, 5, 7, 9, 11, 13, 31, 34, 43, 44, 46, 50, 51, 53, 61, 74, 80, 84, 87, 112, 132, 140, 167
southern, 5, 7, 9, 29, 31, 39, 48–51, 53, 55, 57, 58, 59, 82, 88, 91, 97, 139, 161, 162, 164
western, 1, 3, 8, 11, 29, 34, 38, 80, 214, 219

Flanders, 73, 130
Florence, 46, 49, 55, 58, 64, 65, 72, 74, 76, 93, 98, 99, 100, 101, 114–115, 116, 118, 139, 140, 166
France, 36, 45, 61, 63, 75, 90, 99, 124, 154, 157, 161, 162, 167, 168, 169, 215, 218
Franche-Comté, 158
Frankfurt am Main, 57, 80, 111, 137, 138–139

Geneva, 43, 89, 92, 130
Genoa, 51–52, 61, 62, 64, 65
Germany, 26, 34, 37, 38, 75, 85, 95, 143, 167
Ghent, 65–66, 80, 85, 111
Gouda, 124
Grenoble, 157–158

Haarlem, 125
Hainaut, province of, 73, 110
Holland, 35, 124, 127, 128, 149

Italy, 9, 13, 15, 26, 38, 43, 45, 50, 51, 64, 75, 82, 90, 96, 99, 110, 114, 118, 121, 140, 161, 164, 175, 220

Lancaster, 96
Languedoc, 149
Leicester, 97
Leiden, 85, 113, 124, 126, 130, 132, 137
Loire (French département), 206, 207–208
London, 37, 38, 43, 45, 48, 59, 62, 92, 94, 96, 97, 100
Louvain, 80
Low Countries, 86, 131, 161
Lyon, 133–134, 144, 176, 205, 207

Subject index

Cambridge Studies in Population, Economy and Society in Past Time

DATE DUE